Security, Privacy and Trust in the IoT Environment

Zaigham Mahmood
Editor

Security, Privacy and Trust in the IoT Environment

Springer

Editor
Zaigham Mahmood
Northampton University
Northampton, UK

Shijiazhuang Tiedao University
Hebei, China

ISBN 978-3-030-18074-4 ISBN 978-3-030-18075-1 (eBook)
https://doi.org/10.1007/978-3-030-18075-1

This Springer imprint is published by the registered company Springer Nature Switzerland AG
The registered company address is: Gewerbestrasse 11, 6330 Cham, Switzerland

To:
Rehana Zaigham Mahmood
For her Love and Support

Preface

Overview

The Internet of Things (IoT) is a network of self-configuring sensor-enabled objects connected through wireless and wired connections. It is a vision of pervasive computing where smart devices connect to each other in a seamless manner, to establish a unified physical–virtual world. With the broadband Internet becoming widely available and the cost of connectivity of devices exponentially decreasing, the IoT is becoming a highly promising paradigm for organizations as well as individuals in the society. An unspoken rule for the future digitized world seems to suggest that *anything that can be connected, will be connected*—from industrial machines to wearable devices to driverless vehicles. Gartner, Inc. estimates that there will be over 26 billion interconnected devices through networks such as the IoT, by the year 2020. According to BBN Times as reported in December 2018, the IoT market is predicted to generate an additional $344 billion in revenues as well as to drive $177 billion in cost reductions, by 2020. On a broader scale, the IoT vision is paving the way for developing intelligent cities, autonomic self-driving vehicles, industrial IoT, smarter health care and, in general, smarter environments in a *connected world*. With the passing of time, as the everyday objects and devices are getting smarter, and the number and variety of such devices are growing, users' expectations in terms of adaptive and self-governing environments are also increasing.

The opportunities are limitless as the IoT vision is proving to be hugely attractive and profitable. However, there are also numerous challenges for network specialists, software developers and hardware/devices engineers. Other associated challenges relate to the variety of connected objects, storage and movement of Big Data, complexity of Data Analytics, insufficiency of Internet bandwidth and the unreliable nature of the present-day Internet. The most significant of these, which require urgent attention, refer to the privacy and security of data and applications at all access levels, safety of users of the IoT *things* especially when a smart device malfunctions, connectivity and communication protocols, and the trust and authentication mechanisms within the network. Security and trust issues are probably the greatest obstacles to further growth of the IoT paradigm.

Some of the challenges from a different perspective include gaps in technology sophistication; absence or immaturity of available standards; and also, the industry-specific security- and trust-related limitations. Although safety aspects of the networks are getting better, communication protocols are resulting in more secure connectivity, and data protection mechanisms are becoming more sophisticated, there is still a further requirement for novel network architectures and middleware platforms deploying new emerging communication technologies; as well as adoption of novel context-aware management approaches and development of more efficient tools and devices.

It is in the above context that this book is set. The focus of the volume is on the security, privacy and trust essentials of the IoT environment, in particular the relevant principles, frameworks, architectures and technologies, as well as the practical suggestions and solutions to the inherent limitations and challenges. The majority of contributions in the book focus on device connectivity, pervasive computing, data transfer, security, interoperability, trust and adaptability. Twenty-seven researchers and practitioners of international repute have presented the latest research, current trends and case studies, as well as suggestions for further understanding, development and enhancement of the much attractive IoT vision.

Objectives

The aim of this volume is to present and discuss the IoT in relation to inherent security, privacy and trust within the environment. The objectives include:

- Capturing the latest research and practice with respect to the challenges of security as well as issues of privacy and trust in the IoT environment.
- Presenting innovative ideas, practical solutions and workable frameworks to combat such challenges to ensure better security, privacy and trust.
- Developing a complete reference for students, researchers and practitioners of pervasive computing and smart digital environments.
- Identifying further research directions and technologies with respect to the connectivity, security, privacy and trust in the IoT infrastructure.

Organization

There are 12 chapters in this book: *Security, Privacy and Trust in the IoT Environment*. These are organized in two parts, as follows:

Part I: Security and Privacy in IoT: Technologies and Frameworks

This part has a focus on concepts, principles, underlying technologies and methodologies. There are seven chapters.

- Chapter 1 reviews the cyber-security risks of critical infrastructures and provides security management strategies for infrastructures such as SCADA. A control framework for defining a comprehensive set of security objectives with policies, standards and guidelines is also suggested.
- Chapter 2 explores the use of virtual private networks to adopt authentication protocols to enhance the security and privacy of networks. The proposed framework uses Geographical Positioning System (GPS) for mutual two-way authentication. The proposed approach also helps to detect and reduce the wormhole attacks.
- Chapter 3 addresses major threats related to RFID technologies and reviews the existing public key-based cryptographic solutions to counteract the security and privacy issues. It is suggested that solutions that employ delegation of group exponentiation techniques satisfy much better, the core requirements of privacy and security.
- Chapter 4 focuses on Cyber Threat Intelligence (CTI) concentrations such as OSINT, HUMINT, MASINT, SIGINT, GEOINT and TECHINT to develop a proactive Cyber Intelligence aggregation approach model. The proposed model depends on practical tools and methods that help to provide proactive defences and analysis strategies.
- Chapter 5 investigates a next-generation Firewall-as-a-Service (FaaS), called *Seddulbahir*, and discusses its effectiveness to counter the IoT-powered volumetric cyberattacks. Various features of FaaS, such as detection, mitigation and other related aspects are elaborated upon. Critical analysis of similar exiting mechanisms is also presented.
- Chapter 6 aims at providing the current research and development on the use of blockchain technology for securing Internet of Things (IoT) environments. The conceptual blockchain-based IoT architectures for seven different use case situations, including supply chain, manufacturing, smart cities and homes, and health care, are also presented.
- Chapter 7 proposes an image encryption and authentication algorithm to handle bulky medical images. The suggested quantum cyber-physical system incorporates key generation, permutation, Deoxyribonucleic Acid operation and diffusion. It is suggested that the system is well suited for a versatile hospital management system.

Part II: Privacy and Trust in IoT: Healthcare Applications and IoV

This part of the book comprises five chapters that focus on privacy and trust as related to healthcare applications and Internet of Vehicles (IoV) scenarios.

- Chapter 8 presents an overview of security and privacy issues related to healthcare applications that often operate on cloud or fog computing architectures. Thirty recently published research papers are studied to establish the extent of the problem; results are presented and discussed for the benefit of healthcare professionals.
- Chapter 9 extends the study presented in the previous contribution to analyse the IoT-based telemedicine systems focusing on data security and privacy. Thirty research papers published in 2018 are analysed to identify the related issues, to provide solutions based on ciphertext-policy attributes encryption and secure better portable graphics architectures.
- Chapter 10 provides an in-depth investigation into a diverse range of security attacks challenging the realization of Vehicular Ad hoc Networks (VANET). It suggests the need for trust management for securing networks. The study also illustrates how a reconfigurable and agile infrastructure can help in guaranteeing a more secure VANET platform.
- Chapter 11 presents privacy preserving strategies and proposes a novel solution that allows users to benefit from Cloud-Enabled-IoV (CE-IoV) location-based services and safety applications—anonymously and safely. A simulation of the proposed solution is also presented, with encouraging results.
- The last chapter in this part, and the final in the book, also focuses on Mobile Ad hoc Network (MANET). It discusses the use of least squares time series forecasting method, with interval-based fuzzy mathematics, to forecast the future positions of MANET nodes; with a view to predicting secure shortest paths between the nodes in motion at any given times.

Target Audiences

The current volume is a reference text aimed at supporting a number of potential audiences, including the following:

- *Network Specialists, Hardware Engineers and Security Experts* who wish to adopt the newer approaches to resolving the issues of network security, data privacy and human trust in the IoT paradigm.
- *Students and Academics* who have an interest in further enhancing the knowledge of technologies, mechanisms and practices relevant to security, privacy and trust from a distributed computing perspective.

- *Researchers and Practitioners* in this field who require up to date knowledge of the current methodologies, technologies and practices relevant to the security, privacy and trust-related weaknesses and proposed solutions.

Derby, UK

Zaigham Mahmood

Acknowledgements

The editor acknowledges the help and support of the following colleagues during the review, development and editing phases of this text:

- Prof. Zhengxu Zhao, Shijiazhuang Tiedao University, Hebei, China
- Dr. Alfredo Cuzzocrea, University of Trieste, Trieste, Italy
- Dr. Emre Erturk, Eastern Institute of Technology, New Zealand
- Prof. Jing He, Kennesaw State University, Kennesaw, GA, USA
- Josip Lorincz, FESB-Split, University of Split, Croatia
- Aleksandar Milić, University of Belgrade, Serbia
- Prof. Sulata Mitra, Indian Institute of Engineering Science and Technology, Shibpur, India
- Dr. S. Parthasarathy, Thiagarajar College of Engineering, Tamil Nadu, India
- Daniel Pop, Institute e-Austria Timisoara, West University of Timisoara, Romania
- Dr. Pethuru Raj, IBM Cloud Center of Excellence, Bangalore, India
- Dr. Muthu Ramachandran, Leeds Becket University, Leeds, UK
- Dr. Lucio Agostinho Rocha, State University of Campinas, Brazil
- Dr. Saqib Saeed, University of Dammam, Saudi Arabia
- Prof. Claudio Sartori, University of Bologna, Bologna, Italy
- Dr. Mahmood Shah, University of Central Lancashire, Preston, UK
- Dr. Fareeha Zafar, GC University, Lahore, Pakistan

I would also like to thank the contributors of this book: 27 authors and co-authors, from academia as well as industry from around the world, who collectively submitted 12 chapters. Without their efforts in developing quality contributions, conforming to the guidelines and meeting often the strict deadlines, this text would not have been possible.

Grateful thanks are also due to the members of my family—Rehana, Zoya, Imran, Hanya, Arif and Ozair—for their continued support and encouragement. Every good wish, also, for the youngest in our family: Eyaad Imran Rashid Khan and Zayb-un-Nisa Khan.

Derby, UK
February 2019

Zaigham Mahmood

Other Books by Zaigham Mahmood

Guide to Ambient Intelligence in the IoT Environment: Principles, Technologies and Applications

This reference text discusses the AmI element of the IoT paradigm and reviews the current developments, underlying technologies and case scenarios relating to AmI-based IoT environments. The book presents cutting-edge research, frameworks and methodologies on device connectivity, communication protocols and other aspects relating to the AmI-IoT vision. ISBN: 978-3-030-04172-4.

Fog Computing: Concepts, Frameworks and Technologies

This reference text describes the state of the art of fog and edge computing with a particular focus on development approaches, architectural mechanisms, related technologies and measurement metrics for building smart adaptable environments. The coverage also includes topics such as device connectivity, security, interoperability and communication methods. ISBN: 978-3-319-94889-8.

Smart Cities: Development and Governance Frameworks

This text/reference investigates the state of the art in approaches to building, monitoring, managing and governing smart city environments. A particular focus is placed on the distributed computing environments within the infrastructure of smart cities and smarter living, including issues of device connectivity, communication, security and interoperability. ISBN: 978-3-319-76668-3.

Data Science and Big Data Computing: Frameworks and Methodologies

This reference text has a focus on data science and provides practical guidance on big data analytics. Expert perspectives are provided by an authoritative collection of 36 researchers and practitioners, discussing latest developments and emerging trends; presenting frameworks and innovative methodologies; and suggesting best practices for efficient and effective data analytics. ISBN: 978-3-319-31859-2.

Connected Environments for the IoT: Challenges and Solutions

This comprehensive reference presents a broad-ranging overview of device connectivity in distributed computing environments, supporting the vision of IoT. Expert perspectives are provided, covering issues of communication, security, privacy, interoperability, networking, access control and authentication. Corporate analysis is also offered via several case studies. ISBN: 978-3-319-70102-8.

Connectivity Frameworks for Smart Devices: The Internet of Things from a Distributed Computing Perspective

This is an authoritative reference that focuses on the latest developments on the Internet of Things. It presents state of the art on the current advances in the connectivity of diverse devices and focuses on the communication, security, privacy, access control and authentication aspects of the device connectivity in distributed environments. ISBN: 978-3-319-33122-5.

Cloud Computing: Methods and Practical Approaches

The benefits associated with cloud computing are enormous; yet the dynamic, virtualized and multi-tenant nature of the cloud environment presents many challenges. To help tackle these, this volume provides illuminating viewpoints and case studies to present current research and best practices on approaches and technologies for the emerging cloud paradigm. ISBN: 978-1-447-15106-7.

Cloud Computing: Challenges, Limitations and R&D Solutions

This reference text reviews the challenging issues that present barriers to greater implementation of the cloud computing paradigm, together with the latest research into developing potential solutions. This book presents case studies, and analysis of the implications of the cloud paradigm, from a diverse selection of researchers and practitioners of international repute. ISBN: 978-3-319-10529-1.

Continued Rise of the Cloud: Advances and Trends in Cloud Computing

This reference volume presents the latest research and trends in cloud-related technologies, infrastructure and architecture. Contributed by expert researchers and practitioners in the field, this book presents discussions on current advances and practical approaches including guidance and case studies on the provision of cloud-based services and frameworks. ISBN: 978-1-447-16451-7.

Software Engineering Frameworks for the Cloud Computing Paradigm

This is an authoritative reference that presents the latest research on software development approaches suitable for distributed computing environments. Contributed by researchers and practitioners of international repute, the book offers practical guidance on enterprise-wide software deployment in the cloud environment. Case studies are also presented. ISBN: 978-1-447-15030-5.

Cloud Computing for Enterprise Architectures

This reference text, aimed at system architects and business managers, examines the cloud paradigm from the perspective of enterprise architectures. It introduces fundamental concepts, discusses principles and explores frameworks for the adoption of cloud computing. The book explores the inherent challenges and presents future directions for further research. ISBN: 978-1-447-12235-7.

Cloud Computing: Concepts, Technology & Architecture

This is a textbook (in English but also translated in Chinese and Korean) highly recommended for adoption for university-level courses in distributed computing. It offers a detailed explanation of cloud computing concepts, architectures, frameworks, models, mechanisms and technologies—highly suitable for both newcomers and experts. ISBN: 978-0-133-38752-0.

Software Project Management for Distributed Computing: Life-Cycle Methods for Developing Scalable and Reliable Tools

This unique volume explores cutting-edge management approaches to developing complex software that is efficient, scalable, sustainable and suitable for distributed environments. Emphasis is on the use of the latest software technologies and frameworks for life-cycle methods, including design, implementation and testing stages of software development. ISBN: 978-3-319-54324-6.

Requirements Engineering for Service and Cloud Computing

This text aims to present and discuss the state of the art in terms of methodologies, trends and future directions for requirements engineering for the service and cloud computing paradigm. The majority of the contributions in the book focus on requirements elicitation; requirements specifications; requirements classification and requirements validation and evaluation. ISBN: 978-3-319-51309-6.

User Centric E-Government: Challenges & Opportunities

This text presents a citizens-focused approach to the development and implementation of electronic government. The focus is twofold: discussion on challenges of service availability, e-service operability on diverse smart devices; as well as on opportunities for the provision of open, responsive and transparent functioning of world governments. ISBN: 978-3-319-59441-5.

Cloud Computing Technologies for Connected Government

This text reports the latest research on electronic government for enhancing the transparency of public institutions. It covers a broad scope of topics including citizen empowerment, collaborative public services, communication through social media, cost benefits of the Cloud paradigm, electronic voting systems, identity management and legal issues. ISBN: 978-1-466-68629-8.

Human Factors in Software Development and Design

This reference text brings together high-quality research on the influence and impact of ordinary people on the software industry. With the goal of improving the quality and usability of computer technologies, topics include global software development, multi-agent systems, public administration platforms, socio-economic factors and user-centric design. ISBN: 978-1-466-66485-2.

IT in the Public Sphere: Applications in Administration, Government, Politics, and Planning

This reference text evaluates current research and best practices in the adoption of e-government technologies in developed and developing countries, enabling governments to keep in touch with citizens and corporations in modern societies. Topics covered include citizen participation, digital technologies, globalization, strategic management and urban development. ISBN: 978-1-466-64719-0.

Emerging Mobile and Web 2.0 Technologies for Connected E-Government

This reference highlights the emerging mobile and communication technologies, including social media, deployed by governments for use by citizens. It presents a reference source for researchers, practitioners, students and managers interested in the application of recent technological innovations to develop an open, transparent and more effective e-government environment. ISBN: 978-1-466-66082-3.

E-Government Implementation and Practice in Developing Countries

This volume presents research on current undertakings by developing countries towards the design, development and implementation of e-government policies. It proposes frameworks and strategies for the benefits of project managers, government officials, researchers and practitioners involved in the development and implementation of e-government planning. ISBN: 978-1-466-64090-0.

Developing E-Government Projects: Frameworks and Methodologies

This text presents frameworks and methodologies for strategies for the design, implementation of e-government projects. It illustrates the best practices for successful adoption of e-government and thus becomes essential for policymakers, practitioners and researchers for the successful deployment of e-government planning and projects. ISBN: 978-1-466-64245-4.

Contents

About the Editor

Prof. Dr. Zaigham Mahmood is a published author/editor of 26 books on subjects including Electronic Government, Cloud Computing, Data Science, Big Data, Fog Computing, Internet of Things, Smart Cities, Project Management and Software Engineering, including *Cloud Computing: Concepts, Technology & Architecture* which is also published in Korean and Chinese languages. Additionally, he is developing two new books to appear later in 2019. He has also published more than 100 articles and book chapters and organized numerous conference tracks and workshops.

Professor Mahmood is the Editor-in-Chief of *Journal of E-Government Studies and Best Practices* as well as the Series Editor-in-Chief of the IGI book series on *E-Government and Digital Divide*. He is a Senior Technology Consultant at Debesis Education UK and Professor at the Shijiazhuang Tiedao University in Hebei, China. He further holds positions as Foreign Professor at NUST and IIU in Islamabad Pakistan. He has served as a Reader (Associated Professor) at the University of Derby UK, and Professor Extraordinaire at the North West University Potchefstroom South Africa. He is also a certified cloud computing instructor and a regular speaker at international conferences devoted to cloud computing and e-government. His specialized areas of research include distributed computing, emerging technologies, project management and e-government.

Contributors

Stephen Kwamena Aikins School of Public Affairs, University of South Florida, Tampa, FL, USA

Abdulwahab Aljubairy Intelligent Computing Laboratory, Department of Computing, Macquarie University, Sydney, NSW, Australia

Suvini P. Amaraweera School of Computing and Mathematics, Charles Sturt University, Melbourne, VIC, Australia

N. Ambika Computer Science Department, HKBK Degree College, Bangalore, India

R. Amirtharajan School of Electrical & Electronics Engineering, SASTRA Deemed University, Thanjavur, India

Pelin Angin Computer Engineering Department, Middle East Technical University, Ankara, Turkey

Soham Bandyopadhyay Dr. B. C. Roy Polytechnic, Durgapur, India

Leila Benarous STIC Laboratory, Faculty of Science, Department of Computer Science, University of Tlemcen, Tlemcen, Algeria

Ugur Can Atasoy Department of Management Information Systems, School of Applied Science, Girne American University, Canterbury, UK

Ahmet Erdem Department of Information Systems, Informatics Institute, Middle East Technical University, Ankara, Turkey

Malka N. Halgamuge Department of Electrical and Electronic Engineering, University of Melbourne, Parkville, VIC, Australia

R. John Bosco Balaguru School of Electrical & Electronics Engineering, SASTRA Deemed University, Thanjavur, India

Benamar Kadri STIC Laboratory, Faculty of Technology, Department of Telecommunications, University of Tlemcen, Tlemcen, Algeria

Sunil Karforma The University of Burdwan, Burdwan, India

Matluba Khodjaeva Center for Cybercrime Studies, John Jay College of Criminal Justice, The City University of New York, New York, USA

Adnan Mahmood Intelligent Computing Laboratory, Department of Computing, Macquarie University, Sydney, NSW, Australia

Muath Obaidat Center for Cybercrime Studies, John Jay College of Criminal Justice, The City University of New York, New York, USA

G. A. Pramesha Chandrasiri School of Computing and Mathematics, Charles Sturt University, Melbourne, VIC, Australia

Padmapriya Praveenkumar School of Electrical & Electronics Engineering, SASTRA Deemed University, Thanjavur, India

Douglas Salane Center for Cybercrime Studies, John Jay College of Criminal Justice, The City University of New York, New York, USA

R. Santhiya Devi School of Electrical & Electronics Engineering, SASTRA Deemed University, Thanjavur, India

Arif Sari Department of Management Information Systems, School of Applied Science, Girne American University, Canterbury, UK

Quan Z. Sheng Intelligent Computing Laboratory, Department of Computing, Macquarie University, Sydney, NSW, Australia

Sarah Ali Siddiqui Intelligent Computing Laboratory, Department of Computing, Macquarie University, Sydney, NSW, Australia

C. Subhashi Jayasekara School of Computing and Mathematics, Charles Sturt University, Melbourne, VIC, Australia

Sevgi Özkan Yildirim Department of Information Systems, Informatics Institute, Middle East Technical University, Ankara, Turkey

Wei Emma Zhang Intelligent Computing Laboratory, Department of Computing, Macquarie University, Sydney, NSW, Australia

Part I
Security and Privacy in IoT: Technologies and Frameworks

Chapter 1
Managing Cybersecurity Risks of SCADA Networks of Critical Infrastructures in the IoT Environment

Stephen Kwamena Aikins

Abstract This chapter reviews the cybersecurity risks of critical infrastructures such as supervisory control and data acquisition (SCADA) systems in the IoT environment; and provides security management strategies to beef up the security of SCADA networks. An overview of IoT reference model and related security concerns are reviewed. Vulnerabilities of SCADA systems as well as risk assessment approaches and risk management strategies to help mitigate vulnerabilities and threats are also examined. The chapter concludes that to effectively manage cybersecurity of SCADA systems in an IoT environment, a control framework that defines a comprehensive set of security objectives with policies, standards, and guidelines should be established and enforced. Additionally, it is suggested that existing protocols should be analyzed to understand their vulnerabilities for effective risk control and SCADA networks should be designed to prevent direct access from the Internet.

Keywords Internet of things · IoT · Network cybersecurity · DoS attack · SCADA · Vulnerabilities · Threats risk assessment · Risk management · RFID · WSN · Ipv6 · Sensors · 6LoWPAN

1.1 Introduction

This chapter reviews the cybersecurity risks of critical infrastructures such as supervisory control and data acquisition (SCADA) systems in the Internet of Things (IoT) environment, and provides the risk management strategies to address them. The IoT is a network of intelligent devices—each embedded with sensors—which are connected to the Internet [1]. It entails interconnection of smart devices in a network based on the possibility of seamless integration of physical objects such as sensors or home appliances which can be loosely defined as a network of interface that explores a piece of functionality [2]. In recent years, IoT technology has been applied in several domains including energy, logistics, agriculture, health, homes and office buildings;

S. K. Aikins (✉)
School of Public Affairs, University of South Florida, Tampa, FL, USA
e-mail: saikins@usf.edu

Z. Mahmood (ed.), *Security, Privacy and Trust in the IoT Environment*, https://doi.org/10.1007/978-3-030-18075-1_1

which, in turn, is helping to improve the quality of life in many ways. However, constraints such as limited CPU memory and energy budget on IoT devices such as sensors limit the ability to process information at speed, and have cybersecurity challenges that make it difficult to maintain confidentiality and integrity in the IoT systems.

SCADA systems consist of complex industrial command and control networks that support communication between a central control unit and multiple units on a common communication bus. Critical infrastructures operated remotely by using SCADA systems include telecommunication and information networks, national electrical grids, oil and natural gas plants, water systems, banking and financial systems, etc. To ensure effective communication as well as command and control, the nodes on these networks are embedded with computing devices such as sensors, actuators and programmable logic controllers (PLCs). Many of these infrastructures are interdependent and critical for the survival and growth of a nation's economy and for safeguarding sensitive national assets and information. For example, telecommunication networks require electricity, transportation networks depend on computerized control and information systems, and many electricity generation plants require fuels to operate. Consequently, the incapacity of one or more of these assets through cyber attacks could have crippling effects on national security, the economy, public health, and safety.

From a security standpoint, the devices on SCADA network face many of the same constraints as IoT devices. For example, like IoT devices, SCADA network devices have limited computational capabilities and low-rate data transmission which complicate security solutions. Similar to IoT devices, many nodes on SCADA networks are embedded computing devices that run real-time operating systems (RTOS) and other real-time control software, which can be seriously compromised in the event of cyber attacks. The global interconnectedness through the Internet and the development of network technologies with embedded communication devices have resulted in the ever-increasing use of SCADA systems to remotely operate critical infrastructures through telecommunication networks. In that regard, many modern SCADA networks are connected to their outside corporate network and the Internet, with some of the connections being over mixed cellular, satellite, and landlines. The web-interface capability, coupled with integration to the corporate network, allows for the convenient gathering of data and production information for higher level management. However, given the fact that these SCADA systems are dependent upon open protocols like IoT networks, the integration makes the devices on the SCADA network vulnerable to application layer and TCP/IP-based and/or wireless sensor network-based attacks.

While the integration with corporate networks and the Internet provide improved connectivity and helps to optimize operations of SCADA systems, it also exposes the devices of these safety-critical industrial networks to a myriad of security problems of the IoT environment. Given the criticality of these infrastructures in safeguarding sensitive information and national assets, there is the need to understand the IoT architecture and its inherent security challenges in relation to the security vulnerabilities of SCADA systems over IP-based and wireless networks in order to provide risk management strategies to address the risks of cyber attacks. Consequently, the remaining sections of this study are organized as follows: we begin with reviews of the domain applications of IoT, as well as the IoT layered architecture, followed by an analysis of cybersecurity vulnerabilities of SCADA systems in IP-based and wireless sensor networks. Next, we examine the risk assessment approaches that could provide the foundation for the treatment of identified risks. Finally, we provide risk management strategies that include a control framework for defining a comprehensive set of security objectives with policies, standards, and guidelines that should be enforced to meet the business and IoT security management goals of organizations in charge of critical infrastructures.

1.2 IoT Application Domains

In recent years, IoT has been having significant effects in a number of domains such as various industries, logistics, smart grids, smart buildings and offices, agriculture, as well as entertainment and media [3]. Several scholars have classified the application of IoT in a number of domains, including smart infrastructure and health care [4, 5], transportation, logistics and healthcare [4, 6], smart cities [7, 8], smart water and metering, and smart agriculture and animal farming [7], as well as smart homes, offices and industrial plants [9, 10]. These applications are changing the way we live and improving the quality of lives in diverse ways. Figure 1.1 shows a variety of IoT application domains.

IoT technology can support a critical infrastructure such as a smart grid—an intelligent power system which incorporates information and communication with existing transmission and distribution system. This is made possible by utilizing sensors, digital meters, and controllers with analysis tools to monitor and optimize grid performance, prevent power outages and restore supply [11]. The role of the IoT sensors in smart grid systems is to identify devices connected to the grid and send real-time power information to the consumer [3]. Sensors are also being embedded to form an integral part of transport infrastructure with significant investments. An example is the introduction of England's Smart Motorways Program in the UK [12].

IoT technologies can also support logistics by enabling the service provider to increase operational efficiency with enhanced automation [13]. Additionally, it can improve inventory management, asset utilization, predictive maintenance, and freight management [14]. The application of Radio Frequency Identification (RFID) technology in logistics enables the industry to forecast information, identify future trends, estimate the probability of an accident, and allow for the early adoption of remedial measures to help enterprises to better respond to market and manage supply risks [3].

The application of IoT in homes and office environments has also experienced significant growth in recent years. This includes increased purchases of smart energy management systems such as Nest thermostats, security solutions like August smart locks and personal home assistances such as Google Home, Bosch's Mykie

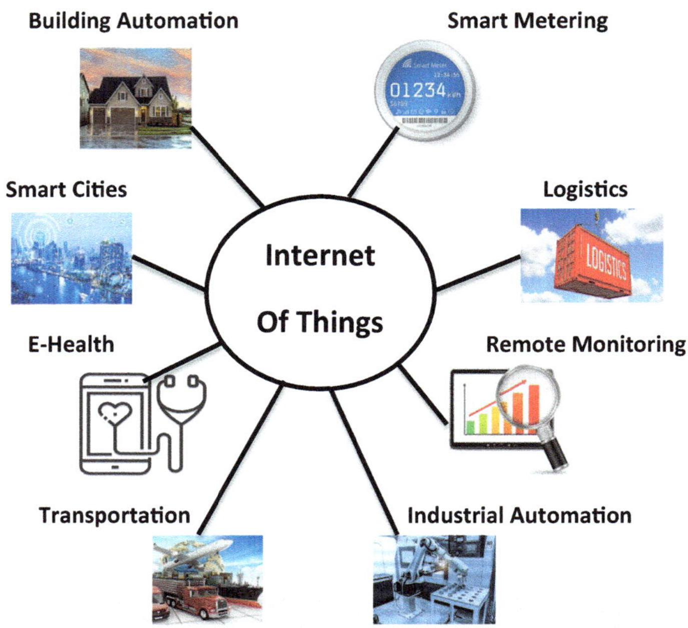

Fig. 1.1 IoT application domains

and Amazon's Alexa. In a survey of 1000 workers, the British Land and Worktech Academy [15] found that 88% of respondents wish to control their work environment better, and that smart office would increase worker productivity by 37%, loyalty by 38%, and well-being and happiness by 40%.

In the area of healthcare, IoT applications involving the use of smart homes allow patient monitoring and care in independent environments. Utilizing semantics, IoT health applications can use medical rule engines to analyze large quantities of sensor data to help make medical decisions [3]. Emerging healthcare technologies have embedded sensors with the potential to aid healthcare services such as ambient assisted living [16, 17]. To maximize efficiency in agricultural production, IoT sensors and technologies can be utilized for cultivation with increased quality through monitoring environmental conditions such as air pressure, humidity and wind direction through wireless sensors.

It is clear from the foregoing that IoT technology is applicable in almost any field. Most importantly, all the domains where IoT is applied rely on the availability of critical infrastructure such as energy system to operate effectively. The foregoing applications notwithstanding, the technology is plagued with numerous security and privacy challenges that need to be addressed if the full potential of IoT is to be realized. With all its advanced capabilities in the information exchange area, IoT presents some serious concerns from security viewpoint; and proper steps need to be taken in the initial phases before going for further development of IoT for effective and widely accepted adoption [18]. Along with the combination of Internet and modern sensor technologies such as RFID, Near Field Communication (NFC) and Wireless Sensor and Actuator Networks (WSAN), IoT itself is suffering from more rigorous security challenges in several areas, including architecture, standard and human involvement [19]. The security issues of IoT are traceable to its architecture which forms the basis of IoT system configuration.

In the next section of this chapter, we review the architecture of IoT framework in order to set the stage for analysis of vulnerabilities and other security challenges of SCADA systems in IoT environment.

1.3 IoT Reference Model Architecture

The IoT reference model [20] consists of four layers, all of which are susceptible to various security issues and require a common standard and compatibility for both hardware and software at each layer in order to ensure effective operation. The layers, as shown in Fig. 1.2, from bottom to the top are: element layer, network layer, service layer, and application layer. Each layer in the IoT system has its own components, communication standards and protocol. Among others, the layered architecture of IoT provides modular management by allowing implementation of different security protocols, security services, and security mechanisms at each layer to enhance overall protection of the IoT network system. The lower layers provide services to the upper layers, and the layered structure is easily expandable, allowing new technologies for both hardware and software to be incorporated into the existing IoT network system. Additionally, it is easy to manage and configure for practical implementations [21]. Figure 1.2 represents the IoT reference model, and the following subsections discuss each layer of the model and their constituent components.

Element Layer:
This is the lowest of the four layers of the IoT. It is the device layer consisting of various kinds of nodes and sensors such as RFID, barcode labels actuators and intelligent devices. The sensors are used to identify the objects as well as transport data to the next layer while the devices gather and upload data to the next layer [21]. RFID is a wireless device using electromagnetic fields to transfer data by identifying and tracking tags attached to the objects. In the context of IoT, RFID technology is mainly used as RFID tags for automated exchange of information without any manual involvement. In an RFID tag, an antenna is embedded in the microchip, and the tag consists of memory units which house a unique identifier known as Electronic Product Code (EPC). The tag stores electronic information, and the function of EPC in each tag is to provide a universal numerical data by which a particular tag is recognized universally. However, RFID tags are prone to various attacks from outside, the four most common types of attack being unauthorized tag disabling, unauthorized tag cloning, unauthorized tag tracking and replay attacks [22, 23].

Unauthorized tag disabling is a DoS attack on authenticity that results in incapacitation of the RFID tags temporarily or permanently. The attack renders the RFID

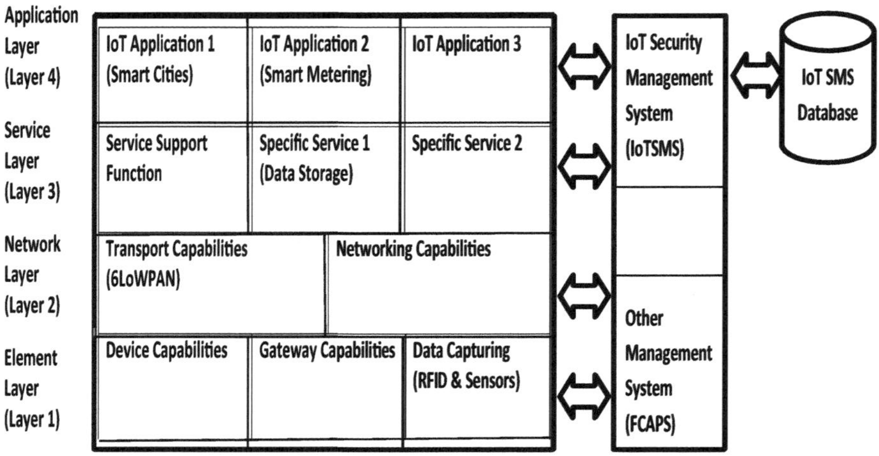

Fig. 1.2 The IoT layered reference model

tag to malfunction and misbehaves under the scan of a tag reader, resulting in its EPC giving misinformation against the unique numerical combination assigned to it [22]. Unauthorized tag cloning is an attack on integrity that results in the capturing of identification information such as EPC through manipulation of the tags by rogue readers. The compromise of the identification information can result in replication of the tag (cloning) which can be used to bypass counterfeit security measures and to introduce new vulnerabilities in any industry using RFID tags automatic verification steps [23].

Unauthorized tag tracking is an attack on confidentiality whereby a tag can be traced through rogue readers, which may result in giving up sensitive information like a person's date of birth or address. This could result in a breach of privacy of a purchaser of a product having an RFID tag. The replay attack is an attack on availability in which the communication signal between the reader and the tag is intercepted, recorded and replayed upon the receipt of any query from the reader at the later time, thereby faking the availability of the tag. In this type of attack, the attacker uses a tag's response to a rogue reader's challenge to impersonate the tag [22].

A key protocol of the element layer is the IEEE 802.15.4 Standard Protocol. This specifies the requirements for the physical layer for low-power wireless personal area networks by focusing on low-speed, low-cost communication between devices [20, 21]. It can be exclusively used with IPv6-based Low-Power Wireless Personal Area Network (6LoWPAN) to build a wireless embedded network for IoT. The major security concerns of the element layer are that the sensors and nodes in the layer are exposed to threats such as unauthorized access, eavesdropping, and spoofing. Additionally, the low communication range of protocols in the layer provides serious limitations. These can be addressed by the use of digital signatures, access control tables, and data encryption.

Network Layer:
This layer transmits data from the element layer to the upper layer through existing communication methods, either wired or wireless network, Internet, cloud, mobile network, satellite network or military network [21]. The data are collected by the nodes and sensors in the layer and transmitted using wireless network sensors. The 6LoWPAN protocol in this layer enables scalability in networking of a large number of devices. This protocol meets the requirements of the low-power consumption devices as well as the weak computing capabilities nodes and sensors of the IoT by allowing packets to be received and sent over the IEEE 802.15.4-based networks [24]. Despite the capabilities of the 6LowPAN protocol, constraints in size and power have serious confidentiality and integrity implications for IoT systems. Other security concerns of this layer include Denial of Service (DoS) attack, man-in-the-middle attack, and malicious code injection. Effective security mechanisms for the network layer include router filtering, encryption, and antivirus software.

Service Layer:
This layer serves as an interface between the different devices in the IoT, provides communication methods between elements and ensures effective functional communication between application and devices. The layer processes the data collected and provides links to the storage for the data received from the lower layer. Additionally, it provides connectivity between sensors and the application layer. For an RFID system, the security weaknesses inherent in the system impacts this layer [25]. Service layer security concerns include DoS, unauthorized access and malicious insider. Intrusion detection systems (IDS), access control tables, and event monitoring can be useful in addressing these security concerns.

Applications Layer:
This layer consists of a variety of practical applications in IoT and uses varying number of different protocols, such as the Constrained Application protocol (CoAp), Message Queue Telemetry Transport (MQTT) protocol, the Advanced Message Queueing Protocol (AMQP) and Extensible Messaging and Presence Protocol (XMPP) [21]. CoAp is a synchronous request/response protocol that runs over the UDP, thereby reducing bandwidth requirements, and targets resource-constrained devices such as mobile phone, tablet, laptop, and low-power consumption devices [26]. MQTT is designed to meet the requirements of low-bandwidth and battery usage.

MQTT protocol runs on top of the TCP and is asynchronous publish/subscribe protocol that decreases network bandwidth, thereby dropping the requirements for computation. The protocol takes advantage of the transport layer security (TLS) secured socket layer (SSL) just as HTTP transaction over the Internet. The Facebook messenger uses the MQTT protocol [21]. AMQP also provides asynchronous publish/subscribe messaging system with the capability of sending large volumes of messages. Research shows the success rate increases directly with bandwidth and helps to provide reliability with message delivery [26]. The TLS/SSL provides security in AMQP. Application layer deals with security concerns such as DoS, unauthorized access and malicious insiders. Appropriate security mechanisms for this layer include IDS, antivirus, and spam filtering.

Supporting SCADA Networks
The IoT offers the advantage of integrating SCADA networks by connecting them with corporate networks and the Internet. However, classical isolated SCADA networks already lack proper security measures. With the integration of complex SCADA architectures based on TCP/IP concepts of IoT and mobile wireless sensor networks, the risk of the vulnerabilities of these SCADA networks being exploited through some of the above-mentioned DoS attacks is high.

1.4 Vulnerabilities of IP-Based SCADA Networks

The IoT is a network system with respect to both the wired and wireless connections that consists of many software and hardware entities such as manufacturing management, energy management, agriculture irrigation, electronic commerce, logistic management, medical and healthcare system, aerospace survey, building and home automation, infrastructure management, large-scale deployments and transportation [27]. There has been tremendous growth in the number of devices connected to the Internet, with some analysts, notably Cisco and Ericsson, predicting nearly 50 billion devices connected to the Internet by 2020. This section of the chapter focuses on SCADA networks of critical infrastructure such as oil refineries, chemical factories, electric power generation plants and large complex manufacturing facilities with IP-based connection to the Internet. As stated earlier, a SCADA system refers to an industrial control system which is used to gather data from sensors and instruments located at remote sites and transmit data at a central or master site for either controlling or monitoring purposes [28]. Based on the information received from the remote stations, automated or operator-driven supervisory commands can be transmitted to remote station control devices which are often referred to as field devices.

Earlier versions of these networks entailed point-to-point networks connecting a monitoring or command device to a remote sensor or actuator. Over the years, these networks have evolved into complex networks that support communication between a central control unit and multiple remote units on a common communication bus. The nodes on these networks are usually special purpose embedded computing devices such as sensors, actuators and remote terminal units (RTUs) or PLCs [29]. RTUs connect to sensors, convert sensor signals to digital data and send the digital data to the supervisory command system. PLCs are used as field devices because they are more economical, versatile, flexible, and configurable than the special purpose RTUs [30].

Typical communications on a SCADA network include control messages exchanged between a command device such as a PC or PLC and a subservient device such as a sensor or actuator. For example, an embedded sensor can send a message to the command device and carry out actions at the instructions of the command. It could also have a communication model that enables peer-to-peer communication between command devices [31]. There are two distinct threats that can affect modern SCADA systems. First, there is the threat of unauthorized access to the control software, whether it is human access or changes made deliberately or unintentionally by virus infections and other software threats existing on the control node. Second, there is the threat of packet access to the network segments hosting SCADA devices [30].

With many modern SCADA networks connected to their outside corporate network and the Internet, the networks are exposed to the risk of cyber attack. As a security measure, the connection to corporate networks and/or Internet are by specialized gateways [32] which provide an interface between IP-based networks on the outside and the Fieldbus protocol-based networks on the factory floor. Additionally, the gateway provides protocol conversion mechanisms to enable communication between the two different networks and provide cache mechanisms for data objects that are exchanged between the networks in order to improve the gateway performance [32]. However, since the SCADA systems are dependent on open protocols for the Internet, they are vulnerable to external remote cyber threats [33].

As stated earlier, although the web-interface capability coupled with integration with corporate network allows for convenient gathering of production information for higher level management, this also makes the devices on the SCADA network vulnerable to the application layer and TCP/IP-based attacks. Thus, while the integration with corporate network and the Internet provides improved connectivity and helps to optimize operations, it also exposes the safety-critical industrial networks to myriad of security problems of the Internet. For example, a malicious attacker can cause significant damage to the SCADA network by targeting the embedded devices that monitor and control operations on the network [29].

With current IoT network technologies and connection of SCADA network to the Internet, there can be serious problems regarding protocol vulnerabilities which could adversely impact protocol conversion mechanisms and prevent effective and intelligible communication between the two networks. The field devices on the older SCADA networks were separated and isolated from cyber threats because they were deployed over serial analog circuits, and the attacker had to make physical contact with the analog circuits to clamp onto the channel and inject serial data into the circuits or otherwise disrupt or capture the protocol [30]. With the advent of IP communications, the risks of cyber attacks are much greater as packets can be routed into the field devices from anywhere and attackers are no longer required to gain physical access to the analog circuits [33].

In complex SCADA architectures, there is a variety of both wired and wireless media and protocols involved in getting data back to the central monitoring site. This allows for the implementation of strong IP-based SCADA networks over mixed cellular, satellite, and landline systems. Figure 1.3 shows SCADA architecture with wired and wireless connections. Given that typical SCADA systems were not designed with security against external threats, IP-based communications can expose the systems to unexpected threats that did not exist with legacy serial communication. An attacker

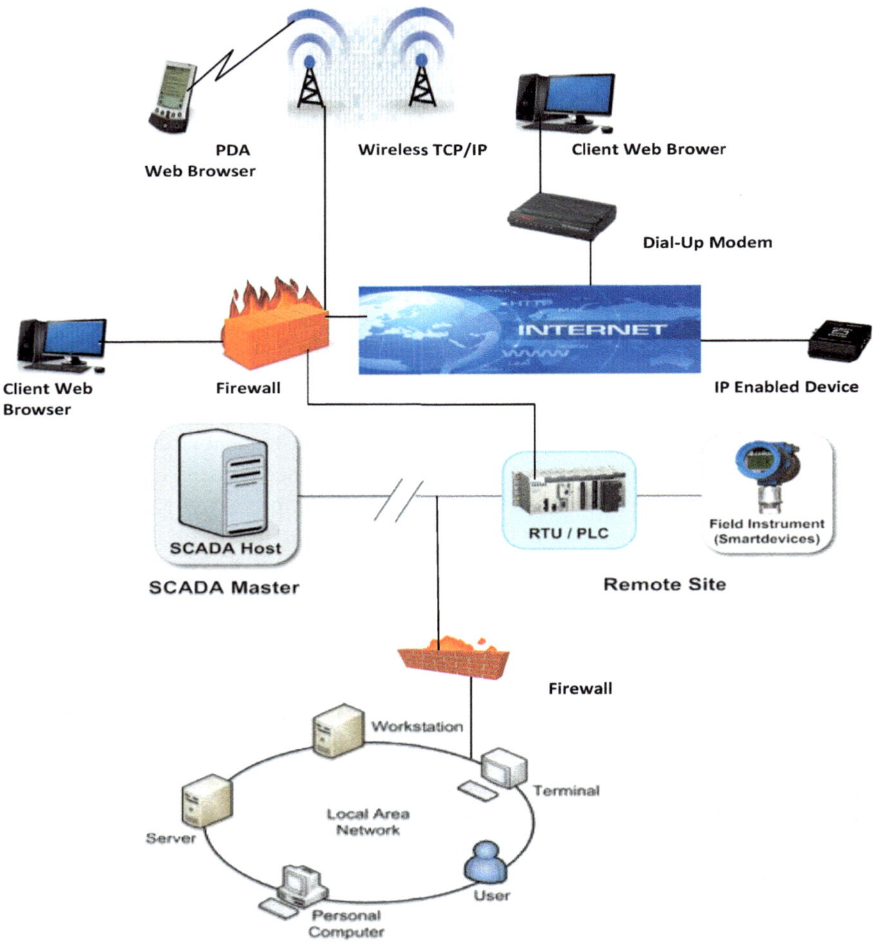

Fig. 1.3 A SCADA architecture with mixed wireless and wired IP-based networks

outside the IP-based SCADA network can initiate an attack on authenticity that can ultimately cause the sensors on the SCADA network to malfunction and provide wrong information to the control device thereby causing serious damage to the operations of the critical infrastructure. Additionally, malicious code injection can ultimately compromise vulnerable nodes and sensors thereby disrupting data transmission between the SCADA network and the integrated web-based network. The use of digital signatures for authentication, IDs for network traffic monitoring, as well as antivirus software to block malicious codes injection can help address these security concerns.

1.5 Vulnerabilities of SCADA Systems Over WSN

A key connectivity technology of IoT is Wireless Sensor Networks (WSN). These are compositions of independent nodes whose wireless communication take place over limited frequency and bandwidth, resulting in multi-hop relay of information between the source and the base station. A typical WSN communication node consists of a sensor, microcontroller, memory, radio transceiver, and a battery [34]. Collaboration among nodes makes possible the collection of data by the wireless sensors, and relaying to the sink node for directed routing towards the base station. This sort of data transmission is facilitated by radio transceivers on the communication network [34].

In WSNs, constraints such as limited CPU memory and energy budget on IoT devices such as sensors limit the ability to process information at speed, and impact most significantly on efforts to maintain confidentiality and integrity in IoT systems. For example, the largest physical layer in IEEE 802.15.4 is 127 bytes [35]. Given that the frame overhead could be 25 bytes, the maximum frame size in the media access control is 102 bytes. Although encryption can be applied to protect confidentiality, it should be noted that the link layer security further reduces this maximum frame size. If AES-CCM-128 (Advanced Encryption Standard using 128 bits designed to provide both authentication and confidentiality) were to be used, this would consume 21 bytes, leaving only 81 bytes available [3]. Consequently, designing appropriately secure and robust systems in the IoT environment is challenging, since communication between nodes is often over 'lossy and low-bandwidth' channels [36].

SCADA networks contain sensors, instrumentation or other metering devices connected to field control devices such as PLCs and RTUs for the purpose of data communication between the field devices and supervisory command units. As stated above, complex SCADA architectures entail a variety of both wired and wireless media and protocols that allow for the implementation of strong IP-based SCADA networks over mixed cellular, satellite, and landline systems. IETF standard enable IPv6 communication over LowPANs. With advances in WSNs, IP-based SCADA wireless networks connected to the Internet may have data communication with devices on WSNs that enable IPv6 communication over 6LowPANs. Indeed, 6LowPAN has the compatibility with respect to stateless address autoconfiguration and neighbor discovery, IPv6 header compression with fragmentation, and support for IP-based routing [37].

Given that IPv6 enables the IoT, having IPv6 network connecting traditional computers in a SCADA network to 6LowPAN with connected smart objects will not be out of place. However, the layers in 6LowPAN are subject to the common security issues plaguing WSNs. Consequently, like all WSNs, the protocol stack of 6LowPAN is vulnerable to DoS attacks in each layer. The protocol stack consists of the physical, data link, network, transport and applications layers or a combination of any of the above. DoS attacks on WSNs can be categorized into three types: attack on secrecy and authentication, silent attacks on service integrity and attacks on network

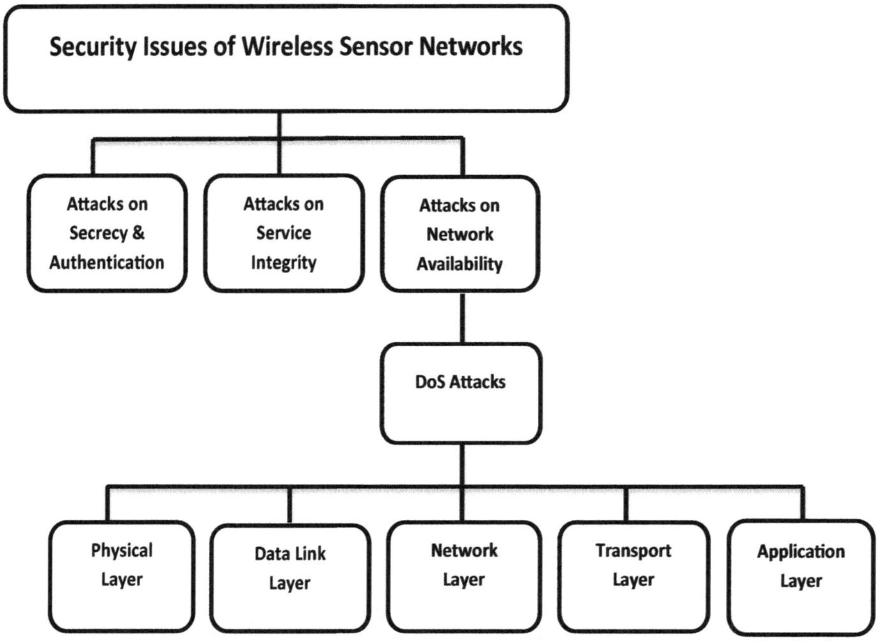

Fig. 1.4 Hierarchical diagram of security issues in WSN

availability [38, 39]. Figure 1.4 shows a hierarchical diagram of the security in WSNs such as 6LowPAN. Various layers of this stack are briefly discussed below.

Physical Layer:
The physical layer of a WSN like 6LowPAN carries the function of selection and generation of carrier frequency modulation and demodulation, encryption and decryption, transmission and reception of data [18]. Attacks on this layer include eavesdropping, jamming and node tampering. Jamming is a DoS attack that occupies the communication channel between the nodes and prevents them from communicating with each other. Node tampering entails physical tampering of the nodes to extract sensitive information [18, 30]. This attack can be prevented by enforcing spectrum techniques for radio communication [30].

Data Link Layer:
The data link layer multiplexes the various data streams, provides detection of the data frame, MAC and error control. Additionally, it ensures point to point or point to multipoint reliability [40]. Attacks in this layer include collision, unfairness, and battery exhaustion. When an attacker induces a collision, two nodes simultaneously transmit packets of data on the same frequency channel, and the collision of data packets results in small changes to the packets. Consequently, the data packets are identified as a mismatch at the receiving end, resulting in discarding of the affected packets for retransmission [41]. A repeated collision-based attack leads to unfairness.

An attacker can also deliberately fragment the packets in the data link layer to bypass the intrusion detection system and disrupt the entire message in the channel. Battery exhaustion is a DoS attack caused by a large number of requests and transmission over the channel, thereby causing unusually high traffic and making accessibility to the nodes very limited. This can be prevented by ignoring excessive requests without identifying authenticity or by adopting proper admission control mechanisms [30, 41].

Network Layer:
Network layer protocols can extend device connectivity from neighboring nodes to all other nodes within the WSN [30]. The function of the network layer in a WSN is routing. Attacks in this layer are numerous, including spoofing, replaying and misdirection of traffic, hello flood attack, homing, selective forwarding, Sybil and wormhole [41]. In hello flooding attack, a single malicious node can send a useless message which is replayed by the attacker to create high traffic and congestion in the communication channel. Such message, if routed to a node on the SCADA network connected to a WSN, can cause disruptive communication between devices on the network and the PLC with potential devastating consequence [18]. In a homing attack, a search is made in the traffic for cluster heads and key managers with the capability to shut down the entire network. These attacks can be prevented by application of commanding encryption mechanisms at the network layer [30]. A Sybil attack replicates a single node on the network and presents it with multiple identities to the other nodes to cause disruption. In a wormhole DoS, an attacker engages in tunneling of bits of data over a link with low latency, resulting in the relocation of the bits of data from its original position in the network. These attacks can be prevented by building durable key management and securing the routing protocol [30].

Transport Layer:
The transport layer of a WSN provides reliability of data transmission and avoids congestion resulting from high traffic in the routers [18]. At the transport layer, attacks can take the forms of flooding, which is a deliberate congestion of communication channels through the relay of unnecessary messages and high traffic. There could also be de-synchronization, an attack whereby fake messages are created at one or both endpoints requesting retransmission for the correction on a nonexistent error, resulting in loss of energy at the affected endpoints. These can be addressed by controlling the number of connections which a node can make or by using proper authentication mechanisms [30].

Application Layer:
The application layer of WSN is responsible for traffic management and for providing software for different applications which carry out the translation of data into a comprehensible form. Additionally, the layer helps in the collection of information by sending queries [40]. Attacks aimed at the application can include message interception, fabrication and modification, subversion and malicious code. Simple malicious code detection, isolation and enforcing a strong encryption mechanism can help prevent these attacks [30]. The security vulnerabilities inherent in both IP-based

SCADA networks and those over WSNs call for effective IoT risk assessment and management in order to help provide workable antidotes to the threats and potential exploits.

1.6 Assessing Cybersecurity Risks of SCADA Systems

IoT creates three kinds of risk: (1) an IoT device can malfunction; (2) it can be hacked; and (3) our efforts to protect privacy or to make IoT devices more secure can create economic harm that outweighs the reduction in risk [42]. Risk assessment is the process of identifying, estimating and prioritizing risk to the organizational assets and operations [43]. It is a critical activity within risk management as it provides the foundation for the identified risks to be treated. Once the risk is assessed, treatment options include risk acceptance for cases where the risk is at an acceptable level considering the organization's risk appetite, risk mitigation using security controls, risk transfer through the purchase of cyber insurance, or risk avoidance by removing the affected assets [44].

From the standpoint of cyber and IoT security, the key concepts to note in risk assessment are assets, vulnerabilities, threats, attack, likelihood, and impact or cyber harm [44]. Assets can be defined as any items of value to the organization, and can have different properties. For example, assets can be tangible, such as SCADA system critical infrastructures like an electrical grid, or intangible, such as the reputation of the government. Vulnerabilities define the weaknesses which can be exploited in assets or in the controls put in place to protect the assets. A threat is the action that could adversely impact, and typically involves exploiting vulnerability. Such actions can be deliberate such as hacking a government's network, or accidental such as not logging off one's computer after work [44]. Cybersecurity risk entails a combination of these concepts, and considers the likelihood of successful exploitation of vulnerability through an attack and the impact of such attack [44].

Most researchers believe that the computing devices used in the Internet of Things will be even more vulnerable than the Internet technologies to which we are accustomed, given the technical limitations of many IoT computing devices. Simply because a SCADA network is connected to the Internet in an IoT environment does not mean someone will exploit it for malicious purposes. An attacker has to decide to exploit a vulnerability after calculating whether an attack will provide economic, political, social or military benefit. When a vulnerability is exploited through a malicious attack, the key thought that should come to mind is the impact or consequence of the attack [42]. Thus, vulnerability is not the sole variable for predicting risk. Therefore, to estimate the risk created by the mix of vulnerable SCADA network devices connected to the Internet, malicious actors and potentially harmful consequences, we need to ask how likely it is that we will see malicious action to exploit vulnerabilities to produce harmful consequences [42].

Catastrophic risk is the probability of an incident where a malicious attack on an IoT device or a device on a SCADA network connected to the Internet would produce mass fatalities or major economic damage. The result of a catastrophic IoT attack on a SCADA network can be likened to the 2003 Northeastern United States blackout, which cost an estimated $6 billion largely through lost production [45]. Thus, it is possible that a well-planned and executed attack on IP-based or WSN-based SCADA system that controls large networks and also lacks safeguards could produce a similar effect. Electrical grid vulnerability to cyber attack has been a topic of concern in many years. Although there has been some progress in making the grid more secure, the progress has been uneven. Given the existing vulnerabilities of the electrical grid, IoT introduces a new kind of vulnerability but how much risk is increased depends on how IoT devices and SCADA networks are designed and used [42].

To strengthen the security of SCADA networks in an IoT environment, it is essential to first analyze existing protocols to understand the vulnerabilities present in the protocols. An understanding of the protocol vulnerabilities would help in developing rules for IDS, and to develop attack signatures for each of the potential exploits which could be included in the IDS. The digital signatures will enable SCADA administrators to monitor the security of their networks. When analyzing any protocol, it is useful to distinguish between two categories of vulnerabilities: those that are inherent in the protocol specification itself, and those that are the result of improper implementation of the protocol [46]. Although, it is easier to address vulnerabilities resulting from improper implementation than those inherent in the protocol specification, both categories of vulnerabilities should be addressed to improve the overall security of the SCADA network.

Within the context of cybersecurity, a considerable variation exists in approach, guides and tools for conducting risk assessments. These vary according to context and the type of organizations for which the assessment is designed. Examples of the most popular and well-regarded approaches are NIST SP800-30, ISO/IEC 27001, OCTAVE, CRAMM and EBIOS [47]. While NIST and ISO/IEC originate from standard-setting bodies, CRAMM and EBIOS originate from the UK government and French government, respectively [44]. Regarding the nature of the approach, some risk assessment processes are grounded around critical assets such as SCADA systems and the harm that may occur to them as a result of vulnerability exploitation. OCTAVE is an approach that emphasizes the identification of critical assets first, and then builds outwards in terms of how those assets can be threatened and the result of the threat [47]. The NIST approach begins with the identification of threat sources and events [43]. This is followed by identifying the vulnerabilities that might be exploited and the respective likelihood and impact of threat events, before determining risks [44]. The benefit of the asset-oriented approach is that it ensures assessments are centered on critical infrastructure rather than ephemeral threats, while the threat-oriented approach tends to be better catered to current threat landscapes [44]. Regardless of the assessment methodology used, there are some inherent weaknesses pertaining to its use in IoT environment that need to be recognized and addressed to ensure a more effective risk assessment.

1.6.1 Weaknesses of Existing Risk Assessment Approaches

Despite the well-known existing risk assessment methodologies, Nurse et al. [44] provide four reasons why the current approaches are inadequate for IoT. These reasons are the shortcomings of periodic assessment, changing systems and boundaries of IoT and yet limited systems knowledge of assessors, the challenge of understanding the glue that enables communication between IoT devices, and the failure to consider assets as an attack platform [44]. Current risk assessment approaches are based on periodic assessment and assume that systems will not significantly change in a short period of time. These assumptions do not hold for the IoT where there is vast variability in scale of system, dynamism and system coupling.

Nurse et al. [44] also argue existing risk assessments typically mandate some reasonable knowledge on assets, threats, probabilities of attack and potential impact but such knowledge is extremely challenging to attain within IoT systems. Furthermore, traditional risk assessment is targeted towards well-known assets, including information, devices, communication platforms and interfaces. Such directed focus is flawed for IoT in that it fails to assess the process through which devices are bound, the connections that allow them to couple and operate, and the inner workings of the actors themselves [44]. Finally, current risk assessment approaches regard assets only as things of value to the organization and ignore the fact that in the IoT environment, assets such as devices on SCADA networks can be the basis for attacks and can be used as distributed cyber weapons [44].

Given the existing flaws in the current assessment approaches, there is the need for automated and continuous risk assessment approaches, as well as the development of new support tools to assist with simulation and modeling for enhancing our predictive powers [48]. Additionally, new assessment methodologies should take into account the fact that the glue that binds IoT systems and their actors will provide a mechanism for risk propagation and creation of harm at physical, social and economic scales [44]. In order to develop and implement solutions for the findings from cybersecurity risk assessments, organizations in charge of SCADA systems in IoT environment need to have a robust risk management system in place.

1.6.2 Managing Cybersecurity Risks of SCADA Networks

To raise the cyber security of SCADA networks in IoT environments to an acceptable level, appropriate risk management and security planning are needed. This begins with establishing a control framework that defines a comprehensive set of security objectives that should be fulfilled to meet the business goals of organizations in charge of critical infrastructure such as SCADA systems. To ensure proper enforcement of the security objectives, the control framework should include a clearly defined security policy followed by a security plan and implementation guidelines. Additionally, there should be a well-defined configuration management plan and an auditing and assessment plan. The security policy must be comprehensive and should cover areas such as communication security policy, data security policy, physical security policy, and audit policy. The control framework should also include a set of standards and guidelines that need to be complied with to ensure maximum enforcement of security policy. These include authorization and authentication standards and guidelines, logging, auditing and monitoring standards and guidelines, vulnerability and patch management standards and guidelines, hardening standards and guidelines, as well as virus management standards and guidelines. Together, these help to form a solid control framework for managing cybersecurity risks of SCADA systems in the IoT environment.

Implementation of a comprehensive risk management system entails developing a key means of protecting SCADA networks from cyber threat. This includes physically separating the SCADA IP network from the corporate network and other untrustworthy networks. To accomplish this, SCADA network design should be such that components and devices inside the SCADA systems should not have direct communication and connection with the Internet. In situations where corporate network infrastructure such as switches, routers, and WAN link are used as transmission media for portions of the SCADA communication, such communication should be encrypted and routed through a VPN tunnel that runs through corporate IT or other noncritical networks [30]. Effective cybersecurity should entail active blocking devices such as firewall, IDS and in-line network antivirus appliances. A basic function of a firewall is to block unauthorized traffic from entering the protected network, and prevent the establishment of a direct connection from the outside Internet to the SCADA network. They can be configured to recognize and allow only traffic belonging to certain protocols, and to control and monitor the activities of authorized entities accessing the network.

From design and procedural standpoint, quality assurance techniques should be implemented to ensure all security and quality requirements are recognized, incorporated into the design and tested with the final product. Those manning an IP-based SCADA network should disable unnecessary services which apply to IP-enabled telecommunication devices, network equipment, PLCs, protocol gateway converters and any other embedded device on the network [30]. In order to enable the filtering and dropping of packets and traffic known to be malevolent based on heuristic and signature matches, in-line network appliances should be deployed at the choke points to perform network intrusion prevention and antivirus functions [30].

Complex SCADA systems over mixed wireless and wired networks share the same security challenges of WSN in addition to security threats from connection to the IP. For networks over 6LowPAN, IEEE 802.15.4 uses IP security Protocol (IPsec) as a default security protocol. However, the key management solution for IPsec, the Internet Key Exchange (IKE), is considered too large due to the high number of signaling messages. Consequently, a smaller packet size and low communication overhead without compromising the security level will be considered as the key management solutions for 6LowPAN [30]. 6LowPANs that require medium to low-security authentications can use symmetric keys for tightening their security communication. In practice, symmetric algorithms are used for encryption and decryption of most data. Riaz et al. [49] presented and evaluated key management schemes against a broad range of metrics, including energy, resource utilization, scalability and resilience to node communication. Depending on the outcome desired by SCADA security expert of a particular network, the appropriate key management may be chosen accordingly [30].

Just as in IP-based SCADA systems, WSN-based SCADA system connected over 6LowPAN must deploy IDS continuously to monitor the network and isolate malicious nodes and detect abnormal activities once the bootstrapping phase between the SCADA master and the registration authority is established. The security of 6LowPAN architecture can be beefed up with IEEE 802.15.4 Advanced Encryption Standard in conjunction with IP security. Additionally, modified IPsec may be a feasible option for securing IoT in terms of packet size, energy consumption, memory usage and process time [30].

1.7 Conclusion

This chapter has reviewed the cybersecurity risks of SCADA networks of critical infrastructures in the IoT environment, and suggested risk management techniques to address them. The literature suggests that devices on IoT and SCADA networks have a lot in common and share similar security challenges. Both IoT and SCADA systems have embedded devices with limited computational capabilities and low rate of data transmission which make them vulnerable to various kinds of DoS attacks with confidentiality, integrity and system availability implications. With advances in IP-based and WSN technologies such as IPv6 and 6LowPAN, many SCADA networks that operated in isolation a few years ago are now connected to corporate networks and the Internet. While this enhances network communication and data transmission for efficiency of operations, it exposes various devices on SCADA networks to the same cybersecurity challenges faced by the IoT.

To effectively manage the security challenges of SCADA systems connected to the Internet, effective risk assessment methodologies and risk management strategies need to be implemented. This begins with establishing a control framework that defines a comprehensive set of security objectives with policies, standards and guidelines that should be enforced to meet the business goals of organizations in charge of critical infrastructures. Effective risk assessment should entail identifying, estimating and prioritizing risk to the organizational assets and operations to provide the foundation for the identified risks to be treated. To strengthen the security of SCADA networks in IoT environments, it is essential to first analyze existing protocols to understand their vulnerabilities, and to help in developing rules for IDS, as well as in developing attack signatures for each of the potential exploits which could be included in the IDS.

Finally, a key means of ensuring comprehensive cybersecurity risk management for SCADA systems is to design the SCADA network such that the component devices do not directly connect and communicate to external devices on the Internet.

This could be done by installing active blocking devices such as firewall, intrusion prevention system and in-line network antivirus appliances.

References

1. IEEE (2014) Special report: the internet of things. Accessed 2 Oct 2018
2. de Leusse P, Periorellis P, Dimitrakos T, Nali, SK (2009) Self- managed security cell, a security model for the internet of things and services. In: Paper presented at first international conference on advances in future internet
3. Maple C (2017) Security and privacy in the internet of things. J Cyber Policy 2(2):155–184
4. Whitmore A, Agarwal A, Xu LD (2015) The internet of things. a survey of topics and trends. Inf. Syst. Front 17(2):261–274
5. Li S, Xu LD, Zhao S (2015) The internet of things. a survey. In Syst Front 17(2):243–259
6. Atzori L, Lera A, Morabito G (2010) The internet of things. a survey. Comput Netw 54(15):2787–2805. https://doi.org/10.1016/j.connect.2010.05.010
7. Libelium (2015) 50 sensor applications for a smarter world. libelium.com/resources/top_50_iot_sensor_applications_ranking/, Accessed 30 Sept 2018
8. Zanilla A, Bui N, Castellani A, Vangelista L, Zorzi M (2014) Internet of things for smart cities. IEEE Internet Things J 1(1):22–32. https://doi.org/10.1106/jiot.2014.2306328
9. Miorandi D, Sicari S, De Pellegrini F, Clamatac I, (2012) Internet of things: vision, applications and research challenges. Ad Hoc Netw 10(7):1497–1516. https://doi.org/10.1016/j.adhoc.2012.02.016
10. Al-Fuqaha A, Guizani M, Mohammadi M, Aledhari M, Ayyash M (2015) Internet of things: a survey on enabling technologies, protocols, and applications. IEEE Commun Surv Tutor 17(4):2347–2376
11. Li L, Xiaoguang H, Ke C, Ketai H (2011) The application of WiFi-based wireless sensor network in Internet of things and smart grid. In: Paper presented at the proceedings of the 6th IEEE conference on industrial electronics and applications, Beijin, China, 21–23 June 789–793
12. Phull S (2012) Intelligent transport systems in the UK. World Scientific. https://ec.europa.eu/transport/sites/transport/files/themes/its/road/action_plan/doc/2012-united-kingdon-its-5-year-plan-2012_en.pdf, Accessed 3 Oct 2018
13. Uckelmann D, Harrison M, Michahelles F (2011) An architectural approach towards the future Internet of thing. In: Architecting the internet of things, Springer, Berlin, Heidelberg, pp 1–24
14. Macaulay J, Buckalew L, Chung G (2015) Internet of things in logistics. DHL Trend Res 1(1):1–27. In: Uckelmann D, Harrison M, Michalelles F (eds) Internet of things. Springer, Berlin, pp 1–24
15. British Land (2017) Smart offices I British Land—the office agenda. https://officeagenda.britishland.com/smart-offices. Accessed 28 Aug 2018
16. Bui N, Zorzi M (2011) Health care applications: a solution based on the internet of things. In: Proceedings of the 4th international symposium on applied sciences in biomedical and communication technologies. ACM, Barcelona, Spain, 26–29 October, pp 1–5
17. Islam SMR, Kwak D, Kabir H, Hossain M, Kwak K (2015) The internet of things for health care: a comprehensive survey. IEEE Access 3:678–708. https://doi.org/10.1109/access.2015.2437951
18. Borgohain T, Kumar U, Sanyal S (2015) Survey of security and privacy issues of Internet of things. https://arxiv.org/abs/1501.02211, Accessed 6 Oct 2018
19. Ning H, Liu H (2012) Cyber-physical-social based security architecture for future Internet of things. Adv Internet Things 2:1–7
20. ITU (2012) Internet of thing global initiative. Recommendations ITU-T Y. 2060

21. Chen L (2017) Security management for the internet of things. A thesis submitted to the faculty of graduate studies through the department of electrical and computer engineering in partial fulfillment of the requirements for the degree master of applied science at the university of windsor. Windsor, Ontario Canada
22. Burnmester M, De Medeiros B (2007) Security: attacks, countermeasures and challenges. In: The 5th RFID academic convocation, the RFID journal conference
23. Padmavathi G, Shanmugapriya D (2009) A survey of attacks, security mechanisms and challenges in wireless sensor networks. aXiv preprint https://arxiv.org/abs/0909.0576
24. Vohra S, Srivastava R (2015) A survey on techniques for securing. In: 5th international conference on communication systems and network technologies, pp 643–646
25. ITU (2005) The internet of things, Geneva, Switzerland. https://www.itu.int/net/wsis/tunis/newsroom/stats/The-Internet-of-Things-2005.pdf, Accessed 29 Sep 2018
26. Karagiannis V, Chatzimisios P, Vazquez-Vallego F, Alonso-Zarete J (2015) A survey of application layer protocols for internet of things. Trans IoT Cloud Comput 1–8
27. Vermesan O, Friess P (2016) Internet of things from research and innovation to market deployment. River Publishers, Aalborg, Denmark
28. National Communications System (2004) Supervisory control and data acquisition systems. Technical Innovation Bulletin, 04–1
29. Igure VM, Laughter SA, Williams RD (2006) Security issues in networks. Comput Secur 25:498–506
30. Kim H (2012) Security and vulnerability of systems over IP-based wireless sensor networks. Int J Distrib Sens Netw 2012:1–10
31. Carlson R (2002) Sandia program: high security SCADA LDRD final report. Sandia National Laboratories Report, SAND, 2002-072 Apr
32. Sauter T, Schwaiger C, (2002) Achievement of secure internet access to fieldbus systems. Microprocess Microsyst 26(7):331–339
33. Ryu DH, Kim H, Um K (2009) Reducing security for critical infrastructures. J Loss Prev Process Ind 22(6):1020–1024
34. Akyildiz IF, Weilan S, Sankarasubramaniam Y, Gayirci E (2002) A survey on sensor networks. IEEE Commun Mag 40(8):102–114
35. Montenegro G, Kushalnagar N, Hui J, Culler D (2007) Transmission of packets over IEEE 802.15.4 networks. RFC, 4994 (Proposed Standard)
36. Heer T, Garcia-Morchon O, Hummen R, Eoh SLK, Kumar SS, Wehrle K (2011) Challenges in the IP-based internet of things. Wirel Pers Commun 61(3):527–542
37. Hui JW, Culler DE, Chakrabarti S (2009) Incorporating IEEE 802.15.4 into IP architecture. Internet Protocol for Smart Objects (IPSO) Alliance, White Paper #3
38. Sharifinejad M, Shari M, Ghiasabadi M, Beheshti A (2007) A survey on wireless sensor networks security, In: SETIT
39. Wang BT, Schulzrime H (2004) An IP trace back mechanism for reflective DoS attacks. In: Canadian conference on electrical and computer engineering, vol 2, pp 901–904
40. Alkhatib AA, Baicher GS (2012) Wireless sensor network architecture. In: International conference on computer networks and communication systems (CNCS 2012) IPCSIT, vol 35, pp 11–15
41. Ghildyal S, Mishra AK, Gupta A, Garg N (2014). Analysis of denial of service (DoS) attacks in wireless sensor networks. IJRET Int J Res Eng Technol. eISSN: 2319-1163, pISSN: 2321-7308
42. Lewis JA (2016) Managing risk for the internet of things. A report of the CSIS strategic technologies program. https://www.csis.org/analysis/managing-risk-internet-things, Accessed 1 Oct 2018
43. National Institute of Standards and Technology [NIST] (2012) Guide for conducting risk assessments SP-800-30—Revision 1. https://nvlpubs.nist.gov/nistpubs/legacy/sp/nistspecialpublication800-30r1.pdf, Accessed 18 Sept 2018
44. Nurse JRC, Creese S, Roure D (2017) Security risk assessment in internet of things environment. https://ieeexplore.ieee.org/document/8057728, Accessed 31 Aug 2018

45. Minkel JR (2008) The 2003 northeast blackout: five years later. In: Scientific American. https://www.uvm.edu/~phines/media/sciam-blackout.pdf, Accessed Aug 13–7 Sept 2018
46. Franz M (2004) Protocol implementation testing challenges and opportunities. In: National infrastructure security coordination center (NISCC) workshop
47. ENISA (2016) Risk management resources and approaches. https://www.enisa.europa.eu/topics/threat-risk-management/risk-management, Accessed 28 June 2018
48. Shameli-Sendi A, Aghababaei-Barzegar R, Cheriet M (2016) Taxanomy of information security risk assessment (IRSA). Comput Secur 57:14–30
49. Riaz R, Naureen A, Akram A, Akbar H, Kim KH, Ahmed AF (2008) A unified security framework for three key management schemes for wireless sensor networks. Comput Commun 31(18):4269–4280

Chapter 2
Energy-Perceptive Authentication in Virtual Private Networks Using GPS Data

N. Ambika

Abstract The Internet of Things (IoT) enables communication between diverse devices from different vendors via a common platform that provides the necessary support in making the communication possible. These are generally unsupervised networks that are liable to threats arising from different kinds of external attacks. Hence, the security of devices, communication, and data becomes a priority issue in this kind of setup. One of the preliminary measures considered to combat these threats is authentication, which acts as a preventive approach. It aids in detecting the legitimacy of the communicating parties, whether humans or other interconnected smart devices. Another approach to enhance security is the use of Virtual Private Networks (VPN), which is slowly replacing the wired networks. The data transmitted in these wireless networks often remains more secure and reliable. This chapter discusses the VPN methodology, presents the relevant analysis and the outcomes. The proposed study utilizes the Virtual Private Network infrastructure setup and adopts mutual authentication protocols, using the Global Positioning System (GPS), before proceeding with the actual data transmission. We establish that authentication using Global Positioning System (GPS) considerably enhances the overall security of the network. Furthermore, considering that energy is a scarce resource, we discuss the preservation of the same. The work we present reduces energy consumption by 82% compared to the previous similar studies. In our proposal, the authentication keys generated are different for every session. This measure also tackles wormhole attacks in the network. It ensures a 4% increase in security in comparison to previously published work. The proposed work also preserves forward-secrecy.

Keywords Virtual private network · VPN · IoT · Markov chain concept · GPS · GPS-enabled transmission · Mutual authentication · Wormhole attack · Energy consumption · Forward-secrecy

---

N. Ambika (✉)
Computer Science Department, HKBK Degree College, Bangalore, India
e-mail: ambika.nagaraj76@gmail.com

Z. Mahmood (ed.), *Security, Privacy and Trust in the IoT Environment*, https://doi.org/10.1007/978-3-030-18075-1_2

2.1 Introduction

Internet of Things (IoT) enables communication between diverse connected devices [1, 2] that fall into several different categories. They have their own capabilities and limitations. IoT provides a common platform where the devices are able to communicate with each other. The provision is also available in wireless media. Wired networks are usually safer than wireless networks. However, Virtual Private Networks (VPN) have now provided a new platform that is much more secure. The devices within VPN are at par with wired networks devices. Security is enhanced between two end-to-end points using Virtual Private Networks. Although wired networks have their own pitfalls, presently, we are beginning to prefer wireless networks over wired ones. The wireless networks aid in transmitting the data to the cloud [3]; and the mobile devices provide a user interface to accomplish the same. These unattended devices are liable to get compromised. They tend to launch different kinds of attacks. Hence safety becomes essential. Virtual Private Network solves the issue by providing a secure communication platform.

Many different types of data breaches can occur in these networks. Using a preventive or detection system solves the problem. Intrusion detection systems [4–6] aids in notifying the respective authorities; the harm caused to the data or the devices are notified on time. This approach provides the deployment to take appropriate measures. Another approach is the use of preventative systems. The intrusion prevention systems aid in preventing an adversary from taking over the devices. One such prevention measure is authentication [7]. Authenticating single communicating party brings in a good amount of security. But the other party has to be a trustable one. Two-way authentication serves a better purpose. This chapter details the mutual authentication approach.

The study proposed in this chapter implements an intrusion prevention system to enhance security in the network. In the proposed work, the Global Positioning System (GPS) is considered to support and aid in the mutual authentication. Both the communicating parties verify their legitimacy. The measures taken avoid the repetition of the same cycle to authenticate. At a different time, the devices need not follow the same approach. Our work adopts exchanging energy conservative approach as well. New derived hash code exchanges provide authentication. The approach minimizes wormhole attacks in the network. The work increases 4% security compared to the previous work. This chapter also considers the limitations of similar previous work. The drawbacks of the previous work are considered and taken care of to aid in the building of a better system. Working on the drawbacks, this chapter narrates the approach used to curtail the problematic steps. It details the analysis and the outcome of the newly adopted approach.

This chapter has six sections. The Introduction section narrates the technology considered and summarizes the outcome of the new approach. The following section discusses the previous researchers' works and details the different approaches suggested by various authors. Section 2.3 details the foreword to provide the background to the development of the proposed work. Section 2.4 presents detailed working of the proposed system. Section 2.5 provides a detailed analysis report and discusses the energy conservation and security aspects. Finally, Sect. 2.6 provides a brief summary and conclusions.

2.2 Literature Survey

VPN is a wireless infrastructure that has aided connected devices to communicate in a secure manner. Many authors have proposed various algorithms to implement security in VPN systems. This section provides further information on such studies.

The authors in [7] have proposed a lightweight authentication protocol. The algorithm consists of a statistical scheme, that provides lightweight per-frame identification at the link layer. It is designed to implement an authentication procedure. The series of packets arriving at the destination are on the constant check. In [8], the authors have come up with mutual authentication between user and the WLAN architecture. Here, a key agreement EAP-SIM encapsulated within the internet key exchange version 2 is used; and the VPN deployed uses IPSec. The setup ensures confidentiality, authentication and integrity to data. The users are also provided with privileges to connect to 3G networks and avail billing services using EAP-SIM authentication protocol. The communication between Network Access Server (NAS) and Authentication, Authorization, and Accounting (AAA) server is based on the diameter the two communicating devices reside. The preset IPSec channel aids in protecting the data communicated between the set diameters. The approach enhances the security level and trust between the two communicating parties.

In a study reported in [9], the authors have proposed a security model for smart home systems. The user convenience is regarded as much more important in their work. The system runs on conventional WiFi network; the implementation is based on Alljoyn framework. Asymmetric elliptic cryptography is used to accomplish the authentication. The system configuration is performed by the WIFI gateway used as the center node. The responsibility of the center node is to authenticate the communicating parties. It also provides mean for user setup, access and control of the system. The user is provided with the android based mobile device running appropriate application program.

Porambage et al. [10] have proposed an implicit certificate-based authentication. The model is considered in a distributed, sensors collaborating to bring in the IoT network. The model provides a platform for the sensors to authenticate each other and initiate secure connections. The system undergoes two phases. Registration phase is used to obtain security credentials from the trusted parties; the Authentication phase is used to commence interactions between two communicating parties. The model uses ECC (Elliptical Curve Cryptography) with equal security similar to the RSA algorithm with less overhead. The certificates generated consume less space and are hence feasible in the considered system. The proposed work is useful to secure the network from DoS attacks.

The original Nyberg's fast one-way accumulator is revised in [11]. The members of the group authenticate each other using one-way accumulator. The model uses two parameters: the first would be shared keys between sender and receiver; and the second one would be multicast data. The lightweight multicast authentication mechanism is built using MAC. The same is used for small scale IoT applications. The proposed work provides similar levels of security as proposed by other authors. The security depends on the properties of HMAC function. The work proves to provide better security. If one of the scheduled receivers is compromised, the same does not affect other scheduled receivers to verify signature and communication doings.

The principles of lightweight identity based elliptic curve cryptography and Lamport's OTP algorithm are proposed in [12]. The sustainability of authentication scheme is based on one-time password (OTP) for IoT is reviewed. Lamport's OTP generation algorithms are based on the successive computation of hash functions. The function is used on some random number of times with initial random seed. The proposed algorithm has proved to be equivalent to the computational Diffie–Hellman algorithm.

In [13], the authors have proposed an ultra-lightweight mutual authentication protocol. The model uses only the bitwise operation. The analysis shows resistance against several attacks like asynchronization, secret disclosure, and traceability attacks. Efficient authentication and access control methods is proposed in [14]. Lightweight ECC is used to accomplish authentication procedure followed by securing the session key. The model aids in providing only legitimate nodes to access resources. The proposed system limits the privileges of the authenticated users using attribute-based access control policy. The model tackles man-in-the-middle attack, eavesdropping attack, node capture attack, DoS attacks and replay attacks.

In the study by Kai Fan [15], the lightweight RFID mutual authentication protocol is proposed. The model helps to reduce computational and transmission cost. The presented work provides forward security by using two different random numbers in every session. The hash function is used to transmit the message and hence eavesdropping is taken care. The communicator uses the parameters obtained before to disguise the tag to communicate with the reader. Hence replaying the attack is taken care of. The protocol also takes care of the spoofing attack and DoS attacks.

A secure authentication mechanism is proposed by a study reported in [16]. The suggested model consists of various kinds of constrained devices with a security manager. The security manager uses the OAuth 2.0 protocol which is an open standard authorization protocol that allows the users to grant the third-party application access to restricted resources without providing access to their credentials. The same protects the network from unauthorized users. The security manager is granted access through the service provider using the protocol service. Impersonation attacks and replay attacks are taken care of by this approach.

In [17], the authors have proposed a two-way authentication security scheme. Public-key cryptography is used; and the model considers the assumption that IPv6 and 6LoWPAN are used in the network. Hydro is used for routing. The model uses a Datagram Transport layer security protocol (DTLS) that employs authenticity, integrity and confidentiality. DTLS handshake employs client and server authentication.

Certificate-based DTLS protocols are used in the design in [18]. The authentication and authorization architecture is evaluated by developing the prototype for IoT-based healthcare system. Pandaboard, T1 smartRF06 boards, and WisMotes are used in the design. CC2538 model is assimilated in the T1 board. This device acts as the smart gateway and the suggested arrangement provides a secure platform between the sensors and the gateway. The design aids in reducing DoS attacks in the network.

2.3 Background to the Proposed Study

The work suggested in this chapter aims to curtail the lengthy process of authentication, that is a multi-cycle process. The first cycle uses the approach similar to the one proposed in [19]. The succeeding cycles use partial hash codes to authenticate the relevant devices. The approach also aims to conserve energy of the devices. Changing the authentication keys minimizes wormhole attack in the network. The work uses some well-known theories, e.g., the Markov chain concept [20–22] is used in the work that aids to camouflage the GPS position of the server. Mutual authentication carried out between the communicating parties uses this outcome.

The new concept in our study provides an improvised version of the idea in [19]. The proposed work minimizes energy consumption; it also enhances security to the devices by adopting mutual authentication using GPS. The method adopted also helps to minimizes wormhole attacks in the network.

2.3.1 Resolving Wormhole Attacks Using Markov Chain Concept

Wormhole attack is an attack introduced by an adversary. The devices under the control of the adversary capture the packets and replay the same. This provides a false illusion of the environment to the receiver. To tackle this attack, the proposed work uses Markov chain concept [20–22]. Changing the related parameters for every session enhances security in the network.

The server is the most trustable source. Securing the GPS position is essential. If the authentication key is compromised, the adversary will be able to gain access to the GPS of the server. It will launch different kinds of attacks into the network. To avoid such incidents the server generates the second derivative of the GPS. This derivative authenticates its client. Markov chain has the property that the probability of transition between any two states depends entirely on the circumstances in the state from which the transition originates, and not on the previous history of the process.

Refer to Eq. (1). Here $X_{n+1}, X_n \ldots X_1$ denote the previous states; while x, x_n denote the derived states

$$\Pr(X_{n+1} = x | X_n = x_n \ldots X_1 = x_n) = \Pr(X_{n+1} = x | X_n = x_n) \tag{2.1}$$

The server is responsible to accept the requests from the users. It is to post service digital signature and parameters. The proposed work does not want to compromise the GPS of the server. But it is willing to change the authentication parameters for every session. The Global Positioning System (GPS) used is the second derivative. The first derived hash code of the GPS is not transmitted. Markov chain concept used generates the second derivative. Hence the GPS location of the server is not compromised. The different authentication code used every time results in better security.

2.3.2 VPN Authentication Using GPS Information

Global positioning system (GPS) takes care to minimize Wormhole attacks in the network. This is one such parameter which would be unique to the device. This parameter is used to authenticate the communicating parties serves the purpose. The approach provides stronger security in the network.

The work proposed in [19] implements one-way authentication using GPS. There, the authors have suggested using GPS information to authentication the devices. The GPS information is dispatched by the client when the request to the server is made. The hash value of the same dispatched replaces the raw value. Hence the method aims in providing security to the information. The system uses the following steps to accomplish the tasks.

1. The client initiates by requesting VPN connection to the server. The server transmits server certificate with the digital signature to the client. The client verifies the received message using stored root certificate authentication (CA). After validating positively, the client extracts the public key from the server certificate.
2. Using the extracted public key, the client encrypts a random string and transmits the same to the server. A pre-shared key using random string is generated by the client. The server also constructs the same pre-shared key using the received random string.
3. The server puts a request for the client certificate. The server receives the same along with encrypted hash value of GPS information and a signature. The server's public key is used to encrypt the GPS information. The signature is derived using the client private key.
4. The server evaluates the client certificate and obtains the public key from the received message.

5. The encrypted GPS information is decrypted using the client private key. The server validates the GPS information with the client private key. The server communicates further upon successful validation.

Limitations of the Above System

The proposed work (as detailed later in this chapter) considers the drawbacks of the previous work as reported in [19] and attempts to make improvements. The existing limitations in [19] have the following core disadvantages:

- Devices undergo authentication before actual data transmission commences. All cycles adopt the same steps. The working becomes laborious. Energy consumption for the same is high.
- The system uses the same authentication parameters, each time. The devices controlled by adversary can also introduce attacks. The procedure increases the occurrences of the wormhole attacks.

Our proposed work aims to remove the above limitations to bring in better security. It also helps to minimize the attacks in the network. GPS information used to tackle wormhole attack [23] proves effective. The proposed study undergoes mutual authentication using the same. The work uses Markov chain concept to conceal the GPS information of the server.

2.4 Proposed Work

The proposed work brings in better reliability and security to the network. It considers the approach similar to the one used in [19] but extends it. The resulting minimization of energy aids in the conservation of the resource. The first cycle of the work is similar to [19]. The succeeding cycles aim to curtail the steps. The approach also aims to deriving new authentication keys for every session. This approach aims to reducing wormhole attacks in the network.

2.4.1 Assumptions Made in the Proposed Work

The proposed work makes certain assumptions as follows:

- The mobile node is capable to move from place to another. It connects to the network before it requires communicating with the server. The network to which it connects is the home network. The home network considered is very secure.
- The router in the home network maintains the information about the mobile node.
- The adversaries are capable of introducing a wormhole attack in the network.
- Measures taken do not store the hash code in the mobile devices. The hash code related to the server is stored. The regenerated hash code aims to prevent forward-secrecy.

Table 2.1 Symbols used in the proposed work

Symbols	Description
U_i	ith user (Client)
R_{VPN}	Request for VPN connection
S_i	ith server
DS_s	Digital certificate of the server
S_c	Server certificate
GPS_{s2}	2 derivate of GPS coordinates using Markov chain concept
PB_{key}	Public key
Str	Random string
R_{cc}	Request for client certificate
DS_u	Digital certificate of the client
U_c	Client certificate
GPS_u	GPS coordinate value of the client

The symbols used in the present study are listed in Table 2.1.

2.4.2 *Working of the Proposed System*

The proposed system uses GPS information to conduct mutual authentication. This approach brings in better security between the communicating parties. The cycle proceeds similarly to the idea in [19]. Changes reflect from the second cycle onwards. After the first attempt, some steps are cut-short. The method conserves energy and brings in better security to the network. The following steps are carried out in the proposed algorithm:

1. The client initiates by requesting VPN connection to the server. In Eq. (2), the client U_i requests for VPN connection with the server S_i. R_{VPN} is the request raised by the client for VPN connection. The server transmits server certificate with the digital signature and second derived the hash value of its GPS location to the client. Equation (3) represents the same. In Eq. (3) server S_i is transmitting server certificate S_c, digital certificate DS_s and second derived hash value GPS_{s2}. The client verifies the first part of the received message using stored root certificate authentication (CA). After validating positively, the client extracts the public key from the server certificate. The second part of the received message is kept for later use.

$$U_i \rightarrow S_i : R_{VPN} \tag{2.2}$$

$$S_i \rightarrow U_i : DS_s||S_c||H(GPS_{s2}) \tag{2.3}$$

2. Using the extracted public key, the client encrypts a random string and transmits the same to the server. Equation (4) represents the same. The client U_i generates a random string str using the public key PB_{key}. A pre-shared key using a random string is generated by the client. The server also constructs the same pre-shared key using the received random string.

$$U_i \rightarrow PB_{key}(str) \tag{2.4}$$

3. The server puts a request for the client certificate. In Eq. (5), the server S_i is requesting client U_i for the client certificate. R_{cc} represents the client certificate request. The server receives the same along with encrypted hash value of GPS information and a signature. In Eq. (6), the client U_i has transmitted digital signature DS_u, client certificate U_c and hash value of GPS_u. The server's public key is used to encrypt the GPS information. The signature is derived using the client private key.

$$S_i \rightarrow U_i : R_{CC} \tag{2.5}$$

$$U_i \rightarrow S_i : DS_u||U_c||H(GPS_u) \tag{2.6}$$

4. The server evaluates the client certificate and obtains the public key from the received message.
5. The encrypted GPS information is decrypted using the client private key. The server validates the GPS information with the client private key. The server communicates further upon successful validation.
6. Using the hash value of both the server and client the new hash value is derived. This generated code is useful to initiate the next interaction. In Eq. (7), the hash value of server GPS_{s2} and hash value of client GPS_u is combined to obtain new hash value GPS_{su}.

$$H(GPS_{s2}) \oplus H(GPS_u) \rightarrow H(GPS_{su}) \tag{2.7}$$

The above procedure aids in conserving energy as some of the steps taken during authentication, as suggested in [19], are eliminated. The same is represented in Figs. 2.1 and 2.2.

2.5 Analysis of the Proposed Work

As mentioned earlier, the proposed work extends the previous work reported in [19]. The new approach increases reliability and reduces energy consumption. The resources are conserved to bring in better practices. Energy is one such resource.

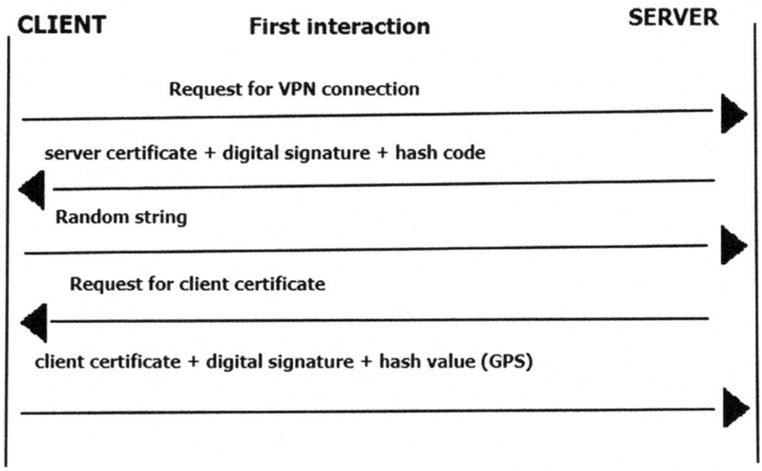

Fig. 2.1 First instance of client and server interaction

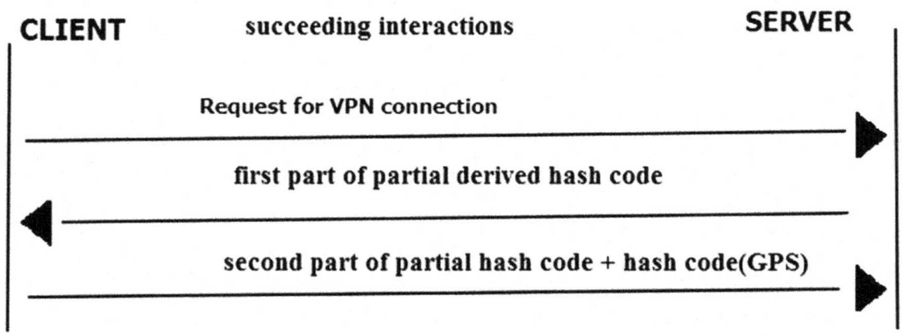

Fig. 2.2 succeding instances of client and server interaction

This section details the comparison of the proposed work with the previous work [19]. The first sub-section provides a comparison. The section details with the narration of the advantages of the proposed study. The second sub-section describes the positive effects of the proposed work; and the proposed work is compared to the previous work. The discussion on wormhole attacks is also presented.

2.5.1 Energy Consumption

Communication between two devices consumes more energy than processing. The receiver and the source consume energy based on the distance between them. The more the distance between the two devices, the higher the amount of energy required. Comparing to the proposed work with [19], the suggested work consumes less energy.

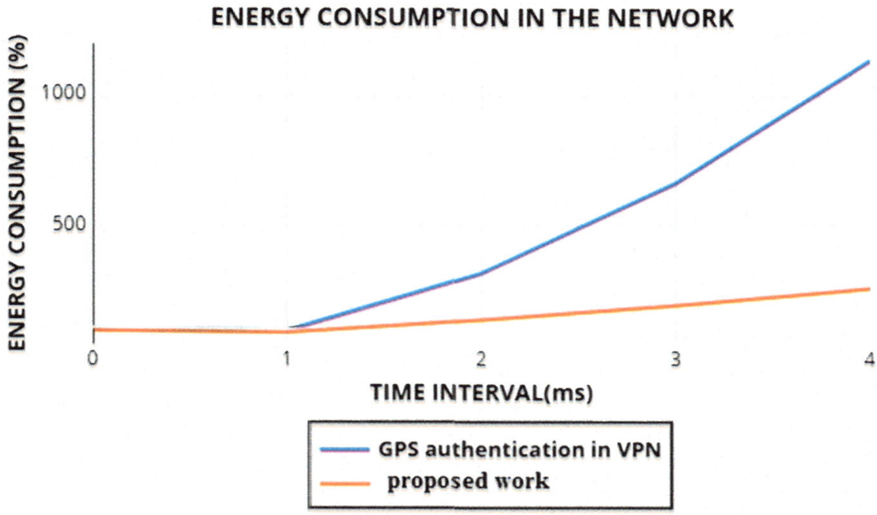

Fig. 2.3 Comparison of energy consumption as reported in [19] and the proposed work

The proposed work undergoes mutual authentication using GPS parameter. Hence the consumption of the energy will be more than the previous work [19]. The authentication between the server and client for first session is similar. Usage of additional parameters consumes 5% more energy than [19]. The succeeding sessions cut-off some of the steps of the process. The curtailing of some of the laborious and unnecessary steps aids in the energy conservation. Hence 82% of energy is conserved by the proposed work compared to the numbers presented in [19]. The graph in Fig. 2.3 represents the same.

2.5.2 *Wormhole Attacks*

The authors in [19] proposed the protocol to establish secure communication. Energy consumption in the work is observed to be high. Every time the two devices communicate, they have to undergo the entire authentication procedure. The authentication parameters are the same for all sessions. Hence the detection rate of wormhole attacks cannot be low if a device gets compromised.

The proposed work tackles different kinds of security attacks. Our proposal undergoes mutual authentication using GPS parameters. When the adversary can gain control of the device, the credentials get compromised. The proposed work takes care of this scenario. Measures taken in the process preserve the forward-secrecy of the keys. The approach alters the authentication key bringing better security to the network. If the mobile device gets compromised, it will be compromising the stored hash code. But the compromised device will not be able to generate the new hash

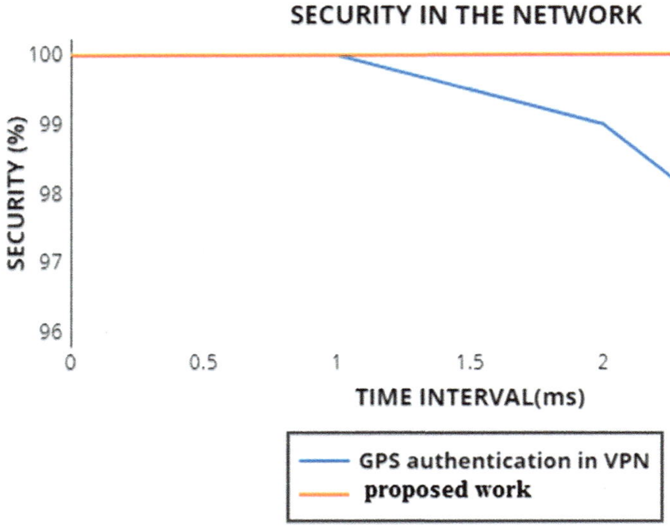

Fig. 2.4 Comparison of security proposed in [19] with that in the proposed work

value. Hence security is increased in the proposed work. The same is represented in Fig. 2.4. The security of the proposed work is increased by 4.16% compared to [19].

2.6 Conclusion

Internet of Things is an attractive paradigm used by a wide range of industries as well as individuals. The connected devices with different caliber aid in communicating with each other. These devices are often not supervised and hence require security. Virtual Private Network is one such technology that can help. This network substitutes wired network in wireless platforms. The resultant technology aids in providing better security than any other wireless system.

In this chapter, previous work reported in [19] is considered and the improvements suggested. The previous work repeats the same steps to undergo authentication every time. The client has to undergo same steps to avail services from the server. The method consumes lot of energy and is also ineffective in the case of wormhole attacks.

The system proposed in this chapter uses GPS coordinates to generate the hash values. The approach aids in secure communication and the mutual authentication adopted aims to better security. The steps of the process are curtailed to fewer steps in the succeeding stages in the proposed work. The approach aids in reducing energy consumption in the devices as well. The hash code exchanged by the two communicating parties is used to generate a new hash code value. To authenticate each other in succeeding interactions, the partial hash value is used. This is transmitted by both the communicating parties. On affirmation, transmission of data using the encryption key is commenced. This procedure enhances security by 4.16%. The method reduces wormhole attacks in the network. It also conserves energy of the devices by 82% compared to the earlier procedure suggested in [19].

References

1. He W, Li S (2014) Internet of things in industries: a survey. IEEE Trans Ind Inform, pp 2233–2243
2. Yaacoub A (2012) Cooperative wireless sensor networks for green Internet of things. In: 8th ACM symposium on QoS security wireless mobile network. Paphos, Cyprus, pp 79–80
3. Huang X (2010) MobiCloud: building secure cloud framework for mobile computing and communication. In: IEEE international conference on service-oriented system engineering (SOSE'10). Nanjing, China, pp 27–34
4. Hodo E (2016) Threat analysis of IoT networks using artificial neural network intrusion detection system. In: International symposium on networks, computers and communications (ISNCC), pp 1–6
5. Le A (2012) 6LoWPAN: a study on QoS security threats and countermeasures using intrusion detection system approach. Int J Commun Syst 25(9):1189–1212
6. Liu C (2011) Research on immunity-based intrusion detection technology for the Internet of things. In: Seventh international conference on natural computation (ICNC). Shanghai, China, pp 212–216
7. Wang H (2003) A lightweight authentication protocol for access control in IEEE 802.11. In: Global telecommunications conference. San Francisco, CA, USA, pp 1384–1388
8. Ntantogian C, Xenakis C (2007) A security protocol for mutual authentication and mobile VPN deployment in B3G networks. In: 18th annual IEEE international symposium on personal, indoor and mobile radio communications (PIMRC'07)
9. Santoso F, Vun N (2015) Securing IoT for smart home system. International symposium on consumer electronics (ISCE). Madrid, Spain
10. Porambage P, Gurtov A, Kumar P, Schmitt C (2014) Two-phase authentication protocol for wireless sensor networks in distributed IoT applications. In: IEEE wireless communications and networking conference (WCNC). Istanbul, Turkey
11. Yao X, Du X, Han X, Zhou X (2013) A lightweight multicast authentication mechanism for small scale IoT applications. IEEE Sens J, pp 3693–3701
12. Shivraj V, Balamuralidhar P, Rajan M, Singh M (2015) One time password authentication scheme based on elliptic curves for Internet of things (IoT). In: 5th national symposium on information technology: towards new smart world (NSITNSW). Riyadh, Saudi Arabia
13. Gupta A (2017) Cryptanalysis of a novel ultra-lightweight mutual authentication protocol for IoT devices using RFID tags. J Supercomput, pp 1085–1102
14. Ye N (2014) An efficient authentication and access control scheme for perception layer of Internet of things. Appl Math Inf Sci, p 1617
15. Kai Fan Y (2016) Lightweight and ultralightweight RFID mutual authentication protocol with cache in the reader for IoT in 5G. Secur Commun Netw, pp 3095–3104
16. Emerson S (2015) An OAuth based authentication mechanism for IoT networks. In: International conference on information and communication technology convergence (ICTC), Jeju, South Korea, pp 1072–1074
17. Kothmayr T (2012) A DTLS based end-to-end security architecture for the Internet of things with two-way authentication. In: IEEE 37th conference on local computer networks workshops, pp 956–963
18. Moosavi S (2015) A secure and efficient authentication and authorization architecture for IoT-based healthcare using smart gateways. Procedia Comput Sci, 452–459

19. Jin Y, Tomoishi M, Tomoishi M (2016) Enhancement of VPN authentication using GPS information with geo-privacy protection
20. Filev D, Kolmanovsky I (2010) A generalized Markov chain modeling approach for on board applications. In: 2010 international joint conference on neural networks (IJCNN). Barcelona, Spain
21. Bolch G (2006) Queueing networks and Markov chains: modeling and performance evaluation with computer science applications. Wiley, Hoboken, NY
22. Ye N (2000) A markov chain model of temporal behavior for anomaly detection. Workshop on IEEE systems, man, and cybernetics information assurance and security. West Point, NY, p 169
23. Bendjima M, Feham M (2016) Wormhole attack detection in wireless sensor networks. In SAI computing conference (SAI). London, UK

Chapter 3
Mitigating Threats and Vulnerabilities of RFID in IoT Through Outsourcing Computations for Public Key Cryptography

Matluba Khodjaeva, Muath Obaidat and Douglas Salane

Abstract The widespread use of IoT devices that rely on Radio Frequency IDentification (RFID) technologies has resulted in numerous benefits; however, device connectivity has also created numerous security threats and vulnerabilities. This is due to the nature of the wireless links and the limited computational capabilities of such devices. However, until now, there has not been a noteworthy practical solution to many of the security issues related to the RFID technology. This chapter addresses the major threats and vulnerabilities related to RFID technologies in the IoT environment. In addition, it reviews some of the recently proposed cryptographic solutions as countermeasures for security and privacy issues. These solutions allow devices with limited computational resources to use asymmetric cryptographic encryption techniques in robust cryptographic protocols. In addition, these solutions, through delegation of exponentiation techniques, satisfy four core requirements, viz., correctness, privacy, efficiency, and security. Moreover, they ensure that the probability, which an untrusted server can convince a client (RFID) of an incorrect computational result, is exponentially small (almost equal to zero). This has a significant impact on the adoption of the said technologies in fields and areas where the use of RFID technology has not been considered. The solutions proposed in this chapter enable RFID technology to be more secure and be part of the IoT vision as a trusted technology, which can be adopted in any field globally without having concerns regarding privacy, security, and trust.

Keywords IoT · IoE · Secure outsourcing · RFID · Security · Modular exponentiations · Discrete logarithm · Privacy · Threat · Trust · Authentication · Reference architecture

---

M. Khodjaeva (✉) · M. Obaidat · D. Salane
Center for Cybercrime Studies, John Jay College of Criminal Justice,
The City University of New York, New York, USA
e-mail: mkhodjaeva@jjay.cuny.edu

M. Obaidat
e-mail: mobaidat@jjay.cuny.edu

D. Salane
e-mail: dsalane@jjay.cuny.edu

Z. Mahmood (ed.), *Security, Privacy and Trust in the IoT Environment*, https://doi.org/10.1007/978-3-030-18075-1_3

3.1 Introduction

Due to the advancements in wireless communications and widespread availability of the Internet, the past decade has witnessed an exponential growth in Information Systems (ISs), networking, and the Internet of Everything (IoE) or Internet of Things (IoT). The projection for the number of IoT devices connected to the Internet is estimated to be in billions, by many studies [1–5], with some estimating over 30 billion devices by 2020 [6]. Cisco projects that the number of devices connected to the Internet by 2020 will reach around 50 billion [7] with an approximate market value of 240 billion dollars by 2022 [8]. Secure connectivity between such a massive number of devices and humans is a key challenge in the IoT community, especially since many IoT applications are mission-critical applications or support real-time exchange of sensitive data. This widespread appearance of IoT devices creates an Internet of vulnerabilities and threats.

A key characteristic of the twenty-first century is the increasing reliance on digital technology in all aspects of life, for example, smart grids and cities, intelligent transportation systems, smart homes and vehicles, networked medical devices, and wearables devices. Sensors are the most prolific aspect of the IoT environment. These devices gather data and report it to a collection point for storage, further processing and analysis.

The most suitable candidate technology to house sensors is Radio Frequency IDentification (RFID) [9]. It is the ideal candidate and leading technology for applications that require continuous real-time monitoring and data collection to ascertain the status of phenomena or its surroundings [10]. RFID enables billions of devices or objects to be part of the IoT and works as a connector interface between the physical environments and the digital world. Security in ISs, networks, and the IoT is only as strong as the weakest link within each system or technology.

The aim of this chapter is to shed some light on the latest vulnerabilities, threats, and attacks on RFID used in IoT devices, and show how to mitigate them by making public key cryptography accessible to computationally weaker devices such as RFID tags. We consider outsourcing group exponentiation to make public key cryptography feasible with RFID tags. In particular, we consider how to overcome the problem of delegating group exponentiation to a single possibly malicious server and establish trust between the RFID and the server responsible for carrying out the computation.

Many attempts have been proposed in the literature to create a standardized IoT architectural model. The following are some of the main proposed architectures:

- Internet of Things-Architecture (IoT-A) [11],
- Industrial Internet Reference Architecture (IIRA) [12],
- Reference Architecture Model Industrie 4.0 (RAMI 4.0) [13], and
- Cisco's Internet of Things Reference Model [14].

Thus far, there has not been an agreed standard architecture for IoT. Initially, the core idea of the IoT was to use RFID, where every object would have an RFID tag. This concept evolved later to include not only RFID but also smart "things" [15]. In this context, sensors, smart technologies, nanotechnologies, and RFID are the main underlying technologies that are used in delivering services in IoT. However, RFID is continuing to be the prominent and the most widespread underlying technology for the IoT. The number of layers in the proposed architectures varies between three to seven layers in each of the proposed reference models for IoT [16–18].

RFID Components

Typically, an RFID system consists of five main components: the RFID tag, the RFID reader, middleware software, a wireless communication link, and a backend database. The following describes, very briefly, the purpose of each component.

- The RFID tag (microchip) or transponder with built-in antenna has a unique identifier called the electronic product code (EPC) that identifies an object universally. These tags are one of three types: either passive, active, or semi-passive. The main difference between these types is whether they have resources such as a power source (battery), computational capabilities, or no computational capabilities [19, 20].
- The RFID reader or interrogator communicates with the RFID tag using the radio frequency [20].
- The middleware is the RFID software that works as an interface between the different hardware parts (i.e., RFID tag, reader, and the antenna), for example, the reader and the application responsible for collecting the necessary information [19].
- The wireless communication link (radio frequency) supports data transfer between the RFID tag and its reader.
- The backend database is the final collection point where data is delivered for processing and analysis [20].

Each component presents opportunities for attacks on the entire system. There are several active research directions that address the computational challenges of deploying cryptographic protocols in RFID systems. The first is to modify known cryptographic protocols to produce lightweight versions that can be executed by computationally weaker devices, such as RFID tags. The second is to employ delegated (also called outsourced, or server-aided) computation of cryptographic primitives.

In this chapter, we describe delegated computation from a computationally weaker client (i.e., RFID) to a computationally stronger server. Specifically, we concentrate on delegating group exponentiation, which is an important operation and among the most widely used for public key cryptosystems and, more generally, cryptographic protocols. Computations on low-powered, resource-constrained devices, such as wireless RFIDs, can also take advantage of delegated computations to implement strong cryptographic protocols without extensive modifications.

The organization of the chapter is as follows. In Sect. 3.2, we discuss vulnerabilities and threats relating to RFID-based systems. Delegation of Group Exponentiation in RFID systems appears in Sect. 3.3. In Sect. 3.4, we present a system scenario and requirements for outsourcing (delegating) computations. We cover delegation of exponentiation in general groups in Sect. 3.5; and in Sect. 3.6, we briefly review delegation of exponentiation in cyclic groups. Section 3.7 summarizes the chapter.

3.2 Vulnerabilities, Threats, and Attacks on RFID

In this section, we discuss the different vulnerabilities, threats, and attacks relating to RFID in IoT-based devices. For the purposes of this study, we base our categorization on the most dominant IoT architecture in the literature which consists of three layers [17, 21, 22], viz.,

- perception (or physical or device) layer,
- network (or transport) layer, and
- application layer.

In addition, we also consider the transport layer with the network layer as some attacks are not solely on the network layer but on the transport as well, as pointed out in [23]. We briefly describe each layer's vulnerabilities, as well as the threats and attacks against RFID systems.

3.2.1 Perception Layer Attacks

Most IoT devices are placed in an open, unstable, unprotected, noisy, and often harsh or even hostile environment [23]. At the perception layer (also called the physical or device layer), the hardware components, and the radio frequency (RF) signals are exposed. Thus, this layer poses many security challenges. These include physical damage and tampering with the IoT RFID tags [24, 25]. The open environment in which these devices are deployed to facilitate attacks that involve counterfeiting information, which we discuss in detail later. Many attacks on RFID in IoT devices are due to the fact that such devices have very limited computational resources for encryption such as power, processor capability, and storage capacity [25–27].

Physical Attacks and Tampering Against RFID Tags
Physical attacks against RFID tags might incapacitate RFID tags permanently or temporarily. These attacks range from destruction or removal of the RFID tags to circuitry manipulation, clock glitching, and probe attacks [28]. Such attacks might be intended to disrupt operations or irritate the owner of the system [23]. In addition, these attacks enable the hacker to gain access to sensitive information from the RFID tag or manipulate the RFID for forgery [25, 28, 29]. Exposing an RFID tag to static electricity will damage the RFID tag permanently. This could be done intentionally using the RFID Zapper [30] that can damage passive RFID tags after their usage purpose ends. Many more physical attacks are investigated by Weingart [28] and are applicable to RFID technology.

RF Interference on RFIDs
The RF interference could be one of the two types: Passive or Active [23]. The passive interference is due to natural interferences from the environment surrounding the RFID tag, for example, the signal from a power switching supply. The active

interference is caused by sending a noise signal to interfere with the RFID to disrupt its normal functionality and operations [31–33]. Once the interference occurs, communication between the RFID and its reader or other devices becomes very difficult which is likely to disable the operation of the IoT device. This situation can ultimately lead to a DoS attack [31, 32, 34, 35].

DoS Attacks Against an RFID Tag
The DoS attack is caused by jamming the radio frequency channels with a noisy signal that prevents the RFID reader from reading the RFID tags [29, 32]. Note that such attacks cannot be prevented using our proposed encryption mechanism.

Physical Attacks Against RFID Readers
Removing or destroying an RFID reader, which might contain sensitive information such as encryption keys, can allow the hacker to gain access not only to the RFID tag, but also to the entire network or system [23]. This could lead to compromises in the integrity and confidentiality of data. Of course, this action can also make the service unavailable.

Relay Attacks
A relay attack is a man-in-the-middle attack where the attacker places a device between the RFID tag and the RFID reader. When communication occurs between the RFID tag and the reader, it actually passes through the illegitimate malicious device. The hacker can then use two different devices: one to communicate with the RFID tag and the other to communicate with the RFID reader [23]. This allows the attacker to impersonate the RFID tag or the RFID reader.

Replay Attacks
In replay attacks, the attacker rebroadcasts communications that are initially intercepted and copied. The information is then collected through an eavesdropping attack. The difference between replay and relay attacks is the time difference between when data is collected and replayed [23]. Descriptions of different types of replay attacks can be found in [36].

Side-Channel Attacks Against RFID Tags
In a side-channel attack, the attacker extracts information by intercepting communications between different parties and processing it. The attacker then looks for patterns to launch the attack [31, 32]. A so-called powerful analysis attack is one of the side-channel attacks used against RFID tags. The attacker tries to correlate power consummation and timing information in the cryptographic algorithms to gain some knowledge about confidential information associated with the RFID tag.

In the simple power analysis (SPA) attack, the attacker exploits the difference in power consumption between processing a one (1) versus zero (0) bit to infer information about the secret key used in the encryption process [37]. A differential power analysis (DPA) attack is similar to SPA; however, it uses statistical analysis to discover differences in analyzing bit power consumption to decipher the secret encryption keys [37, 38].

3.2.2 Network Transport Layer Attacks

The network layer by itself does not perform all intended functions if the transport layer and its protocols are missing. For this reason, we combine both layers into one for the sake of completing the picture. The main function of the network and transport layers is to transmit information between different entities in the RFID system. The challenge is to maintain the availability and functionality of the network since the wireless channel is prone to different security threats and attacks [25].

RFID Spoofing
In this attack, the hacker uses information from a spoofed legitimate tag to communicate with the rest of the devices in the system or network. By impersonating a legitimate RFID tag, the hacker disperses his own data so that it appears to other devices as if it were from a legitimate RFID tag. The goal is to cause harm to the system by conducting various malicious activities [19, 23, 25, 32, 39–41] that allow the hacker to obtain access to the system [31, 34, 35]. This requires full privilege of the spoofed RFID tag, e.g., authentication [23].

Eavesdropping Against RFID Tags
Due to the characteristics of the wireless medium upon which RFID tagged devices operate, eavesdropping attacks are considered one of the most serious threats to RFID systems. These attacks can be carried out from the RFID tag to the reader or vice versa [23]. The hacker intercepts the communications over the radio frequency channel between legitimate RFID tag and its reader by sniffing messages and carrying out traffic analysis [29, 42]. This is a security threat if sensitive confidential information is carried over the channel.

Tag Cloning Against RFID Tags
Cloning attacks penetrate the integrity of the system. The hacker copies the information from the victim's RFID tag into the malicious tag [35] and then gains access to all sensitive data in the cloned RFID tag [29]. This compromises the integrity as well as the confidentiality of the system.

Tracking Attacks Against RFID Tags
Since RFID tags are usually unprotected, they can be read by anyone who has the appropriate technology. This enables the hacker to collect tracking information, which creates security threats and also compromises confidentiality and privacy, especially if the RFID tag is linked to personal information [20, 29, 43].

RFID Unauthorized Access
Authentication is the process of verifying whether an entity (RFID reader) trying to access another entity (e.g., RFID tag) is legitimate and authorized. There is no standardized procedure for authentication for RFID systems. Thus, these tags are vulnerable to different unauthorized access techniques (attacks) that do not require advanced technical skills to conduct the required process [31, 34, 35]. The data stored in RFID tags could be manipulated in different ways such as modification and deletion by the hacker [25, 35, 44, 45].

Traffic Analysis Attacks
The first step in a traffic analysis attack is to launch different reconnaissance techniques to target an RFID technology. Techniques include vulnerability scanning, network sniffing, and port scanning [31, 34, 35, 46]. In an attempt to access sensitive and confidential information, the hacker sniffs the traffic then analyzes it [42, 47, 48]. This is viable because of the characteristics of the wireless medium in IoT which heavily depend on RFID technology.

3.2.3 Application Layer Attacks

As in the Internet protocol stack, the application layer provides services to the user on demand. The application layer is vulnerable to software attacks and those that target the connection between the user and the RFID tags [23, 25].

Unauthorized Tag Access Attacks
Most RFID tags do not possess an authentication mechanism so the attacker can easily read the content of the tag. Moreover, the attacker can modify and/or delete the data on the tag [23].

Malware Attacks
In the following paragraphs, we discuss buffer overflow, SQL injection, code insertion, worms, and viruses; all of which attackers may use to compromise RFID applications.

- Buffer Overflow Attack: This is a well-known vulnerability in software. In this attack, the buffer is exploited by sending data that exceeds its predetermined fixed length capacity. RFID tags are used in this attack to cause buffer overflow on the backend RFID middleware [23, 49]. Buffer overflows allow hackers to perform malicious code injection. RFID tags can be used to launch SQL injection or code insertion attacks that might be fed into the tags. These tags can be used to infect the backend database with different RFID malware [23, 49].
- RFID Worm: An RFID worm is a self-propagating (does not require any user action) malware that has the ability to propagate throughout the system via infected RFID tags. This attack occurs when an RFID middleware server executes malicious code (i.e., worm) over the Internet. The compromised RFID middleware will infect other RFID tags [19, 50].
- RFID Virus: As self-replicating malware, an RFID virus does not need a network connection to propagate. The virus infects a tag which in turn infects the software of the RFID. The middleware of the RFID-infected software infects the backend database which then spreads the virus to other tags in other locations that use the same middleware [19, 50].

To enable RFID to hold sensitive data, an encryption technique as well as an authentication mechanism must be implemented at certain layers of the IoT architecture. This is to guarantee the integrity and confidentiality of transmitted data. Some cryptographic techniques and mechanisms have been implemented but have failed to protect RFID tags against attacks [23]. In the following section, we discuss how delegation of group exponentiation can be used in RFID systems to protect against the majority of the attacks against such systems.

3.3 Delegation of Group Exponentiation in Building Trust in RFID Systems

RFID tags are often limited in resources in terms of battery power, storage capacity, and processing capability. Because of these limitations, most of the RFID tags range from those that have a weak cryptographic mechanism to those that do not employ any cryptographic technique at all. This means that RFIDs typically are vulnerable to different attacks due to the lack of strong authentication mechanisms.

Asymmetric cryptographic (public key) protocols are computationally more intensive than symmetric cryptography (private key) protocols because of their demands in terms of processing, memory, and power usage (e.g., key size is $\approx$ 2048 bits for public key vs. $\approx$ 128 bits for private key).

Delegation of Expensive Computation Operations

Secure delegation of computation allows RFIDs to do some expensive computations with the help of a server (e.g., cloud) without leaking any information about private inputs. Computationally weaker RFIDs delegate the expensive computational tasks. Atallah [51] proposed the first secure delegating of scientific computations using cryptographic techniques involving matrix multiplication, inequalities, and linear equations. Techniques he suggested ensure the privacy of data, but these techniques do not consider the verification of computed results.

In 2005, Hohenberger et al. [52] presented the first formal security definition of secure delegating computation. In particular, they considered group exponentiation. In 2008, Benjamin et al. [53] proposed a verifiable secure outsourcing scheme for linear algebra calculations using homomorphic encryption. In 2009, Gentry et al. [54] proposed fully homomorphic encryption based on ideal lattices. For secure delegation, this idea is helpful; however, the efficiency is low.

Atallah et al. [55] proposed a single server verifiable delegation based on Shamir secret sharing scheme. In the same year, Gennaro et al. [56] proposed outsourcing computation scheme based on any polynomial time computable function and verification is noninteractive, which uses garbled circuits [57] and fully homomorphic encryption [54]. Their solutions are only asymptotically efficient, but not so in a practical setting. Chung et al. [58] proposed an improved generic outsourcing computation protocol without using garbled circuits, but with some values generated by pre-computation to verify the result. In 2011, Chung et al. [59] proposed the new idea about memory delegation; however, the length of the data was limited. In 2012, Parno et al. [60] proposed a verifiable multifunction computation scheme. In 2017, Di Crescenzo et al. [61] proposed batch delegation of exponentiation from batch verification using small exponent test for the first time which was introduced by Bellare et al. [62]. The aforementioned work illustrates that delegating of expensive computations is a promising, active research area.

Delegating Group Exponentiation

Group exponentiation is an effective but somewhat expensive operation in public key cryptography. This has made it a very active research area. In 2005, Hohenberger and Lysyanskaya [52] presented the formal model for delegating cryptographic operations. In this work, the authors focused on outsourcing of modular exponentiation as this is the most computationally intensive operation in many cryptographic protocols. In this model, they have a client, with a private input x, that delegates to one or more servers, the computation of a function F on the client's input. Delegating group exponentiation has four main requirements.

- Correctness: The client obtains the output F(x) of the function evaluated on its input x.
- Privacy: Only minimal or no information about x should be revealed to the servers.
- Security: The servers should not be able, except possibly with a very small probability, to convince the client to accept a result different than F(x).
- Efficiency: The client's computation time should be much smaller than time for computing F(x) without delegating the computation.

In [52], authors proposed two algorithms for delegating modular exponentiation: (1) with two untrusted remote servers of which at most one was malicious, and (2) with one untrusted remote server, which was honest on almost all inputs. Since then the problem of delegating exponentiation to a single, arbitrary malicious server, remains unsolved. In 2014, Wang et al. [63] improved the scheme of [52] and again reiterated the problem by stating "an interesting open problem is whether there is an efficient algorithm for secure outsourcing modular exponentiation using only one untrusted cloud server." We describe several protocols in the coming sections.

The main goal of delegated exponentiation is for the protocols in the RFID to perform a smaller number of multiplications than in a non-delegated group exponentiation. This problem is expected to be of great interest given recent advances. Arbit [64] gives a practical implementation of group multiplication for a specific group. These techniques could be implemented in public key cryptosystems employed in RFID systems.

As mentioned above, many protocols have been proposed with the goal of satisfying four main requirements: correctness, efficiency, privacy, and security. A number of solutions have achieved the three requirements: correctness, efficiency, and privacy; but they satisfy the security probability with a constant probability which is not small (i.e., exponentially small). In the proposed solutions, the main challenge was to introduce a protocol with low-security probability while satisfying the three other requirements, where the RFID delegates computations with only a single malicious server.

Many research studies define security probabilities in various situations. Specifically, in [52], the security probability with two untrusted servers is $\frac{1}{2}$. In 2012, Chen et al. [65] improved the scheme in [52], and the security probability dropped to $\frac{1}{3}$. In 2015, Ye et al. [66] improved the security probability significantly to $\frac{1}{20}$. In 2014, Wang et al. [63] proposed a delegating scheme of modular exponentiation with a single malicious server; however, the security probability of the returned result was $\frac{1}{2}$. In 2016, Ding et al. [67] improved the security probability to $\frac{1}{120}$. In 2015, Cavalo et al. [68] proposed algorithms for delegating group inversion and exponentiation in a general group and showed how to apply the delegation of group inversion to group exponentiation with a single malicious server which resulted in a security probability of $\frac{1}{2}$. In 2018, Di Crescenzo et al. [69] improved the scheme and reduced the security probability to 0.04. In 2017, Di Crescenzo et al. [70] proposed the algorithms for delegating modular exponentiation in cyclic groups and the security probability dropped to an exponentially small value (i.e., $\frac{1}{2^{\lambda}}$) which is described later in the chapter.

3.4 System Scenario and Requirements for Outsourcing (Delegating) Computations

In this section, we introduce delegation protocols and informal definitions for the requirements of correctness, security, privacy, and efficiency for delegation from computationally weaker RFID devices as clients to a computationally stronger server in a single, possibly malicious, server model. These definitions are extensions from [68], as well as [52, 56].

System Scenarios, Entities, and Protocols

Consider a system with two parties: clients (RFIDs) and servers (more powerful computationally devices). An RFID's computational resources are much less than the server's computational resources. Therefore, clients are interested in delegating (outsourcing) the computation of specific functions to servers.

In all protocols we describe below, we consider a single RFID as a client denoted by *C*, and a single server, denoted by S. A client–server protocol (C, S) for the delegated computation of function F is an interactive protocol between *C* and *S*, where both parties have a description of a function F. The RFID client C knows an input *x*, and at the end of a protocol execution, C outputs a value y (intended to be = F (x)). The protocol has two phases:

- Offline phase (i.e., before communications between the RFID and server start) where F is evaluated on another random input other than x at an arbitrary time and
- Online phase (i.e., when communications start), where C's computations are based on an input x, but take less time than what is required to compute F(x).

Such a delegation protocol (C, S) for the function F must satisfy the requirements of correctness, security, privacy, and efficiency. Below is the definition of these requirements. The reader is referred to [70] for more formal definitions.

- Correctness. The natural correctness requirement states that if both parties follow the protocol, at the end of the protocol the RFID client, denoted C, obtains some output y which is equal to the value obtained by evaluating function F on C's input x.
- Security. The most basic security requirement would state the following: if C follows the protocol, a malicious adversary corrupting S cannot convince C to obtain, at the end of the protocol, some output y′ different from the value y obtained by evaluating function F on C's input x. To define a stronger and more realistic security requirement, we can assume that the adversary can even choose C's input x and take part in a polynomial number of protocol executions to convince C with a small probability to output, at the end of the protocol, some y′ different from value $y = F(x)$ (with small probability) or some failure symbol $\perp$ (meaning that C (i.e., RFID) found fraud in this protocol's execution). This small probability is called the security probability, and is denoted ϵ_s . A desirable value for it would be $2^{-\lambda}$, for some statistical security parameter λ, set for instance as, $\lambda = 128$. The security probability would then be 2^{-128}.
- Privacy. The privacy requirement should guarantee the following: if C follows the protocol, a malicious adversary corrupting S cannot obtain any information about C's input x from a protocol execution.
- Efficiency Metrics and Requirements. We scale the efficiency of a client (i.e., RFID)-server protocol (C, S) for the delegated computation of function F by the efficiency metrics (t_F , t_P , t_C, t_S, cc), meaning that

  - t_F: F can be computed (without delegation) using t_F atomic operations;
  - t_P: C can be run in the offline phase using t_P atomic operations;
  - t_C: C can be run in the online phase using t_C atomic operations;
  - t_S: S can be run using t_C atomic operations;
  - cc is the communication complexity: C and S exchange messages of total length at most cc.

In the protocol analysis, we only consider the most expensive group operations as atomic operations (e.g., group multiplication, inversion, exponentiation), and neglect lower order operations (e.g., equality testing, additions, and subtractions between group elements) because these are inexpensive operations. The main goal of the protocol efficiency metrics is to design a protocol where the following hold:

- the client's online calculation should be significantly smaller than evaluations of the function (i.e., $t_C \ll t_F$),
- t_S is not significantly larger than t_F, and
- cc is somewhat larger than the length of F 's input and output.

Note that, according to the "square-and-multiply" algorithm (described below), the complexity on average requires $t_F = 1.5\sigma$ group multiplications, in the worst-case $t_F = 2\sigma$ group multiplications, where σ denotes the length of a group element. This algorithm requires considerable computational processing time, memory capacity, and resources that are not feasible in RFID technology. So, we are proposing a technique with delegation as it is the best technique to enable the utilization of public key cryptosystems at lower cost in terms of computational power, processing time, and resources.

Algorithm: Square-and-Multiply for x^H mod n

Input: Exponent H, base element x, Modulus n

Output: $x^H \bmod n$

```
Determine binary representation H = (h_t, h_{t-1}, ..., h_0)_2
FOR i = t − 1 TO 0
        y = y^2 mod n
        IF h_i = 1 THEN
                y = y * x mod n
RETURN y
```

3.5 Delegation of Exponentiation in General Group

In this section, we describe client–server protocols [68, 69] for delegated exponentiation in a **general class of groups** to a single (possibly malicious) server.

Let (G, $*$) be an efficient commutative group. We define the following functions

- F: G $\to$ G where F(x) $= x^k$ (i.e., private base raised to public exponent in the group) where k is a positive integer
- H : $\mathbb{Z}_q \to$ G where H(x) $= g^x$ (i.e., public base raised to private exponent in the group) and $\mathbb{Z}_q = \{0, 1, 2, \ldots, q-1\}$, $g \in G$ and the order of g is q.

We consider two scenarios for delegating exponentiation for the functions F and H. In function F, the base of the exponent is private while the exponent is public; and in function H, the exponent is private while the base is public as in the above definition. With both protocols for the functions F and H in hand, we could, for instance, implement them in RFID tags. One scenario is where there are two computationally weak parties who want to use an RSA encryption protocol, but who do not have enough computational power to perform exponentiation. In that case, they both can delegate exponentiation to a computationally powerful server S. The sender of a secret message would have to use the function F with a private base and public exponent to encrypt its message, while the receiver would have to use the function H with a public base and private exponent to decrypt the message.

Delegation of these operations for the functions F and H is discussed in Sects. 3.5.1 and 3.5.2.

3.5.1 Delegating Exponentiation: Cut-and-Choose Approach

We first describe the basic protocol (bC1, bS1) for the function F taken from [68] and the basic protocol (bC2, bS2) for the function H taken from [69] where both protocols satisfy a constant security probability. Then we describe the protocols (fC1, fS1) and (fC2, fS2), both obtained as a parallel repetition of the basic protocols, respectively, satisfying the exponentially small security probability property.

Description of the Protocol (bC1, bS1): Let C (the RFID) be the client delegating to S, the computation of function F.

In an offline phase, C randomly chooses group elements u_0, u_1 and computes $v_0 = u_0^k$ and $v_1 = u_1^k$ and stores in its memory two pairs: (u_0, v_0) and (u_1, v_1). Then in the online phase, one of the pairs is used to verify that the answer from S is correct, and the other pair is used to mask the input of C.

The "privacy property" follows from the fact that the message sent by C to S is computationally indistinguishable from random elements in the group G and thus leaks no information about input x. The "security property" follows from the fact that the message sent by C to S does not reveal which of the two pairs of group elements is used for verification and which is used for computation. Therefore, any dishonest answer from S will be detected by C with probability of at least 0.5.

Formal Description of Protocol *(bC1, bS1)*:
Let G be an efficient commutative group.

Input to S: 1^σ, desc(F)
Input to C: 1^σ, desc(F), $x \in \mathbb{Z}_q$

Offline phase instructions:

1. C randomly chooses $u_i \in G$, for i = 0,1.
2. C sets $v_i = u_i^k$ and stores (u_i, v_i) on C, for i = 0,1.

Online phase instructions:

1. C randomly chooses $b \in \{0, 1\}$;
   C sets $z_b = u_b$, $z_{1-b} = x^* u_{1-b}$;
   C sends z_0, z_1 to S;
2. S computes $w_i = z_i^k$ for i = 0, 1;
   S sends w_0, w_1 to C;
3. C checks that if $w_b \neq v_b$
   C **returns** $\perp$ and the protocol halts;
   C computes $y = w_{1-b} * (v_{1-b})^{-1}$ and **returns** y.

The protocol (bC1, bS1) satisfies correctness, privacy, security (with probability of $\frac{1}{2}$), and efficiency (with $t_C = 2$ group multiplications plus 1 inversion, $t_S = 2$ group exponentiations, and $t_P = 2$ exponentiations with random elements in the base). The theorem and proof of the protocol can be found in [68].

Now, we can apply the above protocol (bC1, bS1) to compute the function H (i.e., $H : \mathbb{Z}_q \rightarrow G$ defined where $H(x) = g^x$). Here the public base is raised to the private exponent using group exponentiation where $g \in G$ and the order of g is q. The protocol is described in [69]. The following are the details of the protocol.

Formal Description of Protocol *(bC2, bS2):*
Let G be an efficient commutative group.

Input to S: 1^σ, desc(H), $g \in G$.
Input to C: 1^σ, desc(H), $g \in G$, $x \in \mathbb{Z}_q$.

Offline phase instructions:

1. C randomly chooses $u_i \in \mathbb{Z}_q$, for $i = 0,1$.
2. C sets $v_i = g^{u_i}$ and stores (u_i, v_i) on C, for $i = 0,1$.

Online phase instructions:

1. C randomly chooses $b \in \{0, 1\}$;
   C sets $z_b = u_b$, $z_{1-b} = x - u_{1-b} \bmod q$;
   C sends z_0, z_1 to S;
2. S computes $w_i = g^{z_i}$ for $i = 0, 1$;
   S sends w_0, w_1 to C;
3. C checks that if $w_b \neq v_b$
   C **returns** $\perp$ and the protocol halts;
   C computes $y = w_{1-b} * v_{1-b}$ and **returns** y.

Similar to protocol (bC1, bS1) the above protocol (bC2, bS2) has the properties correctness, privacy, security (with probability of $\frac{1}{2}$), and efficiency (with t_C requires only one group multiplication, $t_S = 2$ group exponentiations, and $t_P = 2$ exponentiations). Note that both protocols satisfy security probability that is equal to a constant (i.e., $\frac{1}{2}$). In order to have lower security probability, parallel repetition of the same protocol could be implemented as described in the next paragraph or decoy elements could be introduced as described in the next subsection.

The protocols (fC1, fS1) and (fC2, fS2) have exponentially small security probability. We can extend the basic protocol (bC1, bS1) to decrease the secure probability from $\epsilon_s = 1/2$ to $\epsilon_s = 2^{-\lambda}$, as follows: first of all protocol (fC1, fS1) consists of λ parallel executions of the basic protocol (bC1, bS1). Then, in step 3 C returns the failure symbol $\perp$ if the value y computed in step 3 is not the same in each parallel execution. The resulting protocol satisfies correctness, privacy, security (with probability $\epsilon_s = 2^{-\lambda}$), and efficiency (with $t_C = 2\lambda$ group multiplications plus λ group inversions, $t_S = 2\lambda$ group exponentiations, and $t_P = 2\lambda$ random base exponentiations to k power). The proof of these properties is a direct extension of the proofs of the properties of (bC1, bS1). Similarly, λ parallel executions can be applied to the basic protocol (bC2, bS2) and we can obtain the protocol (fC2, fS2) in order to get exponentially small security probability (i.e., $\epsilon_s = 2^{-\lambda}$).

3.5.2 Delegating Exponentiation: Improved Probability Reduction

In this subsection we describe an enhanced version of a cut-and-choose approach (see 3.5.1) for computing the function H (i.e., $H : \mathbb{Z}_q \rightarrow G$ defined as $H(x) = g^x$) by introducing random decoy elements [69]. The main goal of the next protocol is to minimize security probability by using a more time-efficient approach than the direct parallel repetition approach described previously.

Description of the Protocol *(bC3, bS3)*:
The idea of the protocol is to increase the number of equality checks, denoted by $c - 1$ number of checks, which the client executes. Note that c represents the number of exponentiations required in the "offline phase" for the RFID's calculations. In previous protocols, there are two exponentiations ($c = 2$) in offline phase and only one equality check. In the resulting protocol, there would be m values in $\mathbb{Z}_q$ sent by the client to the server, one value is used to compute the function output. $c - 1$ values are used to perform equality checks, and $m - c$ values are "decoy elements." The resulting protocol achieves a security probability which is approximately $1/c$ (i.e., linear). Thus to achieve security probability ϵ_s equal $2^{-\lambda}$, the modified protocol performs $\lambda/\log_2 c$ parallel repetitions of the basic protocol. Below is the formal description.

Formal Description of Protocol *(bC3, bS3)*:
Let G be an efficient commutative group.

Input to S: 1^σ, desc(H), $g \in G$
Input to C: 1^c, desc(H), $g \in G$, $x \in \mathbb{Z}_q$.

Offline phase instructions:

1. C randomly chooses distinct $j_1, \ldots, j_m \in \{1, \ldots, m\}$.
2. C randomly chooses $u_i \in \mathbb{Z}_q$, sets $v_i = g^{u_i}$ and $z_{j_i} = u_i$ for $i = 1, \ldots, c$.
3. C randomly and independently chooses $z_{j_{c+1}}, \ldots, z_{j_m} \in \mathbb{Z}_q$.

Online phase instructions:

1. C sets $z_{j_c} = (x - u_c) \bmod q$;
   C sends $z_1, \ldots, z_m$ to S;
2. S computes $w_j = g^{z_j}$ for $j = 1, \ldots, m$;
   S sends $w_1, \ldots, w_m$ to C;
3. if $w_{j_1} \neq v_{j_1}$ or $w_{j_2} \neq v_{j_2}$ or … or $w_{j_{c-1}} \neq v_{j_{c-1}}$ then
4. C **returns** $\perp$ and protocol halts;
   C computes $y = w_{j_c} * v_c$ and **returns** y.

Now observe that protocol (bC3, bS3) satisfies correctness, privacy, security (with probability $\epsilon_s = O(1/c)$), and efficiency (with $t_C = 1$ multiplication in G, $t_S = m$ group exponentiations, and $t_P = c$ exponentiations with random elements in the exponent). The obtained values for ϵ_s when $c = 4, \ldots, 10$ are shown in Table 3.1. For more details, the reader is referred to [69].

Table 3.1 Values of ϵ_s for protocol (bC2, bS2) for c = 4 through 10

c =	4	5	6	7	8	9	10
m = 100	0.10763	0.08403	0.06719	0.05875	0.05118	0.04538	0.04080
m = 1000	0.10568	0.08213	0.06529	0.05686	0.04929	0.04351	0.03894

A protocol (fC3, fS3) with exponentially small security probability. Protocol (fC3; fS3) consists of $r = \lambda / \log(1/\epsilon_s)$ parallel executions of the basic protocol (bC3, bS3), as shown in previous subsection. Protocol (fC3, fS3) satisfies correctness, privacy, security (with probability $\epsilon_s = 2^{-\lambda}$), and efficiency (with $t_C = r$ group multiplications in $\mathbb{Z}_q$, $t_S = mr$ group exponentiation, $t_P = rc$ public base exponentiations to random exponents).

Note that the above protocol (fC3, fS3) described to compute the function H (i.e., $H : \mathbb{Z}_q \rightarrow G$ defined as $H(x) = g^x$, public base, private exponent exponentiation in the group). Similarly, we can apply the same idea to construct a protocol with security probability exponentially small for the function F (i.e., F: $G \rightarrow G$ defined as $F(x) = x^k$, private base, public exponent exponentiation in the group).

3.6 Delegation of Exponentiation in Cyclic Group

Most of the public key cryptography takes place in cyclic groups for the function H (where the exponent is private while the base is public). As we discussed earlier for computationally weaker devices such as RFIDs computing expensive operations (i.e., exponentiation in this case) is infeasible. Thus, the computationally weaker client needs to outsource this operation to a computationally stronger server. The delegation for the function H in a cyclic group is potentially applicable to execute public key cryptosystems (e.g., Diffie–Hellman Key Exchange, ElGamal's encryption/decryption, DSA, etc.).

In the rest of this section, we describe the protocol (fC4, fS4) as devised in [70] for the delegation of exponentiation in **a large class of cyclic groups** from computationally weaker RFID device client C to a single (possibly malicious) server S. This solution is applicable to many cryptosystems in the literature that are based on the hardness of the discrete logarithmic problem. This subsection introduces the protocol (fC4, fS4) that satisfies correctness, privacy, efficiency, and security requirements. This protocol achieves a security probability that is as "exponentially small" as desired (i.e., $\epsilon_s = 2^{-\lambda}$). Moreover, the protocol achieves that without making parallel repetition of the specific protocol as explained previously. However, the previous protocols work in general groups while (fC4, fS4) protocol requires cyclic groups.

Assume that $(G, *)$ is cyclic group, has order q, and denote that g is a generator of the group G. Consider the function: $H : \mathbb{Z}_q \rightarrow G$ defined as $H(x) = g^x$ (i.e., public base, private exponent exponentiation in the group) where $\mathbb{Z}_q = \{0, 1, 2, \ldots, q-1\}$.

Informal Description of the Protocol *(fC4, fS4)*:
The main idea of the protocol is that a computationally weaker RFID device C should be able to verify computations performed by malicious server S efficiently. The way to achieve this is to introduce a "probabilistic verification equation" which is verifiable using only a small number of modular multiplications. More concretely, RFID C inserts an additional random element (i.e., $b \in \{1, \ldots, 2^{\lambda}\}$) in the inputs on which S is asked to compute the value of function H, such that it satisfies the following conditions:

- If S returns correct computations of function H, then C can use the chosen random elements to correctly compute y;
- If S returns invalid computations of function H, then S either does not meet probabilistic verification equation or can only meet it with small probability (i.e., $2^{-\lambda}$).

In order to reach a small security probability (i.e., $2^{-\lambda}$), the domain of the random element should be large enough (e.g., $\{1, \ldots, 2^{\lambda}\}$ where $\lambda = 128$). In this case, the domain is much smaller than the group G. This shows that C's computation is much less costly than evaluating the function. The description of (fC4, fS4) protocol for the function F is given below.

Formal Description of Protocol *(fC4, fS4)*:
Let G be an efficient cyclic group then

Input to S: 1^{σ}, 1^{λ} desc(H), $g \in G$.
Input to C: 1^{σ}, desc(H), $g \in G$, $x \in \mathbb{Z}_q$.

Offline phase instructions:

1. C randomly chooses $u_i \in \mathbb{Z}_q$, for $i = 0,1$.
2. C sets $v_i = g^{u_i}$ and store (u_i, v_i) on C, for $i = 0,1$.

Online phase instructions:

1. C randomly chooses $b \in \{1, \ldots, 2^{\lambda}\}$;
   C sets $z_0 = (x - u_0) \bmod q$, $z_1 = (bx + u_1) \bmod q$;
   C sends z_C, z_1 to S;
2. S computes $w_i = g^{z_i}$ for $i = 0, 1$;
   S sends w_0, w_1 to C;
3. C checks if $x = 0$
   C **returns**: $y = 1$ and the protocol halts;
   C computes $y = w_0 * v_0$ and makes the following tests:

   (a) Distinctness Test: $y \neq 1$.
   (b) Probabilistic Test: $w_1 = y^b * v_1$.
   (c) Membership Test: $w_0, w_1 \in G$.

   If any one of these tests is not satisfied then

   C **returns**: $\perp$ and the protocol halts;

   C **returns**: y

The protocol (fC4, fS4) satisfies correctness, privacy, security (with probability of $2^{-\lambda}$), and efficiency (with $t_C = 2$ group multiplications plus 2 membership tests and 1 exponentiation at most λ bits. Note that λ is much smaller than order of the group G, specially $\lambda = 128$ vs. $\sigma = 2048$, $t_S = 2$ group exponentiations, and $t_P = 2$ exponentiations with random exponent). More details of the proof could be found in [70].

The protocol (fC4, fS4) can be extended further in order to reduce the RFID's online calculation. This will be at the cost of slightly increasing the server's computation by choosing several random elements of smaller size as in [70].

3.7 Conclusion

One of the main underlying technologies that IoT depends on is RFID. This is due to its low cost, ease of deployment, and simple implementation. The IoT provides ubiquitous connectivity between the physical world and the Internet. Embedding RFID into different types of objects with different purposes enabled the widespread adoption of IoT by allowing it to collect and transfer data in real time autonomously for analysis. RFID has some vulnerabilities (that can be exploited) due to the radio frequency and nature of communications between different RFID system components. In particular, authentication, privacy, and security are the main concerns in the IoT that may pose restrictions on the integration of IoT on a global scale. Key concerns are the violation of availability, integrity, and confidentiality in systems that employ RFID.

This chapter illustrates the key role that RFID can play in the IoT and has shed some light on different vulnerabilities, threats, and attacks on RFID system. Furthermore, it discusses how delegation of exponentiation to a single server allows asymmetric cryptography encryption techniques to be used in computationally weaker devices such as RFID systems. Security such system through delegation with a single malicious server has been an open research problem since 2005.

Delegation enables the RFID technology to be more secure and be part of the IoT system as a trusted technology that can be adopted in all fields globally. In addition, the protocols using delegation described here satisfy four requirements: correctness, privacy, efficiency, and security. With these protocols the probability that a malicious server can convince the client of an incorrect computation is exponentially small (i.e., almost equal to zero). These techniques significantly mitigate threats and attacks on RFID systems make them more secure and preserve privacy. However, more work needs to be done to standardize the authentication mechanisms in RFID systems and to incorporate encryption protocols into the communication processes between the RFID tag, reader, and backend databases. Such work is critical in order to prevent most threats and attacks as well as to ensure that the IoT achieves its potential on a universal scale.

References

1. Ericsson (2016) Ericsson Mobility Report, On the pulse of the networked society, Report, Jun 2016
2. Kamble A, Malemath VS, Patil D (2017) Security attacks and secure routing protocols in RPL-based Internet of Things: survey. In: International conference on emerging trends & innovation in ICT (ICEI), Pune Institute of Computer Technology, Pune, India, Feb 3–5, 2017
3. Gartner Inc (2015) Gartner Says 6.4 Billion Connected "Things" Will Be in Use in 2016, Up 30 Percent From 2015. http://www.gartner.com/newsroom/id/3165317, Nov. 2015. Accessed December 2018
4. Karnouskos S, Marrn PJ, Fortino G, Mottola L, Martinez JR de Dios (2014) Applications and markets for cooperating objects. Springer Briefs in Electrical and Computer Engineering, Springer
5. Nokia (2016) A buyers and influencers guide to connected device management, for all things connected in mobile, home and IoT, Strategic Whitepaper, Jul 2016
6. Statista (2015) Internet of Things (IoT) connected devices installed base worldwide from 2015 to 2025 (in billions). https://www.statista.com/statistics/471264/iot-number-of-connected-devices-worldwide/. Accessed Dec 2018
7. Dave E (2011) The Internet of Things: how the next evolution of the internet is changing everything, CISCO. Accessed Dec 2018. http://www.cisco.com/web/about/ac79/docs/innov/IoT_IBSG_0411FINAL.pdf
8. Press Release, Strategy Analytics (2014) M2M market will generate $242 billion revenue by 2022. https://www4.strategyanalytics.com/default.aspx?mod=pressreleaseviewer&a0=5468. Accessed on December 2018
9. Kim S, Mariotti C, Alimenti F, Mezzanotte P, Georgiadis A, Collado A, Roselli L, Tentzeris M (2013) No battery required: Perpetual RFID-enabled wireless sensors for cognitive intelligence applications. Microw Mag IEEE 14(5):66–77
10. Roselli L et al (2015) Review of the present technologies concurrently contributing to the implementation of the Internet of Things (IoT) paradigm: RFID, green electronics, WPT and energy harvesting. In: IEEE Topical conference on wireless sensors and sensor networks (WiSNet), San Diego, CA, pp 1–3
11. IoT-A, (2014) Internet of Things – architecture Io-A deliverable D1.3 updated reference model for IoT v1.5. http://cocoa.ethz.ch/downloads/2014/01/1524_D1.3_Architectural_Reference_Model_update.pdf. Accessed Dec 2018
12. Industrial internet consortium (2015) Industrial internet reference architecture v 1.8, https://www.iiconsortium.org/IIRA.htm. Accessed Dec 2018
13. ZVEI Die Elektroindutrie (2015) The reference architectural model RAMI 4.0 and the Industrie 4.0 component, https://www.zvei.org/en/subjects/industry-4–0/the-reference-architectural-model-rami-40-and-the-industrie-40-component/. Accessed Dec 2018
14. Cisco (2014) Building the Internet of Things. https://www.cisco.com/c/dam/global/en_ph/assets/ciscoconnect/pdf/bigdata/jim_green_cisco_connect.pdf. Accessed Dec 2018
15. Gluhak et al (2011) An architectural blueprint for a real-world internet. The Future Internet, Lecture Notes in Computer Science, vol 6656, pp 67–80
16. Chaqfeh MA, Mohamed N (2012) Challenges in middleware solutions for the Internet of Things. In: Proceedings of international conference CTS, pp 21–26
17. Khan R, Khan SU, Zaheer R, Khan S (2012) Future internet: The Internet of Things architecture, possible applications and key challenges. In: Proceedings of 10th international conference FIT, pp 257–260
18. Tan L, Wang N (2010) Future internet: The Internet of Things. In: Proceedings of 3rd ICACTE, 2010, V5, pp 376–380
19. Grover A, Berghel H (2011) A survey of RFID deployment and security issues, Korea Science. J Informat Process Syst 7(4)

20. Weis SA, Sarma SE, Rivest RL, Engels DW (2004) Security and privacy aspects of low-cost radio frequency identification systems. In: Proceedings of 1st international conference security pervasive computing, pp 201–212
21. Wu M, Lu TJ, Ling FY, Sun J, Du HY (2010) Research on the architecture of Internet of Things. In: Proceedings of 3rd ICACTE, 2010, pp V5-484–V5-487
22. Yang Z et al (2011) Study and application on the architecture and key technologies for IOT. In: Proceedings of ICMT, pp 747–751
23. Mitrokotsa A, Rieback MR, Tanenbaum (2010) Classifying RFID attacks and defenses. A.S. Informat Syst Front 12(5):491–505. https://doi.org/10.1007/s10796-009-9210-z
24. Frustaci M, Pace P, Aloi G, Fortino G (2018) Evaluating critical security issues of the IoT world: present and future challenges. IEEE Internet of Things J 5(4):2483–2495
25. Lin J, Yu W, Zhang N, Yang X, Zhang H, Zhao W (2017) A survey on internet of things: architecture, enabling technologies, security and privacy, and applications. IEEE Internet of Things J 4(5):1125–1142
26. Anderson R, Kuhn M (1996) Tamper resistance-a cautionary note. In: Second USENIX workshop on electronic commerce proceedings, Oakland, California, November 18–21, 1996, pp 1–11
27. Zhao K, Ge L (2013) A Survey on the Internet of Things security. In: 2013 ninth international conference on computational intelligence and security, Leshan, pp 663–667
28. Weingart SH (2000) Physical security devices for computer subsystems: a survey of attacks and defenses. In: Koç ÇK, Paar C (eds) Cryptographic hardware and embedded systems- CHES 2000. CHES 2000. Lecture Notes in Computer Science, vol 1965. Springer, Berlin, Heidelberg
29. Mosenia A, Jha NK (2017), A comprehensive study of security of Internet-of-Things. IEEE Trans Emerg Topics Comput 5(4):586–602
30. C3 Public Wiki (2006) RFID-Zapper (EN). https://events.ccc.de/congress/2005/static/r/f/i/RFID-Zapper(EN)_77f3.html. Accessed Dec 2018
31. Deogirikar J, Vidhate A (2017) Security attacks in IoT: a survey. In: International conference on I-SMAC (IoT in Social, Mobile, Analytics and Cloud) (I-SMAC 2017)
32. Kashif L, Shamsi JA (2015) A study of security issues, vulnerabilities and challenges in internet of things. Secur Cyber-Phys Syst 221
33. Lan L (2012) Study on security architecture in the Internet of Things. In: Proceedings of 2012 international conference on measurement, information and control, Harbin, China, pp 374–377
34. Ahemd MM, Shah MA, Wahid A (2017) IoT security: a layered approach for attacks and defenses. In: International conference on communication technologies (ComTech), Rawalpindi, 2017, pp 104–110
35. Andrea C Chrysostomou, Hadjichristofi G (2015) Internet of Things: Security vulnerabilities and challenges, IEEE Symposium on Computers and Communication (ISCC). Larnaca 2015:180–187
36. Syverson P (1994) A taxonomy of replay attacks [cryptographic protocols]. In: Proceedings the computer security foundations workshop VII, Franconia, NH, USA, pp 187–191
37. Kocher P, Jaffe J, Jun B (1999) Differential power analysis. In: Wiener M (ed) Advances in cryptology CRYPTO' 99. CRYPTO 1999. Lecture Notes in Computer Science, vol 1666. Springer, Berlin, Heidelberg
38. Messerges TS, Dabbish EA, Sloan RH (1999) Power analysis attacks of modular exponentiation in smartcards. In: Koç ÇK, Paar C (eds) Cryptographic hardware and embedded systems. CHES 1999. Lecture Notes in Computer Science, vol 1717. Springer, Berlin, Heidelberg
39. Atamli W, Martin A (2014) Threat-based security analysis for the Internet of Things. International Workshop on Secure Internet of Things, Wroclaw 2014:35–43
40. Puthal D, Nepal S, Ranjan R, Chen J (2016) Threats to networking cloud and edge data centers in the Internet of Things. In: IEEE cloud computing, vol 3, no 3, pp 64–71
41. Sopori D, Pawar T, Patil M, Ravindran R (2017) Internet of things: security threats. Int J Advanc Res Comput Eng Technol (IJARCET), 6(3), ISSN 2278 – 1323
42. Mahmoud R, Yousuf T, Aloul F, Zualkernan I (2015) Internet of Things (IoT) security: current status, challenges and prospective measures. In: the 10th international conference for internet technology and secured transactions (ICITST-2015)

43. Juels A, Rivest RL, Szydlo M (2003) The blocker tag: Selective blocking of RFID tags for consumer privacy. In: Proceedings of ACM 10th conference on computing and communication security, pp 103–111
44. Kim DS, Shin TH, Park JS (2006) Access control and authorization for security of RFID multi-domain using SAML and XACML. In: International Conference on Computational Intelligence and Security, Guangzhou, pp 1587–1590
45. Uttarkar R, Kulkarni R (2014) Internet of things: architecture and security. Int J Comput Appl 3(4):2014
46. Thakur BS, Chaudhary S (2013) Content sniffing attack detection in client and server side: a survey. Int J Advanc Comput Res (IJACR) 3
47. Halim T, Islam Md. R, (2012) A study on the security issues in WSN. Int J Comput Appl (0975 – 8887), 53(1)
48. Khoo B (2011) RFID as an enabler of the internet of things: issues of security and privacy. In: International conference on internet of things and 4th international conference on cyber, physical and social computing, Dalian, pp 709–712
49. Pedro P, Julio H, Juan T, Li T, Li Y (2010) Vulnerability analysis of RFID protocols for tag ownership transfer. Comput Netw 54(9):1502–1508. Research Collection School of Information Systems
50. Rieback MR, Crispo B, Tanenbaum AS (2006) Is your cat infected with a computer virus? In: Fourth annual IEEE international conference on pervasive computing and communications (PERCOM'06), Pisa, pp 10–179
51. Atallah M, Pantazopoulos KN, Rice J, Spafford E (2002) Secure outsourcing of scientific computations. Adv Comput 54:215–272
52. Hohenberger S, Lysyanskaya A (2005) How to securely outsource cryptographic computations. In: Proceedings of the theory of cryptography conference 2005. Springer, pp 264–282
53. Benjamin D, Atallah M (2008) Private and cheating-free outsourcing of algebraic computations. In: Sixth annual conference on privacy, security and trust, PST 2008, Fredericton, New Brunswick, Canada, Springer, October 2008, pp 240–245
54. Gentry C (2009) Fully homomorphic encryption using ideal lattices. In: STOC '09, 2009, pp 169–178
55. Atallah M, Frikken K (2010) Securely outsourcing linear algebra computations. In: Proceedings of the 5th ACM symposium on information, computer and communications security. Springer, New York, 2010, pp 48–59
56. Gennaro R, Gentry C, Parno B (2010) Non-interactive verifiable computing: outsourcing computation to untrusted workers. Advanc Cryptol CRYPTO 2010, Lecture Notes Computer Science 6223, 465– 482
57. Yao AC (1982) Protocols for secure computations. In: Proceedings of the 23rd annual symposium on foundations of computer science, pp 160–168. IEEE Computer Society
58. Chung K, Kalaiand Y, Vadhan S (2010) Improved delegation of computation using fully homomorphic encryption. In: Proceedings of 30th annual cryptology conference, Santa Barbara, CA, USA, in: Lect. Notes Computer Science, vol 6223, Springer, August 2010, pp 483–501
59. Chung K, Kalaiand Y, Liu F (2011) Memory delegation. In: Proceedings of the 31st annual cryptology conference, Santa Barbara, CA, USA. Lecture Notes Computer Science, vol 6841, Springer, pp 151–168
60. Parno B, Raykova M, Vaikuntanathan V (2012) How to delegate and verify in public: verifiable computation from attribute-based encryption. In: Proceedings of the 9th theory of cryptography conference, TCC 2012, Taormina, Sicily, Italy, in: Lect. Notes Comput. Science, vol 7194, Springer, March 2012, pp 422–439
61. Di Crescenzo G, Khodjaeva M, Kahrobaei D, Shpilrain V (2017) Computing multiple exponentiations in discrete log and RSA groups: from batch verification to batch delegation. In: Proceedings of 3rd IEEE workshop on security and privacy in the cloud. IEEE
62. Bellare M, Garay J, Rabin T (1998) Fast batch verification for modular exponentiation and digital signatures. Proc Eurocrypt, Springer, pp 236–250

63. Wang Y, Wu Q, Wong D, Qin B, Chow S, Liu Z, Tao X (2014) Securely outsourcing exponentiations with single untrusted program for cloud storage. In: Proceedings of computer security-ESORICS 2014. Springer, pp 326–343
64. Arbit A, Livne Y, Oren Y, Wool A (2015) Implementing public-key cryptography on passive RFID tags is practical. Int J Inf Sec 14(1):85–99
65. Chen X, Li J, Ma J, Tang Q, Lou W (2012) New algorithms for secure outsourcing of modular exponentiations. In: Computer security–ESORICS 2012, pp 541–556
66. Ye J, Chen X, Ma J (2015) An improved algorithm for secure outsourcing of modular exponentiations. In: Proceedings of 29th international conference on advanced information networking and applications, March 2015, pp 73–76
67. Ding Y, Xu Z, Ye J, Choo K (2017) Secure outsourcing of modular exponentiations under single untrusted programme model. J Comput Syst Sci 90, C Academic Press, Inc., 1–13
68. Cavallo B, Di Crescenzo G, Kahrobaei D, Shpilrain V (2015) Efficient and secure delegation of group exponentiation to a single server. In: International workshop on radio frequency identification: security and privacy issues. Springer, pp 156–173
69. Di Crescenzo G, Khodjaeva M, Kahrobaei D, Shpilrain V (2018) Efficient and secure delegation to a single malicious server: exponentiation over non-abelian groups.Springer Lecture Notes in Computer Science
70. Di Crescenzo G, Khodjaeva M, Kahrobaei D, Shpilrain V (2017) Practical and secure outsourcing of discrete log group exponentiation to a single malicious server. In: Proceedings of 9th ACM cloud computing security workshop (CCSW), pp 17–28

Chapter 4
Multidisciplinary Intel Fusion Technique for Proactive Cyber-Intelligence Model for the IoT

Ugur Can Atasoy and Arif Sari

Abstract Cyber-Threat Intelligence (CTI) is an acknowledged concept both by professionals and academia. This well-known notion was synthesized through interdisciplinary and multidisciplinary subspecialties of Cyber-Intelligence (CI). The CI concept focuses on extracting pure intelligence reports and cyber-perspectives through available information sources, including the deep/dark web. It also discloses possible threats, risks, attack campaigns, espionage, and exposure operations. Focusing on the clear and dark side of the Internet is not enough to feed CI; for an accurate and richer stream of information, the Internet of Things (IoT) concept needs to be clarified and integrated into the entire CI lifecycle. The process includes extracting information through various sources using different methodologies and techniques and by applying the proposed aggregation function/methodology models for continuous development of the CI lifecycle. This chapter focuses on the fundamentals of the CI concentrations such as Open-Source Intelligence (OSINT), Human Intelligence (HUMINT), Technical Intelligence (TECHINT), and the IoT vision in order to propose a proactive CYBer-INTelligence (CYBINT) aggregation approach model. The proposed model depends on practical tools and approaches that are part of the proactive defenses and analyzing strategies.

Keywords Cyber-threat intelligence · Cyber-fusion · Cyber-intelligence framework · Data aggregation · Internet of things (IoT) · OSINT · HUMINT · TECHINT · TCTI · OCTI · SCTI · Proactive security · Shadow intelligence

4.1 Introduction

Today's cyber-space anatomy is much more complex compared to the earlier periods of the Internet. The evolution of Internet Information Systems (ISS), Information and Communication Technology (ICT), and various technological developments in both

---

U. Can Atasoy · A. Sari (✉)
Department of Management Information Systems, School of Applied Science, Girne American University, Canterbury, UK
e-mail: arifsarii@gmail.com

Z. Mahmood (ed.), *Security, Privacy and Trust in the IoT Environment*, https://doi.org/10.1007/978-3-030-18075-1_4

hardware and software aspects have created continuous advancements and hybrid environments that are now called cyber-space. Initially, the main focus areas of the cyber-world were communication (military based) and technology adaptation, but currently, cyber-space plays a vital role in the global authority. Advancements in cyber-space provide various flexible capabilities such as extracting non-cyber-actions from online activities such as advertisements, socializing, military architectures, activists, propaganda, espionage, diplomatic, ideological, and intellectual and battle actions (digital format of armed conflict). Thus, professionalism in cyber-space becomes crucial in the global scope.

Communication, media, entertainment, and defense domains have been the initial digitalized concepts of cyber-space. The other specific domains such as attack–defense, health, education, social life, and intelligence alongside operative actions are added-on concepts of cyber-space. Since cyber-space is essential in our global power balance, some of these add-on concepts such as attack–defense (offensive and defensive aspects) and intelligence (analyst and data processing aspects) have gained significance in terms of usage, development, and flexibility. One of the critical points, since these advancements, is that information may indeed be false in some cases, in cyber-space. Technological adaptations have also added a vast amount of data in the digital zone. Since the processing of information in order to obtain meaningful data which could allow end users to make predictions for the future is based on reliable information, data reliability has gained importance and drew much attention of many data scientists, analysts, activists, and both governmental and nongovernmental intelligence services.

The concept of Data Intelligence is basically the act of extracting meaningful data through data processing. Further processing and transmission of data gives rise to information, and then knowledge and wisdom. The process proceeds to intelligence and associated disciplines like subdisciplines or concentrations of Cyber-Intelligence such as Open-Source Intelligence (OSINT), Human Intelligence (HUMINT), Technical Intelligence (TECHINT), Measurement and Signature Intelligence (MASINT), Signals Intelligence (SIGINT), Image Intelligence (IMINT), Geospatial Intelligence (GEOINT), Social Media Intelligence (SOCMINT), and Communications Intelligence (COMINT).

Various associations of the abovementioned intelligence concentrations lead to specific intelligence types such as Cyber-Threat Intelligence (CTI). There are a variety of tools, techniques, and methodologies that are available for these concentrations in the existing literature. However, the up-to-date usage scenarios and proposed models did not provide a requirement that is determined in this chapter to be a proactive fusion concept of Cyber-Intelligence. This chapter proposes a proactive cyber-intelligence model that depends on aggregating multidisciplinary methods and techniques along with synthesizing the produced intelligence information.

The Internet of Things (IoT) is not a new concept in cyber-space; it was defined by Kevin Ashton in 1999 as physical entities that connect to the Internet via sensors, process abilities, and embedded technologies. In principle, the IoT term is also described as a form of machine-to-machine communication, but there are many devices that are not embedded with such technologies, so machine-to-machine communication is not fully accomplished directly. However, since these device varieties are connecting humans globally, they are accomplishing this expectation indirectly. The IoT concept is becoming popular and a requirement in today's business and professional life, e.g., for Industry 4.0, also known as Industrial IoT (IIoT). Increasing network capabilities of the new generation devices and sensor technology may accomplish direct machine-to-machine communication, but until that time the IoT concept could be regarded as an information source and a new line in cyber-security and development of the Cyber-Intelligence concept [1].

This chapter focuses on the Cyber-Intelligence development concept and provides an analysis of the known intelligence types that help to create a proactive Cyber-Intelligence structure. In the chapter, we provide a review of the various intelligence and data collecting methods that we use for the proposed model. Thus, the proposed model is a synthesis of up-to-date approaches, methods, and life cycles found in the cyber-space literature. As a result of global IoT integration, the chapter also includes IoT factors that have an influence on the proposed architecture. The goal of the proposed architecture is to create a system with the capability to extract more accurate and intelligence-based information in the cyber-space. In other words, the proposed CYBer-INTelligence (CYBIT) model provides a more efficient usage of the current-related models available. Hence, the suggested model offers strong outcomes in terms of scope profit, value, and action. Ultimately, the proposed model extracts information for use in several domains such as threat hunting in the military and in related organizations.

4.2 Background

The main focus of this chapter is on efficient and effective use of Cyber-Intelligence and associated assets. There are a variety of usage methodologies, life cycles, and combinations of intelligence services currently out there. But these services do not cover all of the available sources and intelligence subdisciplines such as OSINT, HUMINT, TECHINT, MASINT, SOCINT, SIGINT, IMINT, and COMINT. This chapter focuses on these concepts and proposes a hybrid Cyber-Intelligence (CYBIT) model for proactive cyber-intelligence in the IoT era.

4.2.1 Issues, Controversies, and Problems

One of the determined problems in cyber-space is appropriating the efficient use of Cyber-Intelligence along with the existing data sources and methodologies. Cyber-Intelligence can provide proactive security, but to achieve this, there must be a hybrid approach that uses a synthesis of the existing methodologies, tools, and frameworks. Previous studies mention this requirement with different viewpoints as summarized in the following.

The increased use of Information Systems (IS) brings with it more threats to digital zones and possibilities for data breaches, so there is a need for a comprehensive security plan that works differently than the traditional approaches and one that also provides proactive security. Hence, the current systems are not able to cover the increasingly sophisticated attacks. What is needed is a hybrid system, a combination of current and up-to-date methodologies in order to fully cover the possible threats against ISs [2].

Without intelligence, the success of operations cannot be realized, making the advantage of having associated secure operations that are unprotected. In the case of a cyber-war, the intelligence always plays a vital role in terms of starting and finalizing cyber-operations. Cyber-Intelligence is most commonly associated with the military concept "cyber-force actions." When the subject comes to cyber-operations, the importance of intelligence comes into the picture once again [3].

Increased data pools and web source alternatives have created a vast amount of data through cyber-space, so the necessity of correctly analyzing and processing this huge amount of data is getting harder. Therefore, the usage of systematic attitudes that depends on scientific approaches and that also works with within the framework of rules is highly desirable [4–6].

From ancient times to the modern day, people have always grasped the importance of information, more specifically, the importance of reliable information for financial, governmental, and warfare strategies. Investigators' methods and methodologies are mainly focused on information-based operations where the significance of the information and the usage of false information are key areas of concern. The usage of information as a service and the integration of information into an applied field created the intelligence concept and started during World War II (WW-II). After WW-II and during the time of the cold war, the intelligence concept raised and became highly integrated with armed force activities and international relations [7].

Smart systems are becoming more popular in this century. Cyber-physical systems have also started to become a necessity in the development of current technology and in trends like Industry 4.0, Web 4.0, Cloud Computing, and the Internet of Things (IoT). Smart grid-like system prototypes lead to smart home systems in terms of security practicability, manageability, and affordability. Today's 24/7 connected digital life brings with it, corresponding technologies and other underlying technologies to the center of people's daily lives. While the IoT trend has started to be part of the daily and professional life, the security of IoT must be included in the security perimeters. Since these systems are like mobile phones and are always in the "on" mode, they have an Internet Protocol (IP) address so there is an open door for the threats. According to respective security authorities, more than 60% of the frequently used IoT structures used to have inherent security vulnerabilities [1, 8].

Existing lack of security architecture in IoT has made the IoT environments a target for hackers. Current privacy and forensics applications are not capable to provide a solid IoT environment that can protect against different attack methodologies. Since Industrial Control Systems (ICS), cars, homes, surveillance units, and router like devices are in an IoT environment, there is a substantial number of devices and users linked to such environments [9]. Therefore, IoT environments must be included in the cyber-intelligence scope in order to progress security operations.

New, IoT technological advancements provide a suitable environment for attackers to launch cyber-attacks against critical and IoT environments. Current approaches are not able to detect, block, and mitigate corresponding attacks fully, and there are a variety of product/system-based solutions that are not able to fulfill the next-generation attacks against critical infrastructures [10–12].

To comprehend the intelligence concept, the stages of data transformation into intelligence must be clarified. The following paragraphs discuss the transformation aspects of the raw data into intelligence.

4.2.2 Data and Data Processing

Data represents a set of numbers and characters that are processed in order to generate information. There are processes that represent the given data in the required structure. By filtering and refining the gathered data, the information generated gets dependent upon the data relationships [7, 13]. Processing transforms the data into significant and operable shapes that are then called information. The transformation process generally comprises a set of actions that include documenting, analyzing, computing, summarizing, categorizing, distributing and finally shaping the data into intelligible, actionable, profitable, and a comparable state [7].

Types of Data

There are three types of data available in cyber-space:

- Raw Data: This is unprocessed data that contains raw figures such as IP addresses, log details, and attacker attributes [14, 15].
- Exploited Data: This is classified and filtered raw data; usually, the process is conducted by analysts and it exhibits the anatomy of data along with its associated themes [14, 15].
- Production Data: This is processed data that contains minimal raw data; this type of data prepares to serve clients and consumers [14].

Information

The function of "informing" lies behind the word *information*. Theoretically, creating the form of intelligence represents accumulated *information*, but the word "information" is mostly used for transmitting messages that contain a refined set of words and numbers, often called *data*. In other words, information is described as a component of the knowledge that it creates [7, 16].

Intelligence and Intel Process

Intelligence produces outputs through information and data processing aspects such as synthesis, transformation, and aggregation. The term is commonly used in military and organizational-based strategies by representing activities against possible opponents and threats/risks in order to predict the next set of moves. The purpose of intelligence is to provide up-to-date, significant, precise, timely, and convenient intelligence information for specialized cases for the requestor [7].

The concept of intelligence is defined by the intelligence cycle, which is classically built by collecting, processing, analyzing, and publishing steps. Traditional intelligence mainly focuses on military and civil cases; however, the shape of intelligence information could differ due to a change of requirements by the customers and requestors [7]. Finally, intelligence information gathering could be summarized as a set of hybrid operations.

The term "Intel Process" refers to the processing of information that makes sense. This process produces predictive and proactive information via purposed intelligence models.

4.3 Cyber-Threat Intelligence (CTI)

Cyber-Threat Intelligence (CTI) is proof-based intelligence information detection identified through accessible and available data. It provides defensive alerts as predictions for the most known and latest threats. The CTI concept also helps practitioners to describe the threats and apply intelligence-based actions against specified cases [17]. There are three levels of CTI [17]: Tactical, Operational and Strategic—as follows.

- Tactical Cyber-Threat Intelligence (TCTI) is focused on rapid and instant reactions and feedbacks. It works on the endpoint level and provides intelligence information through daily events, malware hashes, and common malicious software indicators.
- Operational Cyber-Threat Intelligence (OCTI) is focused on technical details of the cyber-incidents in order to provide support for particular cases. OCTI also focuses on the attacker in order to describe the profile of the attacker. This type of intelligence also investigates the possible effects of the attack vector on the requestor or customer.
- Strategic Cyber-Threat Intelligence (SCTI) mainly draws a big picture for the practitioner by defining the new threat campaigns, the intent of new threats, threat models, and identifies the practitioner's competences to provide instant and executive notifications. SCTI also uses up-to-date information in order to describe technology usage for the benefit of the practitioner.

4.3.1 Characteristics of Efficient CTI

The efficiency of CTI is dependent upon the quality of the resources that are evaluated via the following criteria:

- **Timeliness**: Intelligence must be shared on time in order to handle the corresponding operation/case and to create actions on the intelligence [7, 18].
- **Relevant**: Intelligence must provide required details to the recipient and it must be associated with the recipient. There must be a connection with the intelligence and the recipient in terms of used systems, operations, plans and the sector in terms of vulnerabilities, risks, and opportunities [7, 18].
- **Accurate**: Intelligence must be accurate, objective, balanced, and solid. Corresponding intelligence must fully clarify the indicators/findings and any uncertain information that would corrupt the accuracy of the intelligence [7, 18].
- **Tailored/Specific**: Intelligence must fulfill the recipient's requirements and have crucial details related to the recipient's system and structure. Intelligence must declare how possible threats, vulnerabilities, risks, and opportunities could affect the recipient's systems and infrastructure.
- **Usable**: Intelligence must be in a comprehensible format that makes sense by the recipient. Generated intelligence must be compatible with the recipient's systems and structure [7].
- **Predictive/Actionable**: Intelligence must indicate the applicable and proper operations/activities in order to avoid corresponding risks and vulnerabilities or to obtain opportunities [10, 18].

4.4 Concentrations of Cyber-Threat Intelligence

There is a variety of intelligence gathering subdisciplines, also known as concentrations. This section discusses the most popular of these in order to build a proactive cyber-intelligence model.

OSINT

Open-Source Intelligence (OSINT) is an open information system that publishes/shares and sometimes discovers information from a variety of publicly available platforms such as social media, news, forums, databases, libraries, reports, advertisements, and commercial services. Unpublished documents and human intelligence are also included in the corresponding scope; however, the critical point always focuses on rules and regulations. There are two important and differential characteristics of the OSINT: first, the obtained data is gathered with legitimate approaches; and second, the monetary requirements are relatively low compared to other intelligence concentrations [17–19].

HUMINT

Human Intelligence (HUMINT) is an intelligence collection approach that depends on human resources such as interests, activities, connections, conversations, intentions, and competences. Humans and individuals are the major resources for HUMINT collection, and there are a variety of information gathering tools and techniques used to collect data from a human source. Usually, multimedia items, digital, and physical activities are examined by intelligence collectors in order to have the corresponding intelligence and to create a correlation with different types of intelligence concentrations. Espionage, patrolling, investigation (including background and face-to-face), stalking, and recon actions are commonly used in HUMINT operations [17–19].

SOCMINT
Social Media Intelligence (SOCMINT) is a social media-based information system. It is discovered through a variety of social media platforms such as Ask.fm, Booking, Hotels, Eventbrite, Facebook, Flicker, Foursquare, Google, Instagram, LinkedIn, Pinterest, Quora, Reddit, Skype, Snapchat, Telegram, Tumblr, Twitter, Viber, Vine, VKontakte, WeChat, WhatsApp, Wikipedia, Yandex, YouTube, etc. These channels and platforms are used for communication and create interaction actions so there is a vast amount of personal identifier data that is collected, including data on interests, personality, attitudes, plans, achievements, and suchlike. Due to containing the categorized data and offering a customized data scope, the value of SOCMINT is quite different from OSINT [18, 20].

TECHINT
Technical Intelligence (TECHINT) acquires information through an intelligence analysis cycle and works against technical goods of any target. This type of intelligence focuses on the technical characteristics of the target's properties. Usually, it is used by governmental intelligence purposes in order to identify a target's technological developments and infrastructures. Obtained data through the system provides signs in terms of capacity, limitation, and countermeasures. In consideration of highly governmental usage, TECHINT reports could provide sensitive data for governments and other international actors [18, 19, 21].

MASINT
Measurement and Signature Intelligence (MASINT) acquires information through quantitative and qualitative analysis of technical data in terms of the sender and receiver and is from a variety of communication means. It defines characteristics of the counterparties of the communicators including fixed and dynamic sources. Geographical tracking, recognition, and identification are major results of this type of intelligence. Due to strategic discovery and multi-object analysis features of MASINT, it is highly useful for the military and governmental operations in terms of supplying strategic plans and operations. There is a variety of intelligence concentrations that supply MASINT [17–19] including

- Nuclear Intelligence (NUCINT)
- Infrared Intelligence (IRINT)
- Radar Intelligence (RADINT)
- Acoustic Intelligence (ACOUSTINT)
- Radio Frequency Intelligence (RFINT) or Electromagnetic Pulse Int. (EMPINT)
- Laser Intelligence (LASINT)
- Unintentional Radiation Intelligence (RINT)
- Chemical and Biological Intelligence (CBINT)
- Electro-Optical Intelligence (ELECTRO-OPTINT)

- Directed Energy Weapons Intelligence (DEWINT)
- Image Intelligence (IMINT)
- Signals Intelligence (SIGINT).

SIGINT
Signals Intelligence (SIGINT) acquires information through electronic signals and systems like communication signals transmitted via digital systems such as computers, mobile phones, radars, and both offensive and defensive weapon systems. It depends on the investigation of transferred data and provides signs about a target's capabilities, operations, and objectives. Communication Intelligence (COMINT) is a concentration of SIGINT; it provides intelligence through fax and radio frequencies [17, 19].

IMINT
Image Intelligence (IMINT) acquires information through visual sources such as visualized sensors, radars, and electronic images (information based on visual resources). Both hardcopy and soft copy visual resources are also included in the IMIT scope. Discovering, categorizing, and identifying actions could be done through IMINT [17, 19].

MEDINT
Medical Intelligence (MEDINT) is an intelligence collection model that depends on medical resources and the capabilities of the analyzed target. The scope of MEDINT includes bioscientific, environmental, medical, and infrastructural details of a target in both civilian and military fields [19]. This type of intelligence is highly practical on a global scope in terms of medical assistance and war operations. Due to this sensitive domain, MEDINT may provide exploitable signs in case of a crisis and/or conflict.

4.5 Proposed Proactive Cyber-Intelligence Model (CYBINT)

This chapter outlines the CYBINT, also known as Digital Network Intelligence model and describes how it provides efficient usage of intelligence tools, services, and disciplines. The chapter offers a practical methodology that was created by a variety of intelligence types and tools, some of which are already described in the previous section. Overall, this section focuses on the usage of the discussed concepts via the Cyber-Intelligence (CYBINT) cycle. Figure 4.1 visualizes the proposed CYBINT model.

The primary goal of CYBINT is to provide an extensive knowledge database that works against possible threats as well as against a recipient's systems and infrastructure. It helps to build a database that contains the mentioned intelligence from a variety of sources and shows the results simultaneously for each category in order to

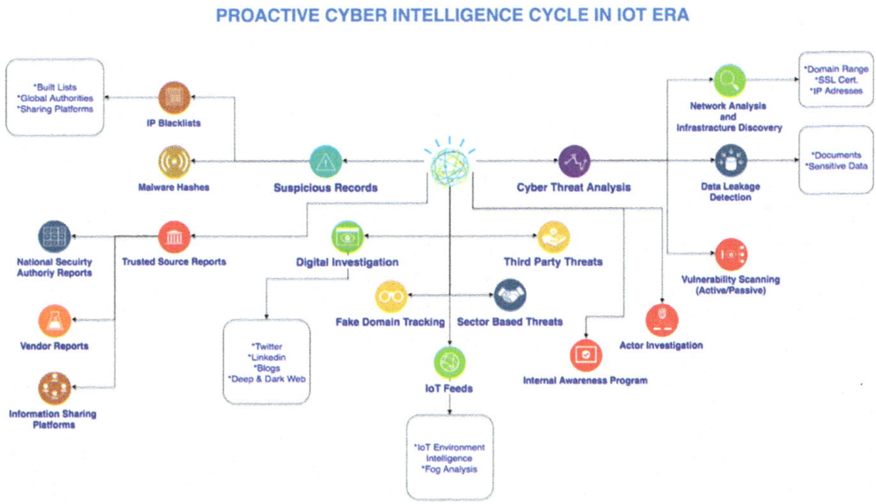

Fig. 4.1 Proposed cyber-intelligence model

help the security officers and the managers who then take appropriate actions. Provided model and intelligence concept are built in a proactive intelligence perspective. The following subsections clarify each major task of the intelligence cycle, as shown in Fig. 4.1, noting that the provided intelligence model is not dependent upon any task list, however, to provide extensive intelligence, all tasks must be achieved.

4.5.1 Components of Cyber-Intelligence Model

This section focuses on the modules of the CYBINT process. Scope of the intelligence highly depends on the success of the core modules as discussed in the following subsections.

4.5.1.1 Suspicious Records

Suspicious logs can mainly be found in the recipient's traffic and in endpoint security logs. Examination of these services with traffic analysis will provide a list of malware, spam e-mail addresses, phishing domains, IP addresses, and suchlike violations. Building lists from suspicious records will keep the recipient's network safer and protected against specialized attacks. Monitoring of network traffic is carried out through combining a variety of logs gathered through specifically located security systems on the network and nodes such as Security Information and Event Management (SIEM) systems, firewalls, intrusion detection systems, endpoint security systems, and e-mail gateway. There are varieties of tools (commercial/open source) which process the corresponding massive information and provide actionable outcomes for the security analysts. Current SIEM/monitoring products are able to tackle the complicacy of managing the massive logs files, and generate local threat lists with the less false positive rate. In addition to local lists, global authorities and national security centers, vendors, and information sharing platforms provide customized and classified information for these purposes.

Mentioned services and authorities will be discussed in a later section of this chapter on Trusted Source Reports. This section of the CYBINT cycle retrieves massive baseline information of the organization; since the results are generated through local user and device logs, it is critical for the CYBIT cycle. Organizational cyber-maturity and risk levels can be defined via gathered activity logs.

IP Blacklists
Malicious IP addresses must be collected in a list and checked systematically. The list must be designed as a dynamic list in order to provide a fully trustable IP blacklist. Systematic controls accomplished by security analysts during predetermined time intervals depend upon the recipient's traffic load. Dynamic list logic is dependent upon banning a malicious IP address until it is not participating in malicious activities anymore. Therefore, tracking the blacklisted IP addresses activities is important to accomplish the cycle.

Malware Hashes
Majority of the security products are able to identify the common malware via their hashes but this countermeasure falls short against specifically designed malware. Organizations should create a malware hash database and support the used security countermeasures with this information against custom malware. Information sharing agreements and platforms provide malicious hashes to their partners—having such a partnership will give the recipient a malware hash block list that could be used like an IP blacklist.

4.5.1.2 Trusted Source Reports

This section provides information about the national security agencies and vendors. Crawling and following these sources will create a great up-to-date vulnerability and threat database. Information provided by these services must be included in CYBINT process in order to accomplish data enrichment.

Governmental Security Authorities Reports
Most of the National Security Authorities are suggesting that nations are targeted and that there are global threats and related operations. Following these sources will help the recipient in terms of notification of the latest threats. National Computer Emergency Response Teams (CERT) and Computer Security Incident Response Teams (CSIRT) are majorly focused on the global and national threats. Every national CERT provides specific information on suspicious/malicious IP addresses, malware hashes,

attack campaigns, and customized attacks. Since threat intelligence is evidence-based information, enriching the evidence/sample size supports the decision accuracy. CERT and CSIRT authorities are gaining importance in the global scope, and today majority of the countries have similar departments. CERT and CSIRT departments tend to provide information on the following:

- Malicious/Suspicious IP Addresses
- Attack Campaigns (Specifically designed against specific nations)
- Phishing Attack Samples
- Security Practices Against Attacks and Threats.

Vendor Reports

The majority of the product vendors provide security and vulnerability reports along with bug fixes/updates. Following the reports about a product will allow vendors to fill in gaps about the intelligence. Updating the products and systems cannot provide security at 100% level; sometimes, new features are able to create bugs that lead to exploitation. However, patching the bugs and fixes are mandatory for the security cycle. Following vendor reports and alerts is another essential source for the CYBINT cycle. Vendors usually provide information on

- Product Updates
- Bug Fixes
- Countermeasures Against Threats.

Information Sharing Platforms

There are varieties of these platforms that perform both in commercial and non-commercial situations. The common purpose of these platforms is to exchange the threat information with the community members. Win-win approach is the basis of these platforms. Organizations share their threat knowledge in terms of suspicious/malicious IP addresses, malware, and attack campaigns with assistive information. Being a member of these platforms will support the CYBINT cycle.

Most common information sharing and threat intelligence platforms are listed below [22]:

- Open-Source Platforms
  - Collaborative Research Into Threats (CRITs)
  - Collective Intelligence Framework (CIF)
  - MANTIS Cyber-Threat Intelligence Management Framework
  - Malware Information Sharing Platform (MISP)
  - MITRE| ATT&CK
  - MineMeld Threat Intelligence Sharing
  - Yeti Threat Intelligence Platform
- Commercial Platforms
  - Recorded Future

  - Anomali
  - Blueliv
  - ThreatSteam
  - EclecticIQ Platform
  - LookingGlass
  - Soltra Edge
  - Threat Central
    ThreatConnect
    ThreatQ Platform
    TruSTAR

- Community Platforms
  - Open Threat Exchange
  - Threat Exchange
  - X-Force Exchange

- Platforms providing information exchange/sharing
  - Malware | Malware Hashes
  - Attack Campaigns
  - Phishing Attacks
  - Sectoral Threat Information.

Majority of the mentioned platforms are using a Structured Threat Information Expression (STIX) and Trusted Automated Exchange of Intelligence Information (TAXII) infrastructure to share the information.

4.5.1.3 Digital Investigation

Tracking social–digital platforms provide up-to-date information. Nowadays, the majority of the actors and attacker groups post messages on social media platforms, blogs, communication channels, forums, both in clear web and the deep dark web. Posted messages generally provide information on data exposures, attacks, attack campaigns, malware, bugs, vulnerabilities, zero days, and sometimes on next attack campaigns. Crawling suchlike specific fields allows early detection against attack campaigns, vulnerabilities, malware, and exploits. Focusing on global and local actors along with attack campaigns is important in the corresponding investigation. Digital investigation mainly focuses on the following:

- Twitter
- Facebook
- Hacker Blogs
- Defacement Achieves
- Paste Sites
- Malware Sharing Platforms

- Exploit and Zero Day Sharing Platforms.

4.5.1.4 Fake Domain Track

Generating possible phishing domains and freezing the similar ones will strengthen the recipient's security both in system and personal aspects. This aspect is an important countermeasure against social engineering and phishing attacks. Since Unicode tricks accomplished via Cyrillic characters, range of the possible phishing domains is increased too. To avoid suchlike cases, tracking similar domain gained importance in the proactive intelligence concept.

4.5.1.5 Cyber-Threat Analysis

Medium scope of the Cyber-Threat analysis is another aspect of the CYBINT model. This analysis should operate for the recipient's partners too. There are a variety of tasks that must be accomplished under the CTI, such as the following.

Network Analysis and Infrastructure Discovery
This step focuses on actions including network analysis in terms of defining the domain range (subdomains and IP addresses) and Secure Sockets Layer (SSL) certification in order to control the domain scope and security. Scheduled internal scans and outsider scan activities are accomplished at this stage. Infrastructure of the system such as operating system, open ports, and services is explored at this stage too.

Corresponding analysis focuses on the techniques, as listed below, for gathering information over organization/recipient:

- Network Reconnaissance
- Subdomain Extraction
- Linked/Associated System and Service Discovery
- Port Discovery.

Data Leakage Detection
This step focuses on periodical analysis on data exposure platforms such as leaked documents, data fraud cases, and personal identification information (e-mail, username, password). Personal activities and their personal entities like social media accounts are analyzed along with corporate accounts. Investigating data leakage platforms and corporate entity usage on social life activities is accomplished at this stage in order to hardening the security level. Majority of the data leak cases are shared via the following platforms:

- Twitter
- Paste Sites
- Leak Forums
- Pwn Exposure Platforms.

Vulnerability Scanning (Active and Passive)
Vulnerability scanning focuses on penetration testing including black, white, and gray ox, along with social engineering attacks. This aspect focuses highly on the recipient's systems strength and configuration quality in terms of vulnerabilities and security flaws. Passive scanning can be accomplished through third-party services such as Software-as-a-Service (SaaS) model and by manual analysis. Active scanning is done via offensive skills; moreover, implementing both black box and gray box penetration testing methodologies will provide more accurate and actionable results.

4.5.1.6 IoT Feeds

Performing the required actions and services in IoT environments such as smart grids, smart offices, and smart home systems will assist in providing extensive intelligence.

4.5.1.7 Sector-Based Threats

Having an agreement and information sharing platform membership provides sector-based intelligence that can help to provide information on sector-based attacks and specialized malware. Another sectoral information source is organizational-level agreements. Establishing threats information exchange agreements on major sectors like defense, banking, and other vital service sectors will also provide massive information on sector-based threats. Mentioned agreements could be established in local and global scope; however, due to field competitions and financial concerns establishing this may be an issue. Consequently, this aspect could be achieved through information sharing platforms.

4.5.1.8 Actor Investigation

Tracking vulnerabilities, risks, exposures, and defacements is not enough for accurate intelligence information. Recipients must define their attacker types (sector based) and focus on their attack styles in order to be ready for the next move of the attacker. Attacker style, defacement history, attack frequency, reactions, and supported campaigns must be tracked in order to create an accurate attacker profile. Proper actor profile must provide attacker skills, target sectors, used methods and malware, activity area, and motivation.

4.5.1.9 Internal Awareness Program

Working with security specialists is not enough to build a tough security system as humans are always the weakest link in the security chain. Conducting periodical phishing attacks for internal network will always influence the recipient's network.

With the help of the gathered massive information on threats, attack campaigns, and actor profiles, internal awareness program must be specifically designed within the scope of the corresponding information in order to achieve the maximum awareness level of the organization members.

4.5.2 Cyber-Intelligence Cycle

Intelligence and building the proactive intelligence concept (proposed model) are now discussed in this section. After collecting the whole information and processing the actionable intelligence, the proposed model is able to produce actionable information that is shown in Table 4.1.

The proactive intelligence concept collects information through various sources. The information fusion, already mentioned, must be supplied with machine crawling and Application Programming Interface (API) connections. This model focuses on multi-source event/threat integration in order to identify the Indicators of Compromise (ICOs) with high accuracy and supports the analyst for taking the most appropriate action. This proactive approach also supports the mitigation of the threats and risks against both insider and outsider ones.

Cyber-Intelligence is one of the hot topics in the cyber-security field, and there is a variety of concentrations of the cyber-intelligence [22, 23], as mentioned in a previous section. Each discipline specifically focuses on certain particular objectives. Table 4.2 shows the most known cyber-intelligence concepts in the cyber-space. It highlights the separation of the duties; however, single countermeasures are not able to cover sophisticated attack types, so the proactive strategies are one of the necessities of the time.

It is in this context that CYBINT infrastructure and intelligence processes are being discussed. Covered information sources provide a vast amount of data gathering information through various methods, technologies, and platforms duplicate the existing data, but verifying an incident or malware via several sources increases the attribute size of the corresponding intelligence. To provide the most accurate Intel, CYBINT process is accomplished with the following steps:

- **Collect**: Collecting and measuring the data systematically through various sources such as information sharing platforms and threat intelligence platforms.
- **Correlate**: This aspect is establishment of the connection between obtained data via complementing and supplying correlation. Aim of this aspect is to provide the most accurate data and increase the attributes of the data.
- **Enrichment and Contextualization**: This refers to complementing the obtained data in order to create an Intel information from different types of data. This aspect provides intelligence information via using different types of data.
- **Analyze**: This is an analysis of threat indicators, processed intelligence information and the relationships between gathered information in order to produce accurate, timely, relevant, and actionable intelligence.

Table 4.1 CYBINT cycle

CYBINT cycle (Intel fusion)		
Scope	Information sources	Provided information
Suspicious records	Traffic records Government CERTs Information sharing platforms	• IP blacklists • Malware hashes • Spam e-mail addresses • Phishing domains
Trusted sources	Government CERTs Vendors Information sharing platforms	• Attack campaigns • Product bug fixes/patches • Customized malware
Digital investigation	Social media Blogs Forums Deep and dark web	• Attacker profiles • Exploited vulnerabilities • Bugs • Attack campaigns • New attacks and malware
Domain track	Owned domains Domain service analysis	• Possible phishing domains
Cyber-threat analysis	Network analysis Pentest services Vulnerability scans Data leakages Pwned accounts Exposed information	• IP range • SSL control • Open ports • Used systems and services • Vulnerabilities • Leaked usernames and passwords • Leaked e-mail addresses • Leaked sensitive data exploration • Personal accounts (Social media)
IoT feeds	Smart grid, office, and home Systems Recon	• IoT vulnerabilities
Sector-based threats	Information exchange	• Customized malware
Actor investigation	Defacement history Associated groups	• Attacker skills • Target sectors • Activity area • Motivation

Table 4.2 Most common intelligence concentration practices

	Threat intelligence	Incident response	Security operations
Focus	Threat investigation	Security incidents	Security monitoring
Actions	Investigating external threats	Investigating security incidents and data breaches	Monitoring security systems against insider and outsider attacks

Table 4.3 Scope of the intelligence fusion architecture

Intelligence scope of the proposed model	
Information database	Services
• Electronic crime • Data breaches • Compromised data • Malware information • Attacker information • Botnet information • Indicators of threats • Malicious hosts • Security incidents • Global incidents • Attack campaigns • Vulnerabilities • Social media threat detection • Crawled sources	• Risk modeling • Risk scoring • Extensive monitoring • Threat/risk filtering

- **Act**: This concept explains that the provided information producing the actionable CYBINT process. Findings and discoveries must be served via dashboard or portal system in order to analyze the data and take appropriate actions. Proposed model is based on this structure.

Multidisciplinary Intel Fusion concept enhances a strong knowledge, threat, and evidence database; and satisfies the big data and artificial intelligence analysis requirements.

Upgrading the current SOC and SIRT concepts through offensive-defensive approaches like red/blue/purple teaming concepts is the crux of the Intel Fusion concept. CYBINT process represents the output of the Intel Fusion process. Table 4.3 presents the specific information that would be gathered via the proposed architecture.

4.5.3 Challenges

This section focuses on the limitations and challenges of the proposed model, as presented above. The major challenges of the CYBINT process are listed below:

- **Voluminous information rate to analyze on the cyber-space**: There is a vast amount of data in the cyber-space, capturing/exploring the relevant data; and processing it to information requires a massive effort.
- **Data collection issues**: Intelligence information is speared across the cyber-space, some resources are depending on commercial platforms, and some of them are located in Deep & Dark Web, so crawling/collecting from these information sources is a big challenge.

- **Lack of toolset determination**: Automatically determining the relevancy of the data and information cannot accomplish completely. There is still a need for a combination of manual and semiautomatic actions.
- **Data storage issues**: Building an intelligence database requires data warehouses specifically dedicated to data collection.
- **Trust Issues**: There are a variety of intelligence platforms and information share agreements; however, there is a trust issue in terms of participants' trust and cyber-maturity levels.
- **Diversity of the data sharing formats**: There is a variety of standards and formats used in data sharing platforms such as STIX, Yara, Sigma, etc. Supporting more than one data type is still an issue for the platforms.
- **Analysts knowledge maturity level**: Nominating cyber-analysts for the CYBINT like platforms requires satisfactory knowledge on threat actors, attack campaigns, malware, tools, and countermeasures. Educating employees in corresponding fields will take time and exploring an expert in the mentioned field is a challenge.

Mentioned challenges are not exactly the obstacles for the cyber-threat intelligence concept. Using currently proposed model and other varieties of cyber-threat intelligence frameworks, information share/exchange services are providing satisfactory information in terms of producing actionable information for mitigation against indicators of compromise and cyber-threats. However, elimination of the mentioned difficulties will enhance the current intensity of the CYBINT varieties.

4.6 Conclusion

Massive traffic flows throughout cyber-space, including cyber-attacks, cyber-operations, communication, entertainment, services, espionage, intelligence, defense, and patrol actions. The mentioned activities are taking place on open systems and affecting the global scope. Currently, cyber-threats and security are protected by several products and by Security Operations Centers (SOCs). However, advancing technology provides a variety of sophisticated tools to counter the threats that can easily cross many of the security countermeasures, so there is a need for a new cyber-intelligence framework that could provide proactive security.

Since there is a need for a new comprehensive Cyber-Intelligence approach, this chapter provided an effective CYBer-INTelligence (CYBINT) model, which is able to meet the current cyber-space requirements for safety and trust. The model focuses on proactive cyber-intelligence in order to cover both the offensive and defensive methodologies and to be open, as well as to be used in both military and civilian/professions and organizations. Additionally, there are several tools and methods that exist but not mentioned in the chapter.

The proposed cyber-intelligence model focuses on the fusion of intelligence in order to provide proactive intelligence to counteract current and possible future threats and attacks. Intelligence fusion depends on multi-source evidence collection and multi-rule/standard correlation. This architecture has compatibility to integrate and optimize with artificial intelligence approaches as well.

The current threat and intelligence models are not able to cover a combination of the existing and up-to-date dataflows, threat actors, next-generation threats, and risks at the same time. SOCs are able to monitor the entire network and notice the threats/attacks on time but they are not able to predict any sophisticated or customized attack campaigns before they occur. This model has focused on fulfilling these aforementioned gaps, and it merges the entire intelligence concept with an added benefit of its monitoring actions. The proposed model blends big data analytics capabilities with CTI and offensive and defensive approaches. This approach creates a proactive intelligence protection for the recipients and their partners. It also provides a multidisciplinary approach for evaluating risks, incidents, threats, and operations on a global scope and generates CYBINT that predicts the overall threats before they occur. Entire CYBINT cycle is able to accomplish, via data enrichment and contextualization, correlation and deep analysis in order to provide a proactive security against defined and undefined threats, risks, and malware. As a result of this proactive approach, the security strength level increases and decision-makers have reliable and actionable information. This helps the recipients to take appropriate actions against security threats before they happen. Ultimately, data aggregation will gain importance at the same time as the big data and intelligence concepts. This is the main motivation for completing this intelligence synthesis. We feel that proactive cyber-security concept will reach its best capabilities by further contributing to the existing Cyber-Intelligence research.

References

1. EY Global (2015) Cybersecurity and the Internet of Things, March 2015. https://www.ey.com/Publication/vwLUAssets/EY-cybersecurity-and-the-internet-of-things/%24FILE/EY-cybersecurity-and-the-internet-of-things.pdf. Accessed 1 Nov 2018
2. Cunningham T (2015) A cyber-threat intelligence program—how to develop one and why it matters (Unpublished doctoral dissertation). Luleå University of Technology
3. Eom J (2014) Roles and responsibilities of cyber intelligence for cyber operations in cyberspace. Int J Softw Eng Appl 8(9):137–146
4. Köseli M (2015) Bilimsel Araştırma Yöntemlerinin İstihbarat Analizinde Kullanılması. J Secur Strateg 21(11):87–117
5. Richards J (2010) The art & science of intelligence analysis. Oxford University Press, USA
6. Marrin S (2011) Improving intelligence analysis: bridging the gap between scholarship and practice. Routledge, New York
7. Antonio A (2013) Open source information, the future of intelligence. http://www.euintelligenceacademy.eu/sites/eia/files/EIA_REPORT_2013.pdf. Accessed 1 Nov 2018
8. Almeida F (2017) Concept and dimensions of web 4.0. Int J Comput Technol V16:N7
9. Sari A, Kilic S (2017) Exploiting cryptocurrency miners with OSINT techniques. Trans Netw Commun V5:N6
10. Sari A (2018) Countrywide virtual siege in the new era of cyber warfare: remedies from the cyber-firewall: Seddulbahir. J Cyber Secur Technol. https://doi.org/10.1080/23742917.2018.1476956

11. Prolexic Attack Report, *Prolexic believes the nature of DDoS attacks are changing: they are becoming more concentrated and damaging*. Quarter 4, 2011, Akamai Technologies, DC, USA
12. Akamai Technologies (2011) Prolexic Attack Report, Financial services firms get hit by DDoS attacks as malicious packet volume increases 3.000% quarter over quarter, Quarter 1, 2012, Akamai Technologies, DC, USA. https://www.akamai.com/us/en/multimedia/documents/content/akamai-quarterly-global-attack-report-q4-2013-white-paper.pdf. Accessed 5 November 2018
13. Burchfield RW (1996) Fowler's modern english usage (3rd ed.). Oxford: Clarendon Press. pp 197–198. ISBN 0-19- 869126-2
14. Felix TM (2018) Unified cyber threat intelligence, (Unpublished doctoral dissertation). Universidade De Lisboa
15. Vardangalos G (2016) Cyber-intelligence and Cyber Counterintelligence (CCI): General definitions and principles. KEDISA
16. Luciano F (2005) Is Information meaningful data? The Standard Definition of Information, Philosophy and Phenomenological Research, pp 351–370
17. Thomas EA (2017) Use of cyber threat intelligence in security operation center. CreateSpace Independent Publishing Platform, USA
18. Sari A (2018) Context-aware intelligent systems for fog computing environments for cyber threat intelligence. Springer International Publishing AG, Part of Springer Nature 2018
19. Bautistia J (2018) Practical cyber intelligence. Packet Publishing, ISBN 978-1-78862-556-2
20. Omand D, Bartlett J, Miller C (2012) Introducing social media intelligence (SOCMINT). IntellNat Secur 27(6):801–823
21. Butler R (2004) Review of intelligence on weapons of mass destruction. UK House of Commons, HC 898, July 14
22. Enisa (2017) Exploring the opportunities and limitations of current threat intelligence platforms. https://www.enisa.europa.eu/publications/exploring-the-opportunities-andlimitations-of-current-threat-intelligence-platforms/at_download/fullReport Accesses 10 September 2018
23. EclecticIQ (2017) A stakeholder-centric approach to building a cyber threat intelligence (CTI) practice. https://www.eclecticiq.com/downloads/EclecticIQ-White-Paper-A-Stakeholder-CentricApproach-to-Building-a-Cyber-Threat-Intelligence-Practice.pdf. Accessed 15 Sept 2018

Chapter 5
Countering the IoT-Powered Volumetric Cyberattacks with Next-Generation Cyber-Firewall: Seddulbahir

Arif Sari

Abstract Volumetric cyberattacks powered by the Internet of Things (IoT) cause critical damage and lead to a significant negative impact on critical infrastructures, such as electricity, telecommunication and water supply. We saw recent evidence of volumetric attacks on the power grid in Ukraine, which left consumers without power for a period of 1–6 h. The volume of an attack depends on the size of the network that attacks the networks, and the resulting attacks can leave catastrophic disruptions of critical infrastructure services for millions of people. Furthermore, since the IoT networks contain numerous vulnerable-interconnected devices used by attackers to form an IoT-powered botnet to maximise the volume and intensity of an attack, the need for protecting critical infrastructure increases due to the catastrophic nature of the attacks. This chapter investigates a system called *Seddulbahir*, which is a Firewall-as-a-Service (FaaS) technology that was developed for the security market. It is one of the newest technologies to counter the IoT-powered cyberattacks; it provides support to cope with the IoT-based threats and vulnerabilities. Later sections of this chapter also elaborate on the previous efforts and solutions used to detect and prevent IoT-based botnets. Finally, the deployment progress, detection, mitigation and various other features of the proposed FaaS technology, and *Seddulbahir,* in particular, are also elaborated in this contribution.

Keywords Seddulbahir · Firewall · Firewall-as-a-Service · IoT · DoS · DDoS · Cyberattack · Cyber-security · Volumetric attacks · Machine learning

5.1 Introduction

For the last decade, organisations have been trying to protect their networks by building an arsenal of tools to monitor, debug and control malicious network traffic via the intrusion detection in the IoT environment. The intrusion detection and volumetric

A. Sari (✉)
Department of Management Information Systems, School of Applied Science,
Girne American University, Canterbury, UK
e-mail: arifsarii@gmail.com

Z. Mahmood (ed.), *Security, Privacy and Trust in the IoT Environment*, https://doi.org/10.1007/978-3-030-18075-1_5

attacks have become a critical issue for organisations. Firewall-as-a-Service (FaaS) technologies have been proposed to provide security at a lower cost with higher efficiency. The machine learning (ML) frameworks have also been introduced to offer intrusion detection in the IoT environment [1–4]. However, the complexity and diversification of the attacks are significant obstacles for suitable detection mechanisms [5–7].

Data mining approaches have been extensively deployed in FaaS technologies to provide better intrusion detection based on specific features of symbolic data and to inform incoming packages of network service flow [8]. Researchers have used the radial basis functions and statistical features to detect intrusion and anomalies. The rate of adoption and feature extraction exposed by the research is around 98% [9]. The KDD CUP 99 dataset has been used for training; however, due to the small number of descriptors used to train the system, the entire system has not successfully functioned on any large-scale networks [9].

The research reported in this chapter investigates the proposed FaaS technologies developed for the security market that deal with the IoT-based threats and vulnerabilities. One of the newest technologies proposed to counter the IoT-powered cyberattacks is called Seddulbahir [9, 10]; it is this that is investigated, in particular, in this research. Within the scope of this research, the architecture and mechanism of Seddulbahir are elaborated and compared to existing firewall mechanisms and architectures.

Seddulbahir is a cyber-firewall that captures TCP/IP packets and filters them based on security policy files. It has been developed based on Lua, a simple, lightweight, fast and high-level programming language that uses LuaJIT [11], a just-in-time compiler. The system uses the multiple packet capture modules packet capture (pcap) [12], nfqueue [13] and netmap [14] and has a modular architecture to apply a user's specified security policy on a live network flow.

The specific security rules written in Lua can detect and filter malicious network traffic. Apart from this, the system can manipulate a live traffic stream and drop, create and inject packets. There are a variety of advantages that exist in this new-generation firewall system that use artificial intelligence (AI) to update security rules and learn from previous attacks to prevent attack variants [9, 10].

In what follows in this chapter, Sect. 5.2 elaborates on the previous efforts to detect IoT-powered botnets and cyberattacks. Section 5.3 explains the advanced features of Seddulbahir, including on-the-fly advanced packet modification (such as altering packets, dropping/resetting packets or creating/injecting new packets into live traffic), advanced packet inspection and a dedicated customisable dashboard. Section 5.4 elaborates further on the complete system architecture of Seddulbahir and investigates the four main system modules. This section also covers the deployment of AI algorithms, such as the radial basis function [15] and multilayer perceptron (MLP) [16], on an AI security engine module. The deployment of this module covers the classification and clustering processes. The security rule module, protocol dissector module and logging and alerting module are the remaining modules in the system architecture. The protocol dissector module covers the deployment of pcap, nfqueue and netmap [12–14]. Each of these modules is explained separately. The events are generated in an intrusion detection message exchange format (IDMEF) [17]. Section 5.5 investigates the dashboard implementation through Kibana [18], which visualises the events. The system architecture uses syslog and elasticsearch with logstash for indexing proposes [19]. Finally, Sect. 5.6 presents a brief summary with conclusions.

5.2 Detection of IoT-Powered Botnets and Cyberattacks

This section aims to review the methods and approaches that have been used in IoT-powered botnet detection by other researchers. The research reported in [20] proposed a study on botnet detection using machine learning (ML) to analyse traffic behaviour by classifying network traffic behaviour. The authors worked on the feasibility of detecting botnet activity without having access to a complete network flow by grouping behaviour based on time intervals. They focused on behavioural analysis of peer-to-peer (P2P) C&C channels. For the detection process, features such as the variance length of the payload at each time interval, the number of packets exchanged at each time interval, the size of the first packet in the flow and the number of flows per address were extracted. The researchers mainly studied detection algorithms and did not propose an analysis of these features over time [20].

Another study [21] has presented a novel approach for classifying traffic and identifying applications with the help of an unsupervised ML technique. The authors used statistical flow characteristics to classify flows automatically. They calculated the efficiency of the proposed method using data collected from different traffic traces. They have used feature selection to find an optimal feature set and determined the influence of different features.

The previous research was followed by a study [22] in which the researchers used online ML algorithms to create a classification model, and they compared it with the baseline classifiers. The authors observed the file system, network and registry activities along the execution traces and patterns, which were analysed using data mining and searching n-grams over application programming interface (API) call sequences to show the behaviour-based features of malware. The voting experts' algorithm was used to extract malicious API patterns over API calls. The model had a 98% malware classification accuracy after being trained and tested with 17,400 malware samples [22].

In another research reported in [23], the authors presented a framework to automatically analyse malware behaviour using ML. The framework helped to detect classes of malware with similar behaviours (clustering) and to place unknown malware into these classes (classification). The authors proposed an incremental approach for behaviour-based analysis. The behaviours of the malware were presented by the malware instruction set, which was inspired by the CPU. A sequence of instructions was used to characterise the behaviours of malware, and the support vector machine (SVM) algorithm was used to classify these malware samples. In addition, using an incremental approach reduced the runtime of the current analysis methods.

Saad et al. [24] verified the success rate of five commonly used ML techniques. The authors studied a method using network traffic behaviours that characterises and detects botnets before they launch their attack. The authors generated a custom botnet dataset to verify the ability of the five most commonly used ML techniques to meet online P2P botnet detection requirements. These requirements were adaptability, novelty detection and early detection. The dataset contained two existing and publicly accessible malicious datasets and a non-malicious 'pcap' dataset. They were joined together to create a new file. This was considered the best dataset that could be obtained for comparison purposes. However, it did not support synchronisation analysis, as there was only one infected machine for each type of botnet.

Another study on AI was proposed by Nogueira et al. [25] in 2010. It was a botnet detection method that utilised an artificial neural network to determine licit and illicit patterns. This method was used in identifying traffic patterns. The authors trained a multilayer neural network using TCP connection-based features to detect HTTP botnets. The results gathered from the experiments pointed to a low false-positive detection rate with efficient detection of HTTP bots. Furthermore, the authors proposed a method for botnet detection that used a multilayer feedforward neural network with an adaptive learning rate. The proposed method focused on extraction of TCP-related features, as HTTP botnets communicate over a TCP connection. In addition, the bold driver backpropagation algorithm was used to optimise the dynamic range of the learning rate coefficient. A comparison with the decision tree, random forest and radial basis function approaches showed actively learned neural networks had better identification accuracy with fewer false positives.

In addition, Chen et al. [26] presented a method for the detection of HTTP bots that included the time slot, mutual authentication and clustering analyses. The presented method was efficient in identifying web bots, which can be found in HTTP protocols.

There are studies, e.g. [26–28], that assessed web bot detection. Since the TCP connection was the most popular communication method among the web-based bots, the researchers used an X-means clustering algorithm to classify the key statistical features, such as the request bytes, response bytes and number of efficient packets. This method had considerable detection accuracy with light computation. However, if the botmaster decides to use a random delay technique to eliminate the periodicity, the proposed method will fail [26–28].

In 2011, Sawaya et al. [29] proposed a study about detecting attackers with a flow-based attack detection method. This method detected attackers regardless of the blacklist/whitelist hosts that were defined previously. They worked on the analysis of traffic flows on a related object port (also known as an open port) and decoy port (also known as a closed port). However, attacks that were injected into the payload were not identified as a flow-based approach and were preferred by the authors [29].

As detection of botnets and attackers using behavioural analysis became popular, Garcia et al. [30] proposed a method to detect them using network behavioural patterns. The proposed method detected bots regardless of the protocol connection of the bot. First, the authors collected network data from infected computers, and information from these data was extracted. Then, the TCP flows were separated. After that, the flows in one-second time windows were divided to monitor and identify bot behaviour. The final step was clustering these data using the expectation maximisation algorithm. In addition, the proposed method had a 0.7% false-positive error rate, which proved that the bot traffic could be separated accurately [30].

Li et al. [31] proposed a firewall system to mitigate cyberattacks against supervisory control and data acquisition (SCADA) systems. The proposed system provided proprietary industrial protocol protection and an out-of-sequence detection algorithm to detect abnormalities within industrial operations [32]. Another interesting research proposed by Clark et al. [31] was based on the firewall policy diagram to propose a behaviour analysis model since the detection of anomalies in the network flow requires modelling behaviour analysis.

5.3 Deployment Features of Seddulbahir

Seddulbahir, the first Turkish national cyber-firewall, is proposed to resist cyberattack threats against Turkey's Internet infrastructure. This section elaborates on the features of the cyber-firewall Seddulbahir in detail. The three main functions of the cyber-firewall are on-the-fly advanced packet modification, advanced packet inspection and a dedicated customisable dashboard. These are now explained below as the key features of the said firewall.

5.3.1 On-the-Fly Advanced Packet Modification

Seddulbahir provides on-the-fly packet modification. This feature is also available in China's Great Cannon attack tool [33]. This enables the security operation centre to interfere with incoming network flows based on rules, regulations or specific security policies. For example, this feature is very useful to hijack some botnet commands and automatically disinfect a set of compromised nodes if the malware supports such C&C commands (e.g. uninstall). Figure 5.1 illustrates the altering of a package in a live network traffic flow. Apart from this, there is also the possibility to drop any malicious incoming network traffic by injecting the RST command [34–36]. Figure 5.2 illustrates the packet drop or reset, and Fig. 5.3 illustrates a new packet creation and injection into a live network traffic flow.

As shown in Fig. 5.1, Seddulbahir provides the possibility to alter any packages in live network traffic. The modification of the message content may be compulsory to expose adversaries in the case of surveillance.

Figure 5.2 shows that the incoming package is dropped by Seddulbahir. This process is done based on specific rules that are generated by the security rule module of the firewall system. Seddulbahir provides the possibility to drop any malicious package or reset connections between two peers if necessary. The detection of malicious activities or connection requests that violate a country's cyber-security policy can be provided by this mechanism.

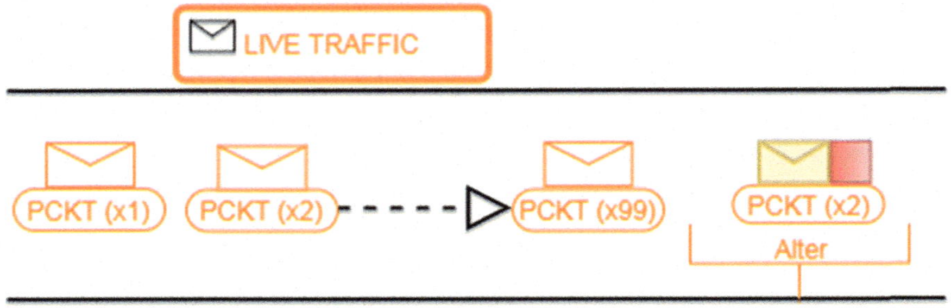

Fig. 5.1 Altering packets in live network traffic

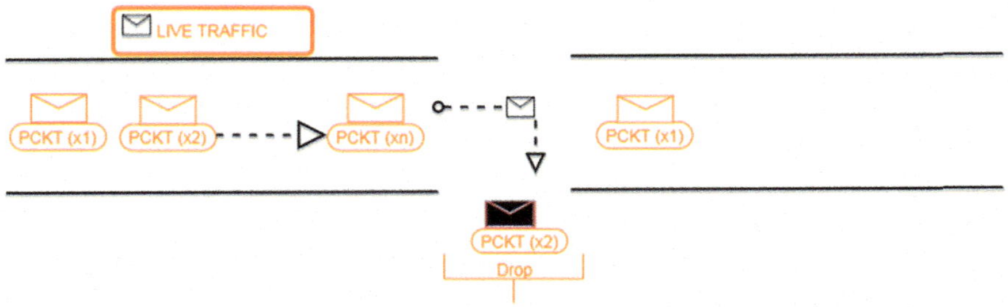

Fig. 5.2 Drop-reset packet connections in live network traffic

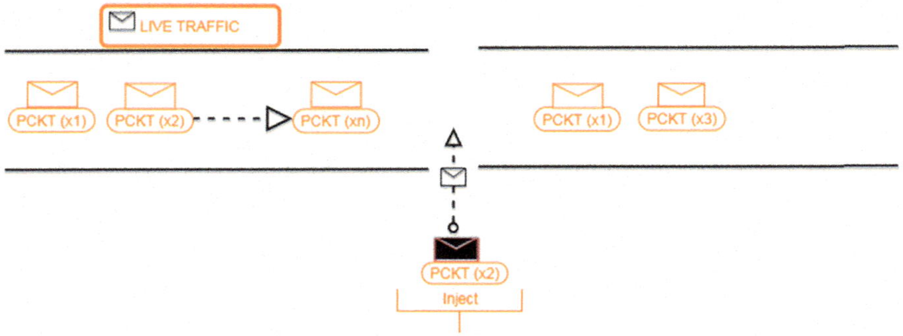

Fig. 5.3 Create/inject new packages into live network traffic

Figure 5.3 illustrates the injection of a new package into the live network traffic flow. This feature provides a possibility to inject customised malicious or benign packages into a live network that may have specific targets for surveilling, tracing and detecting adversaries.

5.3.2 *Advance Packet Inspection*

The system has an interactive mode that enables it to break into particular packets or streams and inspect their content. Seddulbahir is able to check a variety of properties of the incoming network flow such as flags, ip src, src port, dst port, seq, checksum, ip dst, ttl, ackseq and data.

5.3.3 *Dedicated Customisable Dashboard*

Seddulbahir has a dedicated customisable dashboard to provide real-time visualisation of malicious or benign network traffic, network events, firewall rules, bandwidth and network behaviour through Kibana dashboards. More details and screenshots are available in a later subsection on dashboards.

5.4 System Architecture

The Seddulbahir system architecture contains four main modules as illustrated in Fig. 5.4. These are as follows:

- AI Security Engine,
- Security Rule Module,
- Protocol Dissector Module, and
- Logging and Alerting Module.

There is also a dashboard component. As shown in Fig. 5.4, all components of the cyber-firewall system are integrated with each other to function properly. This system provides the overall security for live network flow filtering, anomaly detection and attack mitigation and interference. In this section, each module is explained separately in some detail.

5.4.1 *Artificial Intelligence Security Engine Module*

This module uses a special AI algorithm for feature extraction from the previous attack data/record for classification and clustering [9]. The previous attack data are collected from external sources as pcap files and are used for feature extraction. This provides feature information about previous attacks and becomes the input for the classification and clustering progress. Security rules are kept secure in a separate database and are updated after the clustering and classification progress. This database is not participating live in the system for live network traffic, but

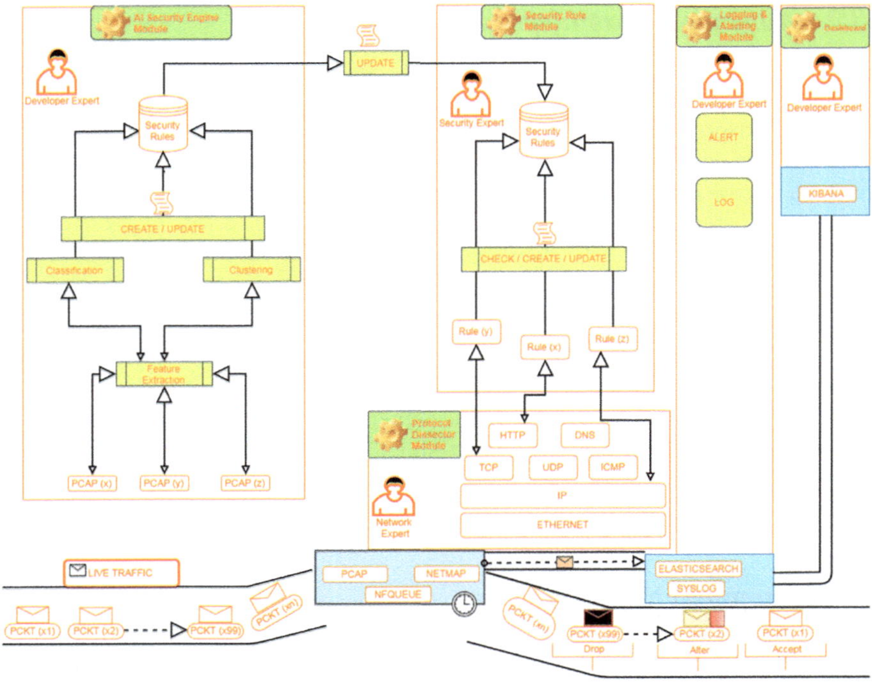

Fig. 5.4 Seddulbahir system architecture

it updates the security rule module database. It is updated with new attack features based on classification and clustering, and the new rules are included in this database. This provides an advantage for Seddulbahir to cope with new variants of existing attacks.

5.4.2 *Security Rule Module*

This is the firewall security rule module that maintains active security rules in a database. This database is updated by an AI security engine module regularly. A security expert can update the rule dataset manually, enter new rules and remove or edit existing rules from the rule table. The incoming live network flow is inspected through this table and is based on security rules. Incoming packages are tagged as malicious or benign.

5.4.3 Protocol Dissector Module

This module specifies several TCP/IP-based protocols (IP, SMTP, TCP, UDP, HTTP, ICMP and DNS) and SCADA protocols (Profibus, Modbus and RP-570). The system supports binary-based protocols (e.g. DNS), text-based protocols (e.g. HTTP), packet-based protocols (e.g. IP) and stream-based protocols (e.g. TCP). The dissector module uses pcap [12], nfqueue [13] and netmap [14] for packet capture purposes. Since firewalls deal with volumetric network traffic, a delay in processing the network operations is one of the most important concerns. The netmap is a framework that gives user-space applications a very fast channel to exchange raw packets with the network adapter. It is not dependent on special hardware features, and its design makes very reasonable assumptions on the capabilities of the NICs [14]. Seddulbahir uses netmap, which provides substantial performance improvements to a wide range of applications using low-level packet I/O (packet capture and generation tools, software routers and firewalls).

5.4.4 Logging and Alerting Module

In this module, the system logs the complete network activities and logs suspicious network activities in a syslog format separately. The logs are interpreted with syslog and elasticsearch [19] for indexing purposes. The alerts are generated in IDMEF which is developed by IETF; the origin of the format is IETF-RFC 4765, which increases the system detection capabilities, particularly through the correlation, to simplify the work of the operators [17]. The logs and alerts are simultaneously visualised through Kibana dashboards by developer experts [18].

5.5 Dashboards

Figure 5.5 illustrates the main dashboard of Seddulbahir. The dashboard illustrates information about network protocols, network flows, bandwidth, open flows and incoming–outgoing network traffic flow locations.

Figure 5.6 shows the DNS queries, HTTP hosts, HTTP user agents, HTTP response (including response codes, e.g. 304, 200, etc.) and all logs collected about these events, including the URL particular to the host and state.

Figure 5.7 illustrates detailed version on the collected logs under the ‘Documents’ menu. This option provides more insight into the collected logs. It indicates that the logs contain a variety of fields, such as time stamp, destination port, flow, source country, destination country, state, destination ip, source ip, source port, destination port, type, etc.

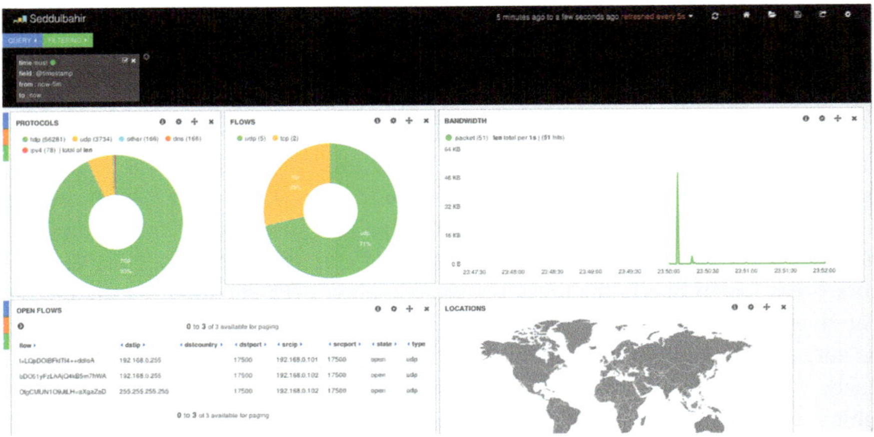

Fig. 5.5 Seddulbahir dashboard—1

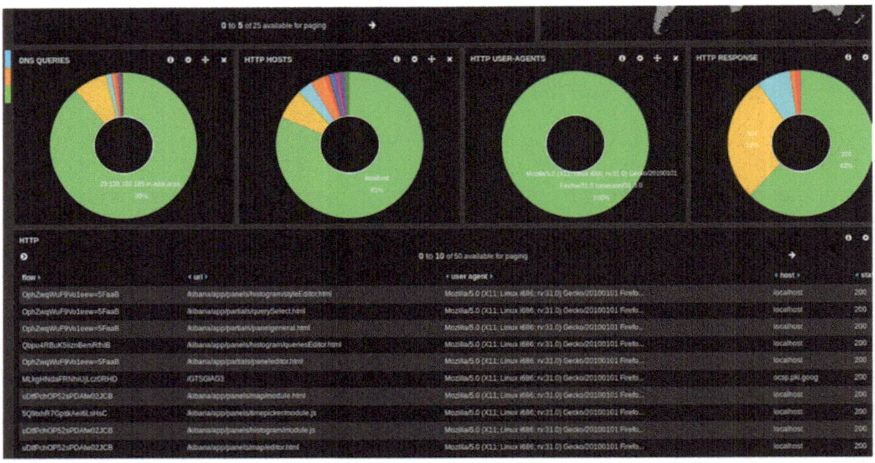

Fig. 5.6 Seddulbahir dashboard—2

Figure 5.8 illustrates one of the collected log details indicated in Fig. 5.7. The displayed selected log is in JSON format and is laid out in specific detail. It can be investigated and filtered through this panel. It is useful when considering a quick search among the volumetric log files.

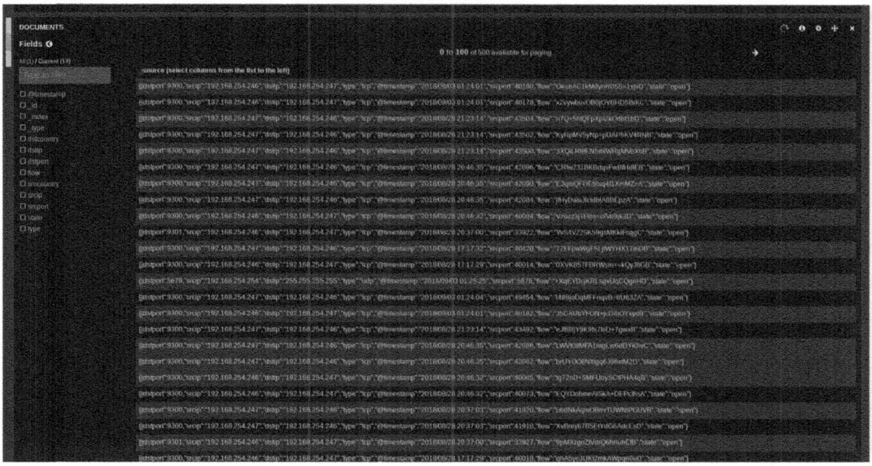

Fig. 5.7 Seddulbahir dashboard—3

Fig. 5.8 Seddulbahir dashboard—4

5.6 Conclusion

While the IoT paradigm brings many benefits and challenges for developed and developing countries, the manufacturers of IoT devices have not paid much attention to the security of the IoT devices. Instead, they focused on fast-track development, ease of use, design, marketing and delivery to the market. There is an increasing need for developing security solutions since numerous vulnerabilities in interconnected IoT devices are one of the main opportunities for attackers to use a volumetric botnet for intensive destructive distributed denial-of-service (DDoS) attacks. The deployment of traditional firewall systems provides conventional security solutions that cannot cope with sophisticated cyberattacks. The deployment of next-generation firewall systems is necessarily required due to the expanding IoT technology vulnerabilities and the complexity of the attack motivation.

The existing implementations and solutions are examined in this research; however, there were no proposed lightweight, unified or AI-oriented solutions. In this context, we have presented a Firewall-as-a-Service (FaaS) model called Seddulbahir that includes deployment features and functionality.

The use of interactive AI modules and ML algorithms are inevitable for both proactive and reactive securities. The detection of the attacks is no longer sufficient. Mitigation is also necessary, and trace back is compulsory. The proposed firewall provides deep packet inspection features to investigate the incoming network flow and to differentiate benign and malicious network traffic. The deployment of Seddulbahir is aimed to satisfy the security policies of any organisation since rules can be proposed manually through the system interface.

References

1. Benqdara S (2018) Anomaly intrusion detection system based on unlabeled data. Int J Comput Appl 181(25):18–26
2. Gavrilis D, Dermatas E (2005) Real-time detection of distributed denial-of-service attacks using RBF networks and statistical features. Comput Netw 48(2):235–245. ISSN 1389-1286. https://doi.org/10.1016/j.comnet.2004.08.014
3. Eskin E (2000) Anomaly detection over noisy data using learned probability distribu-tions. In Proceedings of the seventeenth international conference on machine learning (ICML-2000), June 29–July 2, 2000, Stanford University. Kaufmann, San Francisco, pp 255–262. https://doi.org/10.7916/D8C53SKF
4. Este A, Gringoli F, Salgarelli L (2009) Support vector machines traffic classifi-cation. Comput Netw 53(14):2476–2490. https://doi.org/10.1016/j.comnet.2009.05.003
5. Paliwal S, Gupta R (2012) Denial-of-Service, Probing & Remote to User (R2L) attack detection using genetic algorithm. Int J Comput Appl (0975–8887), 60(19):57–62
6. Wu Y, Meng X, Xie L, Lu R, Su H, Wu Z-G (2017) An input-based triggering approach to leader-following problems. Automatica 75(5), 221–228. ISSN 0005-1098. https://doi.org/10.1016/j.automatica.2016.09.040
7. Wu Y, Lu R (2017) Event-Based control for network systems via integral quadratic constraints. In: IEEE Trans Circuits Syst I: Regul Pap 65(4), 1386–1394 (2018). https://doi.org/10.1109/TCSI.2017.2748971
8. Wu Y, Lu, R, Shi, P, Su H, Wu Z-G (2017) Adaptive output synchronization of heterogeneous network with an uncertain leader. Automatica 76(5):183–192. ISSN 0005-1098. https://doi.org/10.1016/j.automatica.2016.10.020
9. Sari Arif (2018) Countrywide virtual siege in the new era of cyberwarfare: remedies from the. J Cyber Secur Technol 2(1):14–36. https://doi.org/10.1080/23742917.2018.1476956
10. Sari A (2019) Turkish national to mitigate countrywide. Comput Electr Eng 73:128-144. ISSN 0045-7906. https://doi.org/10.1016/j.compeleceng.2018.11.008
11. Lua.org. (2018) The Programming Language Lua. http://www.lua.org/. Accessed 24 Dec 2018
12. Tcpdump.org. (2018) TCPDUMP/LIBPCAP public repository. https://www.tcpdump.org/. Accessed 24 Dec 2018

13. Netfilter.org (2018) netfilter/iptables project homepage—The netfilter.org "libnetfilter_queue" project. Netfilter.org. https://netfilter.org/projects/libnetfilter_queue/. Accessed 24 Dec 2018
14. Rizzo L (2012) Netmap: a novel framework for fast packet I/O. In Proceedings of the 2012 USENIX conference on annual technical conference, 13-15 June 2012, Boston, MA, pp. 9–9 https://dl.acm.org/citation.cfm?id=2342830
15. Akkaya M, Agdelen Z, Haydar A, Sari A (2015) Resolution of relationship be-tween organizational performance and human resource management through nonlinear modeling. Int J Commun Netw Syst Sci 8(12):510–522. https://doi.org/10.4236/ijcns.2015.812046
16. Choo K-KR (2011) The cyber threat landscape: challenges and future research directions. Comput Secur 30(8):719-731. ISSN 0167-4048, DOI:https://doi.org/10.1016/j.cose.2011.08.004
17. Debar H (2007) The intrusion detection message exchange format (IDMEF). Experimental network working group. RFC 4765, The IETF Trust
18. Kibana: Explore, Visualize, Discover Data | Elastic. In: Elastic.co. https://www.elastic.co/products/kibana. Accessed 24 Dec 2018
19. Elasticsearch: RESTful, distributed search & analytics | elastic. In: Elastic.co. https://www.elastic.co/products/elasticsearch. Accessed 24 Dec 2018
20. Zhao D, Traore I, Sayed B, Lu W, Saad S, Ghorbani A, Garant D (2013) Botnet detection based on traffic behaviour analysis and flow intervals. Comput Secur 39, Part A:2–16. ISSN 0167-4048 https://doi.org/10.1016/j.cose.2013.04.007
21. Zander S, Nguyen T, Armitage G (2005) Automated traffic classification and application identification. In: The IEEE conference on local computer networks 30th anniversary (LCN'05), Sydney, NSW, pp. 250–257. https://doi.org/10.1109/lcn.2005.35
22. Pektaş A, Acarman T (2017) Malware classification based on API calls and behaviour analysis. IET Inf Secur (2017). ISSN 1751-8709. https://doi.org/10.1049/iet-ifs.2017.0430
23. Rieck K, Trinius P, Willems C, Holz T (2011) Automatic analysis behavior. J Comput Secur 19(4), 639–668. https://doi.org/10.3233/JCS-2010-0410
24. Saad S, Traoré I, Ghorbani AA, Sayed B, Zhao D, Lu W, Felix J, Hakimian P (2011). Detecting P2P botnets through network behavior analysis. In: 2011 Ninth annual international conference on privacy, security and trust, pp. 174–180. https://doi.org/10.1109/PST.2011.5971980
25. Nogueira A, Salvador P, Blessa F (2010) A botnet detection system based on neural networks. In: 2010 Fifth international conference on digital telecommunications, Athens, TBD, Greece, pp. 57–62. https://doi.org/10.1109/ICDT.2010.19
26. Chen CM, Ou YH, Tsai YC (2010) Web botnet detection based on flow infor-mation. In: 2010 International computer symposium (ICS2010), Tainan, pp 381-384. https://doi.org/10.1109/COMPSYM.2010.5685482
27. Venkatesh GK, Nadarajan RA (2012) HTTP Botnet detection using adaptive learning rate multilayer feed-forward neural network. In: Askoxylakis I, Pöhls HC, Posegga J (eds) Information security theory and practice. Security, privacy and trust in computing systems and ambient intelligent ecosystems. WISTP 2012. Lecture notes in computer science, vol 7322. Springer, Berlin, Heidelberg, pp 38–48. https://doi.org/10.1007/978-3-642-30955-7_5
28. Wang B, Li Z, Li D, Liu F Chen H (2010) Modelling connections behaviour for web-based bots detection. In: 2010 2nd International conference on E-business and information system security, Wuhan, pp. 1–4. https://doi.org/10.1109/EBISS.2010.5473532
29. Sawaya Y, Kubota A, Miyake Y (2011) Detection of attackers in services using anomalous host behaviour based on traffic flow statistics. In: 2011 IEEE/IPSJ international symposium on applications and the internet, Munich, Bavaria, pp 353–359. https://doi.org/10.1109/SAINT.2011.68
30. García S, Zunino A, Campo M (2012) Botnet behavior detection using network synchronism. In: Kabiri P (ed) Privacy, intrusion detection and response: technologies for protecting networks, IGI Global, Hershey, PA, pp 122–144. https://doi.org/10.4018/978-1-60960-836-1.ch005
31. Clark P, Agah A (2015) Modeling firewalls for behavior analysis. Procedia Comput Sci 62:159–166. https://doi.org/10.1016/j.procs.2015.08.429

32. Li D, Guo H, Zhou J, Zhou L, Wong J (2018) SCADAWall: a CPI-enabled firewall model for SCADA security. Comput Secur 80:134–154. https://doi.org/10.1016/j.cose.2018.10.002
33. Marczak B, Weaver N, Dalek J, Ensafi R, Fifield D, McKune S, Rey A, Scott-Railton J, Deibert R, Paxson V (2018) China's great cannon. In: The Citizen Lab. https://citizenlab.org/2015/04/chinas-great-cannon/. Accessed 24 Dec 2018
34. Normile D (2017) Science suffers as China plugs holes in Great Firewall. Science 357(6354):856–856. https://doi.org/10.1126/science.357.6354.856
35. Wasserstrom J (2018) Censored: distraction and diversion inside China's great firewall margaret E roberts princeton Oxford: Princeton University Press xii + 271 pp. $29.95; £24.95 ISBN 978-0-6911-7886-8. The China Quart 236:1206–1208
36. Ensafi R, Winter P, Mueen A, Crandall J (2015) Analyzing the great firewall of China over space and time. In: Proceedings on privacy enhancing technologies, vol 2015, No 1, pp 61–76. https://doi.org/10.1515/popets-2015-0005

Chapter 6
Blockchain for Ensuring Security, Privacy, and Trust in IoT Environments: The State of the Art

Ahmet Erdem, Sevgi Özkan Yildirim and Pelin Angin

Abstract Blockchain (BC) is a framework that saves data records in adjacent blocks that are linked together using cryptography. It is in the form of a distributed database that maintains a continuously growing list of data records that are validated by the nodes participating in the chain. BC presents a decentralized solution, which does not require a third-party organization in the middle for achieving the intra-blocks trust. The information about every transaction ever completed in a blockchain is shared and always available to all nodes. This attribute makes the system more transparent than centralized transactions. The goal of blockchain technology is to provide anonymity, security, privacy, and transparency to all its users. This chapter aims to provide the state-of-the-art information on the use of blockchain technology for securing IoT environments. The advantages and limitations of BC technology for IoT architectures are analyzed. Conceptual blockchain-based IoT architectures for seven different cases are also presented. These being: supply chain management and manufacturing, smart cities, smart homes, healthcare IoT systems, identity management and access control systems, electricity market systems, and insurance systems. The most relevant future challenges for the application of blockchain to IoT environments are also discussed.

Keywords Blockchain · IoT · IoT challenges · Security · Trust · Privacy · Smart contracts · Blockchain-based IoT · Use cases · Blockchain advantages

---

A. Erdem · S. Ö. Yildirim (✉)
Department of Information Systems, Informatics Institute, Middle East Technical University, 06800 Ankara, Turkey
e-mail: sevgiozk@metu.edu.tr

A. Erdem
e-mail: ahmet.erdem@metu.edu.tr

P. Angin
Computer Engineering Department, Middle East Technical University, 06800 Ankara, Turkey
e-mail: pangin@ceng.metu.edu.tr

Z. Mahmood (ed.), *Security, Privacy and Trust in the IoT Environment*, https://doi.org/10.1007/978-3-030-18075-1_6

6.1 Introduction

Blockchain (BC) is a framework that saves data records in adjacent blocks that are chained together using cryptography. It is in the form of a distributed database that maintains a continuously growing list of data records that are validated by the nodes participating in the chain. BC presents a decentralized solution, which does not require a third-party organization in the middle for achieving the trust between nodes [1]. The information about every transaction ever completed in a blockchain is shared and available to all nodes, always. This attribute makes the system more transparent than centralized transactions. It is an open, distributed ledger that can record transactions between two parties efficiently and in a verifiable and permanent way. The goal of blockchain technology is to provide anonymity, security, privacy, and transparency to all its users.

The Internet of Things (IoT) devices acquire information about the surrounding environment, and they communicate with each other and with embedded software systems. They produce large amounts of data; and nodes do not necessarily trust each other while performing transactions. Since connected devices spread sensitive personal data and reveal behaviors and preferences of their owners, issues may arise with respect to devices' critical privacy. Users' privacy is particularly at risk when such sensitive data are managed by centralized companies, which can make illegitimate use of them. In this context, the blockchain technology could be helpful in building privacy-preserving IoT environments.

The blockchain is tamperproof and contains only authentic information; in addition, since it is peer-to-peer (P2P) technology, it is not controlled by any single centralized entity. Blockchain technology can provide peer-to-peer contractual communication between IoT devices and address the scalability, single point of failure, time-stamping, privacy, trust, and reliability challenges of IoT. Blockchain technology can provide a simple infrastructure for IoT devices to transfer data between one another in a secured, consistent, and time-stamped contractual manner. To enable message exchanges, IoT devices can leverage smart contracts, which model the agreements between the parties. This feature enables the autonomous functioning of smart devices and enable artificial intelligence applications. If we then extend this peer-to-peer transaction to human-to-human or human-to-objects/platforms, we end up with a fully distributed trustworthy digital infrastructure. Blockchain-based IoT (BIoT) solutions can be used in various use cases, as discussed later in this chapter.

The focus of this chapter is on the use of the blockchain technology for IoT systems' security. An IoT system can be fostered by a custom blockchain solution, where sensitive data produced and exchanged among IoT devices are stored in a blockchain-based storage system. Blockchain technology can ensure privacy, robustness, and absence of single points of failure. It can register and authenticate all operations performed on IoT device data. Each operation on data (creation, modification, and deletion) is registered in the blockchain: this could ensure that any data compromises can be detected. Moreover, access policies can be specified and enforced by the blockchain, preventing unauthorized operations on data. With blockchain, people are not required to entrust IoT data produced by their devices to centralized companies: data could be safely stored in different peers, and the blockchain could guarantee their authenticity and prevent unauthorized access.

The structure of this chapter is as follows. First, the blockchain technology, its characteristics, transaction processing in blockchain systems, and general advantages and limitations of the BC technology are analyzed. Then, the current IoT solutions are described and their challenges are looked into. Finally, conceptual blockchain-based IoT architectures for seven different cases are presented. These being: supply chain management and manufacturing, smart cities, smart homes, healthcare IoT systems, identity management and access control systems, electricity market systems, and insurance systems.

6.2 Blockchain Technology

"Blockchain is a shared, trusted, public ledger of transactions that everyone can inspect but which no single user controls. It is a distributed database that maintains a continuously growing list of transaction data records, cryptographically secured from tampering and revision" [2]. Blockchain (BC) is distributed in nature; there is no master node and all the participating nodes maintain a copy of the chain. The blockchain technology offers a way of recording transactions or any digital interaction in a way that is designed to be secure, transparent, highly resistant to outages, auditable, and efficient [3]. It has the potential to disrupt industries and enable new business models.

Linked chains in the Blockchain record and relay information and transactional data (actions created by the participants) in blocks. Generators of the transactions remain anonymous. They benefit from security, transactional transparency, speed, and cost efficiency. Data in a blockchain gets recorded in a linear manner, with each new block within a blockchain depending on data from all previous blocks (using cryptographic hashes), which provides immutability of data in the blockchain.

Before being added to a blockchain, transactions need to first pass validation by the network participants. The blockchain technology tackles issues related primarily to the following:

- intermediaries,
- transparency,
- decentralization,
- trust,
- data security,
- accuracy, and
- transactional freedom.

6.2.1 Blockchain Advantages

Some advantages have already been presented. However, a major advantage of blockchain is that it is transparent. If it is a permissioned ledger, every node in the system can see the blocks and the transactions stored in them. There is no need for a central authority for approving the transactions. Every node is responsible for approval of transactions. Since the nodes must reach consensus to accept/validate transactions, all the participant nodes in the network trust other nodes.

The blockchain database can only be extended and existing records cannot be changed. Data and transactions entered into a blockchain are immutable and unchangeable, thus data is both accurate and secure. Once a transaction is sent, it can no longer be reversed. Due to the decentralized and tamperproof environment, the ransactors can place their full trust in the incorruptible and failure-proof blockchain.

The use of blockchain technology can help to end the need to rely on intermediaries in various forms of transactions. Similar to how the world was changed and shaped by the advent of the Internet, the future of the blockchain technology is set to change the world and the way in which individuals carry out their business. Blockchain should make improvements for cutting transaction costs and increasing speeds. According to market estimations [4], there will be a huge increase in blockchain usage in different sectors of the society and industry as presented in Table 6.1.

6.2.2 Blockchain Operation

Blockchain is a linked list composed of blocks. Every block keeps a hash code of the previous block (Fig. 6.1). Immutability is achieved by leveraging strong cryptographic properties such as hashing [5]. Each block contains a set of transactions; and digitally signs its contents by storing the hash of its contents inside the block. Chains of blocks are integrated into a secured data structure. When a malicious agent aims to modify a block, it needs to modify all the previous blocks in a chain. This makes adversary attacks infeasible.

Table 6.1 Blockchain market capacity estimation

Sector	Current as of 2018 (millions USD)	By 2023 (millions USD)	Increase by percentage
Agriculture	60.80	429.70	707
Manufacturing	30.00	566.00	1887
Finance	150,000.00	3,000,000.00	2000
Insurance	64.00	1,400.00	2188
Energy	279.00	7,000.00	2509
Retail	80.00	2,339.00	2924

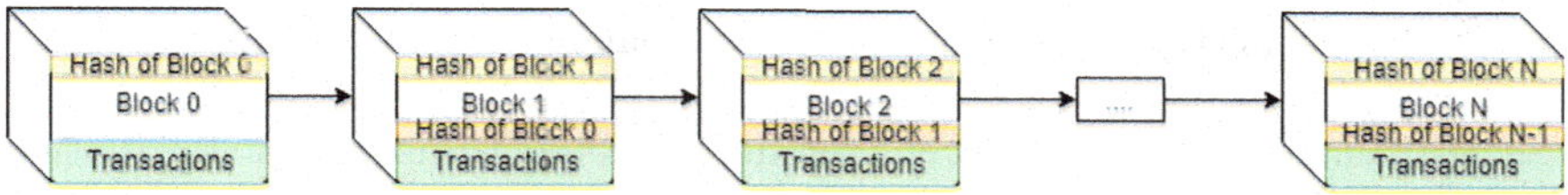

Fig. 6.1 Blockchain block architecture

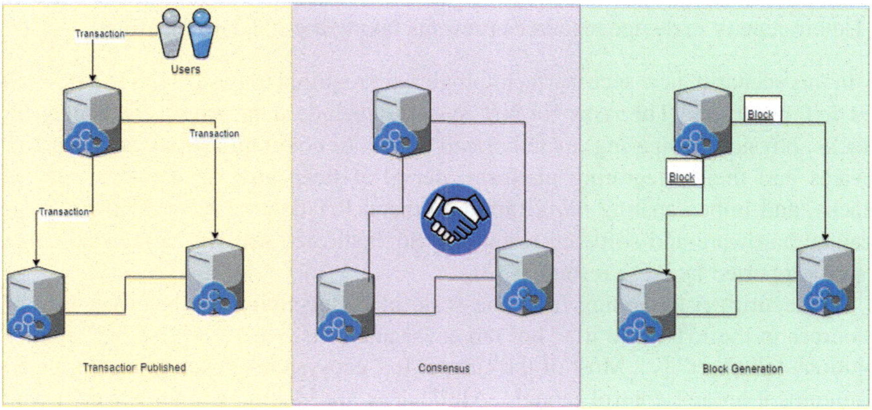

Fig. 6.2 Blockchain transaction processing

When a client wishes to perform a transaction, it broadcasts this transaction to all nodes in the blockchain network. The receiving nodes validate the transaction and initiate a consensus protocol. Based on the result of the consensus protocol (consensus protocols could vary widely), the transaction is inserted into a block and disseminated to other nodes (Fig. 6.2) [6]. The linked list data structure in each node is updated by adding the new block.

6.3 Existing Security Issues Relating to IoT

One of the most challenging aspects of the IoT is achieving a secure ecosystem covering all the building blocks of the IoT architecture. To secure an IoT environment, IoT components need to be examined and areas of vulnerability identified. The components in an IoT architecture being the connected devices, gateways that enable connection of devices, network infrastructure, and cloud infrastructures. Existing security technologies play a role in mitigating the IoT risks, but they are not sufficient due to the following [3]:

- IoT systems use different protocols and technologies, which lead to complexity and conflicts between systems.
- There is limited guidance for life cycle maintenance and management of IoT devices.

- IoT privacy concerns are complex and policies are not always available.
- Standards for authentication and authorization of IoT devices are insufficient.
- Security standards for platform configurations, involving virtualized IoT platforms supporting multi-tenancy are immature.
- The use of IoT technology is expanding and changing.
- Centralized control of IoT devices makes the central unit target of the attacks.
- Heterogeneity in device resources prevents taking the standard measures.

In this scenario, new security technologies are required to protect the IoT devices and IoT platforms. The risks for IoT systems include data privacy and integrity attacks, physical tampering, unauthorized access to communications between IoT devices and their integrating platform, denial-of-sleep attacks, denial-of-service attacks, and impersonating *things* among others. IoT devices have relatively constrained hardware and software resources. Sophisticated security approaches may not be supported by these resources [3].

The security risks arising from the scale of connectivity and heterogeneity of resources in the IoT make it a "hot target for attackers, where centralized security solutions fall short" [7]. Most of the current IoT ecosystems depend on centralized communication and control models. All devices are identified, authenticated, and connected through cloud servers that have huge processing and storage capacities. Connections between devices are exclusively via the Internet. This model has connected generic computing devices and continues to support small-scale IoT networks. However, the growing need of huge IoT systems cannot be satisfied by the centralized communication model [3].

Much of the cost of IoT systems is associated with infrastructure, maintenance, central servers, and networking equipment. As the number of IoT devices increase, the total cost of an IoT system increases exponentially. As Banafa states in [3]: "Even if the unprecedented economic and engineering challenges are resolved, cloud servers will remain a bottleneck and point of failure that can disrupt the entire network." The vulnerabilities in providing proper device authentication and data integrity in IoT networks have devastating effects. A data security architecture for IoT, which can accurately authenticate devices by anyone in the network in a decentralized manner, and prevent unauthorized modification of the stored data becomes a necessity.

A decentralized approach for IoT networking would solve many of these issues. Adopting a standardized P2P communication model to process the hundreds of billions of transactions between devices significantly reduces the costs associated with installing and maintaining large centralized data centers. This approach could distribute computation and storage needs across the billions of devices that form IoT networks [3]. This can also prevent failures in any single node in a network, thus eliminating collapse of the entire network. On the other hand, establishing P2P communications presents its own set of challenges, the most important of which is security. "An IoT security solution will have to maintain privacy and security in huge IoT networks and offer some form of validation and consensus for transactions to prevent spoofing and theft" [3]. In addition to functions of a centralized IoT architecture, a decentralized solution should support P2P messaging, distributed file sharing, and autonomous device coordination.

The current popular approach for IoT devices integration is the *cloud model*. In this model, connections between devices are via the Internet, and it is the cloud servers that identify and authenticate IoT devices. The data processing and storage are carried out in the cloud servers [3]. In the central cloud model, because of data processing requirements, there are high costs. Gartner estimated that in 2016, 5.5 million new IoT devices were connected every day [8]. It is estimated that by 2020, a network capacity that is at least 1,000 times the level of 2016 will be needed [9]. Furthermore, the amount of communication that needs to be handled will increase costs exponentially. Even if economic and manufacturing challenges are addressed, each block of the IoT architecture could act as a bottleneck or point of failure that can then disrupt the entire network [10]. IoT devices are vulnerable to malicious attacks, including DDoS attacks, hacking, data theft, and remote hijacking. The system might be accessed by unauthorized attackers and the data in the system might be modified, deleted, and stolen illegally. If a given IoT device connected to a server is accessed by malicious users, every other device connected to the server can also be affected. Besides, the centralized cloud model is susceptible to manipulation.

Blockchain can eliminate many of these drawbacks. In the bitcoin network, financial transactions are stored in blocks. Similarly, in a blockchain-based IoT system, data generated by IoT devices is stored in blocks and transmitted to other nodes. Data can be accessed by authorized devices or other things. In this case, message passing between devices can be accomplished via the blockchain infrastructure. In blockchain, devices can generate automatic actions by using smart contracts of the blockchain technology. Since blockchain cryptographically signs transactions and verifies cryptographic signatures, the receiver of the transaction can trust the content and the sender. Thus, man-in-the-middle and replay attacks can be eliminated [11].

6.4 Blockchain and the IoT

Blockchain (BC) technology provides an infrastructure for devices to directly transfer a piece of property such as money or data. The transfer can be performed in a secured and reliable time-stamped contractual process. BC has the potential to solve privacy and reliability concerns in IoT by tracking billions of connected devices, enabling the processing of transactions and coordination between devices. This ability can decrease costs of IoT devices as the decentralized architecture is able to eliminate single points of failure. It can provide a more resilient ecosystem for devices to run on. The cryptographic algorithms employed by blockchain also could make consumer data have enhanced privacy.

The blockchain ledger is tamperproof. Since it is decentralized, man-in-the-middle attacks cannot be easily staged. It is the that makes secure, trustless, P2P messaging possible and has already proven its worth in the world of financial services through cryptocurrencies. Blockchain is autonomous, making it a foundational element for

IoT solutions. Enterprise IoT technologies have quickly become early adopters of the blockchain technology.

In an IoT network, the blockchain can keep an immutable record of the history of smart device transactions and interactions. This feature enables the autonomous secure functioning of smart device networks without the need for centralized authority. By using smart contracts, agreements between two or more parties can be verified and validated.

One of the most exciting capabilities of blockchain is the ability to maintain a fully decentralized, trusted ledger of all transactions occurring in a network. This capability also enables IoT systems to comply with regulatory requirements. The blockchain model, based on cryptographically secured, immutable distributed ledger technology and consensus, could enhance IoT frameworks with more automated resource optimization and innate security [12]. The following features of blockchain make it an attractive technology for addressing the security and privacy challenges in IoT:

- Distributed architecture enabling scalability and robustness, eliminating many-to-one traffic flows and single point of failure.
- Ability to keep the identity of *things* private.
- A distributed system for sharing data across a network of key stakeholders.
- Embedded business logic with smart contracts for automating interactions between nodes in the system.
- Hash-based security.
- Verification of identity.
- Origin authentication.
- Consensus and agreement models for detecting problems and mitigating threats.

A blockchain-based IoT system could improve system health and integrity by allowing devices to register and validate themselves against the network. Business logic could be executed automatically by using smart contracts. Since there is no central system to attack, threats like denial-of-service attacks could be inherently mitigated. Applying a blockchain model in an IoT network is able to solve various real-world digital business issues [12], such as

- History tracking: This allows the system to record metadata and results about logic executed at the edge of the network for the purposes of regulatory compliance, and create an immutable history. This enables auditing of certain actions and decisions.
- The ability to publish software updates through a blockchain-based system.
- Payments: Automated payments to business network participants based on sensor data (indicating, for example, service completion or product delivery), as well as micropayments between devices themselves in certain networks for functions and capabilities without human involvement.

There are several studies on blockchain technology and IoT integration. In most studies, the main focus is on enhancing the security of IoT systems using blockchain technology. In some studies, authors proposed models for usage of blockchain-based IoT systems in different use cases.

Huckle et al. [13] explored how blockchain can be utilized to create decentralized, shared economy applications that allow people to monetize, securely, their things to create more wealth, and IoT and blockchain technology can benefit shared economy applications. Huh et al. [14] proposed a management platform for IoT devices using blockchain technology. They manage keys using RSA public key cryptosystems where public keys are stored in Ethereum and private keys are saved on individual devices. They write smart contracts to keep track of data coming from electric meters and smartphones. In their proof of concept study, a meter constantly sends electricity usage data and the smartphone sends policies for usage of air conditioners and light bulbs. Air conditioners and light bulbs constantly check the values on Ethereum to update their device status. When necessary, they switch their mode from normal to energy saving [14].

Ouaddah et al. [15] proposed a framework for access control in IoT based on the blockchain technology. They provided a reference model for the proposed framework within the objectives, models, architecture, and mechanism specification in the IoT. In addition, they introduced Fair Access as a fully decentralized pseudonymous and privacy-preserving authorization management framework that enables users to own and control their data. To implement the model in which they used and adapted the blockchain into a decentralized access control manager. Fair Access introduces new types of transactions that are used to grant, get, delegate, and revoke access [15].

Stavrou and Voas [16] proposed usage of blockchain technology for time-stamping data, generated from different sources. Time-stamping is important for establishing transaction precedence, whenever a race condition or tampering with past events occurs.

Dorri et al. [17] suggested a tiered security framework using blockchain architecture. They tailored blockchain, and added a lightweight consensus algorithm, a distributed trust method, a distributed throughput management strategy, and a separation of the transaction traffic from the data flow. They performed qualitative analysis against 12 relevant cyberattacks and explained the specific defense mechanisms. Their tailored blockchain architecture is resilient to all of the analyzed attacks.

Sharma et al. [18] proposed a new distributed secure IoT network architecture consisting of a software-defined network base network using the blockchain technique, to address the current and future challenges and to satisfy new service requirements. They aimed to generate and deploy protections, including threat prevention, data protection, and access control, and mitigate network attacks such as cache poisoning/ARP spoofing, DDoS/DoS attacks, and detect security threats.

Park and Kim used blockchain for verifying the trustworthiness of an IoT device [19]. Zhang and Wen developed a business model for IoT. In order to provide decentralization, they used a P2P transaction model on the basis of blockchain [20]. Outchakoucht et al. [21] suggested a method for managing access control in IoT using blockchain.

Lee and Lee [22] proposed usage of blockchain for secure firmware update of embedded devices in IoT environments. They aimed to securely check a firmware version, validate the correctness of the firmware, and download the latest firmware for the embedded devices. In the proposed model, an embedded device requests its firmware update from nodes in a blockchain network and gets a response to determine whether its firmware is up to date or not. If it does not have the latest version, the embedded device downloads the latest firmware from a peer-to-peer firmware-sharing network of the nodes. If the version of the firmware is up to date, its correctness is checked. The proposed scheme [22] guarantees that the embedded device's firmware is up to date and not tampered.

As reported in [23], a group of technology and financial companies formed a group to set up a new standard for securing IoT applications using blockchain [23]. Companies joining the group include Cisco, Bosch, Bank of New York Mellon, Foxconn Technology, Gemalto, and blockchain startups Consensus Systems, BitSE, and Chronicled. This group hopes to establish a blockchain protocol to build IoT devices, applications, and networks.

Song et al. [24] presented the opportunities and challenges of implementing blockchains and a use case of integrating blockchain into an IoT framework for securing sensor data acquisition. They proposed a multilayered architecture, comprising a sensor layer, the edge layer collecting data from sensor devices, and the cloud layer as the top layer for collection of data. They used Hyperledger Fabric [25] as the blockchain infrastructure [24].

Angin et al. [7] proposed a blockchain-based approach for IoT systems that introduces transparency and tamper resistance into data storage and retrieval in IoT networks. They proposed an adaptable data security architecture for IoT, addressing limited processing power, battery life, and storage space of IoT devices. The proposed architecture is fit for the decentralized nature of IoT applications. The architecture aims to provide secure device authentication and protect/verify the integrity of data collected from IoT devices. The proposed model is a hierarchical blockchain architecture. The IoT devices are connected to an upper layer of data collectors that are powerful devices with larger storage and less energy constraints (e.g., cloud servers). Data collectors are blockchain nodes.

Table 6.2 presents a summary of the common IoT problems and solutions as provided by the blockchain mechanism.

6.5 Benefits of Blockchain Technology for IoT Systems

Blockchain provides several benefits to IoT systems as illustrated in Fig. 6.3. These are briefly discussed in the following subsections.

Table 6.2 IoT problems and blockchain solution

Challenge	Explanation	Solution with blockchain
Data manipulation risk	Data might be manipulated and can be used inappropriately	Decentralized access and immutability of data. Malicious actions can be detected and prevented. Devices are interlocked: if one device's blockchain updates are breached, the system rejects it with majority voting
Central control risk	In the centralized IoT architecture, the central node acts as a point of failure, which could disrupt the entire IoT system. The central node is open to distributed denial-of-service attacks, hacking, data theft, and remote hijacking Single point of failure in the central server leads to the collapse of the whole system	The lack of central control mitigates single point of failure risk. This ensures scalability and robustness. Blockchain uses resources of all participating nodes. This eliminates many-to-one traffic flows, decreases delay and overcomes the problem of single point of failure In blockchain, secure messaging between devices enables validation of a device's identity, and verification of transactions that only a message's originator could have sent it. Messages are signed. The architecture is decentralized
Unavailability of service as a result of the server node being down	Cloud servers are sometimes down due to cyberattacks, software bugs, power, cooling, or other problems	No single point of failure. Records are kept on many computers and devices that hold identical information
Security	Central cloud leads to security risks	A decentralized, blockchain-based approach would overcome many of the security risks. Blockchain could provide military-grade security for IoT. Blockchain realizes a secure network over untrusted parties, which is desirable in IoT with numerous and heterogeneous devices
Privacy	Privacy of data may not be protected	The inherent anonymity in blockchain is well suited for most IoT use cases where the identity of the users must be kept private

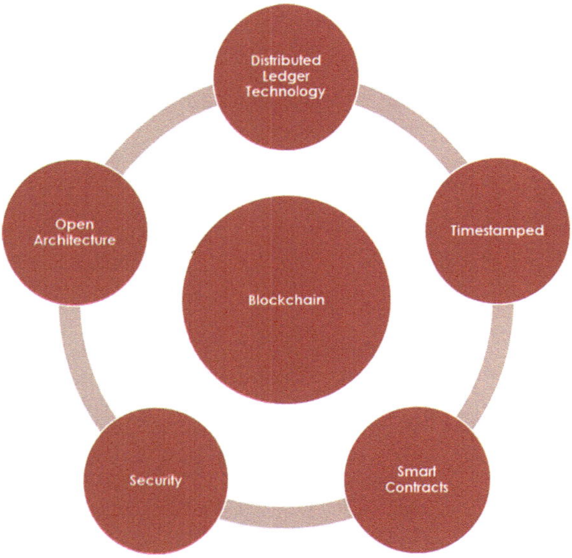

Fig. 6.3 Benefits of blockchain technology

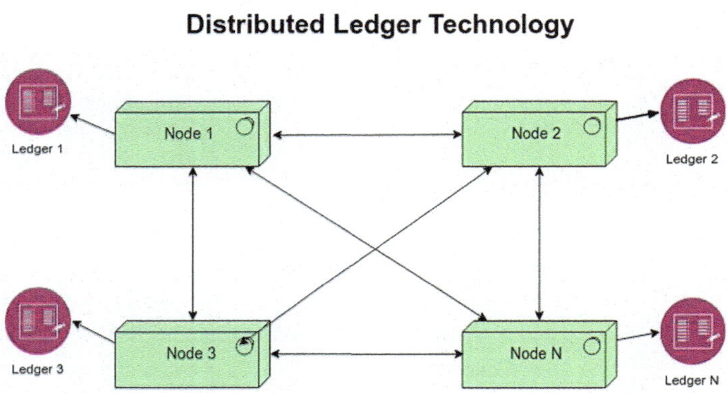

Fig. 6.4 Distributed ledger technology

6.5.1 Distributed Ledger Technology (DLT)

Blockchain has a distributed architecture as illustrated in Fig. 6.4. The International Telecommunication Union defines DLT as "a new type of secure database or ledger for keeping track of who owns a financial, physical, or electronic asset, but without the need for a centralized controller of this data. Instead, the data is shared in a peer-to-peer manner across multiple sites, countries, or institutions" [26].

There are two types of DLT according to accessibility: Permissioned and Permissionless. A permissionless ledger is open to the public and is accessible by everyone (like bitcoin [1]). On the other hand, a permissioned ledger can be public or private. The permissioned ledger can have one or more owners and they can read and write records. Only the permissioned nodes can write records, and anyone can read records in a permissioned public ledger.

Depending on the use case, both permissioned and permissionless distributed ledgers are applicable for IoT structures [27].

6.5.2 *Chronological Time-Stamping*

All records generated within the IoT are time-stamped and shared with the hash-based chain of blocks (Fig. 6.5). The time-stamp operations can help ensure that records cannot be changed without providing the proof of work [1], ensuring that all evidence is interconnected and irreversible.

6.5.3 *Smart Contracts*

A smart contract is a set of instructions or a piece of code embedded into the blocks, which are produced by IoT. The smart contract code is executed by IoT blockchains.

6.5.4 *Security*

Blockchain technology relies on the use of asymmetric cryptography to sign messages and encrypt data using a private/public key pair—Public Key Infrastructure (PKI)-based cryptography. Refer to Fig. 6.6. Each event has the *things* created by the public key. Each record is digitally signed using a hash of the previous record and the public key of the *thing* (owner of the record creator *thing*) [1].

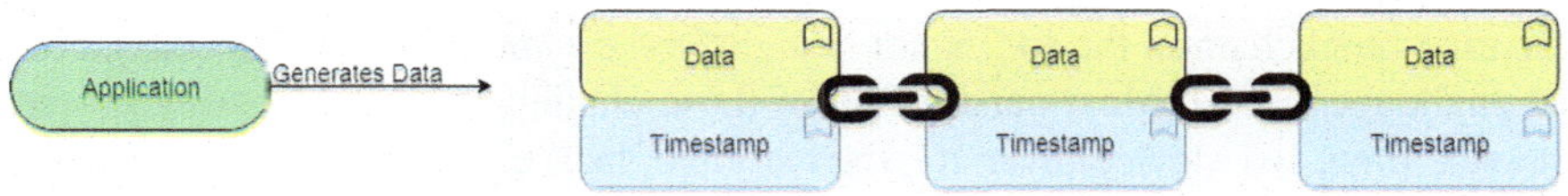

Fig. 6.5 Chronological time-stamped data in blockchain

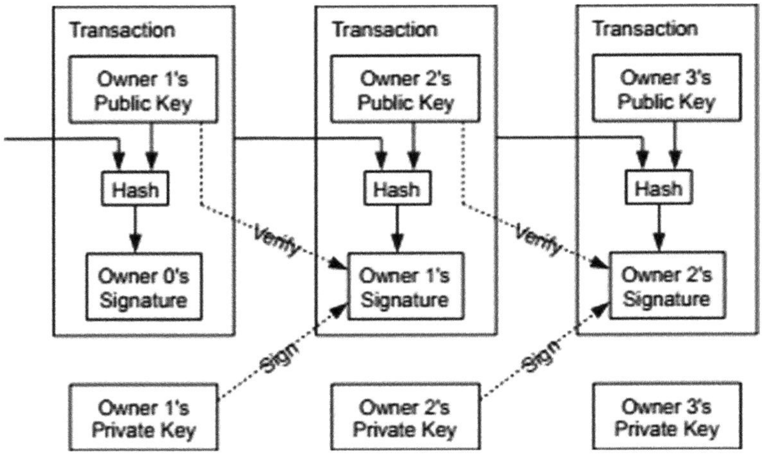

Fig. 6.6 Bitcoin transaction model [1]

6.5.5 *Open Architecture*

Open architecture is defined by Gartner as "a technology infrastructure with specifications that are public as opposed to proprietary. This includes officially approved standards as well as privately designed architectures, the specifications of which are made public by their designers" [28]. The open architecture benefits are as follows:

- Increased competitive innovation opportunities.
- Enabling reuse of components.
- Easier adoption of rapid technology changes.
- Reduced testing and maintenance costs.

The blockchain technology as conceptualized and published by Satoshi Nakamoto in 2008 can be described as an open architecture as presented in Fig. 6.7 [29].

6.6 Challenges of Blockchain-based IoT Systems

Adopting blockchain in the IoT is not straightforward and requires addressing critical challenges [3, 8]. Most outstanding of those challenges are processing power, response time, IoT device diversity, data storage, lack of blockchain development skills, and lack of regulations, as shown in Fig. 6.8 and as briefly defined below:

- Processing power: Mining is computationally intensive and requires processor power for encryption and validation of transactions. Consensus algorithms also add processing requirements.

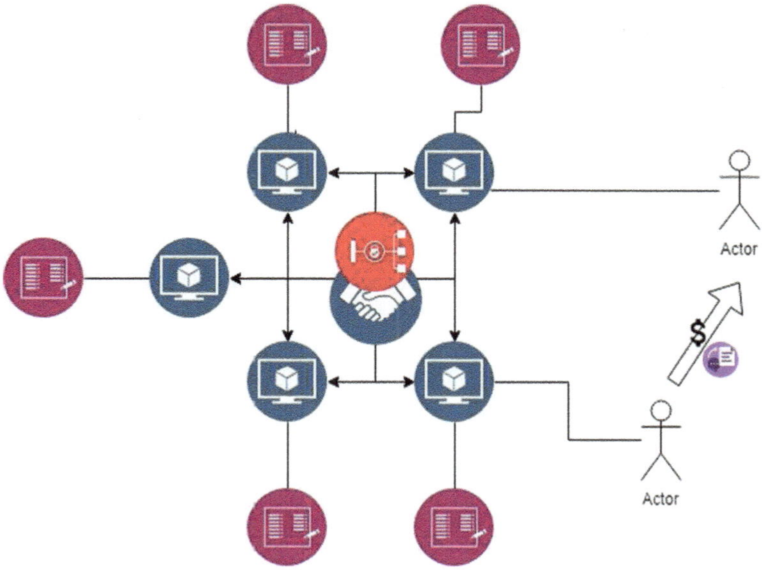

Fig. 6.7 Blockchain's open architecture

Fig. 6.8 Blockchain based IoT system challenges

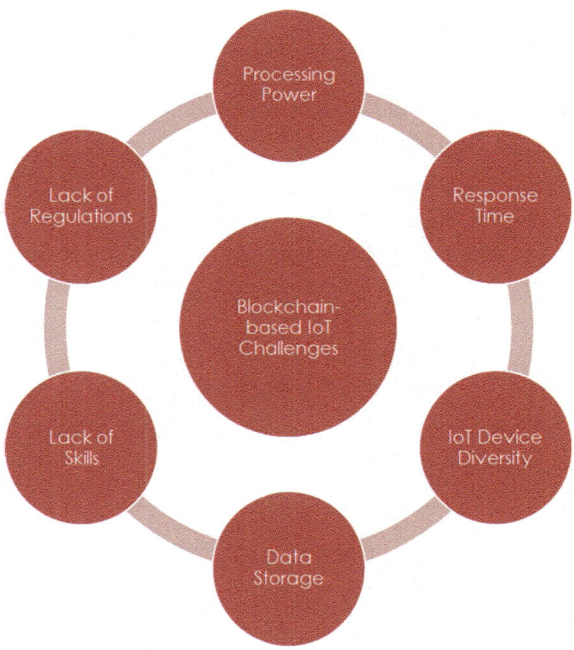

- Response time: Validation of blocks and encryption of transactions and data is time-consuming. IoT systems require low latency.
- IoT device diversity: IoT devices might have different configurations and operation modes. Integration of different devices is a general problem in IoT systems. Running encryption algorithms in all IoT devices may increase the total response time of the system.
- Data storage: Redundancy in blockchain increases data storage requirements. Blockchain eliminates the need for a central server, but the data has to be duplicated in the nodes [3]. The size of the ledger increases as time passes.
- Lack of skills: Since the technology is new, there are insufficient human resources for blockchain implementation.
- Lack of regulations: Since blockchain is a new domain, legal and regulatory guidelines are not in place yet. This is a problem for manufacturers and service providers.

6.6.1 The Optimum Platform

Developing solutions for IoT systems requires collaboration, coordination, and connectivity for each element in the ecosystem, and throughout the ecosystem as a whole. All IoT devices must work together and be integrated with each other. They should communicate and interact with connected systems and infrastructures. These collaborations and connectivity can be expensive, time-consuming, and difficult. The optimum platform [3] for IoT should be able to:

- Acquire and manage data in a scalable and secure manner.
- Conform to standards and regulations.
- Integrate data in a resilient manner.
- Analyze data and extract business value by using artificial intelligence and big data analytics modules, and take actions by using the inferences.
- Manage authentication.
- Perform data validation.
- Encrypt private data and protect privacy.

Blockchain technology will be an attractive option for IoT systems when its drawbacks and limitations are removed.

6.7 Use Cases

There are several proposed implementations of blockchain-based IoT systems in different usage areas. These include smart homes, smart cities, identity and access management systems, supply chain management systems, electricity market management, and insurance systems, among others. Conceptual models for usage areas and proposed solutions for each usage area are described in the subsections below.

6.7.1 Smart Homes

One of the possible use cases for blockchain-based IoT systems is smart home applications (Fig. 6.9). In conventional smart home applications, malicious users can access and change personal data. Blockchain enables smart home device data to become immutable and therefore safe from cyberattacks. With a blockchain-powered smart home system, the owner can enable other parties to access specific areas and devices without giving them access to everything. Comcast Labs is one of the providers of blockchain-based smart home solutions [30].

Dorri et al. [31] have proposed a smart home application with IoT and blockchain. In the proposed system, communication between local devices and nodes use a shared key to secure the communication. All communications to and from the smart home are stored in a local private blockchain. In each smart home, there is a local

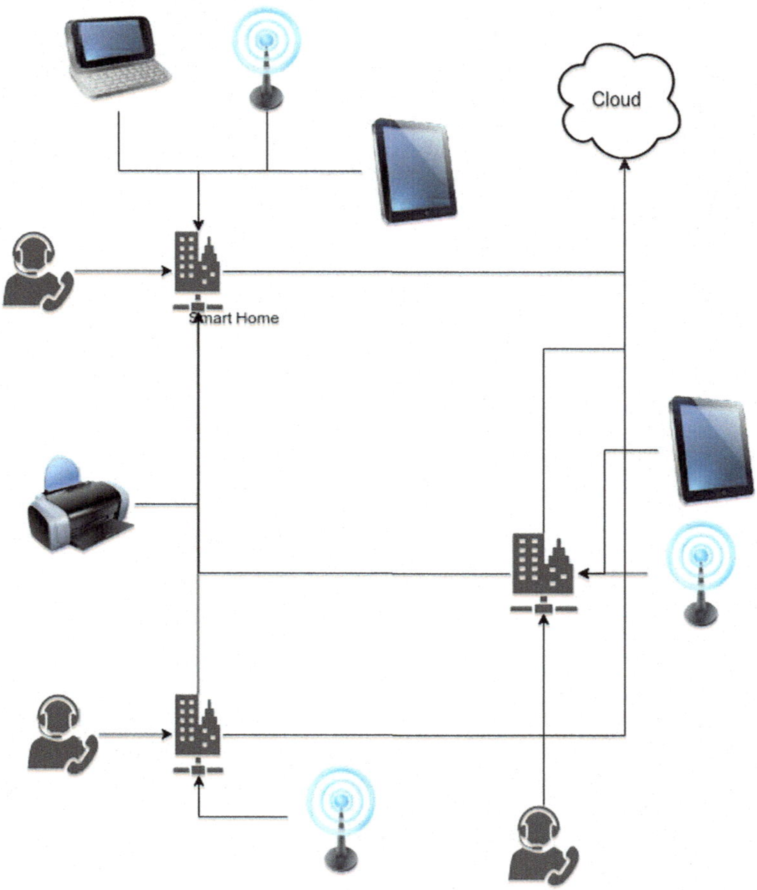

Fig. 6.9 Smart home high-level architecture

private blockchain that keeps track of transactions and has a policy header to enforce user policies for incoming and outgoing transactions. Each device's transactions are chained together in blocks as an immutable ledger in the blockchain. Each block in the local blockchain contains two headers that are the block header and policy header. The block header has the hash of the previous block to keep the blockchain immutable. The policy header is used for authorizing devices and enforcing owner's control policies over his home. In addition, each block contains a number of transactions. There is a local storage for storing data. The storage uses a First-in-First-out (FIFO) method to store data and stores each device's data as a ledger chained to the device's starting point.

6.7.2 Smart Cities

Smart city is a framework for providing solutions to the challenges of urbanization. It depends on new technologies, advanced urban planning, and energy and transportation management. Refer to Fig. 6.10. Possible usage areas of blockchain in the smart city scenario can be as follows [32]:

- Smart payments: Blockchain-based payment systems can facilitate payments in city services.
- Identity and access management: Usage of blockchain for identity management can provide a secure mechanism for storing and validating user identities and reduce identity thefts and related frauds.
- Smart transportation management: Usage of blockchain for transportation can eliminate third-party organizers. Sharma et al. proposed a vehicle network archi-

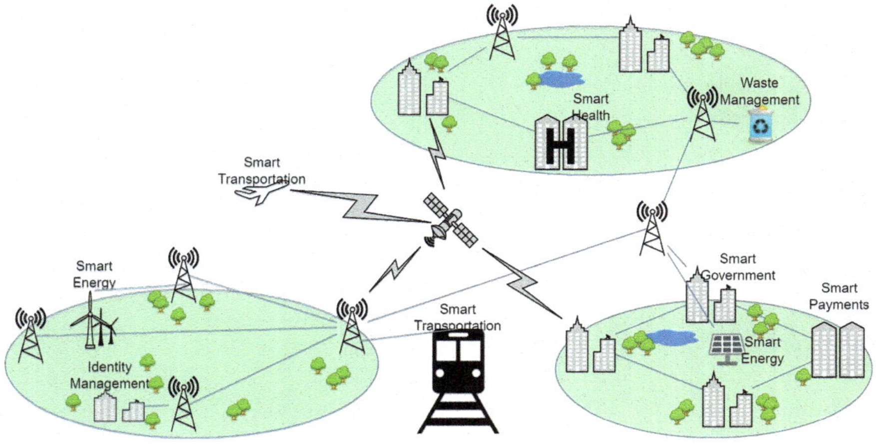

Fig. 6.10 Smart city components

tecture based on blockchain in the smart city [33]. Blockchain leads to better utilization of the transportation infrastructure and resources.
- Smart government services: Blockchain-based solutions improve government services. Identification of citizens, e-elections [34], tax management, and management of ownership of assets can be carried out with blockchain-based solutions.
- Smart energy management and trading: Blockchain-based solutions can enable individuals to trade energy without third-party organizations Energy management systems can be more resilient with blockchain-based solutions.
- Smart waste management: Blockchain-based IoT sensors can be used to improve efficiency of waste management. Artificial intelligence solutions can be developed for prediction of waste amounts and structures.

By supporting smart city solutions, blockchain technology can increase the development capacity for cities around the world.

IOTA [35] combines Internet of Things (IoT) with Distributed Ledger Technology to power the machine-to-machine economy. IOTA is creating an ID-management system called TangleID. The aim of the project is to decrease identity theft, minimize voter fraud, distribute medical records, and provide easy access to social security [36]. Biswas et al. have also proposed a blockchain-based security framework to enable secure data communication in a smart city situation [37].

The integration of blockchain technology with devices in a smart city helps to create a common platform where all devices can communicate safely in a distributed environment. In case of an accident, a vehicle can send relevant data to hospitals, firefighters, the police, and the insurance company by using blockchain technology. The information about road status can be sent to other cars. They can adjust their speed or select other alternative roads and authorities can take action easily.

6.7.3 *Identity and Access Management*

Identity and access management systems (Fig. 6.11), based on blockchain technology, can be developed in order to strengthen IoT security. Some examples of identity and access management are storage of information about the origin of items, identification of items, and digital rights management. In blockchain-based systems properties of physical assets, credentials of users, resource usage of IoT devices, and other relevant data can be stored securely and reliably [38]. As an example usage area, cryptographic hashes of individual device firmware can be stored in a blockchain-based system. Such data can be used to verify that a device's software is not tampered. For connectivity to a network, devices can be directed to such a system, and only allowed to enter the network after validation. Blockchain-based identity and access management systems can solve IP spoofing or IP address forgery attacks. Blockchain-based systems have security solutions to malicious actions. Since approved blockchain data is immutable, it is not possible for devices to connect to a network by disguising themselves by injecting fake signatures into the records [39].

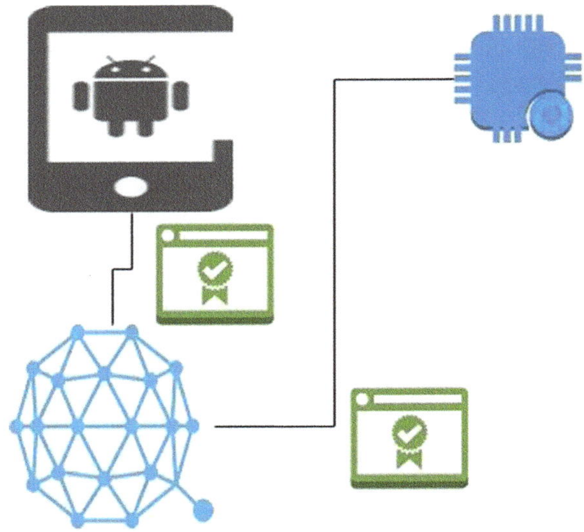

Fig. 6.11 Blockchain based identity management system

Hyperledger Indy [40] is a distributed ledger, developed for decentralized identity management. Privacy-preserving technologies are important for public identity management. Indy has components providing performance, scale, trust model, and privacy [40].

6.7.4 Supply Chain Management

Blockchain can ensure supply chain security and facilitate handling and dealing with crisis situations such as product recalls due to security vulnerabilities. Since it is available to public investigation, it is possible to trace back every product to the origin of the raw materials, and transactions can be linked to identify users of vulnerable IoT devices. Blockchain is suitable for complex workflows. When an item changes ownership, blockchain technology can be used to register the following:

- time,
- location,
- price,
- involved parties, and
- other relevant information for the item.

The user can also track raw materials as they move through the supply chain, which are transformed into circuit boards and electronic components, integrated into products, and sold to customers. Blockchain can be used to register updates, patches, and part replacements applied to a product or device throughout its lifetime. This

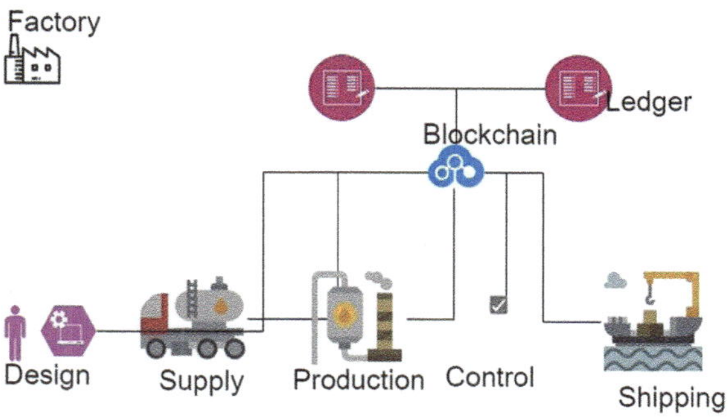

Fig. 6.12 Blockchain based supply chain management system

way, it is easier to track progress in addressing vulnerabilities and send warnings and notifications to owners [41].

For the manufacturing of a product, supply chain management can be automatically performed by IoT devices (Fig. 6.12). Each device can detect required material to be supplied and order record/transaction can be provided to internal Supply Chain Management and Suppliers using blockchain technology (time-stamped and cryptographically sealed). For this specific case, the distributed ledger is a permissioned ledger and private, which means that only the internal supplier department will have all the rights and the other supplier will only have read privileges for transaction/records of each device. Since the architecture is open, it is easy to include new suppliers and seamlessly integrate with the manufacturer. Smart contracts can also be used in this model. For example, if there is a new version of a product, the following operations after production can be written into the smart contract and performed automatically by a connecting device.

Blockchain technology can be used for internal coordination of manufacturing of a product. The internal distributed ledger can be permissioned and public, which means that each node has write and read rights. Blockchain technology adapted to the IoT architecture can help and improve the shipping and sales/order management use cases.

6.7.5 Electricity Market

Zhang and Wen proposed a business model for electricity markets based on blockchain and IoT [20]. The infrastructure of the proposed model is composed of entities and commodities (Fig. 6.13). Entities include Distributed Autonomous Corporations (DACs) and human beings. Entities can produce or buy IoT products. IoT products are sensor data and properties. Sensor data may be human or device processed data. Properties include cars, houses, and parking spaces, which can be controlled by electronic locks or access control systems. Their proposed system

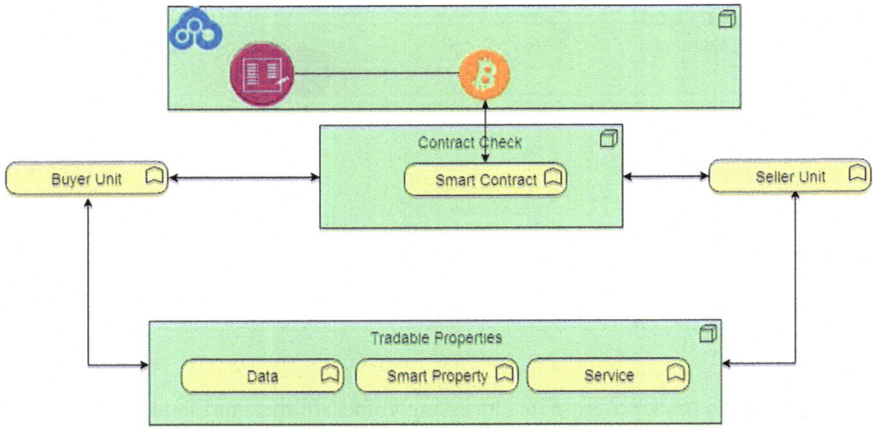

Fig. 6.13 The architecture of IoT for e-business

can also support energy properties (e.g., electricity, water, gas, and oil) that can be controlled and quantified by digital devices [20].

In their proposed model [20], all trade details are written in smart contracts which are used for validation of agreement details of the IoT E-business. Signatures, timestamps, and series numbers of both parties are recorded on the smart contracts. Malicious entities cannot cancel the transaction after this contract is signed by both sides and broadcast to the entire network. The transfer of the encrypted money and IoT commodities are performed according to the content of the smart contract. The system can complete the deal between shareholders without the help of any other third party. In their proposed system [20], they adopted bitcoin as the currency and IoTcoin as the IoT commodity exchange certificate. The primary role of IoTcoin is to act as the title of the property ownership. One of the advantages of the proposed model is removing the requirement for a third party in IoT e-business.

6.7.6 Healthcare Sector

A blockchain-based IoT system (Fig. 6.14) can be developed for medical devices integration. This system can store data from medical IoT devices and medical health records. There are some examples on the usage of blockchain architecture in storing medical health records [42] and pharmaceutical supply chain management [43]. However, combining blockchain and IoT systems in the healthcare domain have some prerequisites like open standards for data sharing and operation, as well as handling of diverse data.

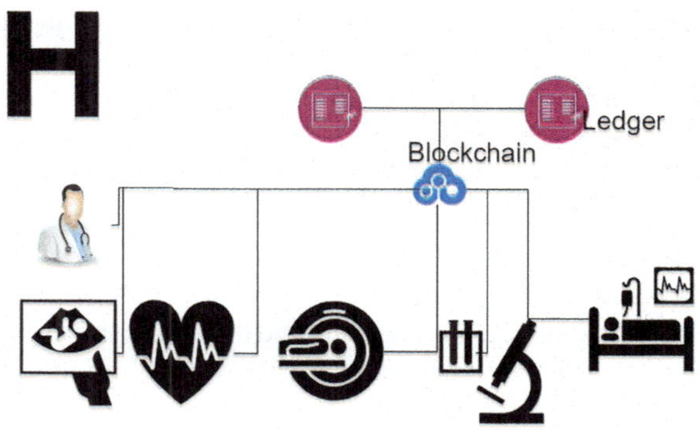

Fig. 6.14 The conceptual model for blockchain in healthcare

6.7.7 Insurance Systems

IoT devices can diagnose their operating state and communicate a failure event. As the number of IoT devices increases, automatic verification of failures, assessment of risks, and ordering the maintenance can improve performance of the insurance domain. Aigang [44] is a project for development of an autonomous insurance network for IoT assets, based on blockchain mechanism integrated with smart IoT devices. In the project, the aim is to issue policies and conduct risk assessment automatically by connecting intelligent devices with insurance policies via smart contracts. Devices can order maintenance and insurance payments can be made automatically.

6.8 Conclusion

Blockchain has the potential to change the way how transactions are conducted in a number of scenarios. Usage of blockchain is not limited to cryptocurrency, and it can be applied in various environments where some forms of transactions are performed.

The IoT environment requires security, reliability, scalability, and endurance to accomplish the network-related tasks. In today's increasingly digitized world, the ability to make sensors, devices, and computational *things* perform tasks autonomously has become a necessity. It is practically impossible to manage big amounts of data manually.

Establishing IoT systems that run securely, efficiently, and independently is not an easy task. Blockchain shows promise for easing secure integration of IoT devices. IDC estimates that, by 2019, as many as 20% of IoT deployments will include blockchain technology in some way [45, 46]. Blockchain is not the answer to everything that challenges IoT, but it can play a powerful role in solving some serious security-related issues. By using smart contracts, IoT devices can perform autonomous transactions. When artificial intelligence is integrated into blockchain-based IoT systems new improvements can be achieved.

Cloud systems also have some security challenges that can be addressed by blockchain. Decentralization, autonomy, trustworthiness, and security properties of blockchain can help to improve IoT systems and provide more secure approaches. By using smart contracts, transferred properties in blockchain can be verified. Since blockchain stores the history of transactions, blockchain-based transactions are easily auditable. It is easier to track the sources of insecurity in systems. In supply chain management systems, handling and dealing with crisis situations will be easier. Since all the transaction data is kept in a blockchain, product recalls after discovery of safety and security vulnerabilities are made easier. IP spoofing is one of the security challenges in identity and access management systems. Blockchain-based systems can address such security risks as well.

Blockchain technology enables peer-to-peer contractual behavior without any third party to certify an IoT transaction. Blockchain proposes solutions to the challenges like single points of failure, time-stamping, privacy, trust, and reliability. In addition, it provides a number of important features such as better fault tolerance capability, faster and efficient operation, and scalability.

Blockchain also faces challenges that require solutions for improved usage. In order to satisfy security requirements, additional processing power is required. In addition, standards and legal regulations should be put in place in order to enable usage of blockchain in different areas. One of the drawbacks of blockchain is the redundant storage of data. Because of data redundancy, amount of storage requirements increases. Another problem is performance. Storing data on a public blockchain is not free and not cheap as in traditional systems; running a single line of code on a blockchain also has an associated cost. The blockchain is only designed for the key–value pair, not large files or a large number of different data formats. Solving the storage problem without giving away decentralization will be a step forward in the utilization of blockchain technology.

References

1. Nakamoto S (2008) Bitcoin: a peer-to-peer electronic cash system. http://www.bitcoin.org/bitcoin.pdf
2. Blockchain Hub (2018) Beginners guide to blockchain. https://blockchainhub.net/blockchain-intro. Accessed 20 Dec 2018
3. Banafa A (2017, Jan) IoT and blockchain convergence: benefits and challenges. IEEE, Internet of things
4. Young J (2018) Use of blockchain in major industries by numbers: retail, manufacturing, finance, and others. https://cointelegraph.com/news/use-of-blockchain-in-major-industries-by-numbers-retail-manufacturing-finance-and-others. Accessed 20 Dec 2018
5. Katz J, Lindell Y (2007) Introduction to modern cryptography. Chapman and Hall/CRC
6. Gupta S, Sadoghi M (2018) Blockchain transaction processing. In: Encyclopedia of big data technologies, pp 1–11. https://doi.org/10.1007/978-3-319-63962-8_333-1

7. Angin P, Mert MB, Mete O, Ramazanli A, Sarica K, Gungoren B (2018, June) A blockchain-based decentralized security architecture for IoT. In: International conference on Internet of things. Springer, Cham, pp 3–18
8. Van der Meulen R (2015, Nov 10) Gartner says 6.4 billion connected 'things' will be in use in 2016, Up 30 percent from 2015. Gartner press release. www.gartner.com/newsroom/id/3165317. Accessed 22 Dec 2018
9. Waterman S (2016, Nov 17) Industry to government: hands off IoT security. Fedscoop. https://www.fedscoop.com/industry-to-government-hands-off-iot-security/. Accessed 19 Dec 2018
10. Banafa A (2016) A secure model of IoT with blockchain. OpenMind. https://www.bbvaopenmind.com/en/a-secure-model-of-iot-with-blockchain/. Accessed 21 Dec 2018
11. Coward J (2016) Meet the visionary who brought blockchain to the industrial IoT. IOT world news. Accessed 14 Dec
12. Petracek N (2018, July 18) Is blockchain the way to save IoT. https://www.forbes.com/sites/forbestechcouncil/2018/07/18/is-blockchain-the-way-to-save-iot/#517d28f55a74. Accessed 20 Dec 2018
13. Huckle S, Bhattacharya R, White M, Beloff N (2016) Internet of things, blockchain and shared economy applications. Procedia Comput Sci 98:461–466
14. Huh S, Cho S, Kim S (2017) Managing IoT devices using blockchain platform. In: 2017 19th international conference on advanced communication technology (ICACT). IEEE, pp 464–467
15. Ouaddah A, Abou Elkalam A, Ait Ouahman A (2016) FairAccess: a new blockchain-based access control framework for the Internet of things. Secur Commun Netw 9(18):5943–5964
16. Stavrou A, Voas J (2017) Verified time. Computer 50(3):78–82
17. Dorri A, Kanhere SS, Jurdak R, Gauravaram P (2017) LSB: a lightweight scalable blockchain for IoT security and privacy. arXiv preprint arXiv:1712.02969
18. Sharma PK, Singh S, Jeong YS, Park JH (2017) DistBlockNet: a distributed blockchains-based secure SDN architecture for IoT networks. IEEE Commun Mag 55(9):78–85
19. Park J, Kim K (2017, Mar) TM-coin: trustworthy management of TCB measurements in IoT. In: 2017 IEEE international conference on pervasive computing and communications workshops (PerCom Workshops). IEE, pp 654–659
20. Zhang Y, Wen J (2017) The IoT electric business model: using blockchain technology for the Internet of things. Peer-To-Peer Netw Appl 10(4):983–994
21. Outchakoucht A, Hamza ES, Leroy JP (2017) Dynamic access control policy based on blockchain and machine learning for the Internet of things. Int J Adv Comput Sci Appl 8(7):417–424
22. Lee B, Lee JH (2017) Blockchain-based secure firmware update for embedded devices in an Internet of things environment. J Supercomput 73(3):1152–1167
23. Brown J (2017, January 30) Companies forge cooperative to explore blockchain-based IoT security. https://www.ciodive.com/news/companies-forge-cooperative-to-explore-blockchain-based-iot-security/435007. Accessed 20 Dec 2018
24. Song JC, Demir MA, Prevost JJ, Rad P (2018, June) Blockchain design for trusted decentralized IoT networks. In 2018 13th annual conference on system of systems engineering (SoSE). IEEE, pp 169–174
25. Hyperledger—Open Source Blockchain Technologies. (n.d.). https://www.hyperledger.org. Accessed 20 Dec 2018
26. Perlman L (2017) ITU-T focus group digital financial services: distributed ledger technologies and financial inclusion. https://www.itu.int/en/ITU-T/focusgroups/dfs/Documents/201703/ITU_FGDFS_Report-on-DLT-and-Financial-Inclusion.pdf
27. Mills D, Wang K, Malone B, Ravi A, Marquardt J, Chen C, Badev A, Brezinski T, Fahy L, Liao K, Kargenian V, Ellithorpe M, Ng W, Baird M (2016) Distributed ledger technology in payments, clearing, and settlement. Finance and economics discussion series 2016–095. Board of Governors of the Federal Reserve System, Washington, DC. https://doi.org/10.17016/FEDS.2016.095
28. Open Architecture (2013, Mar 12) https://www.gartner.com/it-glossary/open-architecture. Accessed 20 Dec 2018

29. How does Bitcoin work? (n.d.). https://bitcoin.org/en/how-it-works. Accessed 20 Dec 2018
30. Davis N (2018) Blockchain for the connected home: combining security and flexibility. http://labs.comcast.com/blockchain-for-the-connected-home-combining-security-and-flexibility. Accessed 20 Dec 2018
31. Dorri A, Kanhere SS, Jurdak R, Gauravaram P (2017) Blockchain for IoT security and privacy: the case study of a smart home. In: 2017 IEEE international conference on pervasive computing and communications workshops (PerCom Workshops). IEEE, pp 618–623
32. Meeting of the minds (2018) Using blockchain in smart cities. https://meetingoftheminds.org/using-blockchain-in-smart-cities-29319. Accessed 22 Dec 2018
33. Sharma PK, Moon SY, Park JH (2017) Block-VN: a distributed blockchain based vehicular network architecture in smart city. J Inf Process Syst 13(1):84
34. Kshetri N, Voas J (2018) Blockchain-enabled e-voting. IEEE Softw 35(4):95–99
35. IOTA (2018) The next generation of distributed ledger technology. https://www.iota.org/. Accessed 31 Dec 2018
36. Buck J (2018) Taipei partners with IOTA to become a blockchain-powered smart city. https://cointelegraph.com/news/taipei-partners-with-iota-to-become-a-blockchain-powered-smart-city. Accessed 20 Dec 2018
37. Biswas K, Muthukkumarasamy V (2016) Securing smart cities using blockchain technology. In: IEEE 14th international conference on smart city on high performance computing and communications. IEEE, pp 1392–1393
38. Catalini (2018, Mar 07) How blockchain applications will move beyond finance. https://hbr.org/2017/03/how-blockchain-applications-will-move-beyond-finance. Accessed 20 Dec 2018
39. Not just for cryptocash: how blockchain tech could help secure IoT. (n.d.). https://internetofthingsagenda.techtarget.com/blog/IoT-Agenda/Not-just-for-cryptocash-How-blockchain-tech-could-help-secure-IoT. Accessed 20 Dec 2018
40. Hyperledger (2018) Hyperledger Indy. https://www.hyperledger.org/projects/hyperledger-indy. Accessed 31 Dec 2018
41. Dickson B (2016, Oct 30) Blockchain could help fix IoT security after DDoS attack. https://venturebeat.com/2016/10/29/blockchain-could-help-fix-iot-security-after-ddos-attack. Accessed 20 Dec 2018
42. Azaria A, Ekblaw A, Vieira T, Lippman A (2016, Aug) Medrec: using blockchain for medical data access and permission management. In: International conference on open and big data (OBD). IEEE, pp 25–30
43. Mediledger (2018) The MediLedger project: an open and decentralized network for the pharmaceutical supply chain. https://www.mediledger.com/. Accessed 18 Dec 2018
44. Aigang platform (n.d.) (2019) https://aigang.network/. Accessed 31 Dec 2018
45. Fritz M (n.d.) The road to a digital upgrade in the enterprise. https://blogs.oracle.com/oraclepartners/the-road-to-a-digital-upgrade-in-the-enterprise. Accessed 20 Dec 2018
46. IDC FutureScape (2018) Worldwide Internet of things 2017 predictions. https://www.idc.com/getdoc.jsp?containerId=US40755816. Accessed 25 Dec 2018

Chapter 7
A Novel Quantum Encryption and Authentication Framework Integrated with IoT

R. Santhiya Devi, R. John Bosco Balaguru, R. Amirtharajan and Padmapriya Praveenkumar

Abstract In the present era of Internet of Things (IoT), communicating medical reports for the concerted diagnosis plays a vital role in any telemedicine network. Here, security of communication, being one of the most important requirements, needs to be appropriately addressed in protecting the transmitted data to ensure authentication, privacy, trust and integrity. In this context, this chapter suggests an image encryption and authentication algorithm to handle bulky medical images integrated with Quantum encryption mechanism. The proposed Quantum Cyber-physical system is established with the help of the security algorithms along with cloud computing framework. In the proposed encryption scheme, initially, the original classical medical image is converted into Quantum image format using Novel Enhanced Quantum Representation (NEQR). Then using Cellular Automata (CA) (Rule:30), the quantum image is confused and diffused and its authentication is provided by cellular automata. Further, encryption takes place in four stages, namely, key generation, permutation, Deoxyribo Nucleic Acid (DNA) operation and diffusion. Additionally, the cloud framework provides a comprehensive platform for individual access to the encrypted files depending on the access privileges granted to the relevant individuals. The approach is well suited for a versatile hospital management system. The strength of the proposed encryption algorithm is validated by evaluating different metrics like Number of Pixel Change Rate (NPCR), Unified Average Change in Intensity (UACI), correlation, histogram and certain chosen-plaintext attacks.

R. Santhiya Devi · R. John Bosco Balaguru · R. Amirtharajan · P. Praveenkumar (✉)
School of Electrical & Electronics Engineering, SASTRA Deemed University, Thanjavur 613 401, India
e-mail: padmapriya@ece.sastra.edu

R. Santhiya Devi
e-mail: santhiya.rathy@gmail.com

R. John Bosco Balaguru
e-mail: rjbosco@ece.sastra.edu

R. Amirtharajan
e-mail: amir@ece.sastra.edu

Z. Mahmood (ed.), *Security, Privacy and Trust in the IoT Environment*, https://doi.org/10.1007/978-3-030-18075-1_7

Keywords NEQR · Quantum image processing · Quantum encryption · Quantum Cyber-physical · Cellular automata · Cloud framework · Correlation · Histogram · DNA · HIPAA

7.1 Introduction

In the current era of the Internet, the developments in the telemedicine applications are increasing exponentially. Some of these are helping to fulfil the core requirements of secure transmission and reception of medical report over the open communication channels such as the Internet of Things (IoT). In this perspective, medical image encryption plays a significant role in enhancing the Confidentiality, Integrity and Authentication (CIA) triad and also withstanding the cyberattacks potentials of medical records. According to the Health Insurance Portability and Accountability Act (HIPAA), there has been 2181 healthcare data breached between 2009 and 2017, which is around 17 crores of health records that were exposed [1]. Health database encompasses patient details, social security number, medical history, health information and healthcare insurance numbers. Fake IDs can be created and forged insurances claimed if such huge amounts of patient data are exposed. As a result, according to the Medical Identity Fraud Alliance (MIFA), over 20% of victims received wither the wrong diagnosis or experienced delayed treatment as a result of this fraudulent use of healthcare data [2].

In telemedicine applications, the number of images handled by the medical systems is huge, and the size of each image is often large. Also, medical images usually have high pixel density as compared to other images. Unlike normal images, medical images have also significant amount of additional information attached to them [3]. Hence, it is imperative that we have high performance methods to process these images, so as to reduce the complexity and hence the computational time.

7.1.1 Rationale and Chapter Objective

Rapid growth in the domain of DNA computing has led to integrating DNA computing with image encryption techniques due to bulky data storage, requirements of massive parallelism and low power consumption. The two main operations involved in DNA cryptography are DNA encoding and DNA computing which incorporate algebraic and biological operations on the encoded DNA sequences like addition, XOR, complement and subtraction.

Recently, a wide range of chaos-based DNA cryptosystems have been implemented due to the fundamental characteristics of chaotic maps such as ergodicity, extraordinary sensitivity towards preliminary seed and aperiodic nature. In order to find the characteristics of RGB (Red, Green and Blue) image and to relate the mathematical expressions into biological problems, Liu et al. [4] have proposed an

RGB cryptosystem based on DNA encoding, addition and complementary operations. Zhang et al. [5], have changed the control parameters of 2-D logistic maps for generating different chaotic sequences which are then incorporated for DNA addition and complement operations for reducing the complexity of the DNA based system. Zhang et al. [6] have proposed an image fusion framework based on the DNA operation and hyper-chaotic maps for encrypting the digital images. However, these one-dimensional and multidimensional chaotic systems have weaknesses including discontinuity in chaotic behaviour and small key space. Liu et al. [4] and Zhang et al. [5, 6] approaches have security weaknesses and are vulnerable to chosen-plaintext attacks [7–9]. Also, researchers have analysed numerous metrics like NPCR, UACI, entropy, correlation, Mean Square Error (MSE), Peak Signal-to-Noise Ratio (PSNR) and chi-square tests to verify the robustness of the cipher image pixels [10–14].

Wolfram in 1983 [15] has suggested that Cellular Automata (CA) can be utilised for generating pseudo-random numbers in an efficient way. CA is a type of discrete dynamic system, which is a good option for various applications like random number generation, confusion and encryption. CA has been implemented in many image encryption algorithms due to huge evolution rule space, parallelism and complex behaviour [16–18]. Therefore, in the current study, CA rule-30 [19] has been implemented for generating the pseudo-random number due to its simple computation and high random nature.

Breakthrough of quantum computation naturally paved the way for the quantum-based cryptosystem due to its exclusive computational features like parallelism, entanglement, superposition of quantum state and quantum coherence which makes quantum computing much more efficient as compared to its classical counterparts. The two main branches of quantum-based cryptosystem include quantum image representation and quantum image encryption algorithms. For the former one, a number of quantum image representation algorithms were proposed, namely, Entangled [20], Real ket [21], Multi-Channel Representation of Quantum Image (MCRQI) [22], log-polar [23], Flexible Representation of Quantum Images (FRQI) [24] and Novel Enhanced Quantum Representation (NEQR) [25]. For the latter, various quantum gates [25 and 26] are used for encrypting the images due to their reversible nature.

Considering the stupendous features of NEQR, such as precise recovery of the original image, less time is required for preparing the quantum image representation. It has been suggested that the quantum image representation can be utilised for many quantum-based cryptosystems [26–28]. Generally, the image encryption algorithms are grouped into two main classifications: Confusion and Diffusion. However, these properties are not fulfilled in these quantum-based cryptosystems [28, 29]. For actively extracting the watermark, and in order to achieve high capacity, Zhou et al. [29] have proposed a watermarking scheme by expanding the watermark image to the size of the cover image and the watermark image is embedded by utilising the Least Significant Bit (LSB) technique. To increase the embedding capacity, El-Latif et al. [27] have suggested a watermarking scheme by embedding the scrambled quantum watermark image into cover by implementing the first three LSB XORing technique. However, the original image cannot be retrieved in these algorithms.

Zhou et al. [30] have suggested an image encryption scheme based on T-DNA cellular automata to meet the criteria of the one-time pad. To reduce the encryption time, Chai et al. [31] have framed a novel encryption scheme based on CA and DNA operations. Chaotic sequences are used for generating 2-D CA, and it is used for selecting different encoding rules. Similarly, Enayatifar et al. [32] have proposed an algorithm where the rule number and CA are determined from the chaotic maps and the proposed algorithm is validated by different metrices.

Motivated by the above analysis and to cope with the problems in quantum authentication algorithms and chaos-based DNA cryptography, a new quantum medical image encryption and authentication algorithm is being proposed for ensuring the confidentiality and authentication of the medical records. This is achieved by combining the quantum computation along with chaotic maps, DNA rule set and CA. The proposed method is divided into four phases, namely, pseudo-random number generation, permutation, DNA operations and diffusion. CA rule-30 is incorporated for pseudo-random number generation and this is used for selecting the rules for DNA encoding phase. So, this acts as the authentication phase, i.e. if there is any modification in the rule set and then the original image will not be retrieved correctly. Further, the diffusion phase includes modulo-arithmetic operations.

In this chapter, Sect. 7.2 provides a detailed description of the methods used in the proposed framework. The proposed encryption, decryption and cloud storage methodologies are projected in Sect. 7.3. In Sects. 7.4 and 7.5, the simulation results, security analysis and conclusion of the proposed framework are discussed.

7.2 Preliminaries

This section provides a comprehensive review of the methods that are used in the current study. The first step in quantum cryptography is to represent the classical image into quantum and this is achieved by utilising NEQR format which is explained in Sect. 7.2.1. The CNOT quantum gate is used for encrypting the message which is explained in Sect. 7.2.3. Encoding and decoding procedures in DNA and CA are explained in Sects. 7.2.3 and 7.2.4, respectively.

7.2.1 Novel Enhanced Quantum Representation (NEQR)

NEQR has been proposed in [25]. For a medical image sized $2^m \times 2^m$ with 2^n grayscale range, its symbolic representation is described as follows:

$$|Image\rangle = \frac{1}{2^m} \sum_{h=0}^{2^m-1} \sum_{v=0}^{2^m-1} \otimes_{i=0}^{n} |p(h, v)\,|hv\rangle \tag{7.1}$$

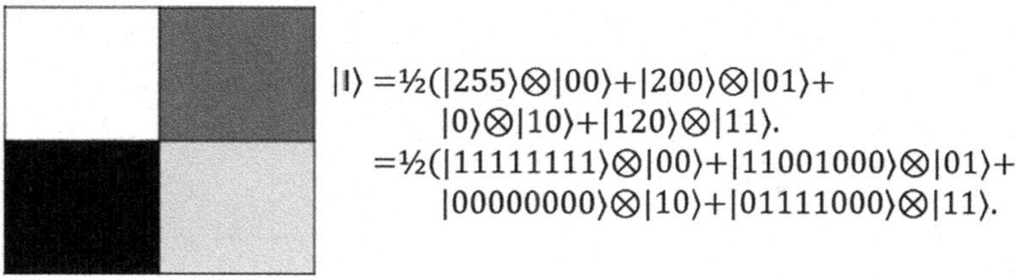

Fig. 7.1 NEQR representation for a $2^1 \times 2^1$ grayscale image

where

h	no. of rows in image ($h = 2^m$)
v	no. of columns in image ($v = 2^m$)
n	grayscale range of the image
p(hv)	pixel value of the image,
$\|hv\rangle$	horizontal and vertical position values of the pixel.

For a 16-bit depth medical image, p (h, v) ranges between 0 and 65,535 and n will be equal to 16. This p (h, v) $\in$ [0, 2^n-1] and can be encoded by the binary sequences as $C_{hv}^0 \ldots . C_{hv}^7 C_{hv}^8 \ldots . C_{hv}^{15} C_{hv}^{16}$. Its horizontal and vertical position values $|hv\rangle$ can be represented as, $|v\rangle = |v_{n-1}\, v_{n-2} \ldots .\, v_0\rangle$ and $|h\rangle = |h_{n-1}\, h_{n-2} \ldots .\, h_0\rangle$. Therefore, $n + 2^m$ qubits are employed for storing both the pixel and position values of a grayscale image sized $2^m \times 2^m$ with 2^n grayscale range. So, Eq. (7.1) can be rewritten as:

$$|Image\rangle = \frac{1}{2^m} \sum_{h=0}^{2^m-1} \sum_{v=0}^{2^m-1} \otimes_{i=0}^{16} \left|C_{\text{hv}}^i\,|hv\rangle,\; C_{hv}^i \varepsilon [0, 1]\right. \quad (7.2)$$

where $\left|C_{hv}^i\right.$ is binary representation of p (h, v).

An example of a $2^1 \times 2^1$ Digital Imaging and Communications in Medicine (DICOM) image in the range [0, 2^8-1] (where referring to Eq. 7.2, m = 1 and n = 8) and its quantum representation is shown in Fig. 7.1.

7.2.2 Controlled-nOT Gate (CNOT)

This is a 2-input gate. The primary input is considered as the controlling qubit and the second input is considered as the target qubit. Controlled-NOT (CNOT) gate operation works as follows: if the controlling qubit is $|1\rangle$, then the target qubit is reversed; else it is unaffected. In the proposed scheme, the key is chosen to be the control qubit and the image is selected as the target qubit. Figure 7.2 portraits the quantum representation of the CNOT gate and the paradigm is provided in Fig. 7.3.

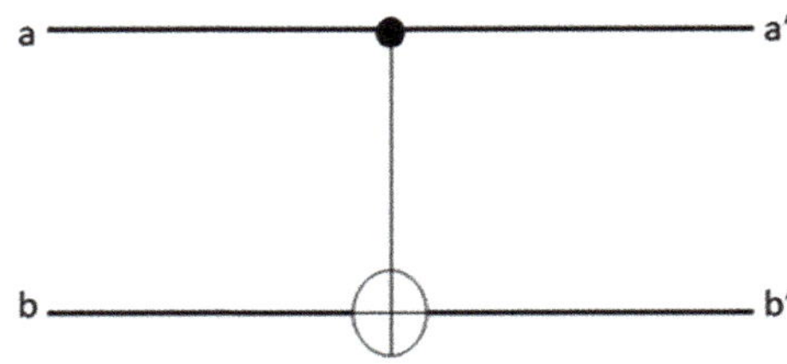

Fig. 7.2 Wire diagram of the CNOT gate

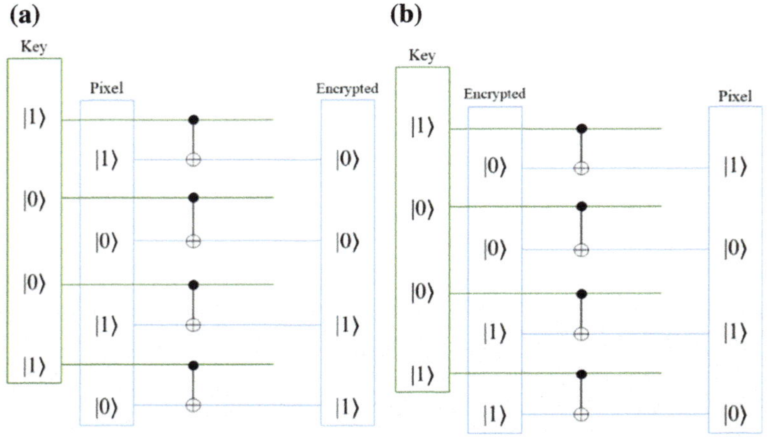

Fig. 7.3 Example of the CNOT gate **a** Encryption **b** decryption

Table 7.1 DNA encoding rules

Rules	1	2	3	4	5	6	7	8
00	A	A	T	T	C	C	G	G
01	C	G	G	C	A	T	A	T
10	G	C	C	G	T	A	T	A
11	T	T	A	A	G	G	C	C

7.2.3 *Encoding and Decoding Procedure in DNA*

A DNA structure comprises four nucleic acid bases, namely, Adenine (A), Cytosine (C), Guanine (G) and Thymine (T). Exploring the base rules, it can be concluded that A and T, G and C are the complementary pairs. Likewise, in a binary system, 00 and 11, 01 and 10 are complement to each other. Therefore, these two bases can be mapped. One can devise 24 varieties of DNA encoding rules. In Watson-Crick's [33] base-pairing schemes, only 8 encoding rule sets satisfy the complementary property and are listed in Table 7.1. Similarly, eight DNA XOR rules can be framed and DNA XOR table based on rule 1 is listed in Table 7.2.

Table 7.2 DNA XOR

⊕	A	C	G	T
A	A	C	G	T
C	C	A	T	G
G	G	T	A	C
T	T	G	C	A

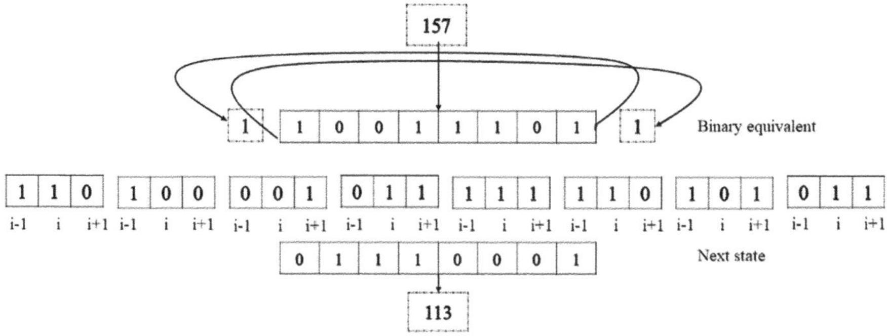

Fig. 7.4 CA rule-30 example

7.2.4 Cellular Automata (CA)

CA is a discrete mathematical pattern, which comprises of an unvarying grid of identical cells in n-dimensional space where each cell has a fixed number of states; such as 0 and 1. In a single dimensional CA, every cell is accompanied by its neighbouring cells. Since there are three cells, its possible binary states are $2^3 = 8$, and the total amount of cellular automata is $2^8 = 256$. Suppose at time t, c_i^t symbolises the state of ith cell, then, the local rule can be indicated by its Boolean function f, and is given as:

$$c_i^{t+1} = f(c_{i-1}^t, c_i^t, c_{i+1}^t) \tag{7.3}$$

Wolfram in [15] coded the collection of rules for the progression of one-dimensional CA. Rule 30 in Cellular Automata belongs to class 3, where the generated sequences result in a pseudo-random sequence exhibiting chaotic behaviour. The evolution always depends on three-bit sequences, with one output Y, where Y = left pixel (XOR) (centre pixel (OR) right pixel). An example of elementary rule 30 is given in Fig. 7.4, where rule 30 is based on the simple XOR and OR operations and its Boolean function is given as:

$$c_i^{t+1} = c_{i-1}^t xor\left[c_i^t \; or \; c_{i+1}^t\right] \tag{7.4}$$

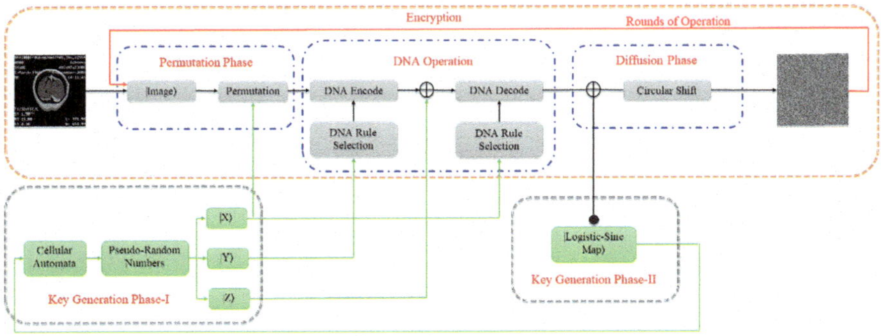

Fig. 7.5 Block diagram of the proposed framework

First, the current cell and the next cell contents are ORed, and then the resultant bit is XORed with the previous cell value as shown in Fig. 7.4.

7.3 Proposed Quantum Encryption and Authentication Algorithm

This section explains the proposed framework for the quantum image encryption and authentication algorithm. It is classified into two stages, namely:

- key generation phase—discussed in Sect. 7.3.1.
- encryption algorithm—discussed in Sect. 7.3.2.

Figure 7.5 demonstrates the block diagram of the proposed encryption and authentication algorithm. Originally, the plain image is represented as a quantum image and then it is permuted. The permuted image is subjected to DNA encoding, DNA XOR and DNA decoding operations and then it is diffused by implementing the CNOT and circular shift operations. Then the NPCR and UACI values are estimated and if the values are not in the optimal range, then rounds of operation are incorporated. Figures 7.6 (a and b) illustrate the wire diagram of the proposed encryption and decryption algorithm, respectively. The proposed framework is practically analysed for a 2 × 2 image which is presented in Fig. 7.7.

7.3.1 Key Generation Phase

The combined chaotic system is a discrete time dynamic system used for generating keys in chaos-based cryptosystems due to its extraordinary features like, huge key space, enlarged chaotic range and randomness. Two chaotic maps are combined as suggested by Zhou et al. [34].

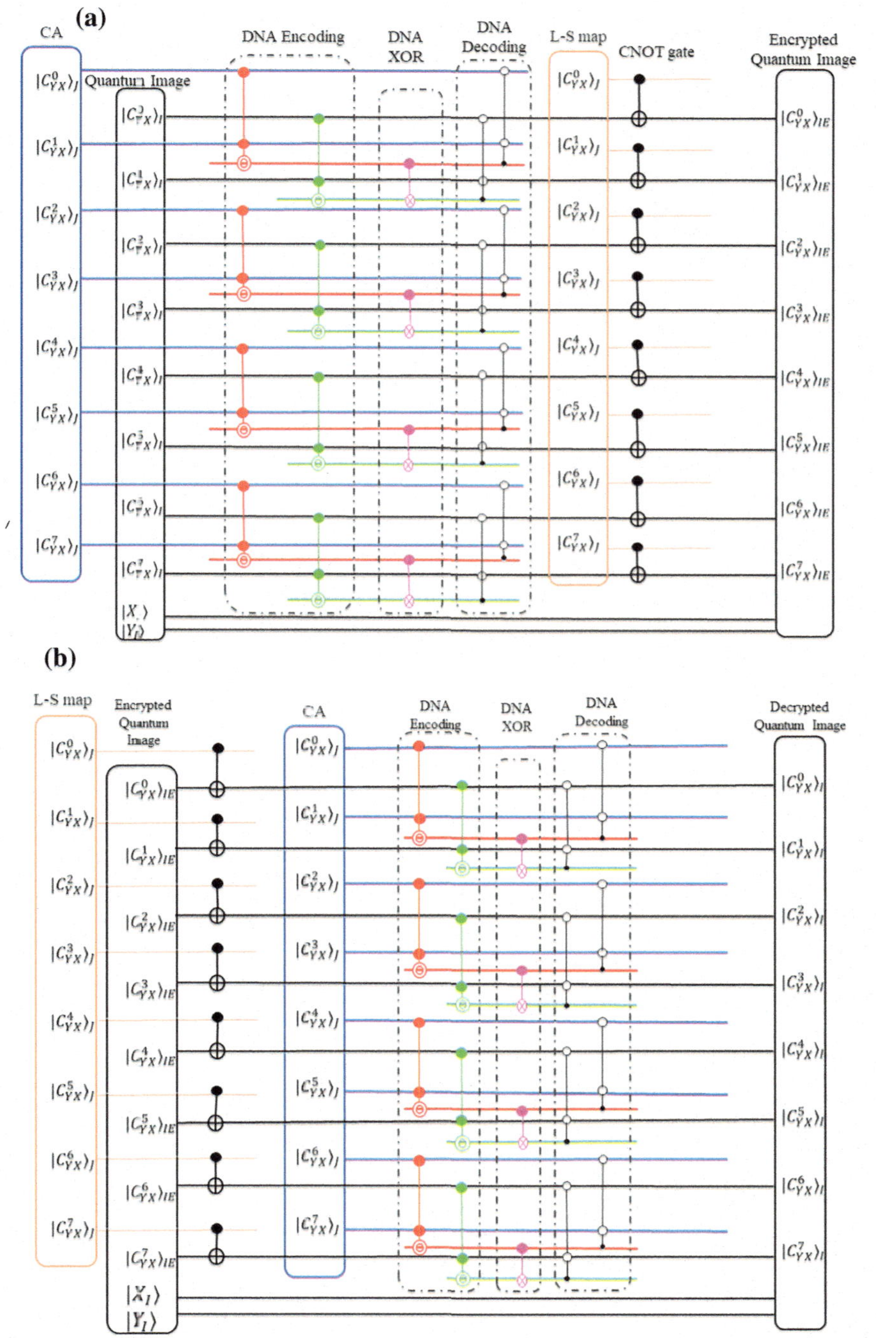

Fig. 7.6 **a** Encryption wire diagram of the proposed framework. **b** Decryption wire diagram of the proposed framework

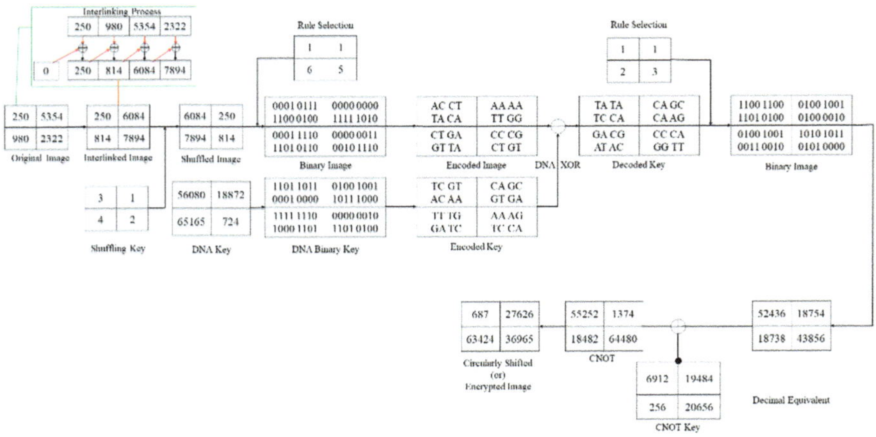

Fig. 7.7 A 2 × 2 example of the proposed framework

Let the two 1-D chaotic maps be G (r1, y_n1) and H (r2, y_n2), where r1 and r2 are the preliminary seeds and y_n1 and y_n2 are the control seeds. The combined map is obtained by using Eq. (7.5i). In the proposed framework, the Logistic map and Sine map are combined. The representation of Logistic-Sine (L-S) map is given in Eq. (7.5ii) as:

$$y_{n+1} = mod((G(r1, y_n1) + H(r2, y_n2)), 1) \tag{7.5i}$$

$$y_{n+1} = [ry_n(1 - y_n) + (4 - r)\sin(\pi y_n)/4]mod1 \tag{7.5ii}$$

where r and y_n are the initial and control values, where r∈ (0,4] and y_n∈ [0,1].

7.3.2 Encryption Algorithm

A detailed explanation of the proposed framework is elaborated in this section. Further, the encryption algorithm is classified into Permutation phase, DNA operation and Diffusion phase.

Permutation Algorithm
The original image was subjected to permutation, i.e. its pixel position values were transformed to make the original image unintelligible. Then, the permuted image was given as input to the DNA operation phase. The process is as follows:
Input: Original image, key X.
Output: Permuted image.

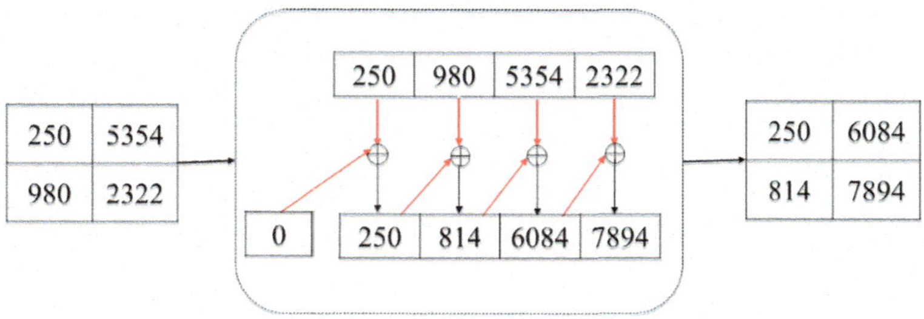

Fig. 7.8 Example of CNOT operation between the current pixel and previous pixel

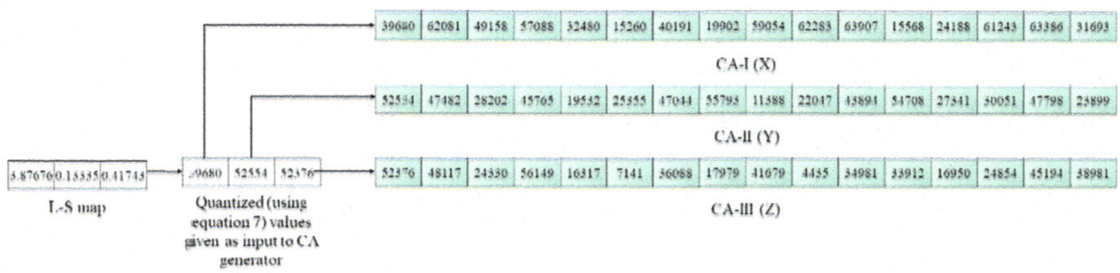

Fig. 7.9 CA key generation using L-S map

Step 1: Represent the medical image of size M × M into NEQR format (2) and Eq. (7.6) operated on the array. Figure 7.8 explains the detailed description of this step.

$$|I\rangle = CNOT(I_{encrypt}(h, v-1), I_{encrypt}(h, v)) \tag{7.6}$$

where

h row value of the image,
v column value of the image

Step 2: The L-S map (5) was iterated three times L = {L(1), L(2), L(3)} and Eq. (7.7) was operated on this sequence to produce the quantised sequence.

$$L_q(\mathrm{i}) = \mathrm{floor}(\mathrm{mod}(\mathrm{L(i)} \times 10^{17}), 65536)\mathrm{i} = 1, 2, 3. \tag{7.7}$$

Step 3: To generate the three pseudo-random sequences X, Y and Z of size M × M, 'L_q' values were fed as the initial condition to the CA generator and the pictorial representation of this is shown in Fig. 7.9. Convert this pseudo-random numbers into NEQR representation |X⟩, |Y⟩, |Z⟩ by using Eq. (7.2).
Step 4: Operate Eq. (7.8) on the sequence |X⟩ to get index values of the sorted sequence (non-repeating numbers) S_X and converted into the M × M size. Then both the S_X matrix and the |I⟩ were compared, then the |I⟩ values were mapped according to S_x's position. For example, in S_X, if the value '1' is in the ith row and jth column

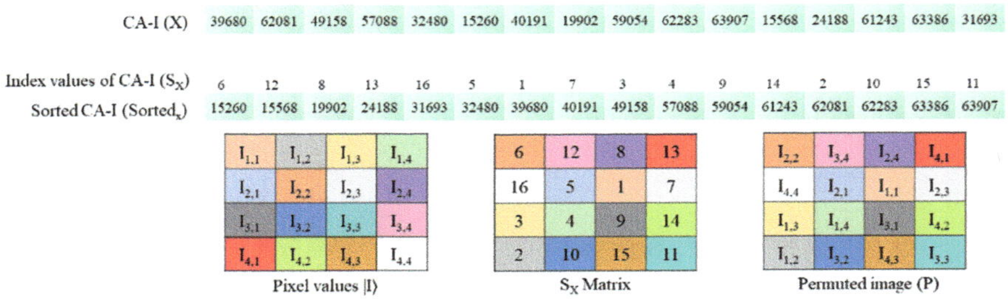

Fig. 7.10 A 4 × 4 example of proposed permutation process

then the first pixel of |I⟩ is mapped to the ith row and jth column of the permuted matrix (P). The detailed illustration is shown in Fig. 7.10.

$$[Sorted_x, S_x] = sort(X); \tag{7.8}$$

where Sorted_x—sorted X sequence,
S_X—index values of Sorted_x sequences.

DNA Operation

In order to achieve the equi-probable pixel values, the permuted image was diffused by utilising the DNA XOR operation.
Input: Permuted image, keys X, Y, Z.
Output: DNA diffused image.
Step 5: Limit the sequence |Y⟩ to a max of 8 values as $|Y_s\rangle$ by operating Eq. (7.9).

$$|Y_s\rangle = mod(|Y\rangle, 8) \tag{7.9}$$

Step 6: The permuted image pixels (P) were converted into binary values (B) and select the encoding rule according to $|Y_s\rangle$ and encode the binary values into DNA sequence matrix as |DNA_encode⟩. The encoding rules are provided in Table 7.1.
Step 7: Like step 6, the first encoding rule from Table 7.1 is used to encode the |Z⟩ as |key_encode⟩.
Step 8: Consider |key_encode⟩ as key and perform DNA XOR operation according to Table 7.2 on |DNA_encode⟩. Let |DNA_XOR⟩ be the XORed matrix.
Step 9: Similar to step 5, operate Eq. (7.9) on the sequence |X⟩ to get $|X_s\rangle$ and decode the |DNA_XOR⟩ according to $|X_s\rangle$.

Diffusion Phase

In this phase, to enhance the security, the DNA output image was further diffused.
Input: DNA diffused image, key LS.
Output: Encrypted image.
Step 10: Equation (5ii) was iterated for 'n' times and, the first 1000 iterations were neglected and the chaotic sequence LS = $\{LS_{1001}, LS_{1002}, \ldots, LS_n\}$ were chosen where n = M×M. The LS sequence was quantised according to Eq. (7.10).

$$|\text{LS'}\rangle = \text{floor}\left(\text{mod}\left(X \times 10^{17}\right), \text{IL}\right) \tag{7.10}$$

where IL refers to intensity level.
Step 11: The CNOT gate was implemented between the |DNA_XOR⟩ and |LS'⟩ as in (11),

$$|I''\rangle = CNOT(|DNA\_XOR\rangle, |\text{LS'}\rangle) \tag{7.11}$$

Step 12: Each row of |I"⟩ was transformed into binary equivalent vector and the number of 1's in each row was computed as N.
Step 13: Calculate 'CS' value using (12), if CS = 0 then the binary vector was right circular shifted by N times otherwise it is left circular shifted by N times.

$$CS = mod(N, 2) \tag{7.12}$$

Step 14: To get the encrypted image, translate the binary vector into decimal values by using Eq. (7.13). The decryption procedure is the inverse of the encryption algorithm.

$$|I_{encrypt} = bi2de(Row, bitdepth) \tag{7.13}$$

7.3.3 *Storage of Encrypted Images in the Cloud*

A real-time management system requires secure and privileged access to the stored encrypted information for different users. Each user will have different privileges depending on their social standing. This scenario is achieved using the Amazon Web Services; S3 (Simple Storage Service) platform using two methods, namely, Identity and Access Management (IAM) for users, and Cross-Region Replication. These methods provide procedures to access the cloud based on single/multi-user cloud accessing. In method 1, single user selective access can be carried out, whereas in method 2, two users can access the stored file via file replication process. The explanation of these now follows.

Method I—IAM Users
This involves the creation of a single cloud which can be accessed by users with login credentials for authentication. To including the selective access, the primary user has to perform the following steps concerning granting permission for a single user:

1. Create a new user with programmatic access.
2. Attach a bucket policy which determines the buckets which the particular user can access.
3. Attach a user policy which determines the read, write and modify permissions for the user.

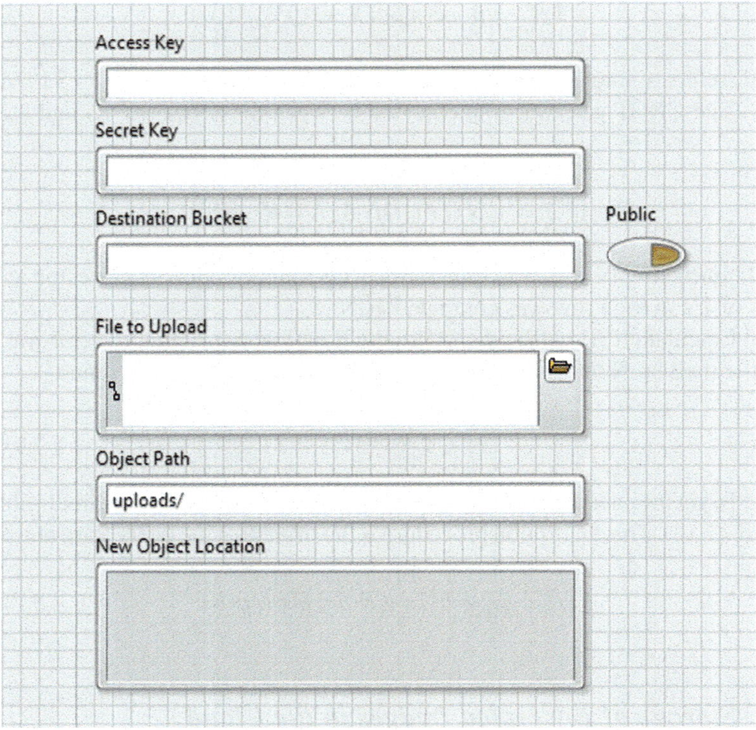

Fig. 7.11 LabVIEW front panel for uploading file to the bucket

4. Provide the user with their login credentials.

The access key and the secret key are provided for each IAM User. They can be updated and changed based on a period provided by the primary user. Only with the knowledge of the access key and the secret key a user can upload a file into a particular bucket of a particular cloud, provided that he has access to it. The LabVIEW front panel and block diagram for file upload to the bucket are shown in Figs. 7.11 and 7.12, respectively. The LabVIEW front panel and LabVIEW block diagram for creating a bucket are shown in Figs. 7.13 and 7.14, respectively.

Method II—Cross-Region Replication

In this method, each user having created their cloud, the replication of a file that is uploaded to a particular bucket of a particular cloud is also replicated to a bucket of a different cloud. Steps involved in this method are as follows:

1. Go to the source bucket's account and enable the versioning for a particular bucket.
2. Include a bucket policy that allows access to all entities in the bucket.
3. Under the same bucket, add a replication rule specifying which contents are allowed.

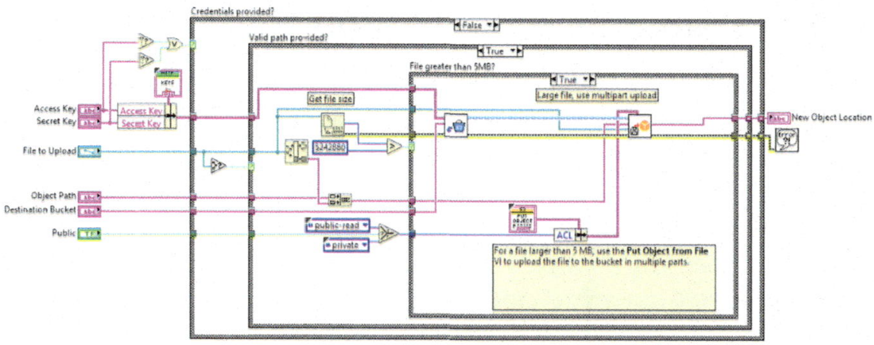

Fig. 7.12 LabVIEW block diagram for uploading file to the bucket

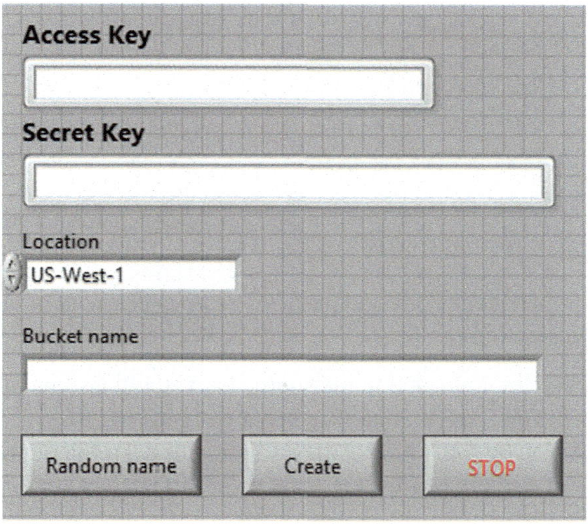

Fig. 7.13 LabVIEW front panel for creating a bucket

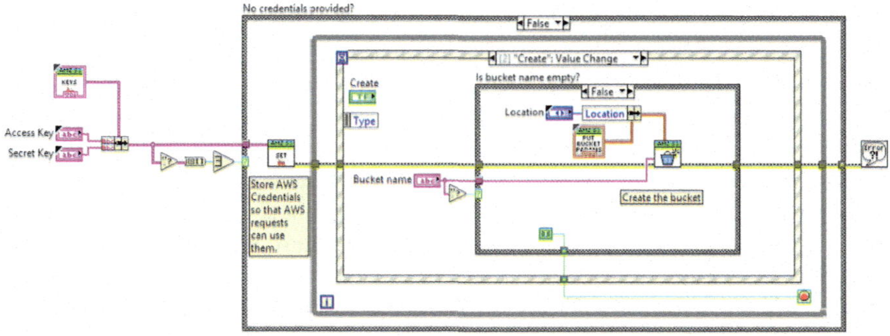

Fig. 7.14 LabVIEW block diagram for creating a bucket

Fig. 7.15 Cross-region replication

4. In the destination bucket, copy and paste the policy generated in step 3 and select the receive files option.

Now the files that are uploaded in the source bucket will also be replicated in the destination bucket. This can be done vice versa by reversing the roles of the source bucket and destination bucket which achieves bidirectional replication. Cross-region replication only works between buckets that exist in different regions as shown in Fig. 7.15.

In case of accessing the cloud as an IAM User, before the user is given access, two different policies are verified as per the flowchart diagram as shown in Fig. 7.16. The first step is to check if the user is an IAM user under that particular account. If this is verified, the next step is to check if that particular user has a user policy that states that he can access that particular cloud. If yes, then the bucket policy is checked. The bucket policy states whether the IAM user has access to a particular bucket in the cloud and also the entities of the bucket for which the IAM user as privileges. If the IAM user has been authorised, then access is granted.

The basic scenario considered for a hospital management system using the cloud framework is shown in Fig. 7.17. Here we consider patient A, Patient B, Physician and an Insurance company. To establish selective authentication system which provides different privileges for different types of users trying to access the content stored in the cloud. A patient may have access to their own records, but they may only be granted privilege to read. They must not have the privilege to modify existing records or write any new records. A physician, on the other hand, can read, write

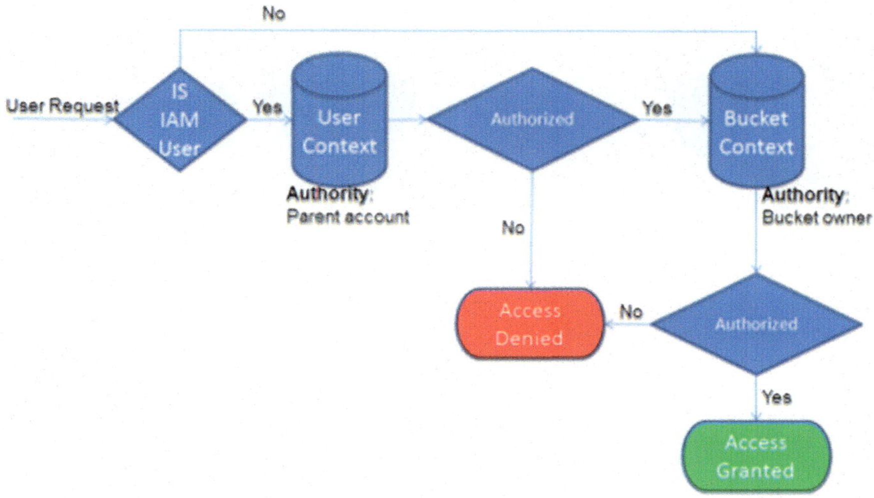

Fig. 7.16 IAM user authentication

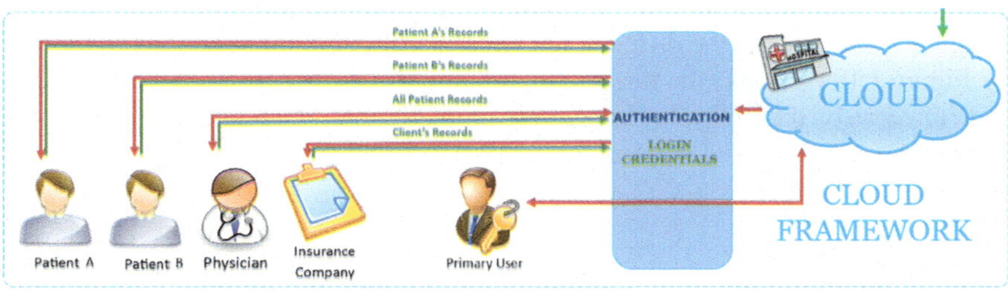

Fig. 7.17 Scenario for a hospital management system using cloud framework

and modify records based on their diagnosis at each stage. The Insurance Company can have access to the basic medical records of the patient as they require only the overall health status of their client and do not require any detailed information. Like this, each user's account is given strict and restricted privileges depending on their designation.

7.4 Simulation Results and Discussion

To validate the proposed scheme, five 256 × 256 DICOM images were considered. Due to the deficiency of quantum computers, the proposed scheme is simulated in a personal lap with Intel Core i5 processor, 2.5 GHz and 8 GB RAM equipped with MATLAB R2016b.

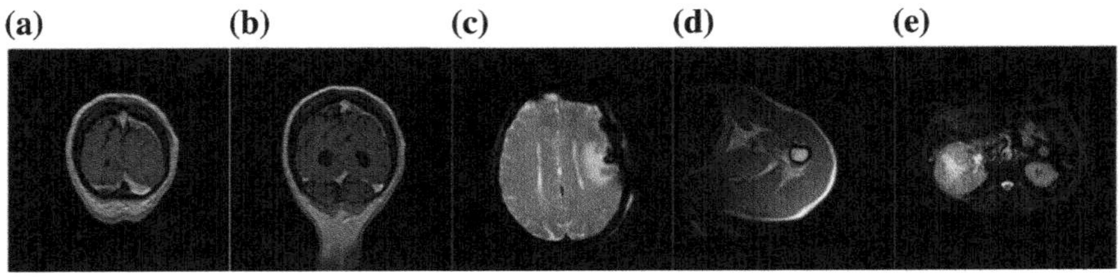

Fig. 7.18 Different MR images. **a** IM-0001-0001, **b** IM-0001-0002, **c** IM-0001-0003, **d** IM-0001-0004, **e** IM-0001-0001

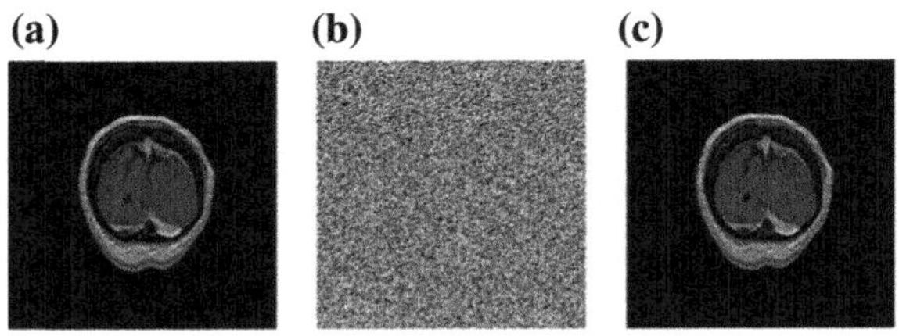

Fig. 7.19 Output of the proposed framework. **a** IM-0001-0001, **b** encrypted image of **a**, **c** decrypted image from **b**

Figure 7.18a–e show the different test images utilised in the proposed methodology. Figure 7.19a–c depict the various stages' output of the proposed encryption algorithm. Obviously, the encrypted images are unintelligible. Then, these are decrypted by using the same key and the decrypted images are recovered correctly.

7.4.1 Security Analysis

An efficient encryption algorithm should withstand the attacks, namely, statistical, differential and chosen-plaintext attacks. To examine the resistive nature of the proposed framework, it is intentionally subjected to various attacks. Also, the pixel correlation, key sensitivity, key space, histogram of the original and encrypted images, entropy, chosen-plaintext attack, differential attacks such as NPCR and UACI are analysed and compared with the existing algorithms available in the literature [10–14].

7.4.1.1 Exhaustive Attacks

These are also known as brute-force attacks. The strength of the projected framework lies in its key. The hacker tries to find the key by checking all the possible key values. Therefore, the key should be huge and also sensitive to minor changes to withstand brute-force attack. The sensitivity of the key and the key space are discussed in this section.

Fig. 7.20 Key sensitivity test. **a** IM-0001-0001, **b** encrypted image of **a**, **c** decrypted image using Key 1, **d** decrypted image using Key 2, **e** decrypted image using original key

Table 7.3 Key sets used in the proposed framework

		Original key	Key 1	Key 2
L	r	3.87676767676767	3.87676767677767	3.87676767676767
	Y_n	0.76767676767676	0.76767676767676	0.76767676767676
LS	r	3.77676767676767	3.77676767676767	3.77676767676767
	Y_n	0.86767676767676	0.86767676767676	0.86777676767676

Key Space Analysis

Key space is the set of all possible permutations of the key. To resist the exhaustive attack, the key space of the proposed framework should be huge. In the proposed framework, the L-S map and CA are considered to produce the secret keys. The proposed framework uses five keys, key = {L, X, Y, Z, LS}. Further, L and LS have two keys, namely, r and y_n. If the precision of L and LS are set to 10^{-14}, then the key space is$(10^{-14})^4 = 10^{56}$. Additionally, the CA generator uses the 16-bit key and the key space is $(2^{16})^3 = 2^{48}$. Altogether, for a single round of operation, the secret keys used in the encryption and decryption process are $10^{56} \times 2^{48}$ which means that the proposed framework has the excessive capability to endure the brute-force attack.

Key Sensitivity Analysis

A good cryptosystem should be sensitive to minor alteration in the secret keys. Both the L-S map and CA are sensitive to the initial and control parameters. Tests are conducted with single bit change in any one of the decryption key values while maintaining the other keyvalues as such. Then the original image is not recovered back. Instead, a new encrypted image is produced. It can be seen from Fig. 7. 20a–e, if there is any small modification in the key, the decryption process will fail. Thus, it can be concluded that the proposed framework is tremendously sensitive to keys. Table 7.3 shows the key values and the modified key sets used in the proposed framework.

7.4.1.2 Statistical Attacks

With different cipher images' statistical values, the hackers try to gain knowledge about the key and encryption algorithm. Therefore, in the cipher image, the probabil-

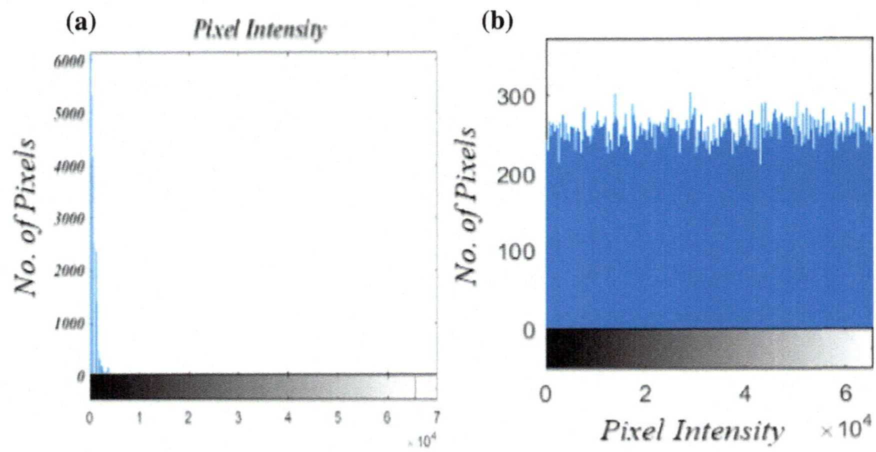

Fig. 7.21 **a** Histogram of IM-0001-0001, **b** histogram of encrypted IM-0001-0001

ity of all the intensity values should be equal and there should not be any relationship between the neighbouring pixel values. The statistical nature of the cipher image can be verified by using histogram, correlation and entropy analysis.

Histogram Analysis
The pixel value distribution of the image is portrayed by using histograms. It is a substantial metric for evaluating the withstanding capacity of the algorithm towards statistical attack by computing the histogram of the cipher image. In the plain image, pixels are not distributed evenly. Therefore, hackers can easily acquire some amount of information from the image. On the contrary, if the histogram is uniform, then it can be concluded that all the pixels are evenly distributed and then it will be hard to obtain the statistical characteristic of the cipher images. Thus, the cipher image's histogram should be flat. Figure 7.21a, b shows the histogram of the original and cipher image, respectively. In the plain image's histogram, the pixels are distributed in uneven fashion, whereas the cipher image's histogram is uniform.

Pixel Correlation Analysis
Correlation gives the linear relationship between the neighbouring pixels and this is calculated in Horizontal (HC), Vertical (VC) and in Diagonal (DC) directions. The plain image is susceptible to statistical attack due to the high relationship between adjacent pixels. A well framed encryption algorithm should breakdown this myth. In Table 7.4, the correlation coefficients are tabulated that afre calculated as follows:

$$Correlation = \frac{cov(a,b)}{\sqrt{D(a)}\sqrt{D(b)}} \tag{7.14}$$

where $cov(a,b) = \frac{1}{N}\sum_{i=1}^{N}(a_i - E(a))(b_i - E(b))$

Table 7.4 Correlation values of original and encrypted images

Images	Correlation					
	Original			Encrypted		
	HC	VC	DC	HC	VC	DC
IM-0001-0001	0.9683	0.9622	0.9426	−0.0017	−0.0015	0.0033
IM-0001-0002	0.9607	0.9575	0.9312	0.0050	0.0040	0.0002
IM-0001-0003	0.9852	0.9898	0.9788	−0.0027	0.0010	−0.0074
IM-0001-0004	0.9757	0.9776	0.9530	0.9530	−0.0006	0.0046
IM-0001-0005	0.9753	0.9819	0.9645	- 0.0037	−0.0035	0.0061

$$D(a) = \frac{1}{N}\sum_{i=1}^{N}(a_i - E(a))^2$$

$$E(a) = \frac{1}{N}\sum_{i=1}^{N} a_i$$

a, b two adjacent pixel pairs,
cov covariance between a and b,
E(a) mean of a,
E(b) mean of b,
D(a) variance of a,
D(b) variance of b,
N total no. of elements in a and b.

Figure 7.22a–f depict the graphical representation of the correlation results of original and the encrypted images. As it can be seen, the relationship between the neighbouring pixels is highly bonded, but it is quite weak in cipher image. Thus, the proposed framework can defend the statistical attack.

Entropy Analysis

Global Shannon Entropy is a qualitative measure used for measuring the randomness of the cipher image and can be calculated using:

$$Ent(\mu) = -\sum_{x=0}^{IL} p(\mu_i)\log_2 p(\mu_i) \tag{7.15}$$

where $p(\mu_i)$—probability of the symbol μ_i,

IL—intensity level.

A random source emitting 2^N symbols tends to have entropy of around N. For a DICOM image with 2^{16}equi-probable level of the grayscale range will have theoretical entropy value of 16. Table 7.5 shows the entropy values of the original image in bit planes. From Table 7.6, it can be seen that the entropy values are close to 1 in all the bit planes. Thus, it can be deduced that the proposed framework can generate random cipher images.

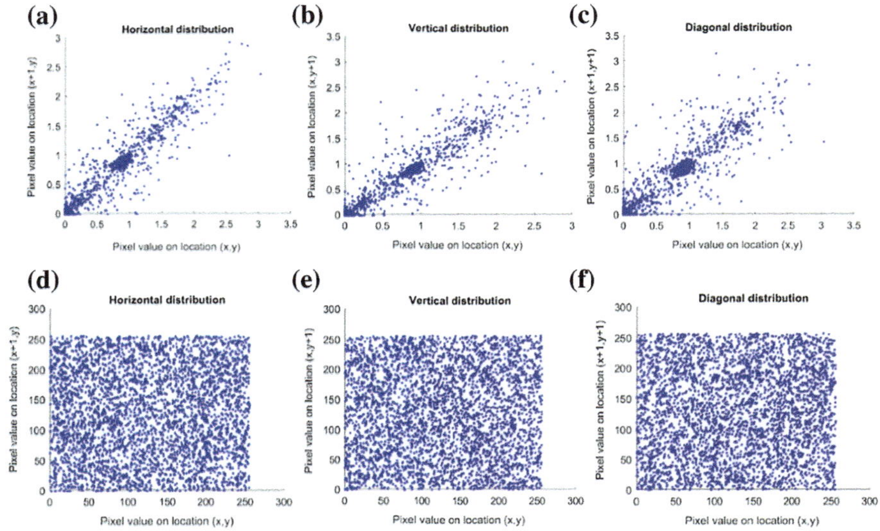

Fig. 7.22 **a** HC of IM-0001-0001, **b** VC of IM-0001-0001, **c** DC of IM-0001-0001, **d** HC of encrypted IM-0001-0001, **e** VC of encrypted IM-0001-0001, **f** DC of encrypted IM-0001-0001

Table 7.5 Entropy values of the original image in bit planes

Bit planes	IM-0001-0001	IM-0001-0002	IM-0001-0003	IM-0001-0004	IM-0001-0005
1	0.717506	0.797527	0.90727	0.951113	0.821513
2	0.687745	0.775308	0.886818	0.946455	0.799487
3	0.643833	0.735148	0.850114	0.944853	0.771511
4	0.589646	0.689941	0.778004	0.939015	0.74677
5	0.544934	0.662875	0.696535	0.925906	0.733844
6	0.555314	0.637775	0.556069	0.914021	0.734467
7	0.588775	0.703864	0.773589	0.949193	0.63227
8	0.577888	0.730625	0.797174	0.837013	0.45646
9	0.377349	0.436101	0.255674	0.679259	0.315817
10	0.090712	0.095769	0	0.620265	0.175038
11	0	0	0	0.438644	0.001563
12	0	0	0	0.116844	0
13	0	0	0	0	0
14	0	0	0	0	0
15	0	0	0	0	0
16	0	0	0	0	0

Table 7.6 Entropy values of encrypted images in bit planes

Bit planes	IM-0001-0001	IM-0001-0002	IM-0001-0003	IM-0001-0004	IM-0001-0005
1	0.99997	1	0.999977	0.999999	0.999978
2	0.999998	0.99999	1	0.9999	0.999991
3	1	0.999994	0.999994	0.999988	0.999995
4	1	0.999986	0.999998	0.999998	0.999991
5	0.999982	0.999978	0.99997	0.999998	1
6	0.999973	0.999991	0.999995	0.999998	1
7	0.999999	0.999984	0.999994	0.999995	0.999991
8	0.999987	0.999982	0.999994	0.999999	0.999992
9	0.999996	0.999981	0.999991	0.999985	0.999999
10	1	0.999989	0.999998	1	0.999971
11	0.999997	0.999995	0.999987	0.999997	0.999998
12	0.999992	0.999995	0.999995	0.999994	0.999994
13	0.999995	0.999981	0.999994	1	0.999996
14	0.999976	0.999978	0.999993	1	1
15	0.999999	1	0.999999	1	0.999997
16	0.999995	1	0.999999	0.999974	0.999986

7.4.1.3 Differential Attacks

Here, the hackers try to trace the similarity between two cipher images typically by changing one-pixel value in the plain image. And using this connection, the hacker tries to recover the ciphertext NPCR and UACI are the two criteria used for measuring the difference between the cipher images. NPCR gives the number of pixels changed and UACI gives the average difference between the cipher images and these are computed by:

$$NPCR = \frac{\sum_{mn} Image(a, b)}{row \times column} \times 100\% \tag{7.16}$$

$$Image(a, b) = \begin{cases} 0\,if\ cipher1(a, b) = cipher2(a, b) \\ 0\,if\ cipher1(a, b) \neq cipher2(a, b) \end{cases}$$

$$UACI = \frac{1}{row \times column}\left(\frac{|cipher1(a, b) - cipher2(a, b)|}{IL}\right) \times 100\% \tag{7.17}$$

where IL is the intensity level, cipher1 and cipher2 are the two cipher images before and after one-pixel change in plain images, respectively. Both the NPCR and UACI values lie within the optimal range as in [35] and these values are shown in Tables 7.7 and 7.8, respectively. This reveals that the proposed framework is sensitive to small variations in the plain image and can defend the differential attacks.

Table 7.7 NPCR analysis

Images	NPCR (%)	NPCR critical values		
		$NPCR^*_{0.05} =$ 99.9960%	$NPCR^*_{0.01}$ = 99.9949%	$NPCR^*_{0.001}$ = 99.9938%
IM-0001-0001	99.9969	Pass	Pass	Pass
IM-0001-0002	99.9984	Pass	Pass	Pass
IM-0001-0003	99.9969	Pass	Pass	Pass
IM-0001-0004	99.9984	Pass	Pass	Pass
IM-0001-0005	99.9984	Pass	Pass	Pass

Table 7.8 UACI analysis

Images	UACI (%)	UACI critical values		
		$UACI^{*-}_{0.05}$ =33.1534% $UACI^{*+}_{0.05}$ =33.5143%	$UACI^{*-}_{0.01}$ =33.0967% $UACI^{*+}_{0.01}$ = 33.5710%	$UACI^{*+}_{0.001}$ = 33.0309% $UACI^{*+}_{0.001}$ = 33.6368%
IM-0001-0001	33.33739431	Pass	Pass	Pass
IM-0001-0002	33.33155992	Pass	Pass	Pass
IM-0001-0003	33.42270674	Pass	Pass	Pass
IM-0001-0004	33.31102852	Pass	Pass	Pass
IM-0001-0005	33.35241249	Pass	Pass	Pass

7.4.1.4 Chosen-Plaintext Attacks

The XOR operation-based algorithm should undergo this test to prove that the proposed algorithm can resist chosen-plaintext attack. This is calculated by:

$$A1 \oplus A1^{'} = B1 \oplus B1' \tag{7.18}$$

where B1 and B1' are the two cipher images obtained from A1 and A1' plain images, respectively. If the equality does not exist, then it can be decided that the proposed algorithm can resist chosen-plaintext attack. Figure 7.23 shows the chosen-plaintext analysis. From Fig. 7.23, the equality does not exist and can be concluded that the

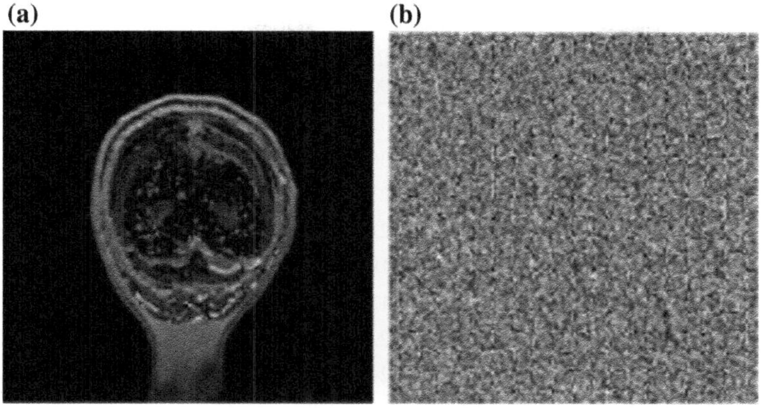

Fig. 7.23 Chosen-plaintext analysis: **a** A1 ⊕ A1' **b** B1 ⊕ B1'

Table 7.9 Performance analysis of the proposed framework with existing algorithms

	Correlation			NPCR	UACI	Key space
	HC	VC	DC			
Praveenkumar et al. [11]	−0.0033	0.0033	0.0117	99.62	33.45	2^{10240}
Ravichandran et al. [12]	−0.0519	−0.0385	0.0004	99.996	33.37	10^{168}
Ravichandran et al. [10]	−0.0025	−0.0016	0.0116	99.5982	33.4399	10^{168}
Fu et al. [13]	NA	NA	NA	99.60	33.48	10^{45}
Wang et al. [14]	−0.0011	−0.0016	0.0012	99.61	33.44	2^{263}
Proposed	0.0099	−0.0001	0.0014	99.9978	33.3510	$10^{56} \times 2^{48}$

proposed algorithm can withstand chosen-plaintext attack Table 7.9. The percentage of 1's in original and in encrypted images is tabulated in Tables 7.10 and 7.11, respectively. From this, it is clear that both the 0's and 1's are evenly distributed in all the bit planes of the image.

7.4.2 *Performance Comparison with Existing Algorithms*

The proposed scheme is compared with existing algorithms [10–14] in terms of entropy, correlation, NPCR, UACI and key space analysis. The values are listed in Table 7.9 and from this, it is obvious that the proposed algorithm can withstand statistical and differential attacks.

Table 7.10 Percentage of 1's in original images

Bit planes	IM-0001-0001	IM-0001-0002	IM-0001-0003	IM-0001-0004	IM-0001-0005
1	19.77997	24.15009	32.26776	37.0575	25.65613
2	18.35327	22.84546	30.45807	36.4624	24.2691
3	16.40167	20.67108	27.6123	36.26404	22.63031
4	14.20746	18.45551	22.99957	35.56519	21.27838
5	12.54883	17.22717	18.76526	34.11407	20.60394
6	12.92267	16.14532	12.95013	32.91168	20.63599
7	14.17389	19.11469	22.7478	36.80878	15.91492
8	13.75885	20.43915	24.12872	26.6922	9.608459
9	7.30896	8.988953	4.295349	17.96265	5.709839
10	1.152039	1.231384	0	15.42053	2.62146
11	0	0	0	9.065247	0.010681
12	0	0	0	1.574707	0
13	0	0	0	0	0
14	0	0	0	0	0
15	0	0	0	0	0
16	0	0	0	0	0

Table 7.11 Percentage of 1's in encrypted images

Bit planes	IM-0001-0001	IM-0001-0002	IM-0001-0003	IM-0001-0004	IM-0001-0005
1	50.32196	49.97101	49.71924	50.04272	49.72687
2	49.9176	50.18311	49.98627	50.58899	50.18005
3	50.01678	49.85199	50.14801	49.79248	50.1297
4	50	50.22278	50.07935	50.09308	49.82605
5	50.24872	50.27924	50.32501	50.0885	50
6	50.30823	49.823	49.86877	50.09003	50.00916
7	50.06104	49.76196	49.85657	49.86572	50.18005
8	50.21362	49.74823	49.85199	50.05035	50.1709
9	50.11597	50.2533	49.82758	50.22583	49.94812
10	50.01526	50.19684	50.08392	50.02136	50.31586
11	50.09918	49.8703	49.78485	49.90387	50.08698
12	50.16479	49.87183	49.87183	49.85352	49.85962
13	50.12665	49.74213	50.14801	50.01526	50.12207
14	50.28687	49.72687	50.15564	49.99237	49.99542
15	50.06561	49.98474	50.05188	49.97559	49.89624
16	50.1297	49.98016	50.06866	50.29755	50.22125

7.5 Conclusion

The protection of sensitive medical information, including medical images, is a top requirement in this digital world. In this contribution, a robust Quantum encryption algorithm that ensures the embranglement of the image using NEQR format has been developed. The Quantum cyber-physical system was established, involving a plain cipher, followed by the enactment of diffusion and confusion. It involves Key generation, Cellular Automata and DNA network as an excellent source of perturbation. The communication becomes esoteric when it happens after this encryption algorithm. The proposed encryption algorithm was validated using the equi-probable $1'$s and $0'$s in the encrypted images. Estimated average correlation values of -0.0027 inform that there exists no correlation between the neighbouring pixels in the encrypted image. Also, average NPCR of 99.99% and UACI of 33.096% proves that the proposed system escapes differential and statistical attacks. Furthermore, large key space and key sensitivity of the projected chapter proves the withstanding capability against brute-force attacks.

To add an extra layer to the proposed scheme, a secure communication platform using Amazon S3 and the cloud platform have also been promoted. The cloud platform provides breach immunity by administrating a set of users who have selective privileges on the access of the uploaded information based on IAM users and cross-region replication models. Hopefully, this system is a perfect fit for any flexible management system.

References

1. HIPAA (2018) Healthcare data breach statistics. https://www.hipaajournal.com/healthcare-data-breach-statistics/
2. HIPAA (2018) MIFA shares industry wisdom on medical identity theft and fraud. https://www.hipaajournal.com/mifa-shares-industry-wisdom-on-medical-identity-theft-and-fraud-3657/
3. Chen J, Zhu Z, Fu C et al (2015) An scheme using nonlinear inter-pixel computing and swapping based permutation approach. Commun Nonlinear Sci Numer Simul 23:294–310
4. Liu L, Zhang Q, Wei X (2012) A algorithm based on encoding and chaos map. Comput Electr Eng 38:1240–1248
5. Zhang Q, Guo L (2010) Image encryption using addition combining with chaotic maps. Math Comput Model 52:2028–2035
6. Zhang Q, Guo L, Wei X (2013) A novel image fusion encryption algorithm based on sequence operation and hyper-chaotic system. Opt—Int J Light Electron Opt 124:3596–3600
7. Ozkaynak F, Ozer AB, Yavuz S (2013) Security analysis of an algorithm based on chaos and encoding. In: 2013 21st Signal processing and communications applications conference (SIU). IEEE, pp 1–4
8. Hermassi H, Belazi A, Rhouma R, Belghith SM (2014) Security analysis of an algorithm based on a addition combining with chaotic maps. Multimed Tools Appl 72:2211–2224
9. Zhang Y, Wen W, Su M, Li M (2014) Cryptanalyzing a novel image fusion encryption algorithm based on sequence operation and hyper-chaotic system. Opt—Int J Light Electron Opt 125:1562–1564
10. Ravichandran D, Praveenkumar P, Rayappan JBB, Amirtharajan R (2017) Chaos blend to secure medical privacy. IEEE Trans Nanobiosci 16:850–858

11. Praveenkumar P, Amirtharajan R, Thenmozhi K, Balaguru Rayappan JB (2015) Medical Data Sheet in Safe Havens - A Tri-layer Cryptic Solution. Comput Biol Med 62:264–276
12. Ravichandran D, Praveenkumar P, Balaguru Rayappan JB, Amirtharajan R (2016) Chaos based crossover and mutation for securing DICOM image. Comput Biol Med 72:170–184
13. Fu C, Zhang G, Bian O et al (2014) A novel medical image protection scheme using a 3-dimensional chaotic system. PLoS One 9:e115773
14. Wang X, Liu C (2017) A novel and effective algorithm based on chaos and encoding. Multimed Tools Appl 76:6229–6245
15. Wolfram S (1983) Statistical mechanics of cellular automata. Rev Mod Phys 55:601–644
16. Guan Sheng-Uei, Zhang Shu (2003) An evolutionary approach to the design of controllable cellular automata structure for random number generation. IEEE Trans Evol Comput 7:23–36
17. Abdo AA, Lian S, Ismail IA et al (2013) A cryptosystem based on elementary cellular automata. Commun Nonlinear Sci Numer Simul 18:136–147
18. Ravichandran D, Rajagopalan S, Upadhyay HN et al (2018) Encrypted biography of biomedical image—a pentalayer cryptosystem on FPGA. J Signal Process Syst 1–27
19. Jun D, Na L, Yixiong G, Jun Y (2009) A high-performance pseudo-random number generator based on FPGA. In: 2009 international conference on wireless networks and information systems. IEEE, pp 290–293
20. Venegas-Andraca SE, Ball JL (2010) Processing images in entangled quantum systems. Quantum Inf Process 9:1–11
21. Latorre JI (2005) Image compression and entanglement. 4
22. Sun B, Le PQ, Iliyasu AM et al (2011) A multi-channel representation for images on quantum computers using the D color space. In: 2011 IEEE international symposium on intelligent signal processing (WISP). IEEE, pp 1–6
23. Zhang Y, Lu K, Gao Y, Xu K (2013) A novel quantum representation for log-polar images. Quantum Inf Process 12:3103–3126
24. Le PQ, Dong F, Hirota K (2011) A flexible representation of quantum images for polynomial preparation, image compression, and processing operations. Quantum Inf Process 10:63–84
25. Zhang Y, Lu K, Gao Y, Wang M (2013) NEQR: A novel enhanced quantum representation of digital images. Quantum Inf Process 12:2833–2860
26. El-latif AAA, Abd-el-atty B, Talha M (2017) Robust encryption of quantum medical images. IEEE Access 6:1073–1081
27. Abd El-Latif AA, Abd-El-Atty B, Hossain MS et al (2018) Efficient quantum information hiding for remote medical image sharing. IEEE Access 6:21075–21083
28. Beheri MH, Amin M, Song X, El-latif AAA (2016) Quantum based on Scrambling—Diffusion (SD) approach. In: 2016 2nd international conference on frontiers of signal processing (ICFSP). IEEE, pp 43–47
29. Zhou RG, Zhou Y, Zhu C et al (2018) Quantum watermarking scheme based on INEQR. Int J Theor Phys 57:1120–1131
30. Zhou S, Wang B, Zheng X, Zhou C (2016) An image encryption scheme based on computing and cellular automata. Discret Dyn Nat Soc 2016:1–9
31. Chai X, Gan Z, Yuan K, et al (2017) A novel scheme based on sequence operations and chaotic systems. Neural Comput Appl 1–19
32. Enayatifar R, Sadaei HJ, Abdullah AH et al (2015) A novel chaotic based using a hybrid model of deoxyribonucleic acid and cellular automata. Opt Lasers Eng 71:33–41
33. Watson JD, Crick FHC (1953) Molecular structure of nucleic acids: a structure for deoxyribose nucleic acid. Nature 171:737–738
34. Zhou Y, Bao L, Chen CLP (2014) A new 1D chaotic system for. Sig Process 97:172–182
35. Wu Y, Member S, Noonan JP, Member L (2011) NPCR and UACI Randomness tests for image encryption. Cyber Journals Multidiscip Journals Sci Technol J Sel Areas Telecommun 31–38

Part II
Privacy and Trust in IoT: Healthcare Applications and IoV

Chapter 8
Internet of Things in the Healthcare Sector: Overview of Security and Privacy Issues

Suvini P. Amaraweera and Malka N. Halgamuge

Abstract The Internet of Things (IoT) in health care is an emerging trend which provides a substantial amount of efficient and effective services for patients as well as healthcare professionals for the treatment of various diseases. Although the IoT paradigm offers numerous benefits, there are also inherent security and privacy challenges in relation to patient data. This chapter aims to investigate such security and privacy-related issues of the IoT healthcare applications that often operate on Cloud and Fog Computing architectures. In this chapter, 30 peer-reviewed publications from the years 2016 to 2018 are reviewed to construct a structured guide for the identification of related problems. Healthcare software applications, service architectures, patient data, and diverse sensory devices used are some of the factors considered for the collection of data, determination of related security and privacy issues, and implications of the said problems. Based on the factors, a comparison table is developed for analysis. Results show that most of these applications are used for remote patient care and monitoring. Furthermore, the results show that most threats occur due to unauthorized access to data, data breaches, and impersonation. Considering the IoT healthcare applications architecture (consisting of application, communication, device, network, and transport layers), we find that the device layer is the most affected layer regarding the security issues. Since most of the similar studies are limited to providing solutions regarding a specific aspect of security and privacy without considering the entire process, we have carried out additional research for a holistic approach to solve the bigger problem. We suggest that application developers should pay particular attention to these threats when designing IoT healthcare applications to provide secure and efficient applications to enhance the services within the healthcare sector. This study could be helpful to plan mitigation methodologies to conquer the inherent vulnerabilities in the IoT healthcare applications.

S. P. Amaraweera
School of Computing and Mathematics, Charles Sturt University, Melbourne, VIC 3000, Australia
e-mail: shonakanz@gmail.com

M. N. Halgamuge (✉)
Department of Electrical and Electronic Engineering, University of Melbourne, Parkville, VIC 3010, Australia
e-mail: malka.nisha@unimelb.edu.au

Z. Mahmood (ed.), *Security, Privacy and Trust in the IoT Environment*, https://doi.org/10.1007/978-3-030-18075-1_8

Keywords IoT · Healthcare applications · Cloud computing · Fog computing · Security issues · Privacy · Vulnerabilities · Device layer · Communication layer

8.1 Introduction

The Internet of Things (IoT) has enhanced the collecting and sharing of data and made it more accessible to software applications and their users. An IoT ecosystem consists of interconnected physical devices which support collecting and exchanging of data. The concept of IoT has improved the connection between computer systems and the physical world. IoT provides numerous opportunities in different fields [1] including health care which is one of the many industries that benefit from various IoT-based computer applications. It offers better health care to patients with improved treatment of various diseases. Researchers in the field have been attempting to find a way to build better and secure IoT healthcare applications to expand healthcare services and provide remote care facilities for patients with chronic illnesses [2]. These applications use various sensory devices to collect patient data and administer treatment. Most of these are wearable devices to promote patients' convenience. Thus, such devices have minimal invasive characteristics compared to implants within the human body.

Components of a typical IoT system are sensor devices, cloud-based interfaces, machine algorithms, and Wireless Sensor Network (WSN). Sensor devices are used to collect data from the human body such as body temperature, heart beat rate, blood pressure, etc. while WSN provides communication facilities [3]. The collected data are processed by the algorithms to perform the necessary analysis. Besides, the cloud services offer storage facilities for the collected data and allow access to users [4], whether patients or healthcare professionals.

Secured and protected IoT healthcare applications are required to improve the well-being of patients with consideration for the security and privacy threats they pose to patients' lives and other implications such as privacy violations and financial risks. This chapter discusses the privacy and security issues in IoT healthcare applications by analyzing the components of the application architecture in depth.

Nodes in the Wireless Sensor Network (WSN) are recognized by their unique identification numbers. Sensor nodes utilize these unique identification codes to maintain communication among the devices while supporting the nodes to collect and exchange data over the sensor network [5]. As a result, the services are provided through the use of various devices in the network. However, this has increased privacy and security challenges in IoT healthcare systems [6]. These issues can be categorized into three main groups as: data collection issues, data exchange issues, and data storage issues [7]. IoT networks are typically hosted by a cloud computing architecture to provide a cost-effective, scalable and efficient environment. This factor presents yet another major security challenge for IoT healthcare applications. Thus, there are serious cybersecurity related issues associated with the cloud environment. However, the cloud paradigm has its advantages such as economies of scale which is financially beneficial for the users [8].

Various healthcare services and applications include clinical diagnosis and emergency medical responses to patients in medical care facilities as well as to patients at home through remote medical processes. The data collected by patients are stored in a data center or database which is operated in a cloud. Cloud also provides access to different healthcare professionals, for example, to perform medical diagnoses to serve the patients. These facilities are rapidly transforming the traditional nature of patient care, and it makes the medical processes more efficient and effective [9]. Furthermore, these healthcare applications provide services through smart devices such as smartphones and wearable sensor devices with remote monitoring options.

Healthcare services and applications provide support for remote patient monitoring processes and alert systems. The most crucial asset of these applications is the data since data collected through these processes is considered as sensitive. The reason is that it has a direct impact on the well-being and safety of patients. The implications of compromising these data are always negative and have a high effect on the privacy and security of the entire system and its stakeholders. Moreover, confidentiality and availability of these data should be maintained. As well as protection from unauthorized access and other threats and risks, sensitive data should be preserved. However, these are challenging areas in an IoT ecosystem due to the volume of data produced through sensor devices and constant communication between the devices in the system. In recent years, healthcare professionals and application developers have been working together to build secure IoT healthcare applications to overcome these challenges alike [10]. They have proposed a number of security and privacy requirements for healthcare applications. These are listed in Table 8.1. The basic architecture of an IoT Healthcare Application is presented in Fig. 8.1.

Table 8.1 Security and privacy requirements of IoT health care

Security/privacy requirement	Rationale
Integrity of data	Accuracy and consistency of patient data should be maintained in the system through the entire data life cycle. Patient data should not be vulnerable to unauthorized access [23]
Usability of data	Access to data should be available for authorized users of the system. IoT generates huge volumes of data which might not be standardized. This issue could lead to various privacy and security concerns [24]
Auditability of data	Auditability is a main requirement in a cloud environment since there are always trust issues between service providers and the users. In order to control and monitor behaviors of the system tools and the techniques that provide, auditability should be available in an IoT healthcare environment [16]
Privacy of data	Patient records contain sensitive information that might be used to violate the privacy of the patient. Therefore, the application architecture should provide appropriate security controls for security of these data such as encryption methods to secure sensitive information from unauthorized access [23]

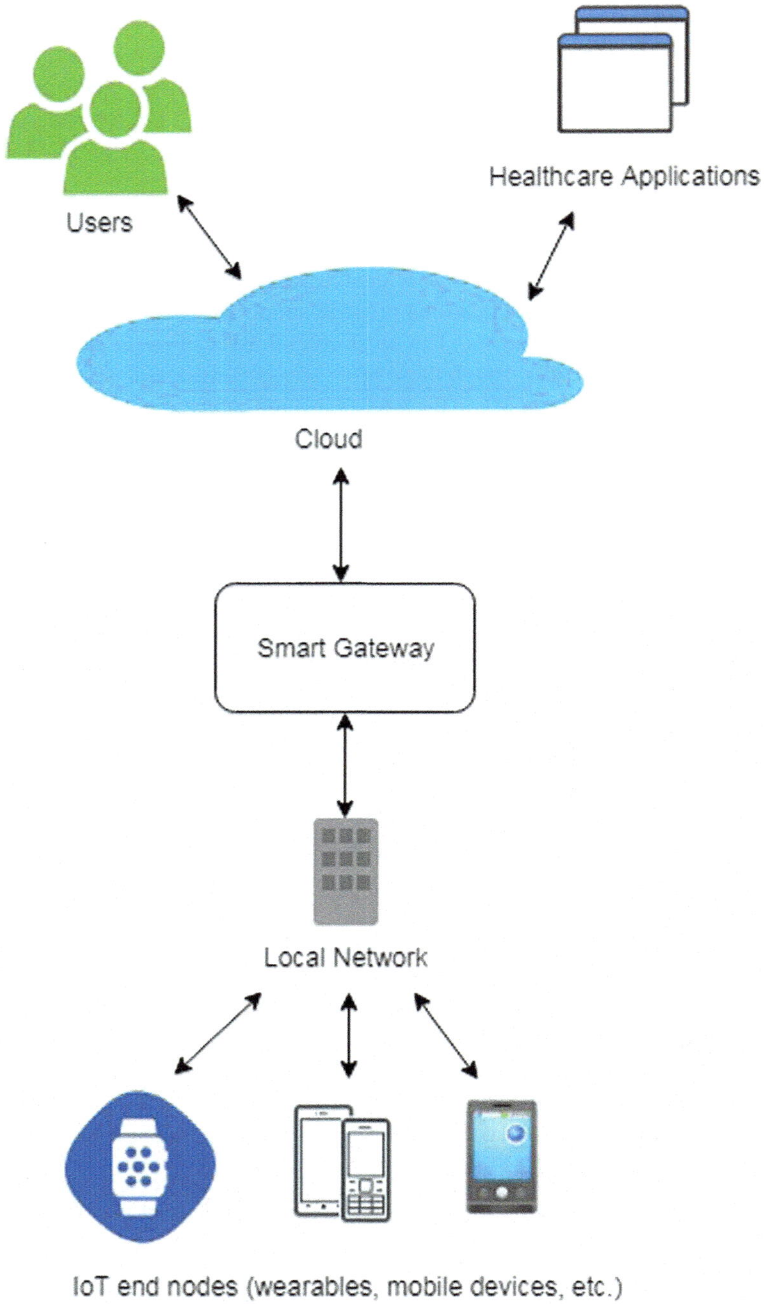

Fig. 8.1 Basic architecture of an IoT healthcare application

Besides, the inherent challenges hinder services that are provided by IoT technology. Also, the issues discourage patients from adopting smart healthcare systems considering privacy and security concerns that the challenges present [11].

MobiCare and MEDiSN are considered to be two of the best healthcare applications available at present. These applications are designed such that these do not interfere with day-to-day patients' lives. Even with minimal invasiveness, the threats landscape they present is significant considering the data exchange through open wireless networks and storage facilities that reside in backend servers. Examples of top threats to IoT health care include: eavesdropping, data breaches, data leak/collusion, and impersonation. Most of these threats affect data integrity as well [12].

Even though there are numerous publications available, it is still challenging to find studies which explore different aspects of the threat landscape. Those research studies have mostly limited their findings to relate to certain chosen aspects of the data process. Since there are three main processes in this context (data collection, exchange, and storage), vulnerabilities in those are also of three varieties. By failing to address all of the weak points and threats, a developer is unable to design an application which would withstand all the possible threats.

Trust is also a crucial factor in a system which deals with sensitive data. Therefore, producing a layout which addresses the entire threat landscape would enhance the effectiveness of the applications and build trust among its users. As a result, more people would allow themselves to benefit from IoT health care. The other issue with the sourced articles is that most of them have targeted an audience of professionals with a more technical background. Researchers have also examined various algorithms and scientific findings in their research studies.

The present research was conducted through reviewing peer-reviewed scientific articles published during years 2016–2018 to discuss different threats and risks to patient data for different kind of healthcare applications. These studies have been conducted by examining data extracted from various sensor-based devices. Most of these sensors are wearable sensors, and very few of them are recognized as implantable sensors.

This chapter is directed towards an audience of potential users, healthcare professionals, application designers, and academics. It is also written with simplicity in mind for nonmedical nontechnical audience. This chapter discusses the latest threats and risks to IoT health care to support the future developers to design and build more secure applications that guarantee fewer vulnerabilities and improved protection. The chapter is structured as follows: Sect. 8.2 presents materials and methods as well as data analysis together with criteria for data collection. Comprehensive analysis of data along with respective graphs is presented in Sect. 8.3. Discussion part which is Sect. 8.4 consists of a literature review that is conducted on similar studies. Finally, the conclusion of the findings and implications is presented in Sects. 8.5 and 8.6 along with ideas for future research work.

8.2 Materials and Methods: Data Collection and Results

As shown in Fig. 8.2, our research was carried out by reviewing 30 peer-reviewed articles published from years 2016 to 2018. The following attributes were considered when reviewing the literature and for further analysis:

- healthcare applications
- service architectures
- patient data
- sensor devices used
- security and privacy issues
- implications of issues
- affected layers of the IoT health application architecture.

The articles chosen for data gathering are related to privacy and security challenges of IoT healthcare applications operated on cloud or fog computing architectures. Some of the initially selected articles have been excluded from the study due to a number of reasons, e.g., insufficient data available in them; papers not being published in peer-reviewed publications; publication year not being in the range 2016–18.

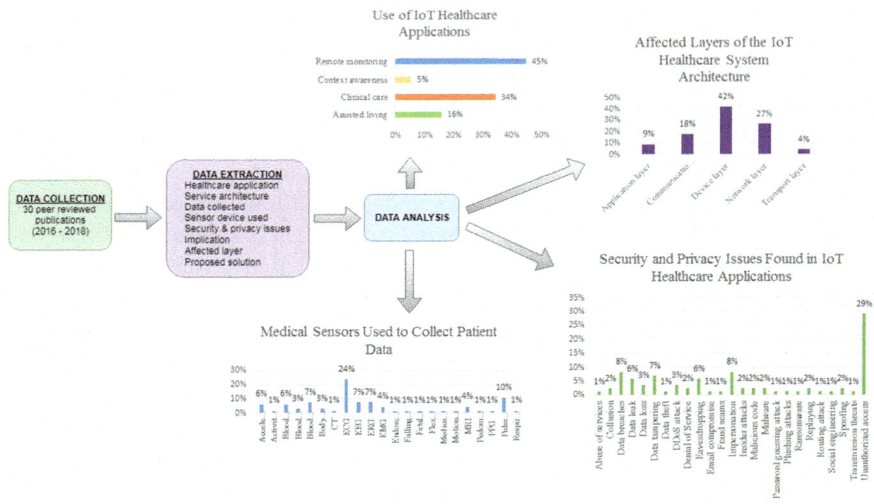

Fig. 8.2 Graphical abstract

Table 8.2 Raw data collection of 30 peer-reviewed articles from 2016 to 2018

No	Authors/ Publications	Healthcare applications	Service architecture	Health data collected	Sensor device used	Security and privacy issues	Implications	Affected layer	Proposed solution
1	Farahani et al 2018 [17]	Assisted living e-Medicine implants Early warning Population monitoring	Fog Cloud	Heart rate Blood pressure Blood sugar	Amped pulse sensor with green LED light Flex sensor	Unauthorized access	Privacy violation	Device layer Network layer Cloud layer Human layer	A holistic eHealth ecosystem covering the layers in fog driven architecture
2	Manogaran et al. 2018 [7]	MobiCare	Fog Cloud	Heart rate Blood pressure Blood sugar Body temperature	EKG Pulse oximeter EMG SpO2 Mica2 Blood oxygen sensor	Unauthorized access	Privacy violation	Communication layer Application layer Security layer	Meta Fog-Redirection (MF-R) for collection and storage of the sensor data
3	He et al. 2018 [9]		Cloud	Heart rate Blood sugar Pulse rate Brain activity Body temperature	EKG	Password guessing attack Unauthorized access DoS attack Data leak Social engineering Phishing attacks	Privacy violation	Network layer	Password strengthen meter

(continued)

Table 8.2 (continued)

No	Authors/ Publications	Healthcare applications	Service architecture	Health data collected	Sensor device used	Security and privacy issues	Implications	Affected layer	Proposed solution
4	Luo et al. 2018 [12]	MobiCare MEDiSN	Cloud	Heart rate Brain activity	EKG	Eavesdropping Impersonation Data breaches Collusion Insider attacks	Privacy violation Data integrity	Device layer	Access control scheme
5	Medvediev et al. 2018 [3]	MySignals	Cloud	Heart rate Blood sugar	Glucometer AD8232 ECG Cardiograph Gyro-accelerometer MPU-6050-MOD Cryptochip Atmel ATECC508A	Unauthorized access	Privacy violation	Network layer	Secured prototype of medical wearable electronic cardiograph
6	Tao et al. 2018 [10]	SecureData	Cloud Fog	Heart rate Blood sugar Body temperature	ECG Fetal monitor	Data breaches Data collusion Ransomware DDoS attacks Email compromise Insider attacks Fraud scams Eavesdropping Impersonation	Privacy violation Data integrity	Device layer	Secure data collection scheme

(continued)

Table 8.2 (continued)

No	Authors/ Publications	Healthcare applications	Service architec-ture	Health data collected	Sensor device used	Security and privacy issues	Implications	Affected layer	Proposed solution
7	Nausheen et al. 2018 [6]	Remote monitoring Clinical care Context awareness	Cloud	Heart rate	Wrist accelerometer	Data tampering Unauthorized access Data theft Malicious code	Privacy violation Data integrity	Application layer Network layer Communication layer	Access control schemes using white box encryption
8	Uddin et al. 2018 [11]	Remote patient monitoring CodeBlue UbiMon MobiCare MEDiSN MeDShare	Cloud Fog	Heart rate	ECG EEG BSC	Data breaches Unauthorized access Spoofing Eavesdropping DDoS attacks	Privacy violation Data integrity Financial losses	Device layer Communication layer	Patient-Centric Agent based healthcare architecture
9	Almulhim and Zaman 2018 [2]	MEDiSN	Cloud	Heart rate	BSC	Data breaches	Data integrity Privacy violation	Communication layer Transport layer	A model with mutual authentication and energy efficient design

(continued)

Table 8.2 (continued)

No	Authors/ Publications	Healthcare applications	Service architecture	Health data collected	Sensor device used	Security and privacy issues	Implications	Affected layer	Proposed solution
10	Elhoseny et al. 2018 [5]		Cloud			Unauthorized access Data tampering	Data integrity Privacy violation	Device layer	A hybrid model for securing the diagnostic text data in medical images
11	Rahmani et al. 2018 [1]	Early warning eHealth mHealth Ambient Assisted Living	Fog Cloud	Body temperature Heart rate Blood sugar	ECG EEG EMG	Data breaches Unauthorized access	Data integrity Privacy violation	Device layer	Fog-assisted system architecture which can cope with many challenges
12	Salahuddin et al. 2018 [8]		Fog Cloud	Heart rate	ECG PPG (photo plethysmography) Endoscopy	Unauthorized access Data tampering	Data integrity Privacy violation	Device layer	A platform using Machine-to-Machine (M2 M) data management system
13	Kim and Kim 2018 [25]		Cloud	High blood pressure Blood sugar	Apple Watch Nike Fuel	Unauthorized access	Privacy violation	Device layer	A guide for IoT healthcare service developers

(continued)

Table 8.2 (continued)

No	Authors/ Publications	Healthcare applications	Service architec- ture	Health data collected	Sensor device used	Security and privacy issues	Implications	Affected layer	Proposed solution
14	Sharma et al. 2018 [26]	kHealth	Cloud	Heart rate Oxygen saturation Body temperature Activity level Respiration flow rate	MRI EEG	Data breaches Unauthorized access	Data integrity Privacy violation	Device layer Communication layer	Analysis the data and analytic requirements for stakeholders
15	Woo et al. 2018 [27]		Cloud	Heart rate Blood sugar Blood pressure	ECG	Unauthorozed access		Communication layer Network layer Application layer	An algorithm to prevent faults on gateways in the M2 M IoT systems
16	Park et al. 2017 [28]		Cloud	Blood pressure Heart rate Blood oxygen saturation	Activity monitor Medication dispenser Pulse oxymeter ECG Blood pressure monitor Falling detector	Unauthorized access	Privacy violation	Communication layer Network layer	A protocol conversion scheme of ISO/IEEE 11073 and oneM2M

(continued)

Table 8.2 (continued)

No	Authors/ Publications	Healthcare applications	Service architecture	Health data collected	Sensor device used	Security and privacy issues	Implications	Affected layer	Proposed solution
17	Shen et al. 2018 [23]		Cloud	Blood oxygen saturation Heart rate Blood sugar	Pulse oxymeter ECG Blood glucose sensor	Unauthorized access Eavesdropping Data modification Impersonation Denial of Service	Privacy violation Data integrity	Device layer	A one-to-many authentication protocol
18	Islam et al. 2015 [29]	iMedPack iMedBox HetNet	Cloud	Blood pressure Body temperature Oxygen saturation Heart rate	ECG Blood pressure meter Pulse oxymeter Body temperature sensor	Unauthorized access Impersonation	Privacy violation Data integrity	Network layer Device layer	Surveys advances in IoT-based health care technologies
19	Gope and Hwang 2016 [30]	BSN-Care CodeBlue UbiMon MobiCare	Cloud	Blood pressure Heart rate	ECG EMG EEG	Eavesdropping Data loss Impersonation Replaying Data leak	Privacy violation Data integrity	Device layer	Highlight the major security requirements BSN healthcare system

(continued)

Table 8.2 (continued)

No	Authors/ Publications	Healthcare applications	Service architecture	Health data collected	Sensor device used	Security and privacy issues	Implications	Affected layer	Proposed solution
20	Laplante and Laplante 2016 [31]		Cloud	Blood pressure Heart rate	EKG Accelerometer	Unauthorized access	Privacy violation Data integrity	Device layer	A study of potential applications and challenges of IoT health care
21	Li et al. 2016 [24]		Cloud		RFID tags	Unauthorized access Spoofing Malicious code Denial of Service Routing attack Transmission threats Data breaches Abuse of services Replaying Impersonation Data tampering	Privacy violation Data integrity	Network layer Service layer Application layer Transport layer	Analyze the security problems in IoT based on four-layer architecture

(continued)

Table 8.2 (continued)

No	Authors/ Publications	Healthcare applications	Service architec- ture	Health data collected	Sensor device used	Security and privacy issues	Implications	Affected layer	Proposed solution
22	Tyagi et al. 2016 [32]	Google Health Microsoft Health Vault MiiM	Cloud	Blood pressure Heart rate Red bloodcell count Blood sugar Cholesterol level Activity level	RFID tags CT MRI	Unauthorozed access	Privacy violation Data integrity	Device layer	Applications of IoT and essential parameters and characteristics
23	Hossain and Muhammad 2016 [16]		Cloud	Blood pressure Heart rate Blood sugar	ECG Glucose monitor Blood pressure monitor	Unauthorized access Malware Impersonation	Privacy violation Data integrity		A Health IoT-enabled monitoring framework
24	Alam et al. 2018 [20]	S-Health	Cloud	Heart rate Blood sugar Blood pressure Oxygen saturation Body temperature	Smartphone sensors Accelerometer ECG	Unauthorized access	Privacy violation Data integrity	Communication layer Network layer	Overview of advances in IoT-based future healthcare

(continued)

Table 8.2 (continued)

No	Authors/ Publications	Healthcare applications	Service architecture	Health data collected	Sensor device used	Security and privacy issues	Implications	Affected layer	Proposed solution
25	Muhammed et al. 2018 [19]	UbeHealth	Cloud Fog	Heart rate Blood sugar Activity level	RFID tags	Unauthorized access Data leak Data tampering	Privacy violation Data integrity	Network layer	An ubiquitous healthcare framework called UbeHealth
26	Gupta et al. 2016 [22]		Cloud	Heart rate Blood sugar Blood pressure	ECG EEG	Unauthorized access Data leak	Privacy violation Data integrity	Device layer	Provide efficient healthcare services to patients through IoT technology
27	Ullah et al. 2016 [33]	k-Healthcare	Cloud	Heart rate Blood pressure Oxygen saturation Blood sugar Activity level	RFID tags ECG RTX-4100 Wireless two-lead EKG Arduino and Raspberry Pi Blood oxygen sensor Pulse oximetry Smart Phone sensors	Unauthorized access	Privacy violation Data integrity	Device layer Network layer	The k-Healthcare model for efficient deployment of IoT

(continued)

Table 8.2 (continued)

No	Authors/ Publications	Healthcare applications	Service architecture	Health data collected	Sensor device used	Security and privacy issues	Implications	Affected layer	Proposed solution
28	Natarajan et al. 2016 [34]		Cloud	Blood sugar Blood pressure Body temperature Oxygen saturation	ECG Blood pressure meter Pulse oxymeter Raspberry Pi	Unauthorized access	Privacy violation Data integrity	Device layer	A efficient machine to machine communication designed for health care data
29	Ahmad et al. 2016 [18]	Microsoft Health Apple Healthkit Samsung S Health Google Fit Fitcoracy RunKeeper Mio DigifitIcardio	Fog Cloud	Sleep patterns Activity level Heart rate	Pedometer Heart rate monitor Accelerometer	Unauthorized access Data leak Malware	Privacy violation Data integrity	Network layer Device layer	A framework of Health Fog

(continued)

Table 8.2 (continued)

No	Authors/ Publications	Healthcare applications	Service architec-ture	Health data collected	Sensor device used	Security and privacy issues	Implications	Affected layer	Proposed solution
30	Sailunaz et al. 2016 [35]		Cloud	Heart rate Respiration rate Body temperature Activity rate Blood pressure Blood sugar	ECG MRI Oximeter Blood pressure sensor Blood sugar sensor Digital thermometer Respiration sensor Smartphone sensors	Unauthorized access Data loss	Privacy violation Data integrity	Device layer	A cloud-based framework for smart healthcare system

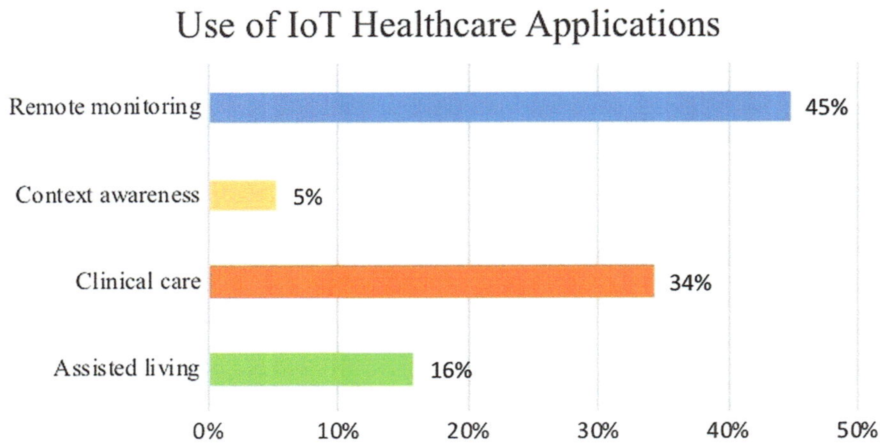

Fig. 8.3 Overview of use of IoT healthcare applications

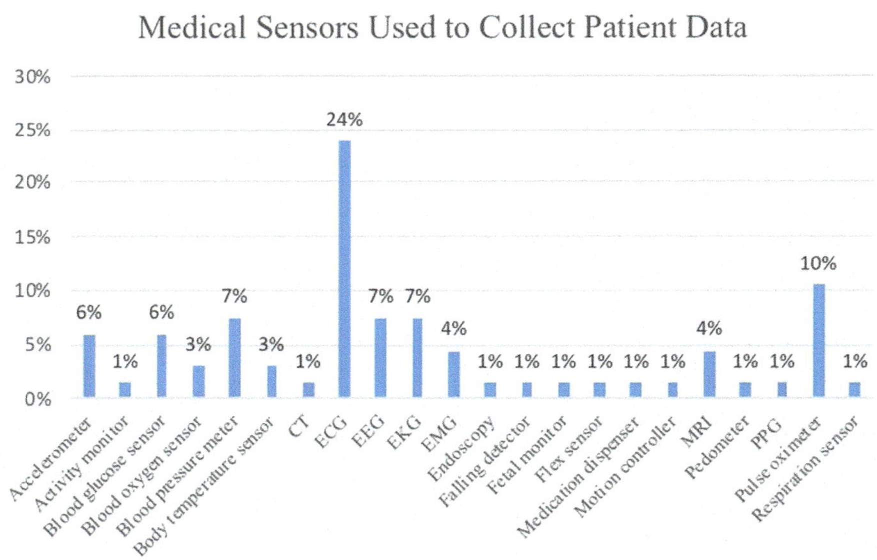

Fig. 8.4 Types of end node medical sensors used to collect patient data

8.2.1 Analysis of Raw Data

The data collected, based on the above seven attributes, is presented in Table 8.2. Based on this, we were able to construct four analysis results as shown in Figs. 8.3, 8.4, 8.5 and 8.6. Summarization of the graphical analysis included the following factors:

- use of IoT healthcare applications
- end node sensors used to collect medical data

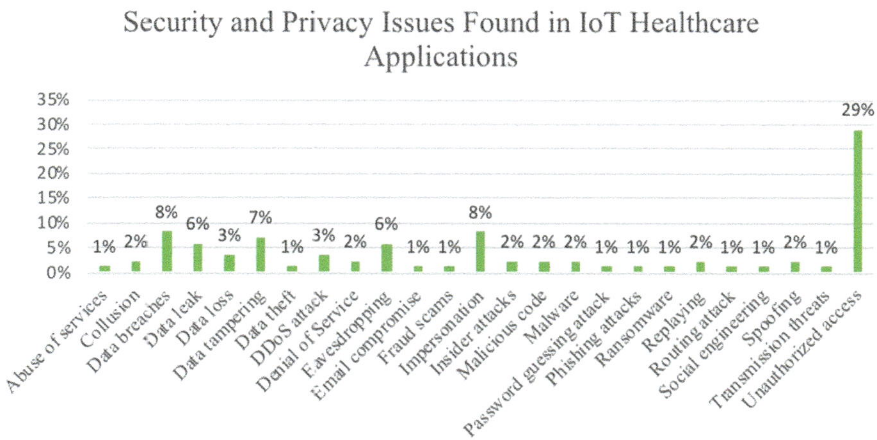

Fig. 8.5 Security and privacy issues found in IoT healthcare applications

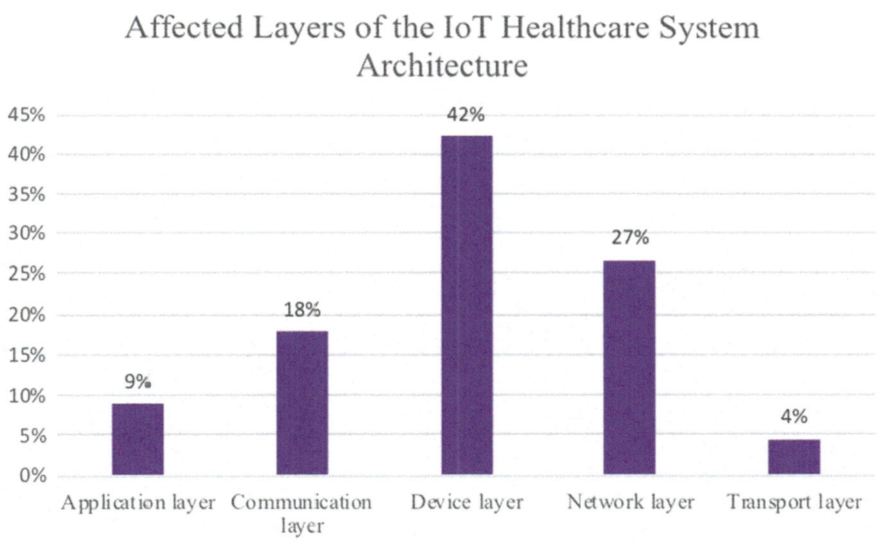

Fig. 8.6 Affected layers of the IoT healthcare system architecture

- privacy and security issues in IoT health care
- affected layers of the service architectures.

8.3 Further Analysis of Results

As mentioned before, data collected from 30 peer-reviewed articles published during 2016–2018 is presented in Table 8.2. As also mentioned in Sect. 8.2.1, further analysis was conducted in terms of the following factors:

- use of IoT healthcare applications
- end node sensors used to collect medical data
- privacy and security issues in IoT health care
- affected layers of the service architectures.

In the following subsections, we first categorize healthcare applications and then present further graphical analysis.

8.3.1 Categorization of IoT Health Applications by Use

IoT healthcare applications found in the literature review, as shown in Table 8.2, can be categorized into four main groups as follows:

- **Assisted living** applications which assist people with disabilities with the form at home smart devices [13]
- **Clinical care** applications to support decision-making by monitoring patients' health information [14]
- **Context awareness** applications which facilitate smartphones to provide location related services for the patients [15]
- **Remote monitoring** applications to assist patients who do not live on conventional healthcare facilities [16].

Table 8.3 represents this categorization.

8.3.2 Use of IoT Healthcare Applications

Figure 8.3 shows IoT healthcare applications concerning their use. Remote monitoring shows the highest 45% rate of use; and the context awareness applications have the lowest rate of use bearing only 5%. Clinical care and assisted living represent respectively 34% and 16% of usage.

Table 8.3 Categorizing the healthcare applications by the use

Use of IoT healthcare application	Healthcare applications
(1) Assisted living	Apple Healthkit [18]
	Fitcoracy [18]
	Google Fit [18]
	Google Health [32]
(2) Clinical care	BSN-Care [30]
	Codeblue [30]
	DigifitIcardio [18]
	eHealth [1]
	e-Medicine implants [17]
	HetNet [29]
	MEDiSN [12]
	MeDShare [11]
	SecureData [10]
	UbeHealth [30]
	UbiMon [11]
(3) Context awareness	mHealth [1]
(4) Remote monitoring	iMedBox [29]
	iMedPack [29]
	k-Healthcare [26]
	Microsoft health vault [28]
	MiiM [28]
	Mio [1]
	MobiCare [18]
	MySignals [32]
	RunKeeper [1]
	Samsung S Health [1]
	S-Health [2]

8.3.3 Use of End Node Medical Sensors (for Collection of Patient Data)

Figure 8.4 demonstrates the type of medical sensors used to collect patient data in an IoT healthcare environment. It shows that the highest number of these (24%) belong to ECG (Electrocardiography) sensors while activity monitor, CT (Computed Tomography), endoscopy, falling detector, fetal monitor, flex sensor, medication dispenser, motion controller, pedometer, PPG (Photoplethysmogram), and respiration sensor each having only 1% of usage.

8.3.4 Privacy/Security Issues in IoT Healthcare Applications

Figure 8.5 shows security and privacy issues found in IoT healthcare applications. With 29%, unauthorized access has been noted as the highest threat to an IoT healthcare system. Data breaches and impersonations are the next highest threats, at around 8%.

8.3.5 Affected Layers of the IoT Healthcare System Architecture

We can consider the IoT healthcare applications architecture as consisting of the following layers:

- Application
- Communication
- Device
- Network
- Transport.

Figure 8.6 presents the affected layers of the IoT healthcare system—affected by the security and privacy threats, that is. Here, we note that the rates of affect are as follows:

- application layer (9%)
- communication layer (18%)
- device layer (42%)
- network layer (27%)
- transport layer (4%).

Device layer suffers the highest impact while the transport layer is affected the lowest.

8.4 Discussion

This chapter is focused on providing an overview of privacy and security issues relating to IoT healthcare applications that normally operate on cloud- and fog-driven architectures. It offers a mechanism for application developers to have information that they can use to enhance the security and privacy features of IoT healthcare applications, when developing healthcare applications. The analysis also delivers awareness to patients and healthcare providers to protect their sensitive data from potential security threats and breaches; especially when healthcare applications contain highly sensitive data. Because of this, threats to these also have the highest impact rate. Research studies show that constant communication between IoT devices has widened the threat landscape of IoT networks. These communication processes are categorized mainly into the machine to machine and people to machine communication [8].

Use of IoT hosted on the cloud offers multiple benefits such as economies of scale, improved efficiency and minimal human effort [3]. The applications built for health care are targeted to care for patients in medical care facilities as well as patients who reside in their own homes. The end node sensors are used to collect data from the patients, gather information through wearable devices and implants.

Examples of data attributes with respect to sensory devices referred to in the study are: heart rate, body temperature, blood sugar level, and brain activity [3, 6, 7, 9, 10, 12, 17]. Unauthorized access, data breach, data leak, data loss, data tampering [6, 7, 9, 10, 12, 17], eavesdropping, impersonation, denial of service and malware [1, 16, 18–20] have been identified as the top threats to an IoT healthcare application. Research has shown that unauthorized access is by far the most common threat to sensitive data in an IoT environment [17]. Other studies are consistent with the findings of our research. Based on these data, we have outlined an overview of the threats landscape to improve the security of data in the system and presented strategies to strengthen the security of the device and network layers (refer to Fig. 8.6). It is also proven that these threats are associated with data exchange. In the current study, we have provided possible solutions to overcome the issues found. Majority of the solutions fall under providing security controls with appropriate measures such as encryption methods to protect data from unauthorized access [6], password protection schemes [5], and access controlling methods [12]. However, some of the solutions are concentrated on a strategic approach—providing users with awareness building programs and training, implementing auditability methods in the systems and data governance frameworks [2].

Even though there has not been a valid evidence to suggest that there are life-threatening risks to a patient's life because of security or privacy breach to a medical sensor, the latest studies have suggested that ransomware would be the next biggest threat to IoT healthcare applications [21]. These threats are believed to extend from wearable medical devices. However, more and more industries are leaning over to the IoT technology due to its cost effective and efficient functionality compared to other technologies. At present, privacy risks associated with IoT healthcare applications are head to head with security issues [21].

This chapter has identified medication dispensers as one of the medical devices that are being used in the IoT healthcare environment. A recent incident has been reported regarding security threats called cyber bugs in those devices. Since then, the FDA has excessively warned the medical care providers against using any medical devices that are prone to cybersecurity threats. The problem of threats increases in magnitude with attackers gaining access to a vulnerable device and using it to gain access to a network which holds even more sensitive information. This vicious cycle is hard to break with meager information security measures. According to Zhang et al. [21], blood pressure meters have been identified as the most commonly used medical device used to collect patient data [22]. However, our findings suggest that the ECG sensor devices are the most used medical devices to collect patient data; and blood pressure meters as the second most used devices. This raises a question regarding the efficiency of the data collected. Nevertheless, due to limitations and constraints during data gathering process, these discrepancies are unavoidable in most researches.

Findings of a few similar studies have failed to use the sensor devices which have limited the data gathering process [7, 17]. As a result, it has hindered developing an inclusive landscape for threats and risks identification. The other main limitation is the size of databases used for the studies. Sometimes, these data sets are restricted to only one area of use and target only one layer of the architecture or form a limited number of end sensor nodes [1, 6, 9–12]. Moreover, the majority of healthcare facilities where patient data are stored, still use legacy systems. The inability to include those data makes a huge difference to such studies. Also, due to issues related to privacy control issues such as patients consent, most medical professionals have been reluctant to provide patient data. The problem arises due to the fact that patient data are considered sensitive information. So, there are a few hurdles to go through to collect such data. There are rules and regulations, not to mention a solid privacy act, which is considered to be one of the most challenging rules to consider when collecting patient data. Besides, there are certain conditions set by government healthcare departments regarding collecting patient data [7]. Furthermore, some of the studies have focused their entire research into analyzing only a limited number of threats [11]. This limits the overall threat landscape. The other main weakness is that a few of the data sets we used are not from recent studies [2].

Although our study is focused on providing the latest threats and risks to IoT healthcare scenario, this issue has a drastic impact on the outcome. Some studies offer additional useful information; however, they lack providing adequate justification for the accuracy of the findings at the same time [5]. These research gaps have restricted us to construct a holistic approach to find out challenges to IoT health care. However, most of the literature review which is completed through similar studies have provided ample useful information to carry out the research in a fruitful manner.

Furthermore, future research should not limit the findings only to the most occurring threats to IoT healthcare applications. Instead, they should attempt to discover the root causes of the threats and find a better way to manage those threats without compromising security and privacy of patient data. Moreover, the concept of IoT health care should be promoted to gain a bigger audience since it could change the way of modern health care, as we know it, and provide better and improved services for people in need. In conclusion, the focus of this chapter is to strengthen the IoT healthcare provision by finding the security and privacy-related threats to the applications and offering an overview to improve and enhance the applications to secure patient data in data collection, and storage processes.

8.5 Future Directions

Even though it is identified that unauthorized access is the most common threat to IoT health care, most of the issues regarding security and privacy occur indirectly mainly due to human error. Human error is often regarded as unintentional and benign; however, they add problems to a threats landscape. The problem in this scenario lies with the fact that there are a huge number of people involved in the process. If the patient is given the control over who can access what data, the control aspect of the issue would minimize dramatically. Since, as recognized with access control, most of the problems identified would be resolved and much more could be accomplished in the entire process. Implementing a data governance strategy with appropriate policies regarding IoT healthcare applications would be the most successful way to overcome these issues. However, it needs to be placed strategically encompassing all the wrongs of current systems from an accessibility viewpoint. Therefore, this is an important issue for future research. Further study with more focus on application information control is recommended.

8.6 Conclusion

This chapter focuses on providing an overview of security and privacy issues of IoT healthcare applications. The analysis of the research was completed by reviewing 30 peer-reviewed publications selected from academic journals databases. The study has shown that data collection, exchange, and storage as the fundamental processes of data management in the IoT environments. The healthcare applications used for this study were further categorized into four groups as: (1) remote monitoring, (2) clinical care, (3) context awareness, and (4) assisted living. Applications used for remote monitoring have shown the highest number of usages. An excessive examination was conducted to analyze the end node medical sensors used to collect data from the patients using wearable smart devices. ECG sensors were found as the most used sensory device. The most critical analysis was carried out to detect privacy, and security-related threats in this environment and the majority of them were recognized as threats mainly to sensitive data. It is discovered that unauthorized access holds the highest rate for security threats. Additionally, the affected layers of the services architectures were identified; it was found that the device layer of the applications architecture has the highest impact as a result of security threats.

Application developers and designers could use the review presented in this chapter as a basis to improve the security of the health-related applications; and to provide a better environment for sensitive patient data by placing appropriate controls to overcome the identified challenges. This study could also be useful to design mitigation strategies to overcome the identified vulnerabilities in the healthcare applications in the IoT environment.

References

1. Rahmani AM, Gia TN, Negash B, Anzanpour A, Azimi I, Jiang M, Liljeberg P (2018) Exploiting smart e-Health gateways at the edge of healthcare Internet-of-Things: a fog computing approach. Future Gener Comput Syst 78:641–658
2. Almulhim M, Zaman N (2018) Proposing secure and lightweight authentication scheme for IoT based E-health applications. In: 2018 20th international conference on advanced communication technology (ICACT). IEEE, pp 481–487
3. Medvediev I, Illiashenko O, Uzun D, Strielkina A (2018) IoT solutions for health monitoring: analysis and case study. In: 2018 IEEE 9th international conference on dependable systems, services and technologies (DESSERT). IEEE, pp 163–168
4. Chako A, Hayajneh T (2018) Security and privacy issues with IoT in healthcare. https://www.researchgate.net/publication/326568227_Security_and_Privacy_Issues_with_IoT_in_Healthcare
5. Elhoseny M, Ramírez-González G, Abu-Elnasr OM, Shawkat SA, Arunkumar N, Farouk A (2018) Secure medical data transmission model for IoT-based healthcare systems. IEEE Access 6:20596–20608
6. Nausheen F, Begum SH (2018) Healthcare IoT: benefits, vulnerabilities and solutions. In: 2018 2nd international conference on inventive systems and control (ICISC). IEEE, pp 517–522
7. Manogaran G, Varatharajan R, Lopez D, Kumar PM, Sundarasekar R, Thota C (2018) A new architecture of Internet of Things and big data ecosystem for secured smart healthcare monitoring and alerting system. Future Gener Comput Syst 82:375–387
8. Salahuddin MA, Al-Fuqaha A, Guizani M, Shuaib K, Sallabi F (2018) Softwarization of Internet of Things infrastructure for secure and smart healthcare. arXiv:1805.11011
9. He D, Ye R, Chan S, Guizani M, Xu Y (2018) Privacy in the Internet of Things for smart healthcare. IEEE Commun Mag 56(4):38–44
10. Tao H, Bhuiyan MZA, Abdalla AN, Hassan MM, Zain JM, Hayajneh T (2018) Secured data collection with hardware-based ciphers for IoT-based healthcare. IEEE Internet Things J
11. Uddin MA, Stranieri A, Gondal I, Balasubramanian V (2018) Continuous patient monitoring with a patient centric agent: a block architecture. IEEE Access 6:32700–32726
12. Luo E, Bhuiyan MZA, Wang G, Rahman MA, Wu J, Atiquzzaman M (2018) Privacy protector: privacy-protected patient data collection in IoT-based healthcare systems. IEEE Commun Mag 56(2):163–168
13. Yang G, Xie L, Mäntysalo M, Zhou X, Pang Z, Da Xu L, Zheng LR (2014) A health-IoT platform based on the integration of intelligent packaging, unobtrusive bio-sensor, and intelligent medicine box. IEEE Trans Ind Inform 10(4):2180–2191
14. Singh B, Bhattacharya S, Chowdhary CL, Jat DS (2017) A review on Internet of Things and its applications in healthcare. J Chem Pharm Sci 10(1):447–452
15. Gomez J, Oviedo B, Zhuma E (2016) Patient monitoring system based on internet of things. Procedia Comput Sci 83:90–97
16. Hossain MS, Muhammad G (2016) Cloud-assisted industrial internet of things (IIoT)-enabled framework for health monitoring. Comput Netw 101:192–202
17. Farahani B, Firouzi F, Chang V, Badaroglu M, Constant N, Mankodiya K (2018) Towards fog-driven IoT eHealth: promises and challenges of IoT in medicine and healthcare. Future Gener Comput Syst 78:659–676
18. Ahmad M, Amin MB, Hussain S, Kang BH, Cheong T, Lee S (2016) Health fog: a novel framework for health and wellness applications. J Supercomput 72(10):3677–3695
19. Muhammed T, Mehmood R, Albeshri A, Katib I (2018) UbeHealth: a personalized ubiquitous cloud and edge-enabled networked healthcare system for smart cities. IEEE Access 6:32258–32285
20. Alam MM, Malik H, Khan MI, Pardy T, Kuusik A, Le Moullec Y (2018) A survey on the roles of communication technologies in IoT-based personalized healthcare applications. IEEE Access 6:36611–36631

21. Zhang Y, Qiu M, Tsai CW, Hassan MM, Alamri A (2017) Health-CPS: healthcare cyber-physical system assisted by cloud and big data. IEEE Syst J 11(1):88–95
22. Gupta P, Agrawal D, Chhabra J, Dhir PK (2016) IoT based smart healthcare kit. In: 2016 international conference on computational techniques in information and communication technologies (ICCTICT). IEEE, pp 237–242
23. Shen J, Chang S, Shen J, Liu Q, Sun X (2018) A lightweight multi-layer authentication protocol for wireless body area networks. Future Gener Comput Syst 78:956–963
24. Li S, Tryfonas T, Li H (2016) The Internet of Things: a security point of view. Internet Res 26(2):337–359
25. Kim S, Kim S (2018) User preference for an IoT healthcare application for lifestyle disease management. Telecommun Policy 42(4):304–314
26. Sharma S, Chen K, Sheth A (2018) Toward practical privacy-preserving analytics for IoT and cloud-based healthcare systems. IEEE Internet Comput 22(2):42–51
27. Woo MW, Lee J, Park K (2018) A reliable IoT system for personal healthcare devices. Future Gener Comput Syst 78:626–640
28. Park K, Park J, Lee J (2017) An IoT system for remote monitoring of patients at home. Appl Sci 7(3):260
29. Islam SR, Kwak D, Kabir MH, Hossain M, Kwak KS (2015) The Internet of Things for health care: a comprehensive survey. IEEE Access 3:678–708
30. Gope P, Hwang T (2016) BSN-Care: a secure IoT-based modern healthcare system using body sensor network. IEEE Sens J 16(5):1368–1376
31. Laplante PA, Laplante N (2016) The Internet of Things in healthcare: potential applications and challenges. IT Prof 3:2–4
32. Tyagi S, Agarwal A, Maheshwari P (2016) A conceptual framework for IoT-based healthcare system using cloud computing. In: 2016 6th international conference cloud system and big data engineering (confluence). IEEE, pp 503–507
33. Ullah K, Shah MA, Zhang S (2016) Effective ways to use Internet of Things in the field of medical and smart health care. In: 2016 international conference on intelligent systems engineering (ICISE). IEEE, pp 372–379
34. Natarajan K, Prasath B, Kokila P (2016) Smart health care system using Internet of Things. J Netw Commun Emerg Technol (JNCET) 6(3)
35. Sailunaz K, Alhussein M, Shahiduzzaman M, Anowar F, Al Mamun KA (2016) CMED: cloud based medical system framework for rural health monitoring in developing countries. Comput Electr Eng 53:469–481

Chapter 9
A Comparative Study in the Application of IoT in Health Care: Data Security in Telemedicine

G. A. Pramesha Chandrasiri, Malka N. Halgamuge and C. Subhashi Jayasekara

Abstract Internet of Things (IoT) is the backbone of telemedicine and its data security has become a significant concern that requires further attention. Therefore, this study was conducted with the aim of analyzing telemedicine systems, focusing on data security measures. Thirty peer-reviewed research studies published in 2018 were reviewed and compared according to certain parameters, viz., algorithms, IoT sensors, data encryption ability, communication mechanisms, mobile accessibility, protocols, software, and platforms. The results illustrate that transmitting sensitive medical data over the Internet has been identified as a major threat, and solutions such as ciphertext-policy attribute-based encryption and Secure Better Portable Graphics (SBPG) architecture have been developed to authenticate and protect data by concurrent encryption and watermarking. Furthermore, the comparison reveals that data encryption is the most frequently used secure data transmission method and 32% of the reviewed studies have focused on this. Regarding the most frequently used technologies, Raspberry Pi3 Edge platform (with the usage percentage of 60), TCP/IP protocol (with usage of 38%), and ECG and temperature sensors (with usage of 20%) have been discussed. Additionally, telemedicine has focused on standalone systems, and, in this context, integrated systems with micro-services are yet to be improved. Therefore, this study compares and analyzes the significant technical trends, security trends, widely used IoT sensors, platforms, and protocols; the aim is to help the researchers to gain a better insight into telemedicine to improve healthcare services by maximizing the capabilities of Internet of Things.

Keywords IoT · Telemedicine · Algorithms · Encryption · Platform · Architecture · Sensors · Big data · Health care

---

G. A. Pramesha Chandrasiri · C. Subhashi Jayasekara
School of Computing and Mathematics, Charles Sturt University, Melbourne, VIC 3000, Australia
e-mail: pramesha_chandrasiri@yahoo.com.au

C. Subhashi Jayasekara
e-mail: subhashi@ieee.org

M. N. Halgamuge (✉)
Department of Electrical and Electronic Engineering, The University of Melbourne, Parkville, VIC 3010, Australia
e-mail: malka.nisha@unimelb.edu.au

Z. Mahmood (ed.), *Security, Privacy and Trust in the IoT Environment*, https://doi.org/10.1007/978-3-030-18075-1_9

9.1 Introduction

The Internet of Things (IoT) in telemedicine involves the inter-connected devices and technologies. Recently, it has raised greater concerns over the security of health-related data. There exist several types of research [1–4], based on the IoT applications in telemedicine suggesting that IoT can be used to monitor patients, provide immediate treatments, and keep track of health records since the IoT approach offers the provision of quick and accurate medical services [1] with real-time connectivity. While security threats are the primary issue in telemedicine area, the other problems of concern include mechanisms such as data storage and data access. To overcome the data security issues, researches have proposed a secure and trusted communication architecture by cyphertext-policy attribute-based encryption [1]. This encryption uses algorithm pattern identification, data filtering, authentication, and authorization, and the proposed model gives security at the communication link by allowing user authentication and privacy management.

Another application of IoT in telemedicine includes telemedicine platform for diabetes control and management called "Saleem" [2]. The proposed architecture collects behavioral and health data from patients and performs data mining to produce useful information. The results are visualized to the end parties including doctors and patients. The proposed platform provides feedback and alerts messages to the patients to avoid complications in the disease. Patients can compare symptoms with other patients, and doctors can give recommendations to patients to prevent severe situations in the future.

An algorithm for IoT-enabled telesonography [3] is another example of the application of IoT in telemedicine. This novel algorithm helps to scan ultrasound to validate data automatically. In this system, the scanned ultrasound videos are sent to an expert for analysis. If the scanned ultrasound video contains a smaller number of representative frames, then the non-expertise can go for rescanning until the representative data for diagnosis is obtained.

Fiber Bragg grating-based monitoring system [4] for age care and nursing facilities uses IoT sensors to monitor pulse rate, temperature, movements, and bed exit. Using this system, residents in aged care facilities can be remotely controlled to provide better care for them. If there are any strange behaviors, they will be detected by the system which will give alerts to the staffs and doctors in their mobile devices, and if the residents need help, the warnings can be made through the system as well.

Big data also plays a significant role in telemedicine as converting big data into meaningful visualized data chunks helps for better understanding of data elements. There are also systems [5, 6] to monitor health using visualizing techniques to check and monitor patient's status and draw a polygon on a map, visualizing the markers in the area where every marker runs in a circular view showing different parameters to monitor patient's health status. These systems are user-friendly because it visualizes graphics that would help to monitor patients remotely by supporting geoJSON standards.

IoT cloud-based network for anesthesia online monitoring [7] is another application of IoT in telemedicine. Through an Android app, the proposed system lets the doctors remain connected to the patients all the time, and the medical data of patients can be shared on the cloud via a web application allowing teleconsulting. Using this method [8], the doctors can check the data shared from any location at any time. It provides three drugs monitoring, body temperature, and pH level monitoring.

PillSense [9] is another system designed to monitor patients. It is capable of reminding patients to take medicines when an unusual health condition is detected, and the messages are sent via emails or SMS (Short Messaging Service). It can monitor health indicators such as blood pressure, body temperature, heart rate, respiration rate, and movements of the body. Also, this system has a set of different sensors and interfaces to detect changes and abnormalities. Finally, the system decreases the human errors and makes the process of providing medications more efficient and effective while tracking the health conditions seamlessly.

Researches have also introduced a cloud-based heart rate variability (HRV) remote monitoring system [10, 11]. It is low cost, easy to apply, and accurate, and ensures the security of data, while the system is acting as the interface between health care and the patient. This novel health monitoring system analyzes the HRV by extracting data from wearable sensors attached to the user. The system has been tested, and all the tests have shown positive and successful results. Also, the proposed method enables warning messages to the patients as well as to the doctors.

IoT in telemedicine has also been used in systems that consist of wireless sensor networks and diaphragmatic electromyogram (EMGdi) [12] for respiratory diseases by introducing a norm-based method where the network collects physiological data (EMGdi), performs compression, and sends signals to a smartphone in a low-cost, reduced-energy consumption way. Also, a novel architecture called BodyEdge [13] has been designed to boost healthcare applications. This has reduced bandwidth and low processing time. It has been tested on different hardware platforms. This system can run on low-cost and data loading, and processing delay can be very low due to network conditions.

Another application of IoT in telemedicine is an experiment focused on SBPG architecture using data protection and authentication with concurrent encryption and watermarking in smart health care [14]. It discusses the requirements of having an automated analysis of biomedical images, and secure communication using IoT infrastructure. This research has been conducted to develop the energy-efficient real-time architecture to validate the security of medical images where the medical data can be stored securely, and integrity can be verified. Further researches should be carried out on nonimage biomedical data as future work.

As discussed above, since the security of medical data becomes more challenging, the researchers have introduced a system which can translate text data into the form of images. This system [15] has been developed using 2-D discrete wavelet transform 1-level, and 2-D discrete wavelet transforms 2-level steganography with hybrid encryption. The proposed system hides the confidential and sensitive medical data by transmitting them into a cover image. As a result of this technique, even when the system has been hacked, the data will not be visible to the hackers.

The m-Green-cardio embedded system [16] proposes a device that is wearable and that detects the immediate situations of patients depending on ECG data that it collects. There are models [17] based on system modeling languages to monitor elderly people by monitoring phycological signals, where the model collects real-time data and is very useful compared to other similar models.

Medication monitoring systems as reported in [6, 18] are useful in the telemedicine field. In previous studies, "sensing techniques" have been used within the IoT-based applications. The medication monitoring systems with the medication bottles include a magnetic switch, an accelerometer, and a load cell to allow mobility, and user acceptance of the system. Actual experiments were carried successfully, and the results of the experiment included monitoring patients and a multisensory system. A significant advantage of this research is the system working on a single-cell battery for 22 days while monitoring multiple health-related tasks.

Considering all those studies conducted so far, it is evident that different researches have been focused on different areas of IoT in telemedicine. However, there were no significant records of any research publication that compares and analyzes the latest trends in applications of IoT in telemedicine. Therefore, this study aims to provide an insight into the areas that require to be addressed in the field of IoT in telemedicine.

As shown in Fig. 9.1, this study aims to compare and contrast the existing and reported applications of IoT applications in telemedicine, by discussing the most frequently used platforms, protocols, data encryption enabled models, and the sensor usages of the IoT in telemedicine.

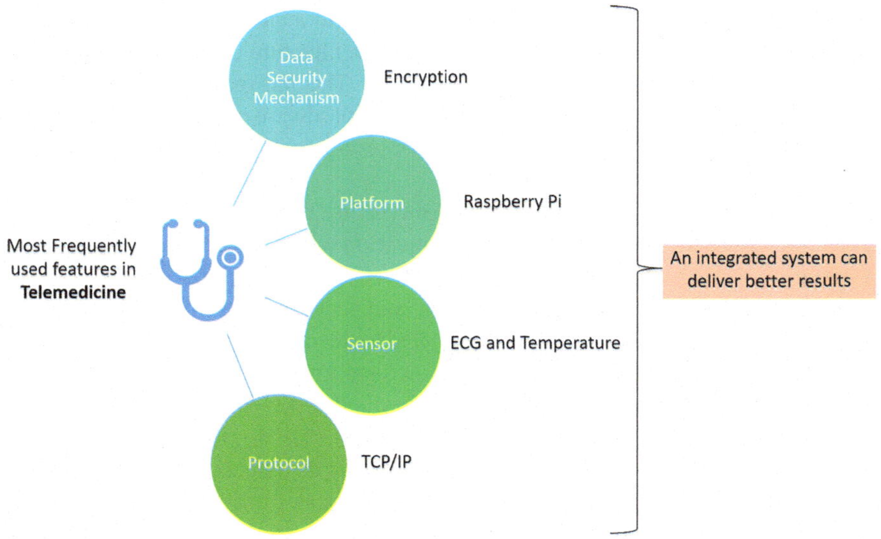

Fig. 9.1 Analysis of peer-reviewed studies and determination of significant and most frequently used features of IoT in telemedicine

9.2 Methodology

The present research was conducted using 30 peer-reviewed research studies published in 2018 and the required data collected from these articles. During the study, 13 IoT sensor devices, 5 platforms, and 7 types of protocols were recognized for further analysis. For the extraction of data, the following data inclusion criteria were used.

Data Inclusion Criteria

A system consists of two major parts: software and hardware. For the software component of a system, we considered the algorithms, the software, and the platforms used in the research papers. The aim was to investigate the encryption mechanisms for security. To study the hardware side of the systems, we considered the IoT devices, mentioned in these studies, as the core components. As IoT requires a communication element to connect with other devices, communication mechanism, protocol, and mobile accessibility were considered for discussion. Therefore, altogether, collected data from the articles were further analyzed according to eight identified criteria in telemedicine and security measures as follows:

- Algorithms,
- IoT devices,
- encryption mechanisms,
- communication mechanisms,
- mobile accessibility,
- protocols,
- software, and
- platforms.

Table 9.1 presents the extracted data according to the criteria as defined above.

9.3 Evaluation of Collected Data

The results were generated after conducting a further analysis of data gathered under each criterion (as mentioned above) from the tabled information (as presented in Table 9.1). The results were in terms of the same eight criteria as were used for the extraction of relevant data (as presented in Table 9.1). Results are presented in the following subsections.

Table 9.1 Comparison of features available in IoT devices in telemedicine

Articles	Algorithms	IOT devices	Encryption enabled?	Communication mechanism	Mobile access allowed?	Protocols	Software	Platforms
Albalawi and Joshi [1]	Secure Communication Algorithm CP-ABE and AES algorithm	IOT sensor IOT adapter contextual sensor	Yes. Ciphertext-policy attribute-based encryption (CP-ABE)	Radio frequency/bi communications	Yes	TCP/IP	IOT hub	Big data platform
Alelyani and Ibrahim [2]	Machine learning deep learning algorithms	IOT sensors, HIS, self-quantification	No	–	Yes	–	–	–
Bharath and Rajalakshmi [3]	Diagnostically driven compression algorithm ultrasound video validation algorithm	–	No	WebRTC peer-to-peer communication	Yes	Session initiation protocol/jingle	–	–
Foo et al. [4]	Simple algorithm using variance	IOT sensor FBG-based optical fiber sensors polysomnography devices, IoT thermometer BCG sensor mat	No	–	Yes	Internet protocol	Service application-programming interfaces	Tomcat platform

(continued)

Table 9.1 (continued)

Articles	Algorithms	IOT devices	Encryption enabled?	Communication mechanism	Mobile access allowed?	Protocols	Software	Platforms
Kuusik et al. [5]	Data visualization algorithm	Motion sensor units (IMUs) IoT sensor Wireless sensors	No	–	Yes	Internet protocol (IP)		PIP platform
Aldeer et al. [6]	PillSense operation algorithm	Motion sensors Weight sensors Magnetic switch sensor Accelerometer	No	–	Yes	–	–	–
Hussein et al. [7]	Pan-Tompkins QRS detection algorithm	IOT sensor	Yes Homomorphic encryption (HE)	Two-way wireless communication	Yes	–	–	Cloud computing along with the BSN data stream middleware
Elhoseny et al. [9]	Combination of advanced encryption standard, and Rivest, Shamir, and Adleman algorithms	IP camera	Yes steganography technique and a hybrid encryption	–	Yes	Communication protocol	MATLAB R2015a	–

(continued)

Table 9.1 (continued)

Articles	Algorithms	IOT devices	Encryption enabled?	Communication mechanism	Mobile access allowed?	Protocols	Software	Platforms
Zagan et al. [11]	–	Temperature sensor	No	Modbus Poll	Yes	GSM/GPRS/3G/TCP-IP	Microcontroller software	MCBSTM32 kit and Keil development platform hSensor platform
Aloi et al. [12]	Stress detection algorithm	Body sensors Communication engine	No	Multi-radio and multi-technology Client–server communication BE-GTW interface management	Yes	IoT device management protocol Application protocol CoAP, MQTT, LwM2M	–	Azure cloud platform Raspberry Pi3 edge platform
Saha et al. [13]	–	Heartbeat sensor Blood pressure sensor Respiration sensor Temperature sensor Accelerometer sensor	No	–	Yes	–	Putty software	Raspberry Pi

(continued)

Table 9.1 (continued)

Articles	Algorithms	IOT devices	Encryption enabled?	Communication mechanism	Mobile access allowed?	Protocols	Software	Platforms
Mohanty et al. [14]	BPG compression algorithm., novel algorithm called the scale adaptive object tracking (SAOT)	CMOS sensors, digital signal routing and a complex system CPU, SDC (Secure digital camera) BPG encoder, BPG decoder, Javascript decoder, and BPG viewer	Yes, two layer encryption seamless integration of water-marking, encryption facility is secure better portable graphics (SBPG)	–	Yes	–	–	–
Kotronis et al. [15]	–	IOT medical sensors	No	Bluetooth low energy (BLE) or ZigBee	Yes	IPSec	–	Healthcare network internet
Aloi et al. [12]	–	Multi-radio and multi-technology communication Mall range communication ZigBee, ZWAVE, Wi-Fi, Bluetooth, Bluetooth low energy, ANT+, Z-wave, ZigBee, Wi-Fi, LTE/5G	Yes	Application protocol, CoAP, MQTT, LwM2M	Yes	Public/private cloud platforms Raspberry Pi3 single board and ii) Zotac CI540 NANO Pc Edge (Raspberry Pi3) Edge (Nano PC) Azure cloud	–	BodyEdge, a novel architecture BE-GTW architecture

(continued)

Table 9.1 (continued)

Articles	Algorithms	IOT devices	Encryption enabled?	Communication mechanism	Mobile access allowed?	Protocols	Software	Platforms
Wu et al. [17]	Compressed sensing algorithm	WBAN sensors	No	Wireless body area network (WBANs) Diaphragmatic electromyogram (EMGdi),	Yes	–	–	–
Hussein et al. [7]	Pan-Tompkins QRS detection algorithm	WBAN sensors	Yes. Using advanced encryption standard (AES)	ZigBee wireless communication system	Yes	–	–	Cloud computing platform along with the BSN Data stream middleware
Guo et al. [19]	–	WBAN sensors	No	On-the-go (OTG) wire to keep communication	Yes	–	–	The medical network platform
Stradolini et al. [10]	–	WBAN sensors	No. But uses pre-shared access feature, to secure transfer data	Bidirectional communication	Yes	TCP/IP	Qt Creator 3.2 software with Qt 5.3 libraries.	Therapeutic drug monitoring (TDM) platforms

(continued)

Table 9.1 (continued)

Articles	Algorithms	IOT devices	Encryption enabled?	Communication mechanism	Mobile access allowed?	Protocols	Software	Platforms
Islam et al. [20]	–	WBAN sensors	No	Short-range communications technology	Yes	Standard protocol	–	–
Saha et al. [13]	–	WBAN sensors	No. But uses a role-based user authentication	–	Yes	–	Raspbian	Raspberry Pi
Santos et al. [21]	Sliding window algorithm	WBAN sensors	No	Physiologically-aware communication architecture	Yes	Communication protocol	–	–
Hamici et al. [22]	Novel genetic algorithm Genetic cryptography algorithm	WBAN sensors	No	–	Yes	TCP/IP	–	–

(continued)

Table 9.1 (continued)

Articles	Algorithms	IOT devices	Encryption enabled?	Communication mechanism	Mobile access allowed?	Protocols	Software	Platforms
Nadrag et al. [23]	Pulse detection algorithm Video-based heart rate Detection algorithm AdaBoost learning algorithm	WBAN sensors	No	–	Yes	–	–	Android and Raspberry Pi
Hamici et al. [22]	Novel genetic algorithm End-to-end node-server security algorithms Cryptographic algorithms	WBAN sensors	Yes	–	–	TCP/IP protocol	–	–
Rajagopalan et al. [24]	AES and gold code algorithm AES algorithm	WBAN sensors	Yes symmetric block cipher	Image communication mechanism	Yes	–	–	–

(continued)

Table 9.1 (continued)

Articles	Algorithms	IOT devices	Encryption enabled?	Communication mechanism	Mobile access allowed?	Protocols	Software	Platforms
Galletta et al. [25]	Nonlinear regression algorithm	WBAN sensors	No	Video communication	Yes	–	–	MyGene Friends Web platform
Satyanarayana et al. [26]	A K-NN (K-Nearest Neighbor) based algorithm	WBAN sensors	No	Cellular IoT communication	Yes	–	–	Raspberry Pi
Chakravorty et al. [18]	–	WBAN sensors	No	–	Yes	–	–	Raspberry Pi
Lavanya et al. [27]	Signature verifying algorithm	WBAN sensors	Yes	–	Yes	–	–	PREDIX iFOGSIM
Enciso-Quispe et al. [8]	–	WBAN sensors	No	–	Yes	–	–	DHIS2

9.3.1 Use of Algorithms, Communication Mechanisms, Mobile Accessibility, and Software

According to the analysis on algorithm, only 66.67% of the reported studies have discussed these and 50% of them have used data analysis algorithms once the data were collected from sensors. The rest have only displayed detected data without analyzing. Moreover, the algorithms are specific to the purpose and the output of the system and therefore, we were unable to compare algorithms to find the most suitable algorithms for the development of integrated systems.

As for the communication mechanisms, it is noted that a variety of 16 different mechanisms have been considered. However, the most common mechanisms have been: Radio frequency, two-way wireless communication, ZigBee wireless communication system, and image communication mechanism for the enablement of encryption. Considering the mobile accessibility of the system, it is noted that all the systems allowed mobile accessibility. Moreover, only 23% of the reviewed studies have discussed the used software; and these were of seven different varieties. Out of these, only IoT hub and MATLAB R2015a were the software systems that enabled encryption.

As for the analysis of the remaining four criteria (usage of IoT sensors, encryption ability, used platforms, and used protocols), and for the possibility of their application to a generic integrated system, results are presented in the following four subsections.

9.3.2 Use of IoT Sensors in Telemedicine

Figure 9.2 shows that the frequently used sensor types in 2018 have been ECG sensors and the temperature sensors: their usages being 20% each. Blood pressure sensors and motion sensors were used moderately, and the sensing devices such as fiber sensors, motion sensors, and contextual sensors were used less frequently.

9.3.3 Use of Encryption in IoT Data Transmission in Telemedicine

Figure 9.3 shows the Encryption Usage of Data Transmission in the IoT in telemedicine. 32% of the conducted research has enabled encryption as an extra feature in the application of IoT in telemedicine, while the majority of remaining 68% have enabled encryption in earnest.

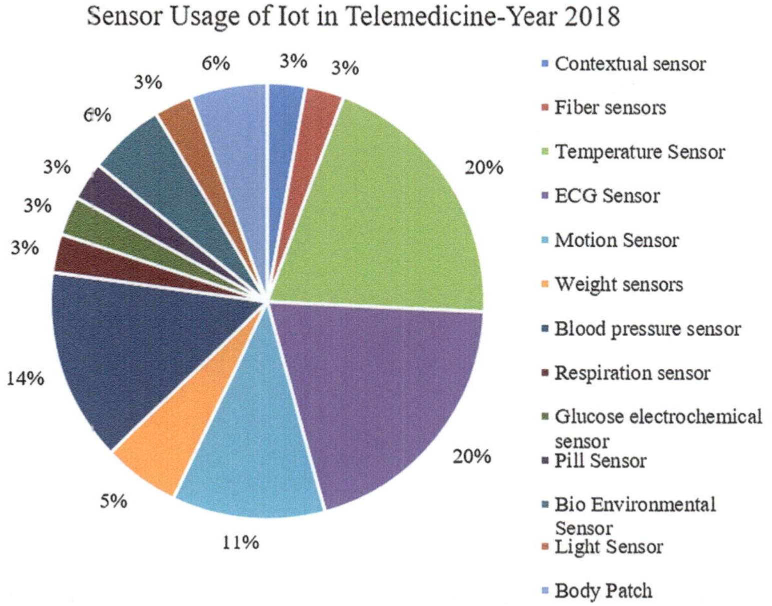

Fig. 9.2 Usage of IoT sensors in telemedicine

Fig. 9.3 Encryption usage of data transmission in IoT in telemedicine

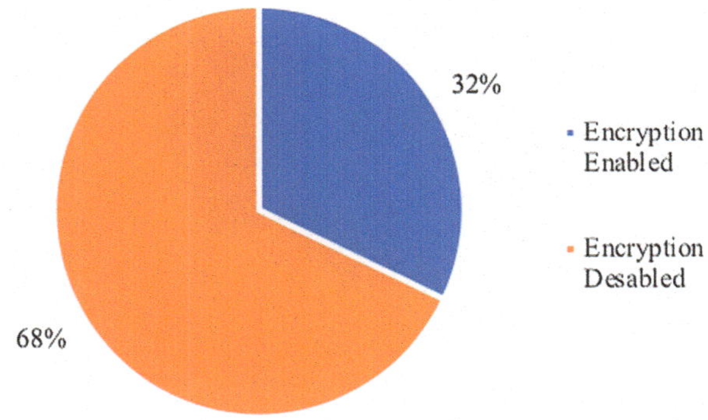

9.3.4 Use of IoT Platforms in Telemedicine

Considering the platform usage of IoT in telemedicine, Fig. 9.4 shows that the majority of 60% of the research used Raspberry Pi and the platforms such as PIP, hSensor, Tomcat, and big data are equally and moderately common in the telemedicine field showing approximately 10% of the usage in each case.

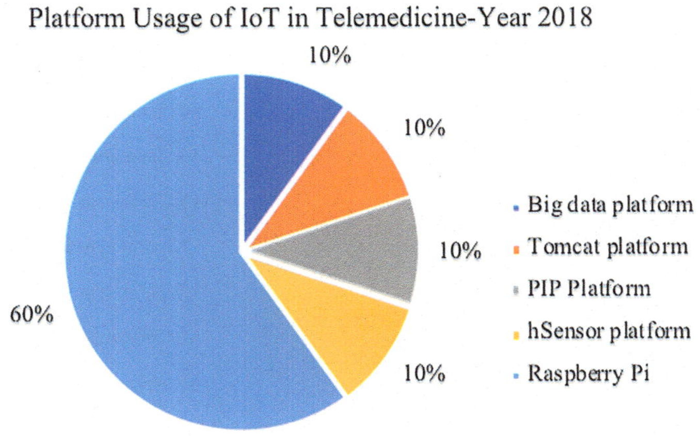

Fig. 9.4 Platform usage of IoT in telemedicine

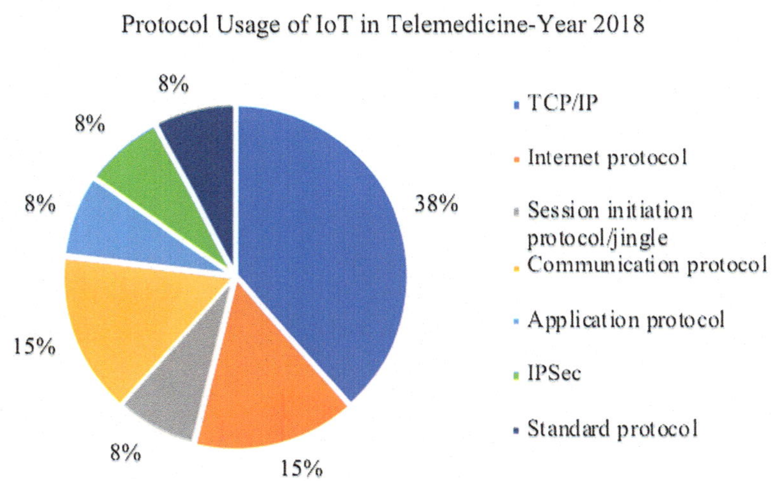

Fig. 9.5 Usage of IoT protocols in telemedicine

9.3.5 Use of IoT Protocols in Telemedicine

Figure 9.5 presents the usage of IoT protocols in telemedicine. It is found that most used protocol is TCP/IP where the contribution is 38% of the total usage. The second most used protocols have been Internet protocol and communication protocol where its contribution is around 15%. Moreover, protocols such as session initiation, standard, IPSec, and Application contributed only 8% each, of the total.

9.4 Discussion

The current study focuses on comparing and analyzing the IoT-based applications in the telemedicine sector as reported in the literature published during the year 2018. Telemedicine and IoT technologies are typically dealing with an extensive number of connected devices and health data stores and exchange data between those devices. Thus, the security and privacy are the utmost important factors in such telemedicine application and related applications. Also, the platforms must be able to fulfill the data security requirements in every aspect. During the study, we have explored various IoT-based sensors used in telemedicine. Further, we have examined 30 peer-reviewed articles and analyzed the proportion of the use of encryption features for data transmission in different telemedicine applications. Moreover, we have also investigated related platforms and protocols used in telemedicine in the 2018 publication year.

Many research articles related to IoT in telemedicine published in the year 2018 [1, 14] have focused on general security issues [1] and have proposed algorithms to overcome the problems. There is no detailed discussion on specific telemedicine services related issues, which can be generally applied as "Security data transmission" [13]. Most of the proposed systems [9] have not been tested in the real environment, and further experiments and observations should be carried out to test and prove their accuracy and reliability.

Another drawback in the research is that most of the proposed architectures [2] can detect only one disease, although these could have been applied to detect multiple diseases simultaneously as well as increasing the accuracy of determination. For instance, the studies conducted to validate videos in the telemedicine sector [3] have only 96.5% accuracy in identifying a representative frame in the ultrasound video. There is a risk of 3.5% where it is not able to locate representative frames. Since there still is a risk of not recognizing a disease accurately, further researches should be conducted to increase the probability closer to 100%. Moreover, the systems are generally based on the data that are collected by sensors only [4]. If there are faulty sensors that can harm the patient, there is no method to identify them in advance. Although there are machine learning algorithms [5] that can be helpful to analyze data, still, there is a possible risk of converting collected data into a visual form. However, systems should be further developed to be more intelligent with fault detection in advance and alert the necessary authorities.

Developing "Integrated" systems is another area that should be addressed in IoT-based telemedicine. For instance, Pill sensing system [6] which can only be used in pill-based medication systems can be improved for non-pill used monitoring systems as a part of IoT-based patient monitoring systems. A lot of other sensors could be connected to monitor various body conditions enabling the "Integrated" system features. A system designed for IoT for telemedicine practices enabled by Android™ Application with Cloud System Integration [7] has been proposed as an application to alert about critical patients one at a time. This can be further developed to alert about multiple critical patients simultaneously.

Another research reported in [9] has proposed a system to change the room environment depending on the data collected by the sensors. There is still a risk to rely on a few sensors as the measurements can be limited and a patient can have more complex and complicated health situations which cannot be detected by the available sensors. Furthermore, the research article [12] targeting low-cost and energy-saving communication capacity has not focused on the quality of the signals. This is a very important area which required attention, as the data transmitting plays a significant role in IoT in telemedicine.

Considering the quality of experiments, there is a study [13] conducted using 100 participants. This sample size is too small—if there was possibility of using data from a large number of participants, the quality of the research would have been increased. Also, efficiency is another area that should be discussed although there are systems that give less attention to that [14]. A proposed "Model-based Approach" as reported in [15] translates text data into the form of images. It is a unique way of transmitting medical data over the Internet. In the system, encryption mechanisms and other security mechanisms have been used. However, it requires to focus on high capacity, unpredictable, high deterioration steganography techniques where even though the system is been hacked, the data will not be visible to hackers.

The most effective method to anchor Electronic Medical Records (EMR), Electronic Health Records (HER), and Personal Health Records (PHR) is for the biological community to guarantee the privacy and integrity of the information. This is a functioning examination region where methodologies incorporate utilizing cryptographic natives, for example, those dependent upon basic public foundation and public clouds to guarantee information confidentiality and privacy [28]. In this scenario, data are encrypted before redistributing to the cloud. Nonetheless, this restrains the accessibility of the data, as for healthcare suppliers, we need to unscramble the (conceivably noteworthy) data [29]. Moreover, exploring diverse techniques for big data databases [30, 31] and accurate estimation of sensor power consumption would be another critical aspect of the IoT platform [32, 33].

Another exciting method as discussed in [34] provides multilevel security mechanism by exploiting the watermarking and chaotic encryption technique for telehealth applications. A delicate watermarking strategy which depends on singular value decomposition (SVD) and Arnold change for giving secure medical image transmission is presented in a study in [35]. Examining the proposed approach against different attacks demonstrated its enhanced execution. It concerns the peak-signal-to-noise ratio (PSNR) and accuracy of altering recognition in contrast with a portion of the ongoing methods [36–39]. The other comparable medical image watermarking procedures are introduced in many more studies as well [40–45].

In this research, we have investigated the IoT sensor usage in IoT-based telemedicine context as addressed in recent studies. We have explored different types of sensors and found that the ECG and temperature sensors are the most commonly used sensors. Besides, we have studied and analyzed the encryption facility usage in IoT telemedicine applications and found that most studies were not able to fulfill the encryption facility in data transmission. Consequently, we have seen that big data platforms, tomcat platforms, pip, hSensor platforms, and Raspberry Pi3 edge platform are the most common types of platforms that allow the data encryption feature.

Our research demonstrates that the significant research areas including IoT sensor usage, platforms, and protocols used in IoT telemedicine segment have also been used by previous similar research studies. During the survey, we found that investigations have only focused on one disease or two at a time. Thus, we can see that the future researches should be focusing on inventing a system that detects several disorders together as an integrated system. Moreover, future research in telemedicine context could consider implementing an integrated system that can remotely monitor patients.

9.5 Conclusion

This study compares and analyzes the applications of IoT in telemedicine sector in the research publication year 2018 showing that the data security in telemedicine is a significant concern. Having the ability to collect data, analyze, and distribute it fast has become the main reason for this concern although it facilitates the medical field to work more efficiently. However, according to our study, the available algorithms can be used to minimize the risk of security and privacy of data. Moreover, big data platforms, Tomcat platforms, pip, hSensor platforms, Raspberry Pi3, and Edge platform are the most common types of platforms that allow data encryption. The research also shows that the communication mechanisms such as two-way wireless communication and ZigBee wireless communication system enable the data security. Therefore, we can conclude that a combination of an underlying software that enables encryption along with a communication mechanism that ensures the privacy of data over transmission can provide a more secure system for IoT systems in telemedicine. Furthermore, we also conclude that the researchers have been focused on a single disease or health condition or a few at a time in the recent past. Hence, the future researchers should ideally focus on inventing systems that detect several illnesses together as an integrated system to make the maximum use of IoT technology to help the medical field. Considering the vast number of available sensors to detect different symptoms, robust algorithms to analyze, and finally transmit to different channels, it opens the possibilities for integrated systems. Furthermore, future research in telemedicine could consider an integrated system that can remotely monitor patients without direct human interactions. This automation process can be helpful to increase accuracy and also to alert the doctors and care workers whenever the sensors detect an anomality in a patient's body. With the end goal of accomplishing a unified structure, our current study hopefully provides critical technical and security trends with the most frequently utilized IoT sensors, platforms, software, and protocols in 2018. In conclusion, it will hopefully also guide the researchers and related authorities to improve telemedicine sector by expanding the capabilities of the Internet of Things in this field.

References

1. Albalawi U, Joshi S (2018) Secure and trusted telemedicine in internet of things IoT. In: IEEE 4th world forum on internet of things (WF-IoT)
2. Alelyani S, Ibrahim A (2018) Internet-of-things in telemedicine for diabetes management. In: 2018 15th learning and technology conference (L&T)
3. Bharath R, Rajalakshmi P (2018) WebRTC based invariant scattering convolution network for automated validation of ultrasonic videos for IoT enabled tele-sonography. In: 2018 IEEE 4th world forum on internet of things (WF-IoT)
4. Fook V, Jayachandran M, Jiliang E, Yongwei Z, Jianzhong E (2018) Fiber Bragg grating-based monitoring and alert system for care of residents in nursing homes. In: 2018 IEEE 4th world forum on internet of things (WF-IoT)
5. Kuusik A, Alam M, Kask T, Gross-Paju K (2018) Wearable m-assessment system for neurological disease patients. In: 2018 IEEE 4th world forum on internet of things (WF-IoT)
6. Aldeer M, Martin R, Howard R (2018) PillSense: designing a medication adherence monitoring system using pill bottle-mounted wireless sensors. In: 2018 IEEE international conference on communications workshops (ICC work-shops)
7. Hussein A, Kumar M, Burbano-Fernandez G, Ramirez-Gonzalez E, Abdulhay E, De Albuquerque V (2018) An automated remote cloud-based heart rate variability monitoring system. IEEE Access
8. Enciso-Quispe L, Sarmiento S, Zelaya-Policarpo E (2018) Personalized medical alert system based on internet of things with DHIS2. In: 2018 13th Iberian conference on information systems and technologies (CISTI)
9. Elhoseny M, Ramirez-Gonzalez G, Abu-Elnasr O, Shawkat S, Farouk A (2018) Secure medical data transmission model for IoT-based healthcare systems. IEEE Access
10. Stradolini F, Tamburrano N, Modoux T, Tuoheti A, Demarchi D, Carrara S (2018) IoT for telemedicine practices enabled by an Android™ application with cloud system integration. In: 2018 IEEE international symposium on circuits and systems (ISCAS)
11. Zagan I, Gaitan V, Iuga N, Brezulianu A (2018) m-Green CARDIO embedded system designed for out-of-hospital cardiac patients. In: 2018 international conference on development and application systems (DAS)
12. Aloi G, Fortino G, Gravina R, Pace P, Caliciuri G (2018) Edge computing-enabled body area networks. In: 2018 32nd international conference on advanced information networking and applications workshops (WAINA)
13. Saha J, Saha A, Chatterjee A, Agrawal S, Saha A, Kar A, Saha H (2018) Advanced IOT based combined remote health monitoring, home automation and alarm system. In: 2018 IEEE 8th annual computing and communication workshop and conference (CCWC)
14. Mohanty S, Kougianos E, Guturu P (2018) SBPG: secure better portable graphics for trustworthy media communications in the IoT. IEEE Access
15. Kotronis C, Nikolaidou M, Dimitrakopoulos G, Anagnostopoulos D, Amira A, Bensaali F (2018) A model-based approach for managing criticality requirements in e-Health IoT systems. In: 2018 13th annual conference on system of systems engineering (SoSE)
16. Perez Z, Memeti S, Pllana S (2018) A simulation study of a smart living IoT solution for remote elderly care. In: 2018 third international conference on fog and mobile edge computing (FMEC)
17. Wu F, Yang K, Yang Z (2018) Compressed acquisition and denoising recovery of EMGdi signal in WSNs and IoT. IEEE Trans Ind Inform 14:2210–2219
18. Chakravorty D, Islam S, Rana T (2018) IoT based patient guidance system using Raspberrypi. In: 2018 2nd international conference on electronics, materials engineering & nano-technology (IEMENTech)
19. Guo J (2018) Smartphone-powered electrochemical biosensing dongle for emerging medical IoT applications. IEEE Trans Ind Inform 14:2592–2597

20. Islam S, Hossain M, Hasan R, Duong T (2018) A conceptual framework for an IoT-based health assistant and its authorization model. In: 2018 IEEE 8th annual computing and communication workshop and conference (CCWC)
21. Santos J, Peng D, Hempel M, Sharif H (2018) Towards a physiologically-aware architecture for transmission of biomedical signals in BASNs/IoT. In: 2018 IEEE international conference on communications (ICC)
22. Hamici Z (2018) Towards data-centric genetic cryptography for telemonitoring and ambient assisted living systems. In: 2018 13th annual conference on system of systems engineering (SoSE)
23. Nadrag V, Poenaru, Suciu G (2018) Heart rate measurement using face detection in video—IEEE conference publication. In: 2018 international conference on communications (COMM)
24. Rajagopalan S, Janakiraman S, Rengarajan A, Rethinam S, Arumugham S, Saravanan G (2018) IoT framework for secure medical image transmission. In: 2018 international conference on computer communication and informatics (ICCCI)
25. Galletta A, Carnevale L, Bramanti A, Fazio M (2018) An innovative methodology for big data visualization for telemedicine. IEEE Trans Ind Inform 15:490–497
26. Satyanarayana P, Sujitha K, Kiron V, Reddy P, Ganesh M (2018) Assistance vision for blind people using k-NN algorithm and Raspberry Pi. In: Proceedings of 2nd international conference on micro-electronics, electromagnetics and telecommunications
27. Lavanya R, Nivetha M, Revasree K, Sandhiya K (2018) Smart chair-a telemedicine based health monitoring system. In: 2018 second international conference on electronics, communication and aerospace technology (ICECA)
28. Hammami S, Moungla H, Afifi H (2018) Proactive anomaly detection model for eHealth-enabled data in next generation cellular networks. In: 2018 IEEE international conference on communications (ICC)
29. Nepal S, Ranjan R, Choo K (2015) Trustworthy processing of healthcare big data in hybrid clouds. IEEE Cloud Comput 2:78–84. https://doi.org/10.1109/mcc.2015.36. Poh G, Chin J, Yau W, Choo K, Mohamad M (2017) Searchable symmetric encryption. ACM Comput Surv 50:1–37. https://doi.org/10.1145/3064005
30. Halgamuge M, Guru S, Jennings A (2018) Centralised strategies for cluster formation in sensor networks. In: Classification and clustering for knowledge discovery. Springer, Berlin, pp 315–331
31. Halgamuge M, Kotagiri R, Zukerman M (2006) High powered cluster heads for extending sensor network lifetime. In: Proceedings of 6th IEEE international symposium on signal processing and information technology (ISSPIT'06)
32. Parra V, Syed A, Mohammad A, Halgamuge M (2016) Pentaho and Jaspersoft: a comparative study of business intelligence open source tools processing big data to evaluate performances. Int J Adv Comput Sci Appl. https://doi.org/10.14569/ijacsa.2016.071003
33. Kalid S, Syed A, Mohammad A, Halgamuge M (2017) Big-data NoSQL databases: comparison and analysis of "Big-Table", "DynamoDB", and "Cassandra". In: IEEE 2nd international conference on big data analysis (ICBDA'17), pp 89–93
34. Thakur S, Singh A, Ghrera S, Elhoseny M (2018) Multi-layer security of medical data through watermarking and chaotic encryption for tele-health applications. In: Multimedia tools and applications. Springer, Berlin, pp 1–14
35. Shehab A, Elhoseny M, Muhammad K, Sangaiah A, Yang P, Huang H, Hou G (2018) Secure and robust fragile watermarking scheme for medical images. IEEE Access
36. Dhole V, Patil N (2015) Self embedding fragile watermarking for image tampering detection and image recovery using self-recovery blocks. In: Proceedings of international conference on computing communication control and automation (ICCUBEA), pp 752–757
37. El'arbi M, Ben Amar C (2014) Image authentication algorithm with recovery capabilities based on neural networks in the DCT domain. IET Image Proc 8:619–626. https://doi.org/10.1049/iet-ipr.2013.0646

38. Patra B, Patra J (2012) CRT-based fragile self-recovery watermarking scheme for image authentication and recovery. In: 2012 international symposium on intelligent signal processing and communications systems
39. Preda R (2014) Self-recovery of unauthentic images using a new digital watermarking approach in the wavelet domain. In: 2014 10th international conference on communications (COMM)
40. Al-Haj A, Amer A (2014) Secured telemedicine using region-based watermarking with tamper localization. J Digit Imaging 27:737–750. https://doi.org/10.1007/s10278-014-9709-9
41. Al-Haj A, Mohammad A, Amer A (2016) Crypto-watermarking of transmitted medical images. J Digit Imaging 30:26–38. https://doi.org/10.1007/s10278-016-9901-1
42. Kannammal A, Subha Rani S (2014) Two level security for medical images using watermarking/encryption algorithms. Int J Imaging Syst Technol 24:111–120. https://doi.org/10.1002/ima.22086
43. Parah S, Ahad F, Sheikh J, Bhat G (2017) Hiding clinical information in medical images: a new high capacity and reversible data hiding technique. J Biomed Inform 66:214–230. https://doi.org/10.1016/j.jbi.2017.01.006
44. Singh A, Dave M, Mohan A (2014) Hybrid technique for robust and imperceptible image watermarking in DWT–DCT–SVD domain. Natl Acad Sci Lett 37(4):351–358
45. Singh A, Kumar B, Dave M, Mohan A (2015) Robust and imperceptible dual watermarking for telemedicine applications. Wirel Pers Commun 80(4):1415–1433

Additional References

46. Marjani M, Nasaruddin F, Gani A, Karim A, Hashem IAT, Siddiqa A, Yaqoob I (2017) Big IoT data analytics: architecture, opportunities, and open research challenges. IEEE Access 5:5247–5261
47. Hashem IAT, Chang V, Anuar NB, Adewole K, Yaqoob I, Gani A, Ahmed E, Chiroma H (2016) The role of big data in smart city. Int J Inf Manage 36(5):748–758
48. Elhoseny M, Abdelaziz A, Salama AS, Riad AM, Muhammad K, Sangaiah AK (2018) A hybrid model of internet of things and cloud computing to manage big data in health services applications. Futur Gener Comput Syst 86:1383–1394
49. Gardašević G, Veletić M, Maletić N, Vasiljević D, Radusinović I, Tomović S, Radonjić M (2017) The IoT architectural framework, design issues and application domains. Wireless Pers Commun 92(1):127–148
50. Dastjerdi AV, Gupta H, Calheiros RN, Ghosh SK, Buyya R (2016) Fog computing: principles, architectures, and applications. In: Internet of things, pp 61–75

Chapter 10
Trust Management for Software-Defined Heterogeneous Vehicular Ad Hoc Networks

Adnan Mahmood, Wei Emma Zhang, Quan Z. Sheng, Sarah Ali Siddiqui and Abdulwahab Aljubairy

Abstract Over the past few decades, a considerable amount of interest has been observed (in both academia and industry) for improving the overall road transportation across the globe, primarily to enhance the safety of vehicular passengers and vulnerable road pedestrians. Vehicular Ad hoc Networks (VANETs) are anticipated to play a critical role in smart cities and Internet of Things (IoT) domain. Instead, it is expected that a new paradigm of Internet of Vehicles (IoV) will soon become an important component of the IoT. Also, since the connected vehicles primarily disseminate safety-critical information, it is imperative to have an extremely secure and trusted network so that critical data information (or any other sort of sensory data information) could be traversed with extreme reliability and authenticity. Unlike conventional wired networks, vehicular networks are highly dynamic, distributed and of open nature, and are, therefore, susceptible to various attacks such as replay, spoofing, eavesdropping, man-in-the-middle, distributed denial-of-service, blackhole, grayhole, Sybil and other malware attacks. To address the same, numerous mechanisms have been proposed in the literature, mainly relying on traditional cryptography techniques. Nevertheless, cryptography-based solutions are not effective in VANETs since nodes in this network are highly dynamic and distributed across the network. Moreover, the network infrastructure cannot be guaranteed permanently, and cryptographic solutions may also get compromised due to insider attacks in a network. This chapter aims to provide an in-depth investigation of a diverse range of security attacks challenging the actual realisation of vehicular networks. In contrast to conventional security (cryptography-based) solutions, it brings forth the need for trust management for securing vehicular networks (a concept still in its early stages of development) for ensuring reliability, authenticity and relevance by revoking both malicious and selfish nodes. It also briefly highlights the need for trust models and illustrates the characteristics of data-oriented trust models, entity-oriented trust models and hybrid trust models. Furthermore, since the conventional networks are being transformed via the promising yet emerging notion of software-defined networking (SDN), a brief discussion is presented so as to

A. Mahmood (✉) · W. E. Zhang · Q. Z. Sheng · S. A. Siddiqui · A. Aljubairy
Intelligent Computing Laboratory, Department of Computing, Macquarie University, Sydney, NSW, Australia
e-mail: adnan.mahmood@mq.edu.au

Z. Mahmood (ed.), *Security, Privacy and Trust in the IoT Environment*, https://doi.org/10.1007/978-3-030-18075-1_10

illustrate how a reconfigurable, reprogrammable and agile infrastructure can help in guaranteeing more secure vehicular networking platforms which are indispensable for futuristic Intelligent Transportation System (ITS) applications and services.

Keywords Vehicular Ad hoc Networks (VANETs) · V2X communication · Software-Defined Networking (SDN) · Heterogeneous networks · Trust management · Internet of Vehicles (IoV) · Cryptography

10.1 Introduction

Over the years, a rapid surge in demand for improved road safety and highly efficient ITS has prompted the researchers in both academia and the automotive industry to develop and fully integrate state-of-the-art wireless networking technologies within the vehicles. Accordingly, a considerable amount of advancement in Vehicular Ad hoc Networks (VANETs) has been observed over time, wherein vehicles communicate with one another via Vehicle-to-Vehicle (V2V) communication, with the roadside infrastructure via Vehicle-to-Infrastructure (V2I) communication, within the network via Vehicle-to-Network (V2N) communication and with the vulnerable pedestrians via Vehicle-to-Pedestrian (V2P) communication. All of this development points towards the emergence of a promising paradigm referred to as Vehicle-to-Everything (V2X) communication which has enabled the automotive industry to enter into a completely different but exciting era. The notion of connected and semi-/fully autonomous vehicles has now become a reality [1, 2]. An illustration of V2X communication is presented in Fig. 10.1.

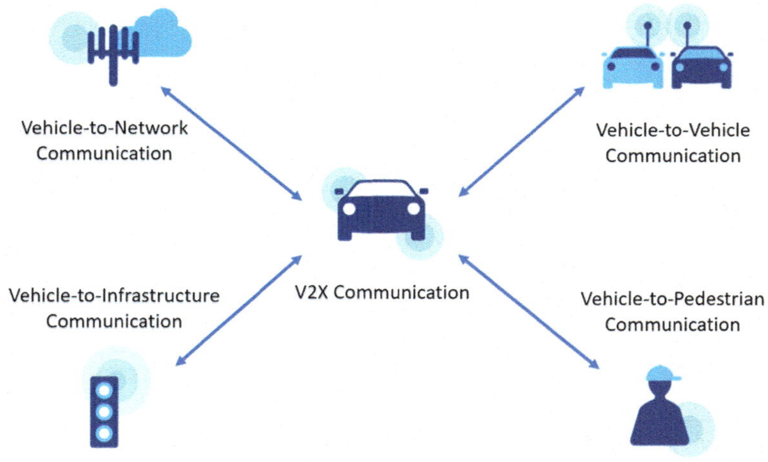

Fig. 10.1 Towards a seamless ubiquitous V2X communication

In VANETs, vehicles and their supporting roadside infrastructure are generally equipped with various sensing, compute or processing features and a wide variety of wireless networking capabilities. In terms of sensing, ambient intelligence plays a key role as vehicles not only sense their immediate surroundings but also become sufficiently intelligent to take low-latent safety-critical runtime decisions for protecting lives and other vehicles on the roads. Today, modern connected vehicles are equipped with approximately 100 sensors onboard, and this number is expected to exceed over 200 by the end of the year 2020. These sensors are diverse in types and their nature and generally include other smart devices such as radar sensors, accelerometers, GPS, LIDARs, video cameras, ultrasonic sensors, gyroscopes, infrared sensors and odometry sensors. Subsequently, a massive amount of data is generated by these sensors which is then analysed and processed on a runtime basis for intelligent decision-making. As per an estimate by Intel, connected vehicles are expected to generate 40 Terabytes (TB) of data for every eight hours of their driving. This would yield a flood of data which, if sent over the communication network, could choke the entire backhaul and lead to considerable delay and disruption in the network service and overall deterioration not only in the Quality-of-Service (QoS) but also in the Quality-of-Experience (QoE) of vehicular users. In order to mitigate such a network management overhead, it is essential to deal with this massive volume of big vehicular data at the localised level for the first-hand observations or results. Thus, only the tasks which cannot be handled by the local compute and storage can be referred to the backend servers since they possess sufficient resources to address the same. This has led to the accelerated deployment of edge and fog computing for VANETs. Researchers in academia and industry have recently proposed many edge- and fog-based vehicular networking architectures. It is pertinent to mention here that several authors have treated both edge and fog computing paradigms to be the same, though, in fact, there is subtle difference between the two approaches. For the sake of clarity for the readers, edge computing pushes the network intelligence, communication capabilities and processing power directly into the devices (vehicle's onboard units). Contrarily, fog computing drives the intelligence into the local area network level of a network's architecture, hence carrying out processing operations in the IoT gateway [3–5].

Traditionally, cellular technologies, e.g., 4G LTE, have been employed for vehicular communication purposes, and the proponents of the paradigm of cellular Vehicle-to-Everything (C-V2X) communication have been pushing for the same over the past few years. However, cellular communication is limited to only 100 Mbps in high mobility scenarios though much lower data rates are typically usual. In addition to the cellular technology, Direct Short-Range Communication (DSRC) has been proposed as a short-to-medium range wireless technology for ensuring highly secure V2V communication. Nevertheless, maximum data rates for DSRC in practice are also around 6–27 Mbps. Lately, millimetre wave (mmWave) communication has been rolled out in the form of IEEE 802.11ad and is capable of supporting a data rate of 7 Gbps. However, several bottlenecks related to its beam alignment overhead and insufficient penetration rates have not yet realised the full potential of a mmWave V2X communication system [6]. Therefore, the optimal solution is to use the notion of heterogeneity such that the disadvantages of one technology could be easily offset via the advantages of the others and the vehicles (and their vehicular users) remain seamlessly connected in an 'Always Best Connected' mode [7, 8].

While heterogeneity brings a number of potential advantages to the networking architectures in order to ensure high bandwidth and low-latency communication, it also opens numerous security concerns since it facilitates multipath communication; and if any one of these paths gets exploited, the whole network could become subsequently exploited and compromised. Security is thus one of the biggest concerns for the next-generation autonomous vehicles. It is therefore imperative to secure such dynamic networks as they have a direct influence on human lives.

Over the past several years, numerous security solutions have been proposed in the research literature for vehicular networks. However, most of them relied on the traditional cryptography schemes, wherein vehicles utilise certificates and public key infrastructures for guaranteeing security [9]. Nevertheless, these schemes are not feasible for vehicular networks as vehicles are highly dynamic in nature and are usually dispersed throughout the network. Also, the availability of infrastructure cannot be guaranteed for vehicles at all times (i.e. especially in rural areas); and lastly, traditional cryptographic solutions are vulnerable to insider attacks which are instigated by the vehicular nodes with authorised access of the network and thus pose serious threats. It is due to this reason that *trust* has been lately introduced for vehicular networks and is generally defined as the confidence of one node over the other [10–12].

In this context, the objectives of this chapter are manifold. It presents an overview of the possible security attacks in the realm of vehicular networks supported by appropriate examples and use cases. Then, trust management has been brought into deliberation, and its existing state-of-the-art is summarised. Moreover, the emerging, yet promising, paradigm of SDN has been discussed as a possible solution to better understand the dynamics of highly distributed vehicular networks and to facilitate the notion of trust management in order to ensure that vehicular networks always remain secure against a diverse range of malicious activities. Finally, in the last section, conclusions are presented.

10.2 Types of Security Attacks in VANET

Over the past several decades, a number of malicious attacks have disrupted the networks worldwide, thereby causing a significant amount of financial losses (in the order of hundreds of billions of dollars worldwide) as well as dissatisfaction from the network users. With the advent of vehicular networks and the promising notion of IoV, similar attacks have been launched by the malicious intruders for disrupting the vehicular networks. The key difference between security attacks on traditional networks and vehicular networks is that the former results more in financial losses and a higher service delay, thus affecting the QoS and QoE, whereas the latter in addition to these factors is associated with the human lives, and therefore demands careful attention and resolution. In this section, we outline some of these security attacks which are a continuous source of threats for the deployment of futuristic IoV networks and act as bottlenecks in the realisation of the smart city domain [13–15], which includes smart living including smart transportation.

10.2.1 Denial-of-Service and Distributed DoS Attacks

A Denial-of-Service (DoS) attack floods the target network with an excessive amount of traffic than it was meant to handle, subsequently choking the entire network and in turn blocking both safety-critical and non-safety (i.e. infotainment) contents to the vehicles and the vehicular users. This sort of attack in vehicular networks is instigated by a malicious vehicle generating an overwhelming amount of traffic to either temporarily or entirely choke some or all services for vehicles in a given geographical location. In some instances, DoS attacks are either stimulated by more than one malicious source via multiple compromised systems or also in the form of an organised group or crime ring. Such an attack is referred to as the Distributed Denial-of-Service (DDoS) attack and is difficult to handle since these malicious intruders' attack from more than one network address, which makes it difficult to trace and evict them from the network. There are a number of types of DoS and DDoS attacks, and the most common ones include ping of death attacks, teardrop attacks, smurf attacks, botnets and TCP SYN flood attacks [4, 16, 17].

It is pertinent to mention that conventional networks are usually orchestrated by the network administrators in a centralised manner and are capable of tracing the malicious intruders and subsequently restoring the network in a timely fashion. On the contrary, vehicular networks are highly distributive in nature, and hence a self-governing and self-healing nature is highly appropriate for their security purposes. This requires intelligent mechanisms to be devised such that a vehicular network (or a vehicular cluster/platoon[1]/cloud) can identify malicious intruders and accordingly take appropriate corrective actions on the same at the localised levels. Failing to do so could transpire grave challenges especially in the context of connected and autonomous vehicles as trajectories of nearby vehicles and vulnerable pedestrians may not be timely disseminated, and such a delay could result in the loss of precious human lives. Unless and until appropriate security mechanisms are in place, the potential of next-generation smart cities would not be fully and successfully realised [18].

[1]Vehicle platooning considerably reduces the inter-vehicular distances in contrast to the ones recommended for conventional (manual) driving. This helps in achieving shared objectives instead of uncoordinated individual decisions, increasing the road capacity as a large number of cars can be packed in finite road space and an increase in energy efficacy due to a reduction in aerodynamic drag [49].

10.2.2 Man-in-the-Middle Attacks

A man-in-the-middle attack transpires when a malicious intruder (or a hijacker) injects itself between a client (vehicle) and a server. Some common forms of man-in-the-middle attack include session hijacking (TCP session hijacking), IP spoofing and replay attack (playback attack) [4, 19].

In the case of TCP hijacking, an attacker hijacks a communication session between the trusted client (vehicle) and its local or backend server. The malicious intruder takes control of the trusted client, disconnects its session with the corresponding server, substitutes its own IP address with that of the client's, spoofs the client's sequence numbers and keeps communicating with the server while the server believes that it is still communicating with the original client. This is also referred to as active session hijacking. On the contrary, in the case of passive session hijacking, the malicious attacker tends to remain hidden so as not to raise any suspicion and quietly monitors the flow of network traffic. An attacker could morph any passive session hijacking into active session hijacking as soon as it finds any profitable opportunity to gain an advantage.

In case of vehicular networks which are highly dynamic in nature and require a runtime highly accurate information of all the vehicles in ambience of one another, both active and passive session hijacking may become a potential threat for the safety-critical and non-safety applications.

In the case of safety-critical applications, a connected vehicle approaching the blind intersection could have its trajectory and ambient information blocked subsequently leading to fatal road accidents. Also, in case of non-safety (infotainment) applications, either the user preferences could be amended by the malicious intruder, thereby deteriorating the QoE or the users trying to access online banking or e-commerce websites for shopping purposes could have their critical credit card information stolen.

In case of IP spoofing, the malicious intruder broadcasts a packet with the IP source address of a trusted host instead of its own, which the target host may accept and subsequently act upon it; thus sourcing critical network information which is not accessible to the malicious intruder otherwise. Moreover, in case of a replay attack, valid data transmission is intercepted and fraudulently sent later by a malicious intruder. Since the said data is correctly encrypted, the trusted host may potentially treat it as a correct request and act as per the will of the intruder. Nevertheless, a replay attack is easy to trace and could be intercepted via the nonce or session timestamps. An illustration of a man-in-the-middle attack is depicted in Fig. 10.2.

10.2.3 Eavesdropping Attacks

Modern-day connected vehicles remain seamlessly connected with one another and with the backbone network and are, hence, vulnerable to a diverse range of malicious

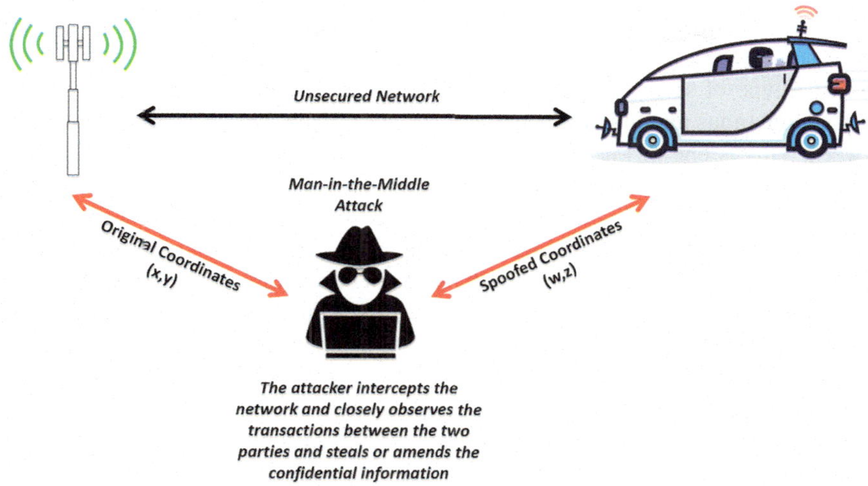

Fig. 10.2 A typical illustration of a man-in-the-middle attack in VANETs

attacks. Eavesdropping, also usually referred to as sniffing or snooping, is an unauthorised real-time interception of communication between the two parties by a malicious third party. Eavesdropping is difficult to trace as no abnormality could be observed in the data transmission. Hackers, over the years, have continued to evolve new forms of eavesdrop which are capable of capturing the credit card and other confidential information and even the login details of social networking accounts, e.g. Facebook, Twitter and Instagram, which a vehicular user may send over the vehicular network [20].

Eavesdropping generally transpires in the digital world in the form of network eavesdropping, wherein a protocol analyzer could be potentially utilised to sniff and record packets of data communication over the network without being even noticed by the users, and the same is subsequently listened to via specialised software packages. Over the past several years, there have been numerous instances, whereby the speakers of IP-based devices were turned on remotely by the malicious intruders with callers put on mute and confidential information was listened without the user's knowledge and consent. In the case of connected vehicles, the hackers can infiltrate the telematics system of a vehicle and accordingly eavesdrop on confidential conversations within the connected vehicles through their in-cabin microphones.

Data encryption is usually regarded as one of the best countermeasures for this purpose. Thus, appropriate security mechanisms need to be in place in order to build a more secure network. Such mechanisms should not only be capable of withstanding the attacks of the malicious intruders (by primarily blocking their access to the valuable information propagating between the network's nodal points) but should also be immune to the repeated attempts of digital eavesdropping [21, 22].

10.2.4 Sybil Attacks

Sybil is a type of security threat wherein a malicious node claims to have multiple pseudonymous identities for gaining disproportionally larger influence within a network. This is one of the most prominent attacks in the context of peer-to-peer networks, i.e. a type of network, whereby each node possesses a unique identity and participates in trust-based ranking or recommendation systems. Some typical examples of Sybil attacks include rigging of critical internet polls by malicious identities via different IP addresses, fraudulent enhancement of rankings via page ranking system (i.e. Sybil attacks have been carried out by some companies to gain significantly better ratings on Google PageRank) and reputation enhancement of certain products on various e-commerce websites (e.g. eBay has also been a victim of such sort of attacks in the past) [23–25].

Sybil attacks can prove extremely intimidating in case of vehicular networks as modern-day connected vehicles communicate and exchange messages with other vehicles in their immediate vicinity based on trust, and further participates in trust management systems to opt for the optimal cluster heads for communicating with the backhaul network. It is pertinent to mention that connected vehicles generally resolve their computational and storage matters on a localised level (i.e. at the edge and/or in the fog) and only the cluster head communicates the statuses and other critical information of all vehicles to the backend server, as and when required, hence mitigating the network management overhead. In such sort of scenarios, the cluster head plays an important role by not only navigating the vehicles to their intended destinations but also by allocating the precious network resources among its members. Thus, a malicious vehicle with the assistance of a Sybil attack can artificially boost its rating (a phenomenon also known as self-promoting) and can become a cluster head, thereby causing a considerable level of threat to its member vehicles and their users, and to other vehicular clusters, independent vehicles and vulnerable pedestrians in the immediate surroundings. Also, a malicious cluster head could disrupt communication of its members by making the cluster to completely go off the radar, thereby posing threat to the other nearby autonomous vehicles since they would not be able to obtain the coordinates of such a malicious cluster until these coordinates have been re-ascertained and reported back to the traffic management authorities. These authorities, in turn, can then send a warning broadcast to vehicles in nearby vicinity or in the anticipated travelling trajectory of the malicious cluster. Although Sybil attacks are much difficult to detect, nevertheless, blockchain-based solutions have been recently explored to prevent critical systems against such sort of attacks. One possible solution could be to rely on a trust-based reputation system, wherein only the established (or long-term) users are allowed to vouch for new entrants in a network or via allowing new entrants to stay active and unique for a certain period before being provided with any voting privileges. An illustration of a Sybil attack in a VANET is depicted in Fig. 10.3.

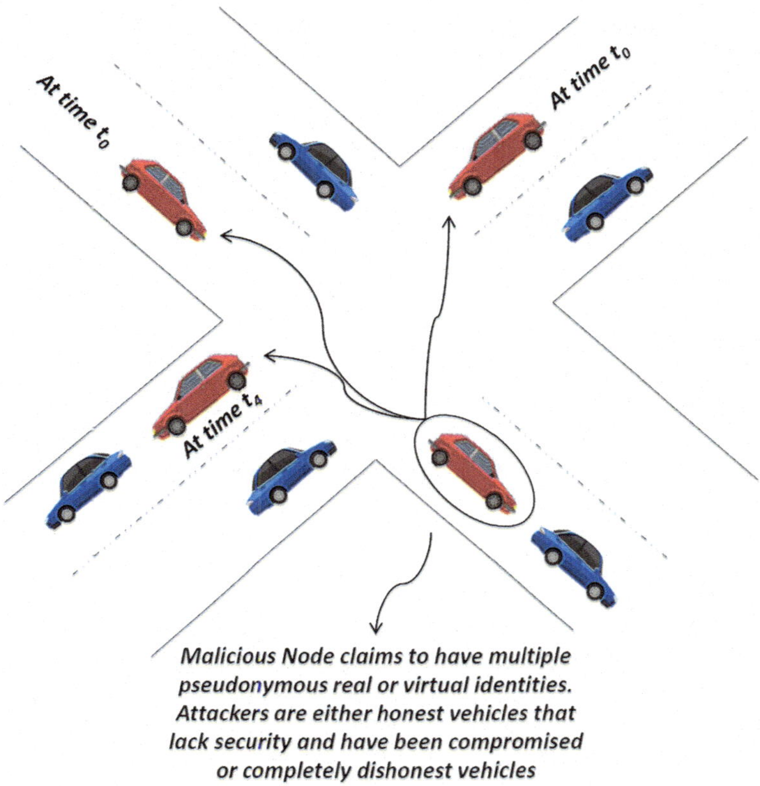

Fig. 10.3 An illustration of the Sybil attack in VANETs

10.2.5 Malware Attacks

In addition to the aforementioned security attacks faced by the VANETs, there also exist several malicious software which could be installed onboard a vehicle without the consent of the vehicular owners. These may be directly injected or by embedding malicious codes in the macros of the data files by the malicious entities, and such data files could be either injected in a vehicle directly through V2V communication or by sending it via cloud-based connection or supporting roadside units. Some of these malware include the following [26]:

- Macro-viruses—These are malicious content generally embedded in the macros of the data files, and hence run as soon as the vehicles or the vehicular users open the respective data files. Macro-viruses are generally spread via phishing emails containing the malicious contents and replicate themselves instantaneously and get attached to other computerised systems too. They also spread easily as vehicular users downloading and opening malicious attachments in an autonomous vehicle could infect the other onboard systems and sophisticated operations of the vehicle.

Moreover, vehicular users may become a source of spreading these malicious contents provided they have to share some data files (and even the infotainment contents) with other vehicles or users in a vehicular cluster.

- File Infectors—These usually associate themselves with various sorts of executable files and are usually loaded once the vehicles or vehicular users execute these files. These can severely harm a vehicle's onboard unit as vehicles typically request software to be installed onboard either as per the requirements of the vehicular drivers or may require upgraded executable files or supporting patches for a number of other purposes. Once the malicious file is executed, it has the potential to overcome onboard systems of the autonomous vehicles subsequently becoming a potential source of threat for its passengers as well as for the passengers of other vehicles and vulnerable pedestrians on the road.
- Trojans—These, also referred to as trojan horses, are malicious programmes (mostly in disguise of an authentic software) which can hide in an important programme in order to launch a potential attack on a vehicle's onboard unit. While trojans do not self-replicate like viruses, they open backdoors for attackers so that they may easily exploit the system. One of the most common forms of such backdoor is opening up of a high numbered port to facilitate a hacker for spying and/or stealing valuable information through these ports and then accordingly take malicious actions such as deleting, blocking, modifying or copying valuable data or even completely disrupting the performance of an autonomous vehicle.
- Stealth Viruses—These are capable of going unnoticed by any specialised antivirus scan, and conceal changes made to any infected file and even to its size and last time and date of modification. This is also known as a silent killer in a VANET context and has the potential of completing disrupting a VANET without being even noticed by a vehicle's anti-malware capabilities and the traffic management authorities. Nevertheless, the traffic management authorities, upon noticing a strange behaviour of any vehicle, could put it off the network and mark it as malicious along with disseminating warning messages to other vehicles in the immediate vicinity to warn them for not communicating with the malicious vehicle and making it part of a cluster or platoon.
- Logic Bombs—These are malicious instructions appended to an application or a programme which triggers once a specific condition or logic is satisfied. This specific condition may depend on the time and date or a specific geographical position. Logic bombs in the past have known to wipe out the records in the banking sector, media industries and for driving down a company's financial standing within the stock market. A sophisticated logic bomb attack could be launched on a vehicular platoon for diminishing its trust values to not let the other neighbouring vehicles in the immediate vicinity to join the same or for completely dissolving the platoon before it can realise any useful objectives. Moreover, in a sophisticated manner, this sort of an attack could be launched once a platoon has a specific number of vehicles (or even once a specific vehicle joins the platoon) in order to consume the platoon's network resources for some other malicious tasks.
- Adware—These, also referred to as advertisement malware, often employ intrusive and usually specific harmful mechanisms to present unwanted advertisements.

While not all of these advertisements are threatening, they are often irritating and a possible source of distraction too. It is also pertinent to note that future connected and autonomous vehicles are anticipated to have Augmented Reality (AR) capabilities installed onboard the vehicles; the AR-enabled windscreens are currently in advanced testing stage by various automotive companies and are due to appear in the market fairly soon. AR augments real world with runtime supporting contextual information and objects which exists in the same world as the real world. Thus, while the vehicular users see this useful context on their windscreens (i.e. speeds, and possibly the behaviour of vehicles in their immediate vicinity, terrain information, weather details, warning notifications for blind intersections, speed alerts or other relevant safety-critical information), an instantaneously popped-up adware would not only cause distraction but would inevitably become a possible source of threat subsequently leading to fatal accidents. This is especially true in the event where a vehicular user is manually navigating the car through dense driving environments or in semi-autonomous modes. Adware may get injected via installing any freeware or shareware applications or by visiting the infected websites where they can get installed without a user's consent. As one part of its heritage lies in the spy family, adware track users' activities for determining their preferences of internet traffic and advertisements. In worst scenarios, adware may completely alter the users' preferences, thereby directly having an impact on caching systems since modern caching techniques store the frequently accessed or requested content for a specific duration of time for minimising the end-to-end latency and for mitigating the network management overhead. Also, adware is responsible for consuming the processing power of a vehicular onboard unit since loading and running advertisements consume the processing power and subsequently slow down the overall performance of an autonomous vehicle. Furthermore, adware also eats up the data just like data is consumed once any picture, movie or supporting software is downloaded by the end user. Although adware is capable of hiding itself within the system, nevertheless, specialised anti-adware cleaners with abilities to distinguish among the authorised and unauthorised installations help to detect the unwanted adware (and the badware) and subsequently eradicate them.

In addition to the above-stated malware, there further exists some other malware such as system or boot-record infectors, polymorphic viruses, worms, droppers, ransomware and spyware which needs to be effectively tackled for devising and deploying efficient next-generation ITS architectures and platforms. An illustration of blackhole attack, grayhole attack, DoS attack, and injected and amended message is depicted in Fig. 10.4.

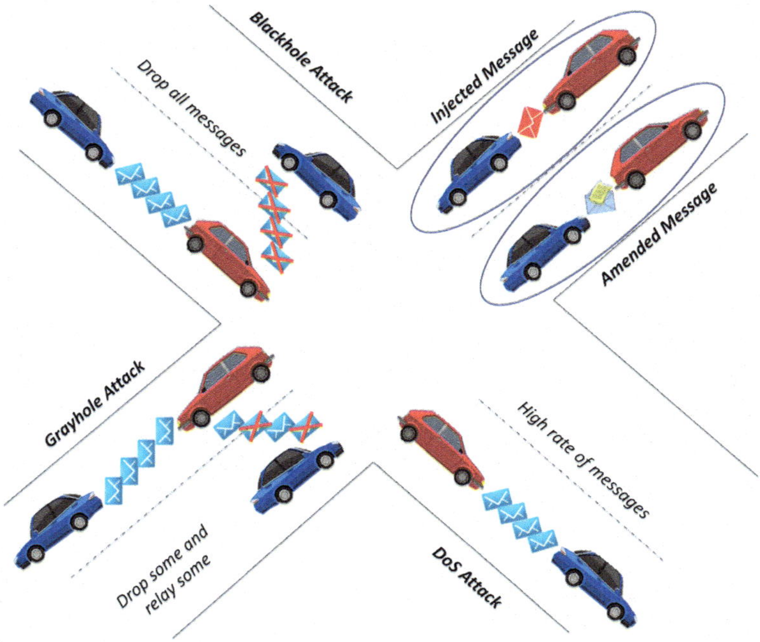

Fig. 10.4 An illustration of various other security attacks in VANETs (blackhole attack, grayhole attack, DoS attack, and injected and amended message)

10.3 Need for Trust Management in VANETs

In order to overcome the shortcomings of traditional cryptographic techniques, 'trust' has been recently proposed as an alternate mechanism for strengthening the security of VANETs. Trust, as discussed earlier, can simply be defined as the confidence of one vehicle over another depending on a specific set of tasks or actions. Thus, just as humans interact with one another and form relationships, vehicles could interact with other vehicles and establish a relationship purely based on trust. However, unlike conventional networks, vehicular networks are highly dynamic in nature, and hence trust values of a vehicle keep on changing abruptly with changes in its geographical neighbours and immediate surroundings. This practically means a rapid change in the ambient context and vehicles have to keep on evaluating trust on a frequent basis (while they are on the move), and this, therefore, puts an extra network management overhead on the vehicles and accordingly waste their precious network resources—a phenomenon that needs to be mitigated as much as possible.

Also, trust is categorised in terms of direct trust and indirect trust. Direct trust is usually a vehicle's direct observation about the other vehicle, whereas indirect trust is computed using recommendations (opinions) from the neighbouring vehicles about a target vehicle, as illustrated in Fig. 10.5. Nevertheless, researchers have also computed direct trust by assessing the quality of exchanged messages between the

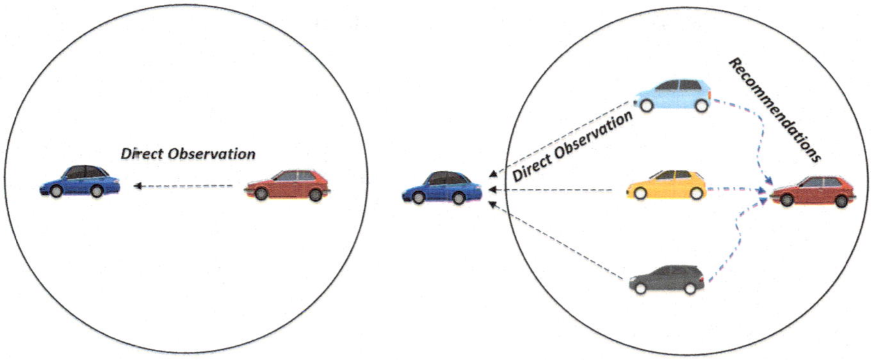

Fig. 10.5 An illustration of direct trust (left) and indirect trust (right) in VANETs

vehicles and indirect trust depending on the broadcast drop ratio (originating) from the sender. While direct trust is more relevant than indirect trust, both are generally taken in unison for better trust evaluation. Furthermore, the primary intent of the trust models in a VANET is to guarantee a highly secure and trusted dissemination of data among the vehicles by not only revoking the compromised messages but also by identifying and evicting any malicious vehicles from the network. While several trust models have already been proposed for VANETs; all of these could be broadly classified into three types as discussed below [27]:

- Data-oriented Trust Models—These primarily rely on the accuracy and authenticity of the data (e.g. messages) exchanged between the vehicles, and information contained therein. Several schemes have been proposed in the research literature for such data-centric trust models, wherein

  (a) trustworthy reports are usually obtained from the neighbouring vehicles and weights are assigned to each of these reports based on a vehicle's location and time closeness with an event on the road, i.e. the closer a vehicle is to an event, the more updated and reliable information it would possess [28].
  (b) by grouping the neighbouring vehicles into two sub-groups, i.e. one with similar content information and other with conflicting content and trustworthiness of messages is evaluated by taking into account the information similarity and conflict and received routing path similarity, and so forth [29].

- Entity-oriented Trust Models—These are well regarded for evicting malicious nodes from the vehicular networks primarily by evaluating the trustworthiness of a vehicle. Such models heavily rely on the recommendations and reputation endorsed by the (honest) neighbouring vehicles on the message originator, i.e. a source vehicle generating or sending messages. A brief glimpse of the literature reveals a number of studies proposing the entity-oriented trust models, wherein

(a) cluster heads act as 'watchdogs' to seek recommendations from their neighbouring vehicles regarding a misbehaving vehicle and subsequently strip it from the list of trusted vehicles.
(b) by applying an economic incentive model whereby a credit value is assigned to the vehicles in a distributed manner. The credit increase or decrease depends on a vehicle's behaviour in the network, and the vehicle is excluded from the network once all the credit value has been depleted [30–33].

- Hybrid Trust Models—These assess trust based on the trustworthiness of the vehicles and the data they exchange. Both quality of data, i.e. messages exchanged, and a particular vehicle's reputation and its neighbourhood opinions play an indispensable role in evaluating the trust. Literature reveals that hybrid trust models have been employed for (a) evaluating the trustworthiness in the presence of packet duplication and Sybil attack; and (b) to identify malicious nodes and disseminate safety-critical messages to improve the overall security of VANETs via employing reputation and various plausibility checks [34–37].

Thus, once a message is received by a cluster head or any other evaluating node in this context, trust is computed on the vehicles or its transmitted/exchanged data in the form of 'role-based trust' or 'experience-based trust'. Role-based trust refers to the trust assessment of the vehicles which are highly trusted in the network. Such vehicles include (a) law enforcement vehicles and ambulances—also referred to as higher authority vehicles since messages originating from such public authorities are authorised and treated as trusted; (b) public transport such as trains, taxis and buses as their respective transport agencies and departments certify these vehicles; and finally, (c) the driving authorities may certify professional drivers with several years of travelling experience in contrast to the ordinary drivers having either very limited or almost no experience of driving. On the contrary, experience-based trust is used for the assessment of the quality of messages received from the vehicles and is generally dependent on the location and time closeness of a vehicle with a particular event. Thus, if a vehicle is transmitting the correct message and of a higher quality, its trust value is increased by an honesty factor. Similarly, if the vehicle is transmitting a malicious message, its trust value is decreased by a punishment factor [38, 39].

A use case/scenario of trust-based message evaluation is depicted in Fig. 10.6. A somewhat similar use case has been deliberated in [9] and regards both message validity and relevance as critical dimensions for evaluating trustworthiness within a VANET context. These two dimensions are deliberated as follows:

- Message Validity—This is generally dependent on the validity of a particular event and can be verified via the time stamps. For instance, information pertinent to road congestion is associated with the peak hours and not with non-peak hours or with the whole day. Furthermore, road closures due to temporary road repair(s) or accident(s) would be for a maximum of 30–120 min depending on how quickly the road authorities and emergency services respond to the same.
- Message Relevance—This ensures that appropriate information gets delivered to the vehicular users. For instance, if a vehicle located in Sydney starts receiving

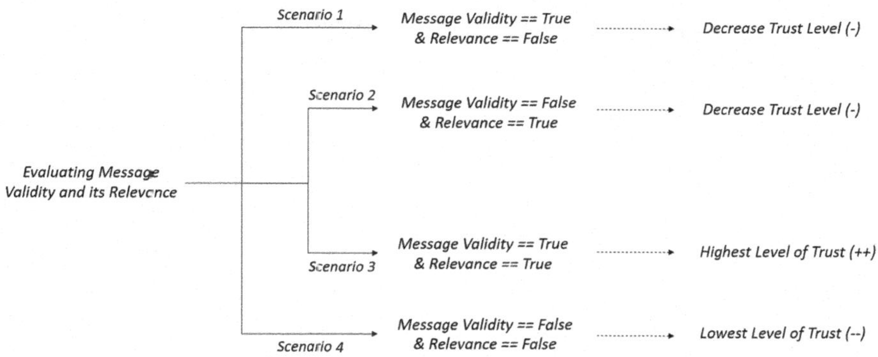

Fig. 10.6 Use case/scenario of trust-based message evaluation (the significance of message validity and relevance)

messages about road conditions in Melbourne, then this information is not relevant to the vehicle at the receiving end.

In addition to tackling the 'malicious' vehicles, trust management models also focus on 'selfish' vehicles. Unlike malicious vehicles, selfish vehicles are generally defined as the ones that serve their own interests only. In other words, selfish vehicles refuse to act as a relay for transmitting messages so as to preserve their resources for satisfying their own individual needs. This implies that their cooperation rate is comparatively lower. In this case, appropriate incentive mechanisms need to be in place for enticing these vehicles to participate in the network. One possible solution is to employ game theory approaches through which the selfish vehicles can be motivated to cooperate in the network either by enhancing their reputation or by offering them some privileges depending on their contribution within the network. Nevertheless, these reputation enhancements and privileges should not exceed beyond a particular threshold since selfish vehicles may employ the entire network to meet their interests before acting again in the selfish mode. Hence, every effort should be made to entice the selfish nodes to participate in the network; however, they should not be ideally selected as cluster heads or proxy cluster heads. Cluster heads usually have access to the resources of their member vehicles and possess the liberty to utilise these resources for satisfying any of its member's objectives or the overall cluster's objectives. In this way, reasonable participation of the selfish vehicles could be ensured, and at the same time, the network integrity could be kept intact. However, attackers may not always persist a malicious and selfish behaviour.

Existing research has only taken into consideration the fact that a malicious vehicle always maintains a stable adversary behaviour at all times. Nevertheless, to avoid detection, intelligent attackers keep on alternating between a legal (non-malicious) and malicious behaviour and each of these sessions can be smartly varied in time to make detection of malicious patterns more difficult. In this manner, intelligent attackers keep pursuing their malicious activities without even being marked as malicious and subsequently removed out of the network. Figure 10.7 depicts the dishonest

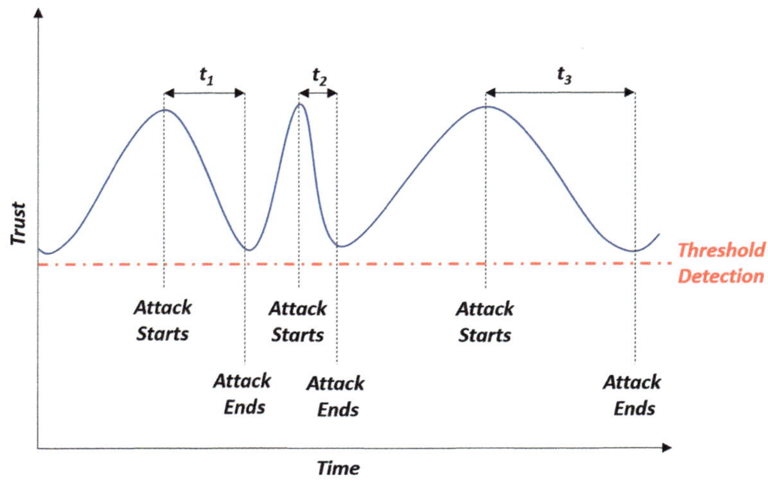

Fig. 10.7 Dishonest behaviour of intelligent attackers over time

behaviour of intelligent attackers over time. It could be observed that the malicious vehicle launches its attack for different durations across all the three time intervals, i.e. t_1, t_2 and t_3, to ensure that its behavioural pattern changes dynamically to avoid identification by the neighbouring vehicles or the localised or centralised network traffic monitoring authorities.

One possible solution for addressing such dishonest behaviour could be to employ an adaptive threshold detection mechanism. Thus, once a vehicle detects that the trust value of its neighbouring vehicle is decreasing, it adjusts the corresponding detection threshold for the respective neighbouring vehicle to ensure early detection of malicious patterns. In this manner, while a malicious vehicle is still busy pursuing malicious activities in its attacking time window, it could be identified and accordingly eradicated out of the network. Refer to Fig. 10.8.

The increasing number of malicious, selfish and dishonest vehicles results in lower network efficiency. Trust, therefore, serves as an ideal metric to evaluate the behavioural patterns of the vehicles and helps network operators to reward or punish vehicles according to their behaviour. Vehicles and service providers generally query the trust values of other vehicles before interacting with them. The question arises as to how quickly the trust for a target vehicle could be ascertained to facilitate a timely interaction. Furthermore, there is a need to regularly update the trust values with low-latency since vehicular trust changes due to several factors which are cognizant to their behaviour over time, interaction with the other vehicles and immediate ambience. Also, this is trivial in order to keep an eye on the dynamic changes in the behavioural patterns (i.e. malicious and non-malicious) of intelligent dishonest vehicles. In large networking environments, distributed trust management is indispensable for coping with these challenges especially as an unprecedented increase in the number of vehicles form part of the vehicular edge networks. In short, efficacious

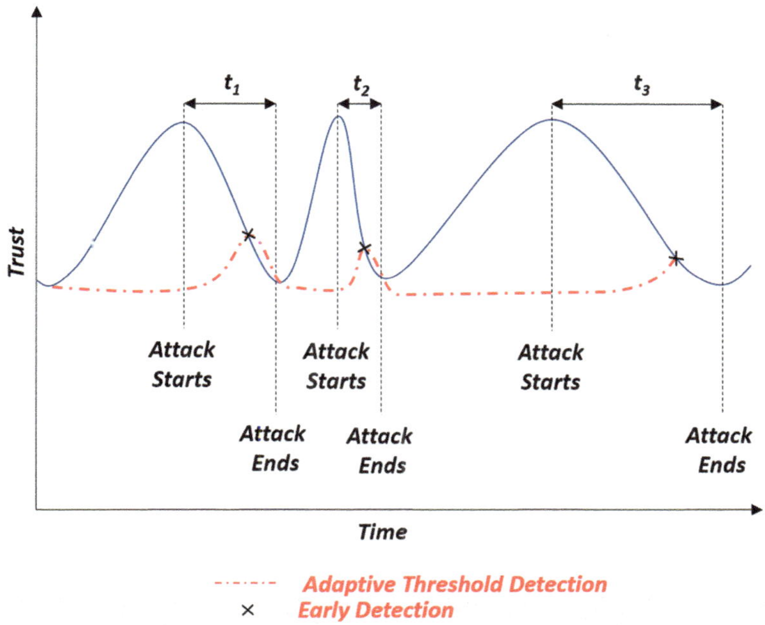

Fig. 10.8 Adaptive threshold detection mechanism for identifying dishonest behaviour of intelligent attackers (dishonest vehicles)

trust management systems help to avoid malicious attacks, steer user behaviour and promote network evolution.

For the sake of clarity for the readers, Table 10.1 depicts a comparison of the state-of-the-art of trust management vis-à-vis VANETs along with their key contributions and evaluation platforms.

10.4 SDN Vis-à-Vis Trust Management in VANETs

The emerging yet promising paradigm of Software-Defined Networking (SDN) is capable of offering a highly efficacious way of orchestrating the communication and networking resources for highly dynamic vehicular networks. SDN decouples the data plane from the control plane to achieve a highly flexible, reprogrammable, agile and scalable networking architecture [43]. Although originally conceived for the wired networks with a single point of centralised control (i.e. primarily for the conventional data-centric operations), a number of research studies have lately employed SDN for the wireless networks and in particular for the VANETs [44–47]. Nevertheless, several challenges still entail its true realisation for highly dynamic wireless networks, a subject which is currently being investigated by a large cohort of scientists and researchers in both academia and industry.

Table 10.1 A comparison of state-of-the-art vis-à-vis trust management in VANETs

Ref.	Proposed heuristic	Salient contributions	Simulation platforms
[40]	An attack-resistant trust management scheme for VANETs	Capable of detecting and tackling malicious nodes within a VANET environment by evaluating the trustworthiness of data (messages and contents contained therein) as well as mobile nodes. Data trust is evaluated based on the sensed data, whereas node trust is assessed in two ways, i.e. functional trust (evaluating the probability that how likely a node would fulfil its assigned functionalities) and recommendation trust (indicating that how trustworthy will be the recommendations of one node for the other).	GloMoSim 2.03
[33]	A job market signalling heuristic for incentive and trust management in VANETs	A Markov chain of distributed trust model for VANETs (conceived from the well-known economic model, i.e. job market signalling model). The proposed heuristic creates a self-selection mechanism among the network's nodes and the nodes with unacceptable or poor behaviour have their credits (which are an indication of their available resources) exhausted/depleted. While the selfish nodes primarily serve their interests and accordingly use resources for satisfying their own needs, this heuristic improves cooperation among the selfish nodes by proposing inciting rewards. The reward is usually attractive but only granted once neighbouring nodes validate the data sent by the source vehicle.	NS2-34, VanetMobiSim and SUMO

(continued)

Table 10.1 (continued)

[41]	Distributed reputation management system for security protection and efficiency optimisation in vehicular edge computing (VEC)	Proposed a multi-weighted subjective logic for improving the reputation update mechanism, wherein all the reputation segments of a target vehicle are collected, weighted (as per familiarity, similarity and timeliness[a]), and subsequently aggregated from its 1-hop neighbours for forming a localised knowledge of reputation update. This is considered along with the vehicle's historical reputation values in order to update the reputation values. VEC servers are scheduled for maintaining the reputation of local vehicles.	Dataset pertains to the actual urban area of San Francisco (details regarding simulation tools have not been provided)
[9]	A trust evaluation and management framework in context-enabled VANETs	A state-of-the-art trust framework which is capable of evaluating various trust models, i.e. data-oriented trust models, entity-oriented trust models and hybrid-oriented trust models, under various contexts pertinent to the mobility of both honest and malicious vehicles. Realistic evaluation criteria have been adopted for evaluation of the trust models based on the QoS and network security. Furthermore, vulnerabilities are mapped with threats in order to perform risk assessments in VANETs.	VEINS (an open-source simulation tool incorporating both SUMO and OMNET++)
[42]	Decentralised trust management scheme for vehicular networks based on blockchain technology	Enables all roadside units to participate in updating the trust values in a decentralised fashion and provide all roadside units with the trust information of all the vehicles in a vehicular network. Decentralisation, tamper-proofing, consistency, timeliness and seamless availability are the key features of this approach. A joint proof-of-work and proof-of-stake consensus mechanism has been proposed for enabling all the supporting roadside units to compete to be a miner for updating the trust values (i.e. by adding a new trust block in the blockchain).	MATLAB

(continued)

Table 10.1 (continued)

[11]	A hybrid trustworthy cluster selection scheme in VANETs based on mobility similarities and trust factors	Proposes a hybrid cluster head selection protocol based on stability (measured as mobility similarities) and trust factors (based on data trust and communication trust) subsequently leading to dissemination of safety-critical vehicular messages in a highly secure and ubiquitous manner and in turn mitigating the excessive network management overhead. Unlike conventional trust schemes with static trust functions, the proposed protocol is event-specific in nature, i.e. safety-critical events have more impact on a reporting vehicle's trust in contrast to non-safety (infotainment) messages.	VEINS (an open-source simulation tool incorporating both SUMO and OMNET++)

[a]Familiarity—refers to the acquaintance among two vehicles (*between a rater/evaluator and ratee*) and describes whether a rater has any prior knowledge of the ratee or not;
Similarity—relates to the context similarity and deliberates on the similarity of the travelling statuses of the rater and the ratee; and
Timeliness—defines the measure of the freshness of the reputation segments. Reputation segments are the opinions of the 1-hop neighbours in the vicinity of a target vehicle
(*the difference between the formation time of the reputation segment and the current time is estimated for predicting this particular measure*)

SDN possesses a globalised view of underlying networking architecture. Thus, it is capable of monitoring the behaviour of any entity (or node) within the network. This is of essence especially in the case of a vehicular platoon or cluster, wherein a malicious vehicle may try to consume the network resources, or a malicious attack may be launched on a particular vehicle forcing it to behave bizarrely, thereby becoming a possible source of threat for the other vehicles, vehicular passengers and vulnerable road pedestrians. SDN in this scenario can immediately act and offline the malicious vehicle from the network and broadcast warning messages to the neighbouring vehicles (i.e. in the immediate vicinity) or to other vehicles in the anticipated travelling trajectory of the malicious vehicle in order to ensure that the malicious vehicle does not become part of any vehicular platoon so as to further disrupt the entire road and network traffic. In worst cases, if a malicious entity can launch an attack on either the southbound or northbound interface of the SDN controller, the vehicles can still act in a conventional manner until the SDN controller has not been fully restored and acquired all of the trajectories and updated vehicular traffic information [5, 48].

Moreover, a number of malicious attacks are fully capable of consuming a vehicle's resources. Such malicious attack types include the following: (1) presenting or displaying excessive unwanted adware without the vehicular user's consent thereby consuming its bandwidth, or (2) in case where the malicious entity lets a vehicle to deliberately broadcast without any particular reason, or (3) utilises a vehicle's resource for intelligently taking over entire network by either generating self-proclaimed higher trust values to become the platoon or cluster head or (4) by inclining the network favorability to its side.

SDN with its globalised view of the underlying networking topology can keep an eye on susceptible behaviours, e.g. (1) sudden increase in the trust values of a vehicle with historically recorded low trust values, (2) sudden broadcasting of data traffic from a vehicle (or even from the cluster head) more than the normal thresholds, (3) zig-zag vehicular trajectories on the road, (4) downloading of any malicious and prohibited content, etc. Accordingly, it can take appropriate actions and reinstate recovery mechanisms.

SDN probably has a better understanding of the ongoing dynamics of the network, and much earlier than the vehicles which themselves are a victim of the malicious attacks tend to realise that they are maliciously controlled. Hence, SDN-based VANETs are highly recommended in contrast to the conventional vehicular networks.

10.5 Conclusion

It is beyond any doubt that the demand for a safe and secure travelling experience has increased over the past decades. Accordingly, engineers and scientists in both academia and industry have promulgated the notion of smart cities in order to enhance the safety of drivers and vulnerable road pedestrians by not only improving the existing transportation infrastructures but by also strengthening the vehicular communication platforms via introducing promising diverse radio access technologies which guarantee higher bandwidths, lower latencies and thus support the notion of heterogeneous networking. Consequently, the notion of IoV has emerged making vehicles an integral component of the IoT landscape. As vehicles are increasingly being connected to the Internet, a number of security challenges have also transpired, which if not adequately addressed could have grave challenges for both the vehicular users and the pedestrians. In this aspect, this chapter discusses the diverse security attacks typically encountered by the vehicular networks.

Moreover, since vehicular networks are highly dynamic and distributed in nature, the traditional security techniques (such as cryptography) which primarily utilise certificates and public key infrastructures for ensuring security are not feasible especially as the network availability could not be guaranteed at all times. Therefore, this chapter also deliberates on the notion of trust management vis-à-vis vehicular networks whose salient characteristics not only ensure the eviction of both malicious and selfish vehicles but further take into account the quality of data (i.e. messages) exchanged and the behaviour of vehicles within the network. Finally, the emerging and promising paradigm of SDN has been brought into consideration for reaping its benefits to ensure a safe and secure trust-based vehicular networking landscape.

Acknowledgements The corresponding author acknowledges the generous support of the *Government of the Commonwealth of Australia* for funding the research-at-hand via its International Research Training Program (Allocation No. 2017560).

References

1. Sun SH, Hu JL, Peng Y, Pan XM, Zhao L, Fang JY (2016) Support for vehicle-to-everything services based on LTE. IEEE Wirel Commun 23(3):4–8
2. Seo H, Lee KD, Yasukawa S, Peng Y, Sartori P (2016) LTE evolution for vehicle-to-everything services. IEEE Commun Mag 54(6):22–28
3. Choi J, Prelcic NG, Daniels R, Bhat CR, Heath RW (2016) Millimeter wave vehicular communication to support massive automotive sensing. IEEE Commun Mag 54(12):160–167
4. Hu P, Dhelim S, Ning H, Qiu T (2017) Survey on fog computing: architecture, key technologies, applications and open issues. J Netw Comput Appl 98(September):27–42
5. Deng DJ, Lien SY, Lin CC, Hung SC, Chen WB (2017) Latency control in software-defined mobile-edge vehicular networking. IEEE Commun Mag 55(8):87–93
6. Va V, Shimizu T, Bansal G, Health RW (2016) Millimeter wave vehicular communications: a survey. Found Trends Netw 10(1):1–113
7. Mabrouk A, Kobbane A, Sabir E, Ben-Othman J, Koutbi ME (2016) Meeting always-best-connected paradigm in heterogeneous vehicular network: a graph theory and a signaling game analysis. Veh Commun 5:1–8
8. He Z, Zhang D, Liang J (2016) Cost-efficient sensory data transmission in heterogeneous software-defined vehicular networks. IEEE Sens J 16(20):7342–7354
9. Ahmad F, Franqueira VNL, Adnane A (2018) TEAM: a trust evaluation and management framework in context-enabled vehicular ad-hoc networks. IEEE Access 6(3):28643–28660
10. Gai F, Zhang J, Zhu P, Jiang X (2017) Ratee-based trust management system for internet of vehicles. In: Wireless algorithms, systems, and applications. Lecture notes in computer science, vol 10251, pp 344–355

11. Oubabas S, Aoudjit R, Rodrigues JJPC, Talbi S (2018) Secure and stable vehicular ad hoc network clustering algorithm based on hybrid mobility similarities and trust management scheme. Veh Commun 13:128–138
12. Sedjelmaci H, Senouci SM, Bouali T (2017) Predict and prevent from misbehaving intruders in heterogeneous vehicular networks. Veh Commun 10:74–83
13. Contreras J, Zeadally S, Guerrero-Ibanez JA (2017) Internet of vehicles: architecture, protocols, and security. IEEE Internet Things J 99:1–9
14. Lu N, Cheng N, Zhang N, Shen X, Mark JW (2014) Connected vehicles: solutions and challenges. IEEE Internet Things J 1(4):289–299
15. Xu W et al (2018) Internet of vehicles in big data era. IEEE/CAA J Autom Sin 5(1):19–35
16. Akhunzada A, Khan MK (2017) Toward secure software defined vehicular networks: taxonomy, requirements, and open issues. IEEE Commun Mag 55(7):110–118
17. Maio A Di et al (2016) Enabling SDN in VANETs: what is impact on security? Sensors (Switzerland) 16(12):1–24
18. Cui L, Yu FR, Yan Q (2016) When big data meets software-defined networking: SDN for big data and big data for SDN. IEEE Netw 30(1):58–65
19. Hasrouny H, Samhat AE, Bassil C, Laouiti A (2017) VANet security challenges and solutions: a survey. Veh Commun 7:7–20
20. Singh J, Pasquier T, Bacon J, Ko H, Eyers D (2016) Twenty security considerations for cloud-supported internet of things. IEEE Internet Things J 3(3):269–284
21. Wang L, Liu G, Sun L (2017) A secure and privacy-preserving navigation scheme using spatial crowdsourcing in fog-based VANETs. Sensors (Switzerland) 17(4)
22. Mosqueda AG, Morales-Sandoval M, Villarreal-Reyes S, Galeana-Zapién H, Rodríguez RR, Alonso-Arévalo MÁ (2017) Multi-hop broadcast message dissemination in vehicular ad hoc networks: a security perspective review. Int J Distrib Sens Netw 13(11):1–21
23. Feng X, Li C-Y, Chen DX, Tang J (2017) A method for defensing against multi-source Sybil attacks in VANET. Peer-to-Peer Netw Appl 10(2):305–314
24. Boeira F, Barcellos MP, Freitas EPD, Vinel A, Asplund M (2017) On the impact of Sybil attacks in cooperative driving scenarios. In: 2017 IFIP networking conference (IFIP networking) and workshops, pp 1–2
25. Sakiz F, Sen S (2017) A survey of attacks and detection mechanisms on intelligent transportation systems: VANETs and IoV. Ad Hoc Netw 61:33–50
26. Bouali T, Senouci S-M, Sedjelmaci H (2016) A distributed detection and prevention scheme from malicious nodes in vehicular networks. Int J Commun Syst 29:1683–1704
27. Gai F, Zhang J, Zhu P, Jiang X (2017) Trust on the ratee: a trust management system for social internet of vehicles. Wirel Commun Mob Comput 2017
28. Raya M, Papadimitratos P, Gligor V, Hubaux J-P (2008) On data-centric trust establishment in ephemeral ad hoc networks. In: Procecedings of 27th IEEE conference on computer communications - INFOCOM, pp 1912–1920
29. Gurung S, Lin D, Squicciarini A, Bertino E (2013) Information-oriented trustworthiness evaluation in vehicular ad-hoc networks. Lecture notes in computer science, LNCS, vol 7873, pp 94–108
30. Jesudoss A, Raja SVK, Sulaiman A (2015) Stimulating truth-telling and cooperation among nodes in VANETs through payment and punishment scheme. Ad Hoc Netw 24(A):250–253
31. Khan U, Agrawal S, Silakari S (2015) Detection of malicious nodes (DMN) in vehicular ad-hoc networks. Procedia - Procedia Comput Sci 46:965–972
32. Haddadou N, Rachedi A, Ghamri-Doudane Y (2013) Trust and exclusion in vehicular ad hoc networks: an economic incentive model based approach. In: Proceedings of computing, communications and IT applications conference (ComComAp 2013), pp 13–18
33. Haddadou N, Rachedi A, Doudane YG (2015) A job market signaling scheme for incentive and trust management in vehicular ad hoc networks. IEEE Trans Veh Technol 64(8):3657–3674
34. Yao X, Zhang X, Ning H, Li P (2017) Using trust model to ensure reliable data acquisition in VANETs. Ad Hoc Netw 55:107–118

35. Hussain R, Nawaz W, Lee J, Son J, Seo JT (2016) A hybrid trust management framework for vehicular social networks. In: CSoNet 2016. LNCS, vol 9795, pp 214–225
36. Sedjelmaci H, Senouci SM (2015) An accurate and efficient collaborative intrusion detection framework to secure vehicular networks. Comput Electr Eng 43:33–47
37. Dhurandher SK, Obaidat MS, Jaiswal A, Tiwari A, Tyagi A (2010) Securing vehicular networks: a reputation and plausibility checks-based approach. In: 2010 IEEE Globecom work. GC'10, pp 1550–1554
38. Soleymani SA et al (2015) Trust management in vehicular ad hoc network: a systematic review. Eurasip J Wirel Commun Netw 146:1–22
39. Yang S, Li J, Liu Z, Wang S (2015) Managing trust for intelligence vehicles: a cluster consensus approach. In: IOV 2015. LNCS, vol 9502, pp 210–220
40. Li W, Song H (2016) ART: an attack-resistant trust management scheme for securing vehicular ad hoc networks. IEEE Trans Intell Transp Syst 17(4):960–969
41. Huang X, Yu R, Kang J, Zhang Y (2017) Distributed reputation management for secure and efficient vehicular edge computing and networks. IEEE Access 5:25408–25420
42. Yang Z, Yang K, Lei L, Zheng K, Leung VCM (2018) Blockchain-based decentralized trust management in vehicular networks. IEEE Internet Things J, 1–10. https://doi.org/10.1109/jiot.2018.2836144
43. Camacho F, Cárdenas C, Muñoz D (2017) Emerging technologies and research challenges for intelligent transportation systems: 5G, HetNets, and SDN. Int J Interact Des Manuf 12(1):327–335
44. He Z, Cao J, Liu X (2016) SDVN: enabling rapid network innovation for heterogeneous vehicular communication. IEEE Netw 30(4):10–15
45. Fontes RDR, Campolo C, Rothenberg CE, Molinaro A (2017) From theory to experimental evaluation: resource management in software-defined vehicular networks. IEEE Access 5:3069–3076
46. Correia S, Boukerche A, Meneguette RI (2017) An architecture for hierarchical software-defined vehicular networks. IEEE Commun Mag 55(7):80–86
47. Azizian M, Cherkaoui S, Hafid AS (2017) Vehicle software updates distribution with SDN and cloud computing. IEEE Commun Mag 55(8):74–79
48. Wang K, Yin H, Quan W, Min G (2018) Enabling collaborative edge computing for software defined vehicular networks. IEEE Netw 32(5):112–117
49. Mahmood A, Butler B, Jennings B (2018) Potential of augmented reality for intelligent transportation systems. In: Lee N (ed) Encyclopedia of computer graphics and games. Springer, Cham, pp 1–7

Chapter 11
A Novel Privacy Preserving Scheme for Cloud-Enabled Internet of Vehicles Users

Leila Benarous and Benamar Kadri

Abstract The Internet of Vehicles (IoV) is the Internet of Things where "things" refer to vehicles. Due to its huge amount of shared data and various types of offered services, relying on the use of cloud as infrastructure is fundamental. Most of road services, regardless of whether they are of an infotainment or a safety type, use location and identity information. As a consequence, the privacy of road users is threatened, and therefore preserving such privacy and safety has also become essential. This chapter presents an overview of existing privacy-preserving strategies and develops a proposal for a novel solution which allows its users to benefit from cloud-enabled IoV location-based services and safety applications, anonymously and securely. The performance of the proposed solution is studied by simulating it against a modeled global passive attacker and comparing it to a state-of-the-art solution. The results are optimistic and out-perform the ones compared with. The scheme ensures that the privacy is preserved with more than 70% against semantic, syntactic, observation mapping, and linkage mapping attacks.

Keywords IoT · Internet of Things · Privacy · Safety · Cloud computing · Internet of Vehicles · IoV · Cloud-Enabled IoV · VANET

11.1 Introduction

The Internet of Vehicles is part of a larger network known as the Internet of Things (IoT) which is composed of connected smart devices and objects of various types and functionalities. The IoT is an attractive paradigm that is now widely commercialized.

L. Benarous (✉)
STIC Laboratory, Faculty of Science, Department of Computer Science, University of Tlemcen, Tlemcen, Algeria
e-mail: leilabenar@yahoo.fr

B. Kadri
STIC Laboratory, Faculty of Technology, Department of Telecommunications, University of Tlemcen, Tlemcen, Algeria
e-mail: benamarkadri@yahoo.fr

Z. Mahmood (ed.), *Security, Privacy and Trust in the IoT Environment*, https://doi.org/10.1007/978-3-030-18075-1_11

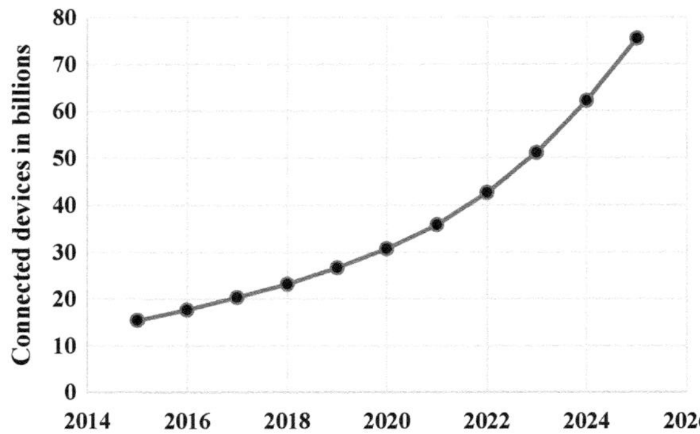

Fig. 11.1 The number of IOT connected devices (adapted from [29])

It has many real-world applications in areas such as smart homes, medical care, and transportation systems. Figure 11.1 shows the rapid growth of the number of connected devices since 2015; it is estimated that it would transcend 30 billion by 2020 and surpass 75 billion by 2025 [1].

Although the Internet of Vehicles appeared after the popularity of the IoT, the concept of connected vehicles is actually not new. It dates back to 2004 when the concept of Vehicular Ad hoc network or VANET was first introduced. However, unlike the concept of Internet of Things that has flourished and got commercialized, the concept of VANET is stagnating for its lack of real-world implementations and some other technical and juridical reasons. Presently, it is being replaced by Internet of vehicles or IoV [2]. In what follows, we briefly discuss what the Internet of Vehicles (IoV) refers to.

IoV is defined by Pasha et al. [3] as a component of the Internet of Things that uses the vehicular cloud computing (VCC) as its infrastructure. Here, vehicles communicate via vehicle-to-vehicle (V2V) and vehicle-to-infrastructure (V2I) wireless connections using Dedicated Short-Range Communication (DSRC) developed by IEEE or Cellular Vehicle-to-Everything (C-V2X) developed by 3GPP which enables lower latency time and bigger range—twice as that of IEEE 802.11p/DSRC [4]. The vehicles can also communicate with other objects, sensors, and humans via vehicle-to-everything (V2X), vehicle-to-sensors (V2S), and vehicle-to-human (V2H) communications, respectively. This enables the IoV to provide various stable services via the cloud computing paradigm that stores and processes information provided by individuals, vehicles, sensors, and other "things".

To recap, the Internet of vehicles is a particular case of the Internet of things which has the vehicles as the main type of its composing nodes. It provides both safety applications just like in VANET and stable cloud-based infotainment services.

The offered services of the IoV are alluring. However, the fact that it exposes the user's identity and real-time location is gravely perilous that it may even waver the decision-makers of whether to continue using it or no. To resolve this issue, numerous solutions are being developed; the majority of them rely on the use of temporal identifiers for the vehicle to preserve the identity privacy; nevertheless, it is not enough to protect the location privacy and avoid tracking.

We illustrate this with an example. Suppose that a vehicle with real identifier "*A*" is using temporal identifier "Temp-ID" to protect its identity, and let "Attacker 1" be the interested person who aims to resolve the owner of "Temp-ID". Now s/he could track "Temp-ID" from its emitted messages and match its owner's habits, routines, frequented places, workplace, and home address to know the real owner of vehicle "*A*". Therefore, the "attacker 1" is not only able to track the vehicle and expose its location privacy but can also resolve the owner of the vehicle and expose the identity privacy at the end.

To avoid such case, researchers proposed to change these temporal identifiers frequently and undetectably so as to ensure the unlinkability, to avoid the tracking, and to preserve the location privacy. In a nutshell, to preserve both the identity and location privacy, it is recommended to use temporal identities that are changed frequently using a robust change strategy.

This chapter is organized as follows: Sect. 11.2 entitled terminology is meant to expand the abbreviations used as well as the essential concepts needed to ease the understanding of the situation. Section 11.3 introduces the reader to the Cloud-Enabled Internet of Vehicles (CE-IoV), its model, and functionality. Section 11.4 defines the CE-IOV characteristics that distinguish it from other kinds of networks. Section 11.5 explains the privacy issue and highlights its importance by stating examples of the possible consequences of its violation. Challenges that make the privacy-preserving difficult to achieve are also stated. Section 11.6 provides an overview of existing IoV privacy preservation schemes and discusses the possibility to adapt VANET privacy protection schemes in the IoV paradigm. Section 11.7 defines the attacker model aiming to break the privacy of the IoV users and explains relevant executed linking attacks which are semantic, syntactic, linkage mapping, and observation mapping. Section 11.8 explains our proposed solution to preserve the identity and location privacy for cloud-enabled Internet of vehicles users. Section 11.9 illustrates the simulation of our solution, its settings, and the realized steps to process the trace files to obtain results. It also looks into its performance against a global passive attacker and analyzes its resiliency with respect to its linking attacks. Section 11.10 resumes the comparative study done between our proposal and a state-of-the-art solution. Both solutions were simulated against the defined attacker model, and both of their performances were compared. Section 11.11 concludes this chapter and provides directions for future work.

In the rest of this chapter, the terms Cloud-Enabled Internet of Vehicle (CE-IoV) and its shorter version, IoV, are used both to refer to the same concept.

11.2 Terminology

Before deepening into the hardcore of the chapter, it is essential to introduce the reader to the key notions that would smoothen its understanding. In this section, we define the terminology used in the chapter starting by a list of abbreviations, and then the explanation of key concepts. The abbreviations used in the chapter are as follows:

BSM	Basic Safety Messages
CAM	Cooperative Awareness Messages
CE-IOV	Cloud-Enabled Internet of Vehicles
CM	Cloud Manager
DC	Do the Change of identifier
DSRC	Dedicated Short-Range Communication
GPA	Global Passive Attacker
IOT	Internet of Things
IOV	Internet of Vehicles
LBS	Location-Based Service
PKI	Public Key Infrastructure
RA	Regional Authority
RDC	Ready to Do the Change of identifier
RSU	Roadside Unit
TA	Trusted Authority
TPD	Tamper-Proof Device
V2H	Vehicle-to-Human communication
V2I	Vehicle-to-Infrastructure communication
V2S	Vehicle-to-Sensor communication
V2V	Vehicle–to-Vehicle communication
V2X	Vehicle to Everything
VANET	Vehicular Ad hoc Network
VCC	Vehicular Cloud Computing
VM	Virtual Machine
VMID	VM Identifier

Now, we briefly explain some of the essential related concepts that would facilitate the understanding of the rest of the chapter.

- ***Vehicular network***: This refers to all networks in which a vehicle is a composing node, e.g., *vehicular* ad hoc *networks* where the vehicles communicate with each other and with an infrastructure to ensure safety on road and enjoy infotainment services; *autonomous vehicles* in which the vehicles receive their data and instructions from a server to drive autonomously; *vehicular clouds* which are clouds formed by vehicles that decide to share their processing, storage, or sensing resources; *vehicular fogs* [5] which also utilizes vehicle computational and communication capacities to ensure the functionality of the network; *Internet of vehicles* which we already defined is the largest network englobing them all.

- ***Beaconing***: This refers to maintaining the stability of the vehicular network and ensuring the safety. Each vehicle has to send periodic messages containing its location, speed, direction, and identity with a frequency of 1 Hz (10 messages per second). These messages are called BSM (in IEEE wave standard) or CAM (in the ETSI standard). We denominate them as beacons and in the rest of the chapter, we continue to use this term to refer to them.
- ***Pseudonym***: This is a short-lived public key certified by a trusted authority [6] also known as Public Key Infrastructure (PKI).
- ***Linkability***: This refers to the ability of the attacker to track the vehicle on road even though it changes its temporal identifier by linking these identifiers to the same vehicle.
- ***Tracking***: This is the possibility to remotely follow the vehicle position on road.
- ***Anonymity***: Being anonymous means hiding the real identity. This can be achieved either using temporal identities in the emitted messages or removing the identity information from them. The identity in vehicular networks is the public key used to sign and encrypt messages. It is fundamental and cannot be removed because only the signed messages can be authenticated and accepted by other vehicles, while others are rejected. Thereby, the anonymity in most of works is ensured using temporal identities and few works only suggested its removal as a solution.
- ***Identifier change strategy***: It a set of methods that are applied by the vehicle before changing its identifier to thwart linkability. Such as changing in a mix-zone, applying silence or at changing at a specific context such as traffic jam, slow speed, at intersections, at roundabout, traffic light, hotspots or when having a specific number of cooperative neighbors, etc.
- ***Eavesdropping***: It is a passive attack where the wirelessly broadcasted messages are intercepted by the attacker's widespread receivers.
- ***Conditional privacy***: Privacy includes ensuring the confidentiality and security of data, the anonymity of users, the unlinkability, and un-traceability of the vehicle on road. However, ensuring complete anonymity, unlinkability, and un-traceability contradicts with other security requirements such as the accountability and non-repudiation. Furthermore, it gives the chance for malicious users to abuse other network users. Thus, limiting the privacy is required. The vehicle should be anonymous and unlinkable to other peer vehicles but if it misbehaves, it shall be held accountable. Thus, the authorities should be able to trace it and know its identity. This is called the conditional privacy.
- ***Accountability and non-repudiation***: It ensures that the sender (originator of the message) cannot deny the fact of having sent the message, and thus, s/he can be legally held accountable for his/her actions [7, 8].
- ***Misbehavior***: The vehicles on roads may not act as honest nodes all the time. They may generate erroneous data either unintentionally because their hardware malfunction or deliberately to mislead other vehicles [9] to take advantage of the road situation or to inject malwares in the network. This type of actions is considered as a misbehavior. The list is not exhaustive and other malicious actions are not mentioned here.

- ***Revocation***: When the vehicles detect a misbehavior, they report it to the authority which in its turn investigates it and revokes the reported node. It is a method to hold the vehicle responsible for its abusive behavior on road also to maintain the correct functionality of the network. It concerns the vehicle's long-term key and the pseudonyms; they are stored in certificate revocation lists (CRL) which are distributed to the vehicles to inform them to not interact with the misbehaving vehicle [10]. The revocation may be followed by legal pursuit of the vehicle's user.
- ***Service messages***: In vehicular networks, a vehicle sends three types of messages: *Beacons* which are periodic messages required to ensure the stability of the networks and the safety of its users; *event-based messages* that are sent when reporting emergency cases such as accidents, landslide, road works, etc.; and *service messages* which are sent by the user to obtain infotainment services, such as navigation systems, weather forecast, restaurants advertisements, coupons, mail, and Internet services.
- ***Authorities***: The vehicular network needs to be maintained by authorities to ensure its functionality, stability, and security. The authorities are responsible for providing certified long-term or short-term (pseudonyms) public keys, of revoking misbehaving nodes and for maintaining the clouds and service provision.

11.3 Cloud-Enabled Internet of Vehicles (CE-IOV)

In this section, we discuss the cloud-enabled Internet of vehicles scenario together with its components, model, functionality, and characteristics.

11.3.1 Generalities

Although the existing literature mentions various proposals for the Internet of vehicles network models [1, 11, 12], no definitive mature standard model exists. However, the model of Kang et al. [13] is the closest to our proposed one. In this model, the CE-IOV contains the LBS provider, an infrastructure-based local cloud with a cloud manager, a central cloud with a registration authority which generates the virtual machine identities (VMID) and sends them to local clouds that distributes them to the registered vehicles.

Our proposed model has similar basic components but, hopefully, is more flexible, realistic, and adaptive to the different constraints of vehicle networks. It satisfies the following requirements:

- Connectivity, ensured by the vehicle-to-vehicle and vehicle-to-infrastructure communications, besides the cellular communication to access the cloud or the Internet services.

- Continuous service in different kinds of environment (Urban, Sparse, or highway) guaranteed by the use of different communication technologies and the use of different kinds of vehicular clouds.
- Availability, reliability, and load balancing, noting that
  - In urban environment, infrastructures (Roadside Units—RSU) are available but the existing obstacles may hinder the connectivity.
  - In sparse environment, the infrastructures may not be deployed or not enough which affects both the connectivity and the continuity of service.
  - In highways, the number of deployed RSUs can be sufficient to form local clouds.

In what follows, we explain the modification made to the Kang et al. model [13] to make it more flexible and to satisfy the abovementioned requirements:

- The *local cloud* should be of VWC (Vehicle with Cloud) type, i.e., a hybrid cloud, made up of an infrastructure-based cloud formed by adjacent RSUs and a cloud manager, and an infrastructure-less cloud formed by vehicles which can contact the cloud manager either by V2V connection or by cellular connection (3G, 4G, or 5G).
- The *central cloud* should be managed by the global registration authority which generates the VMIDs and maintains global revocation list. It can be accessed by the Internet. It is not a single authority but a set of distributed entities who have the same role. This balances the load on this entity and avoids the single point of failure.
- Both the central and local clouds customize virtual machines to satisfy the queries of the users; each machine has a unique identifier known as VMID.
- We assume that there are regional intermediary authorities managing the local clouds. A Regional Authority (RA) gets a VMID list from the central trusted authority (TA) to distribute them to local clouds; it also maintains intermediary revocation list. The organization of the TA and RA can be metaphorically compared to the DNS hierarchical organization. There could be a TA by government per example and RAs per each State/County of it. TAs can be connected together so do the RAs.

Figure 11.2 illustrates the hierarchical organization of the network components. Some of the benefits of using this model include the following:

- The use of distributed TAs connected together balances the load and avoids single point of failure.
- The use of RAs balances the load and on the TAs. It also reduces the verification and revocation process costs in terms of time of response and effectiveness of the revocation.
- The hierarchical organization makes the network flexible; also, it allows the re-usage of used non-blacklisted identifiers cross region.
- The use of Hybrid clouds (Vehicle with Clouds) ensures the connectivity and the continuity of the service in different environment (sparse, urban or highway).

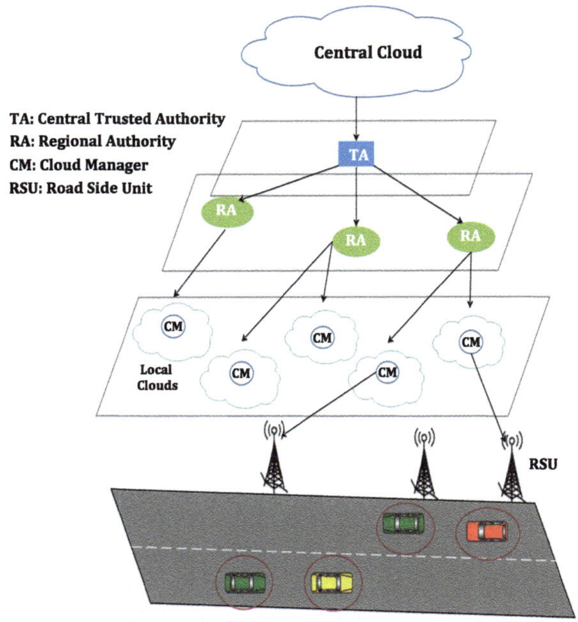

Fig. 11.2 Components of the proposed network model

- The live virtual machine migration from one infrastructure to another, from a vehicle to another or between clouds avoids the interruption of services and the repetitive authentications as the vehicle travels through the road.

11.3.2 The CE-IoV System Functionality

To be able to use the IoV services, a vehicle needs to be registered at the trusted authority TA to obtain a long-term certified key and credentials which it uses to register at the regional authorities RA and to authenticate itself to the cloud manager CM. Each of these functions is explained below:

- **Registration at the TA**: Initially, the vehicle registers at the trusted authority TA to help the vehicle to subscribe to different Regional Authorities (RAs) as it moves from one region to another. Once registered, the vehicle obtains a pair of long-term private/public keys. The keys are used for encryption and digital signature of messages and beacons. Furthermore, once it registers to cloud services maintained by the TA, the vehicle is assigned with a virtual machine responsible for handling future queries (Fig. 11.3 phase 4). This virtual machine has a unique identifier called VMID. The user is provided with credentials to authenticate to the cloud services. A copy of the registered members is forwarded to the RA (Fig. 11.3 phase 5). We note that the initial registration at the TA happens upon the purchase of

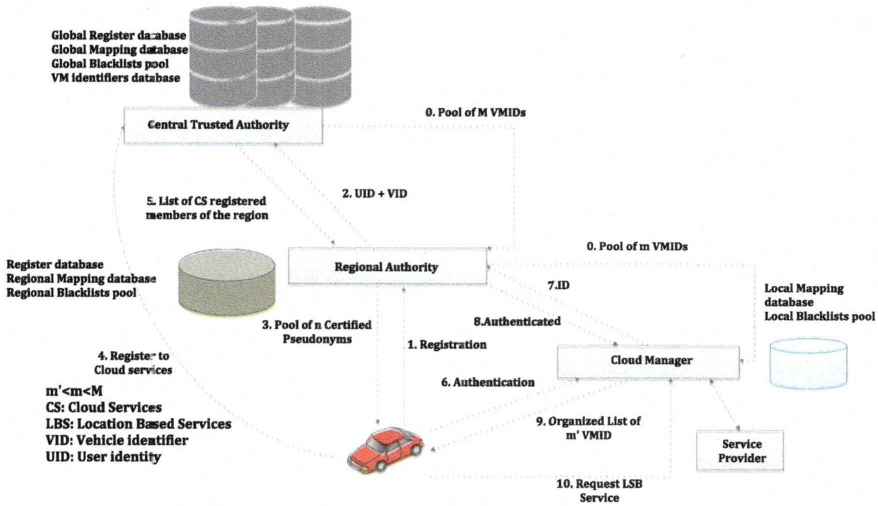

Fig. 11.3 General description of the CE-IoV (numbers refer to phases)

the vehicle only, the keys, and identifiers can be stored either in the vehicle's TPD (tamper-proof device) or separately in external smart key/card or dongle.

- **Registration at the RA**: Upon entering a new region, the vehicle registers at the RA of this region (Fig. 11.3 phase (1)) using the provided credentials and public key. The RA first checks this vehicle with the Trusted Authority (TA) (Fig. 11.3 phase (2)). Once confirmed as a registered member, the RA assigns a pool of certified pseudonyms to this vehicle (Fig. 11.3 phase 3).
- **Authentication with Cloud Manager CM**: The vehicle uses its credentials and VMID to authenticate itself to the CM broadcasting advertisement of a service of interest (Fig. 11.3 phase 6). The cloud manager checks with the RA if the user is registered (Fig. 11.3 phase 7). If it is the case (Fig. 11.3 phase 8), then it provides it with an organized list of short-lived VMIDs (Fig. 11.3 phase 9). The cloud manager CM maps the provided VMIDs with the vehicle's public key and credentials locally in its database, for ensuring traceability, accountability, and protentional blacklisting in case of misbehavior.
- **Request of LBS**: Once the vehicle receives its VMIDs, it can use them to request LBS and cloud services securely and while ensuring the privacy in one hand and the continuity of the service in another hand (Fig. 11.3 phase 10).

It should be noted that the RA provides each CM with a large number (m) of VMIDs from a larger list of (M) VMIDs which it has received from the TA (Fig. 11.3 phase 0). Figure 11.3 illustrates the registration, authentication, and use of CE-IoV services processes with the phases explained above.

11.4 Characteristics of CE-IoV

After explaining the cloud-enabled Internet of vehicles (CE-IOV) model and functionality, we can extract some of its characteristics that would distinguish it from other types of networks.

One of the main traits is that it allows humans, vehicles, and things interactions. This means that there is a large quantity of various data types that are being provided or used as a service. Consecutively, other characteristics of CE-IoV may be marked as follows:

- The CE-IOV is larger than conventional vehicular network in terms of participating nodes and exchanged data and services.
- It is more stable, because it does not rely on one technology of communication but a mix such as vehicular communications or cellular communications to access Internet services. Besides its usage of cloud computing to ensure the diversity, the security and the continuity of service without repetitive authentications.
- It provides more services as the variety of needs of its users is larger, so does the offered applications.
- It is global. Unlike the vehicular networks, there is a limit of connectivity to the neighbors or a certain area of coverage. The IoV extends its area by the use of Internet and cloud computing so as the user can benefit from its services anywhere, anytime.
- It is scalable. The more the users, the more the services, the better is the IoV, just like the Internet of Things.

11.5 Privacy in CE-IOV

As explained in the previous section, CE-IoV allows humans, vehicles, and things to interact. The humans are the individuals using or providing data or services to the networks; they include drivers, onboard passengers, pedestrian, cyclists, etc. The vehicles are the nodes that provide or consume data and services. The things are all other devices that consume or provide data and services such as sensors, checkpoints, etc. Consecutively, this makes the CE-IOV larger than conventional vehicular network, more stable, and provides more services locally and globally.

After introducing the reader to the relevant concepts and characteristics of this network, we now focus on a core issue, namely, the privacy issue. We first explain what privacy is, its types, and importance; then we highlight the challenges that should be taken into consideration when developing a privacy-preserving solution for IoV.

11.5.1 What Is Privacy?

The privacy concept has always existed, although its definition varied from one era to another as it depended on what to consider as private, for whom and from whom. However, the modern privacy definition as was first defined by Warren and Brandeis [14] as *the right to be left alone.* Adrienn Lukács, in his paper [15], presents the history of privacy and its diverse definitions through the different eras with the evolution of the technology and society. To sum up, we define the privacy as the right of the users to decide what is being known about them, to whom, when, and where. We take an example of cyberworld users. They would strongly object to the idea of their identity, data such as photos, or location being sent implicitly without their knowledge from their devices, just like how they object being stalked; however, they may voluntarily share their data on their social media accounts. The reason is that individuals can decide what to share, to whom, when, and where.

Despite the awareness of the privacy as one of the fundamental rights, the users are still generously purchasing technologies, owing to the fact that the advertisers focus on the positive side of their exposed products and they would not mention its negative sides. If you would visit any showroom or venture, they would start convincing you about the services that would be beneficial for you if you use a vehicle that is part of IoV. The variety of continuously available services would tempt any user and blind him/her from the risks of such technology on his/her privacy. So, they may choose to ignore the risks either because they do not take themselves as subjects to privacy attack or they take lightly the consequences of such a threat.

Before continuing with the explanation of the privacy types, we first state some of the consequences of privacy leakage to highlight its importance. We enumerate the possible ramifications from least to the most dangerous, as follows:

- Targeted advertising: Through this, the frequently visited places and user's interest can be known. Likewise, more directed advertisement will be sent to him/her. Per example, if someone frequents a library, they would receive book ads; if they regularly go to the gym, then sports sessions and equipment ads would be sent.
- Trajectory tracking, planning, and control: If the user frequents a specific road, and if someone can track this, they may control the traffic on it either by controlling traffic signals or spreading fake information that it is jammed either to delay him/her or to reroute him/her.
- Stalking and intimacy invasion: By tracking the vehicle, information about his/her frequented places, secret hideouts, habits, and favorite routes can be collected. Being under someone's radar not only gives the feeling of insecurity but also the invasion of privacy.
- Blackmailing: Following someone's whereabout out of liking or interest is less dangerous than blackmailing him/her with the collected information to oblige him/her to make a specific decision, an action or even to ask for money.
- Vehicle theft: If a thief can locate the targeted vehicle, they can plan when to steal it and how to do it. It makes the stealing process and transportation of the stolen vehicle effective and undetectable.

- Planning road traps, kidnapping, or assassination: Similarly, if the vehicle real-time location is known, arranging road causalities, ambushes, abductions, and executions would become successfully and untraceably plausible.

The above examples are enough to demonstrate the seriousness of this issue (i.e., the lack or inadequacy of privacy) and the significance of its preservation and assurance. Having highlighted the importance of the privacy preservation, we continue to explain the types of privacy in the IoV, viz., data privacy, identity privacy, and location privacy [16].

- Data privacy is the confidentiality of the content of the query; it is protected by encryption [16].
- Identity privacy is the global identity of the vehicle or its owner which is its public key used to encrypt messages.
- Location privacy concerns broadcasted real-time positions, the parsed trajectories, frequented places, routinely routs, etc.

Since the data privacy is protected by encryption, most CE-IoV researchers working on preserving the privacy focus on protecting the identity and location.

11.5.2 Privacy Challenges

Previously, we explained the privacy, its importance, and types. In this subsection, we briefly discuss some of the difficulties and key points that should be kept in mind when developing a privacy-preserving scheme especially in relation to CE-IoV.

- First, in CE-IoV, every vehicle needs to send periodical messages that contain its position, direction, speed, and certified public key. These messages if intercepted by malicious eavesdropper can lead to the tracking of the vehicle through its parsed trajectories.
- Second, the wireless communications between vehicles and with infrastructure make the eavesdropping easy.
- Third, the non-repudiation imposed by the juridical system conflicts with the user's demands to be anonymous and unlinkable. Therefore, there should be trade-off when developing a solution to satisfy both sides.
- Fourth, eavesdropping is passive and undetectable type of attack which gives the snooper more advantages, such as long tracking period.
- Fifth, the privacy-preserving solution should not interfere with functionality of the network or cause the discontinuity of services. Therefore, propositions suggesting the cessation of beaconing or the elimination of the identity and location information from it affect negatively the performance of the networks and should not be accepted as a solution.

11.6 Related Works

So far, we have explained the cloud-enabled Internet of vehicles and the privacy issues therein; we emphasized its importance and the necessity of preserving it. In this section, we give an overview of the various strategies reported in the literature that aim to preserve the privacy in vehicular networks [17, 18]. Then, we give a classification of some of them and investigate their feasibility in case of CE-IOV.

We already said that there are two approaches to preserving the privacy using temporal keys, viz., (1) the standard approach where the keys are certified by the TA or its subsidiaries; and (2) the self/group-generated keys which are not certified by the authority. We now continue below to explain each approach.

The IEEE 1609.2 standard [19] specifies that each vehicle uses certified and revocable PKI-based pseudonyms which are pairs of public and private keys used for digital signatures and encryption. To preserve the privacy, these pseudonyms are changed upon their expiry using one of the following strategies: adding silent periods [20], being within a cooperative crowd [21], inside mix zones [22–26], or in hotspots [17, 27]. Some other approaches also exist and the list is not exhaustive; more details can be found in Table 11.1.

Researchers who support the second approach suggested the use of self-generated keys to protect the privacy. However, because they are not certified, they cannot be revoked if the vehicle misbehaves; besides, the receiving vehicles cannot trust messages signed with non-certified keys. The group signature and the hybrid approaches were also proposed and both suffer from the large computation overhead [16], the difficulty to form and maintain the groups in a dynamic environment, the lack of revocation process and the repudiation. The first one proposes that each vehicle uses a non-certified individual private key to sign its messages and a shared public key for the verification of signatures where all the keys are generated by the group manager. In the latter, the vehicle generates its own pseudonyms and signs their certificates using the group private key. The group public key is used to verify the certified pseudonyms [16].

Table 11.1 summarizes the existing identifiers (pseudonyms and/or VMIDs) changing approaches by category, their advantages, drawbacks, and the possibility to apply existing VANET location privacy-preserving solutions in CE-IoV.

11.7 Attacker Model

In the previous sections, we focused on the discussions on the IOV, the privacy issue, and the existing solutions. However, although we mentioned that the privacy is threatened by an adversary/eavesdropper or attacker, we have not specified who is this attacker, what are the privacy attacks, and how are they executed. This section is dedicated to answering these questions.

Table 11.1 Pseudonym changing strategies in VANET and IoV

Privacy approaches	VANET					CE-IoV	
	Cooperative			Noncooperative		Noncooperative	Cooperative
	Collaborative change	Mix-Zone	Context-based	Periodical pseudonym change	Silent period	Kang et al. [13]	Our strategy
Principle	The vehicles synchronize the pseudonym change either by the use of encrypted messages or flagged messages [30, 31]	The RSU creates, maintains, and advertises the existence of a mix-zone. It is defined as a zone where the attacker cannot track the pseudonym change, because vehicles within it are undistinguishable either because they are silent or because they exchange encrypted messages that cannot be read by the attacker or outside of this zone [30]	The vehicle changes its pseudonyms based on context parameters (Internal/external) [30], such as low speed (Traffic jam) [32], number of neighbors, social spots [27], etc.	The vehicle changes its pseudonym at fixed or random times, i.e., it changes its pseudonym independently upon its expiry without adding any extra measure or strategy [30]	The vehicle stops broadcasting beacons for a period of time called the silent period before changing its pseudonym. Once the change is done, it resumes its activity with the new pseudonym [30]	– The pseudonyms and VMIDs are changed simultaneously – The vehicle synchronizes with the CM to do this change. The synchronization process implies the request to change, getting the approval, checking the time continuously, choosing VMID, and informing the cloud manager to record it	The identifiers (pseudonym, VMID) are changed simultaneously using flag-based cooperative change strategy to ensure the unlinkability and anonymity. The cloud manager does not need to be included and synchronized with to do the change. Instead, it is just informed to record it

(continued)

Table 11.1 (continued)

Privacy approaches	VANET					CE-IoV	
	Cooperative			Noncooperative		Noncooperative	Cooperative
	Collaborative change	Mix-Zone	Context-based	Periodical pseudonym change	Silent period	Kang et al. [13]	Our strategy
Advantage	– Increases the unlinkability – Optimizes the number of used pseudonyms – Infrastructure-less which means that it can be used in any environment	– Enhances the unlinkability	– Enhances the unlinkability	– Reduces the overhead of synchronization and mix-zone creation – Simple and fast – Easily implemented	– Enhances the unlinkability and confuses the adversary	– The simultaneous change of identifiers protects against observation and mapping linkage attacks – Prevents repetitive authentications	– Preserves the identity and the location privacy – Prevents services interruption and repetitive authentication – The use of flags and organized list of identities (CE-IoV) optimizes the network overhead – Protects against observation mapping, linkage mapping, syntactic and semantic attacks

(continued)

Table 11.1 (continued)

Privacy approaches	VANET					CE-IoV	
	Cooperative			Noncooperative		Noncooperative	Cooperative
	Collaborative change	Mix-Zone	Context-based	Periodical pseudonym change	Silent period	Kang et al. [13]	Our strategy
Drawback	Does not guaranty the unlinkability when there are road restrictions (one-way roads with vehicles A, B, C in order, even after the change the adversary can link the new pseudonyms X, Y, Z with old A, B, C, respectively)	– Infrastructure dependent – Cannot avoid linkability if the vehicle is alone – A study is required to place the mix-zone at the appropriate locations – Can affect safety applications (use of silent periods) – Overhead and Overload caused by encryption (CMIX: Encrypted Mix-Zones)	– Related to a specific context and conditions which may not be satisfied all the time – Overload and/or overhead caused by the verification of context	– Does not guaranty the unlinkability even if the change happens within a crowd of vehicles – Overconsumption of pseudonyms unnecessarily when the change cannot guaranty the unlinkability and privacy preserving (when within noncooperative crowd)	– Vehicle changing pseudonyms after random silent periods can still be linkable. – The silent period should be studied because long periods affect the safety applications, and short periods can be linkable – Using silent periods when within a noncooperative crowd of vehicles is linkable	– The strategy used to change the pseudonym is not mentioned. However, judging by the given details and seeing that there was no cooperation between adjacent vehicles before or after the change. Thus, it does not protect against syntactic linking attack – The synchronization process causes overhead to the network	–

(continued)

Table 11.1 (continued)

Privacy approaches	VANET					CE-IoV	
	Cooperative			Noncooperative		Noncooperative	Cooperative
	Collaborative change	Mix-Zone	Context-based	Periodical pseudonym change	Silent period	Kang et al. [13]	Our strategy
Application in IoV	It can be applied to IoV. However, it is vulnerable to the same drawback as in VANET	– If applied to IoV, it can cause the discontinuity of service due to requirements of mix-zones (Silence or encryption)	– It can be applied to IoV if the context condition includes those of IoV to ensure the continuous service and avoid packet loss	– It is applicable in IoV. However, it will have the same drawbacks as in VANETs	– If applied to IoV, it causes packet drop and service discontinuity	Applied to IoV	Applied to IoV

To be able to track a vehicle, various methods can be used. Probably, the cameras are the first idea that would come to the reader's mind when we mention the tracking. Indeed, cameras can be an excellent tracking tool but they are costly, and they require individuals to watch all the recordings to track the victim which is both tiring and time-consuming. Although implementing advanced object tracking techniques may present an optimistic solution, it suffers from a variable false-negative and false-positive values which are affected by the light conditions and quality of the captured images. Another approach is the tracking of radio signal patterns which may be subject to interferences, if the vehicle is within a large crowd such as being in rush hours.

In fact, the most potential and appropriate method is the tracking by GPS which is already implemented in the vehicles because of the network requirements. This makes the eavesdropping easier and cheaper. The attacker can simply install low priced receivers across the observation regions to eavesdrop a vehicle's beacons containing pseudonyms and real-time positions, also application messages when using LBSs of CE-IoV containing VMIDs and positions, noting that these positions are provided by the vehicle's onboard GPS.

In this chapter, we have implemented a Global Passive Attacker (GPA) that intercepts the beacons and LBS messages and executes four types of linking attacks [13, 16] to track the vehicles. These attacks are now explained in the following subsections.

11.7.1 Observation Mapping Attack

Let V_A be a vehicle having A as its pseudonym and VM_A as its VMID. We also suppose that V_A is currently at position Pos_1. For the network requirements, V_A that is using LBS would send both beacons and LBS messages like this: V_A sends Beacon (A, Pos_1) and LBS (VM_A, Pos_1). Consequently, the GPA concludes by observation mapping that A and VM_A belong to the same vehicle V_A that is currently at Pos_1.

11.7.2 Linkage Mapping Attack

Following the same notation and hypothesis as in the previous subsection, we suppose that the vehicle initially had the pseudonym A and VMID VM_A and that it only changes its pseudonym to A′ while keeping VM_A. We give below the messages sent before and after this change:

- Before the change of pseudonym, V_A sends: Beacon (A, Pos_1) and LBS (VM_A, Pos_1).
- After the change of pseudonym, V_A sends Beacon (A′, Pos_2) and LBS (VM_A, Pos_2).

The GPA can deduct from the messages sent before the change that Vehicle V_A uses A and VM_A and from the messages sent after the change that V_A uses A′ and VM_A. By combining the obtained knowledge, the GPA deduces that A, A′, and VM_A belong to the same vehicle. A similar conclusion is obtained if the VMID changes more frequently than the pseudonym.

11.7.3 *Syntactic Linking Attack*

Using the same notations, let V_A be a vehicle having three neighbor vehicles V_B, V_C, and V_D. Each vehicle sends Beacon (A, Pos_A) and LBS (VM_A, Pos_A); Beacon (B, Pos_B) and LBS (VM_B, Pos_B); Beacon (C, Pos_C) and LBS (VM_C, Pos_C); and Beacon (D, Pos_D) and LBS (VM_D, Pos_D), respectively.

Supposing that only V_A changes its identifiers , the messages sent by each vehicle after this change are Beacon (A′, $Pos_{A'}$) and LBS ($VM_{A'}$, $Pos_{A'}$); Beacon (B, $Pos_{B'}$) and LBS (VM_B, $Pos_{B'}$); Beacon (C, $Pos_{C'}$) and LBS (VM_C, $Pos_{C'}$); and Beacon (D, $Pos_{D'}$) and LBS (VM_D, $Pos_{D'}$), respectively.

By comparing the old set with the new set of received messages, the GPA presumes that A, A′, VM_A, and $VM_{A'}$ belong to the same vehicle V_A. We remind the readers that the captured and compared messages are consecutively separated by one-tenth second which eliminates the possibility that A′; $VM_{A'}$ belongs to a completely new vehicle.

11.7.4 *Semantic Linking Attack*

The GPA, who intercepts beacons, can learn the direction, speed, and position of each vehicle. Therefore, with simple calculations using these data, s/he can predict their future position. Moreover, when the vehicle changes its identifiers and sends messages with them, the GPA can match the positions on the received messages with the predictions s/he made earlier. If these positions are a match, the GPA can successfully track the vehicle even though it has changed its identifiers.

11.8 Proposed Scheme for the Preservation of Privacy

After explaining our implemented attacker model, we continue in this section to discuss the proposed solution that preserves the privacy, and in the section that follows, we give the simulation result of using it against the attacker model described in the previous sections. This scheme has two levels of protection:

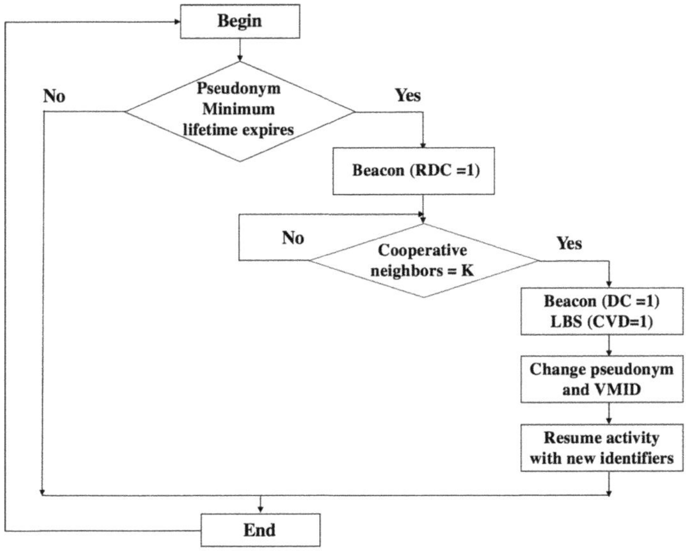

Fig. 11.4 Diagram of the proposed identifier changing scheme

- Safety beaconing level and
- CE-IOV LBS level.

Each of these will be explained below in its separate subsection. Figure 11.4 illustrates the overall proposed change strategy.

11.8.1 Anonymity and Location Privacy at Safety Beaconing Level

To ensure the anonymity, we use pseudonyms; and to preserve the location privacy, we have to avoid linkability. Therefore, the use of a robust change strategy is fundamental. Our change strategy relies on the cooperation of neighbors. To implement our solution, we used two bits from the beacon header: one is RDC (ready to change pseudonym), and the other is DC (Do the change). When the minimum stable lifetime of the vehicle's pseudonym expires, it sets its RDC bit in beacon header to one and sends it. If it receives k beacons from k neighbor vehicles with RDC set to one as well, it sets the DC bit in the beacon header to one and does the change. Vehicles receiving DC flagged beacon do the change simultaneously and continue to broadcast beacons with their new pseudonyms.

11.8.2 Anonymity and Location Privacy at CE-IoV LBS Level

Similarly, as at the VANET level, we use a bit from the header of service messages which we named CVD (Change VMID). The CVD bit is used to inform the cloud manager of the VMID change as explained in Sect. 11.3.2. Once notified, the CM can track and record this change. We remind the readers that the list is organized, and both the CM and the vehicle have the same copy. An example of such a list is [VM_1, VM_2, VM_3, …, VM_n]; if a vehicle is using VM_1 and informs the CM that it will change its VMID, the CM would automatically know that it will be using VM_2, since the vehicle is set to use the VMIDs in the list sequentially.

The change of VMIDs happens simultaneously with the change of pseudonyms. The vehicles cooperate with neighbor vehicles to change its pseudonym, and when it sends DC flagged beacons to its neighbors, it simultaneously informs the CM by setting the CVD flag in the request service message to one, which will in turn records this change. The vehicle and its cooperating neighbors change their identifiers and resume their activities with their new VMIDs and Pseudonyms.

11.9 Simulation and Performance Results

This section explains the simulation settings and the results obtained when testing the performance of our solution against the Global Passive Attacker (GPA) defined in Sect. 11.7 that executes four linking attacks which are semantic, syntactic observation mapping, and linking mapping attacks.

11.9.1 Simulation Settings

The proposed solution was implemented and simulated using NS2 [28] on Manhattan map grid created by MobiSim. It was tested on five scenarios on the same map which have the same simulation time (900 s). We varied the number of vehicles starting at 10 vehicles per scenario (low density), then 50 and 100 vehicles per scenario (medium density), and lastly 150 and 200 vehicles per scenario (high density). Each car sends periodic BSM/CAM to its neighbors and LBS messages to a service provider after authenticating itself to the CM. Additionally, we implemented the global passive attacker as static nodes which have the role of receivers distributed as grid across the map to fully cover it. The simulation parameters are shown in Table 11.2.

Table 11.2 Simulation parameters

Simulation parameters	
Tools	NS 2, MobiSim
Mac layer	802.11p
Simulation time	900 s
Map	1000 × 1000, Manhattan Grid
Pseudonym minimum lifetime	30 s
Vehicle range	300 m
Number of attackers	100
Attacker coverage range	500 m
K cooperative neighbors	2
Scenario 1: number of vehicles	10
Scenario 2: number of vehicles	50
Scenario 3: number of vehicles	100
Scenario 4: number of vehicles	150
Scenario 5: number of vehicles	200

11.9.2 Results and Discussion

Here, we discuss how we obtained, sorted, and extracted the results which are illustrated in the graphs below. We also analyze and comment on them. The simulation generates two types of trace files: trace files of the vehicle activity (beaconing and LBS messages) and trace files of the attacker intercepted messages and tracked vehicles.

We first used the trace file of the vehicle and separated them by activity, so we have the beaconing traces in a file and the LBS messages in another. We used these files to extract the number of identifier changes in each level and to check that this change happened simultaneously. Furthermore, these files were needed to check the correctness of the attacker's tracks.

As for the files generated by the attacker, we also separated them by attacks to have a trace file for each type (the semantic, the syntactic, the linkage mapping, and the observation mapping). For each file, we extracted the number of correctly tracked nodes and correctly linked identifier change. We used the extracted information from each file to calculate the ratios which are represented in the figures below.

We now define how we calculate each ratio using the following equations:

$$\text{Ratio of tracked vehicles per attack} = \frac{\textit{number of correctly tracked vehicles per attack}}{\textit{total number of vehicles per scenario}} \tag{11.1}$$

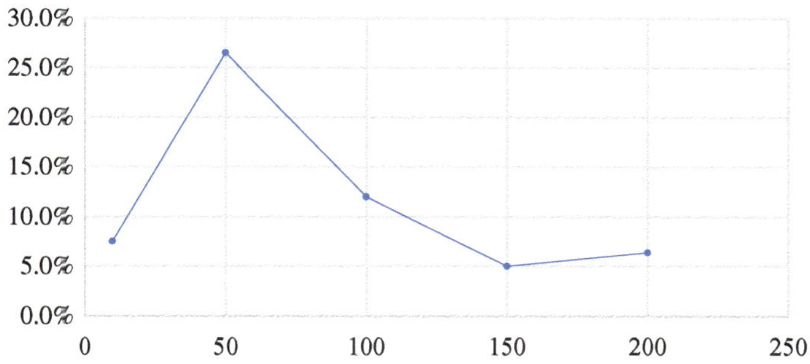

Fig. 11.5 Ratio of tracked vehicles

$$\text{Ratio of tracked vehicles} = AVERAGE\,(ratios\ of\ tracked\ vehicle\ per\ attack) \tag{11.2}$$

$$\text{Ratio of linked identifier per attack} = \frac{number\ of\ correctly\ linked\ identifiers}{total\ number\ of\ changed\ identifiers\ per\ scenario} \tag{11.3}$$

After explaining how we processed the generated files to extract the results and calculate the ratios, we continue now to analyze the figures that display the results obtained.

Figure 11.5 illustrates the calculated ratio of correctly detected vehicles by the modeled GPA when using our proposed scheme. We notice that, overall, it was low and it did not exceed 30%. For most of scenarios, the detected ratio was less than 15% except for the second scenarios which was less than 27% when the number of vehicles was 50. One possible explanation is that in this scenario, the vehicles may have been distributed sparsely and the chances of having cooperative crowd were less which reflected the slightly higher detection ratio compared to other scenarios. We remind the reader that the vehicles' distribution was random. It is true that the more the vehicles, the more the chances of them being neighbors, but we set no rules when generating the scenarios to ensure this case, so as to avoid having programmed and predictable scenarios that generate desired results; instead, we preferred to give realistic results to analyze the performance of our solution objectively. We also observed that, generally speaking, the ratio decreased as the number of vehicles increased, noting that a low tracking ratio reflects a high level of privacy preservation.

After studying the overall tracking ratio, we illustrate in Fig. 11.6 the ratios of tracked vehicles per each attack separately for each scenario.

To facilitate the understanding of the results shown in Fig. 11.6, the numbers 1–5 reflect the simulated scenarios, where in number 1, the number of vehicles is 10 and in numbers 2, 3, 4, and 5, the number of vehicles is 50, 100, 150, and 200, respectively. The tracking ratios for semantic and linking mapping attacks were approximately null for all scenarios because the vehicle changes its identifiers synchronously and

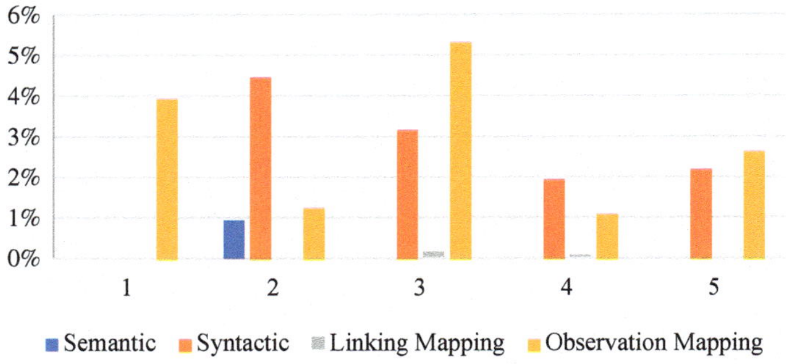

Fig. 11.6 Ratio of tracked vehicles per each attack

cooperatively with its neighbors. The syntactic attack tracking ratio was less 5%, while the observation attack tracking ratio was less than 6%. Both ratios were less than 10%; this indicates that we can ensure with more than 94% certainty that the solution is almost resilient to these attacks, and therefore it preserves the privacy.

11.10 Comparative Study and Performance Analysis

In the previous section, we explained how we tested the performance of our solution against the modeled GPA and how we processed the generated files, extracted the tracking ratios, and analyzed the results. We concluded that both the obtained results (global and detailed) are reasonably satisfying in preserving the privacy. To further analyze our contribution, we decided to compare the resultant performance with a state-of-the-art solution. To do so, we simulated the solution of Kang et al. [13] and compared its results with ours. The simulation was done on the same settings as mentioned in Table 11.2 (except that this solution does not need cooperation of neighbors) and the files generated by the simulation were processed similarly like ours to obtain the ratios, which we illustrate them with the orange graph in Figs. 11.7, 11.8, 11.9, and 11.10, while our results are in blue in the same mentioned figures.

Figure 11.7 provides the global ratio of detected vehicles by the GPA for both solutions. For all the scenarios, our detected ratio is lower than that of Kang et al. [13] which means that our proposed scheme outperforms that of Kang et al. because the lower is the ratio of tracked vehicle, the more robust is the solution in preserving the privacy—given that we are using the same settings and protecting against the same modeled attacker.

Figures 11.8, 11.9, and 11.10 show the tracking ratio obtained by each attack for both solutions. Our solution results for syntactic attack are better than that of Kang et al. (see Fig. 11.8). Besides, both solutions are almost resilient to semantic attack with an identifier linking ratio of less than 2% in overall for Kang et al. solution and less than 1% in ours. The results for all the scenarios are illustrated in Fig. 11.9.

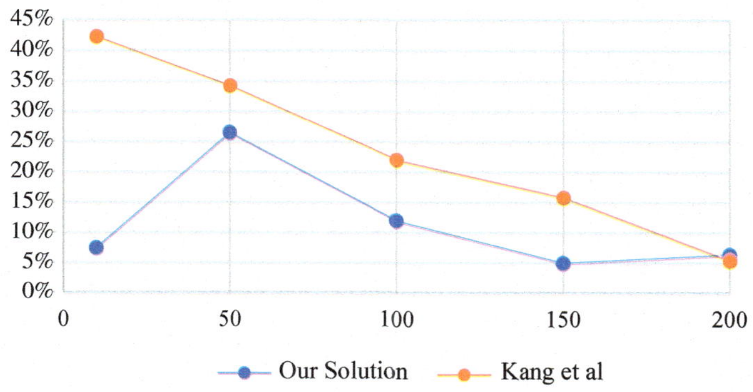

Fig. 11.7 Ratio of tracked vehicles

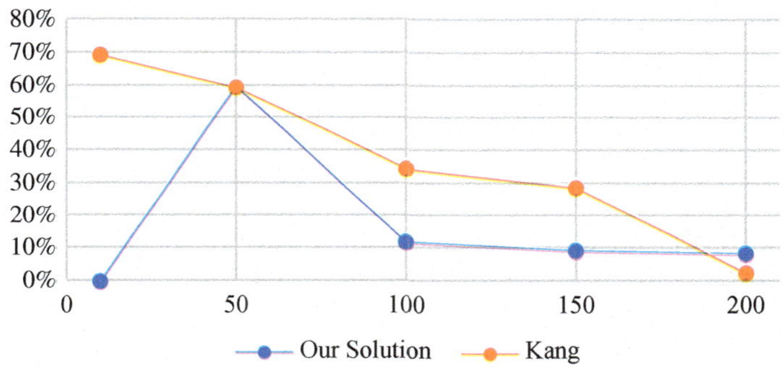

Fig. 11.8 Syntactic attacker's ratio of tracked vehicles

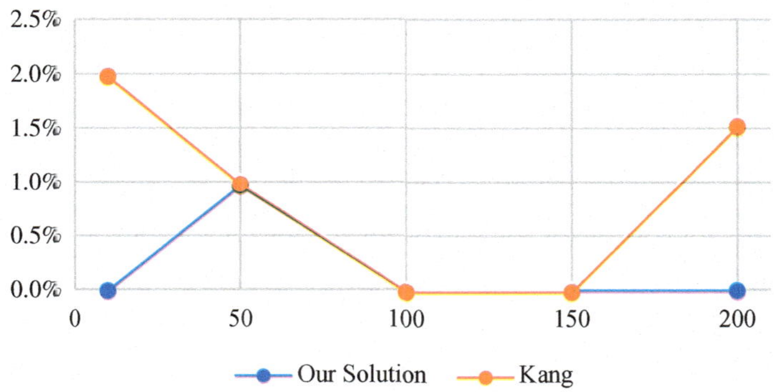

Fig. 11.9 Semantic attacker—ratio of linked identifiers

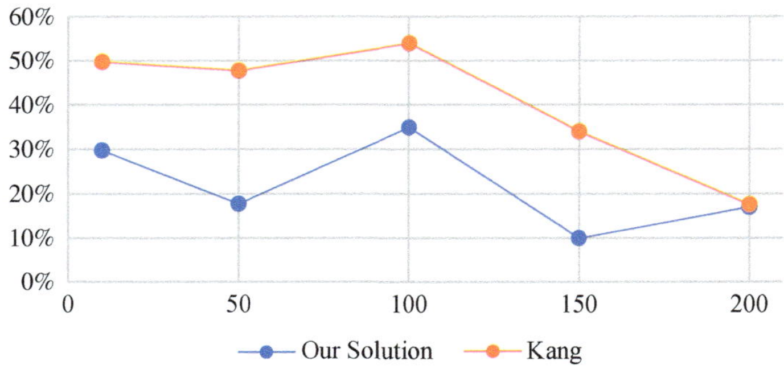

Fig. 11.10 Observation mapping attack—ratio of tracked vehicle

The performance of both solutions is equally good against linking mapping attack with a ratio nearly null for all scenarios.

Our solution also surpasses Kang et al. against observation mapping attacks. Figure 11.10 illustrates the ratio of tracked vehicles for both solutions.

Another comparison metric that should be taken into consideration is the number of identifier changes for each solution. As we believe that the identifier frequent change in unfavorable context does not necessary enhance the privacy level; on the contrary, it leads to the service interruption and to the overconsumption of identifiers. We ensured in our solution that the vehicle changes its identifier only within a cooperative crowd. Unlike, the solution of Kang et al. where identifier change happens independently upon expiry. To prove this supposition, we compared between the average numbers of identifier changes for both solutions during the simulation. We found that this number is about 3 times greater on average in Kang et al. solution than in ours. Despite that, their level of privacy was lower than ours, which further proves our beliefs and hypothesis.

Additionally, our solution reduces the overhead caused by the synchronization in comparison to Kang et al. which requires the exchange of messages with the cloud manager (CM) to request the change, get the approval, check the time, do continuous synchronization, choose a VMID, and inform the CM to record it. While in our solution, the CM delivers an organized list of VMID to the vehicle which only needs to inform it before doing the change so as to record it. Both the CM and the vehicle are aware of the next VMID to use, because they both have the same list.

11.11 Conclusion and Future Perspectives

In this chapter, we introduced the cloud-enabled Internet of Vehicles (CE-IoV) along with its characteristics and network model. We explained the importance of the privacy issue and the major challenges to keep in mind or to resolve in order to develop a good preservation solution. Later, we gave an overview of the existing CE-IoV privacy-preserving solutions with advantages and shortcomings. We also investigated the possibility of adapting VANET privacy-preserving solutions in CE-IoV. Lastly, we presented a novel solution for preservation of privacy that ensures the user's anonymity and unlinkability, i.e., both the identity and location privacy. The solution achieves the underlined aim by the use of temporal identifiers instead of permanent real identities to ensure anonymity. The identifiers are the pseudonym used in beaconing and the VMID used in CE-IOV LBS. Both identifiers are changed simultaneously within a cooperative crowd; this change strategy thwarts the linkability.

The simulation results were optimistic because they were less than 27% overall, and almost null to semantic and mapping linking attacks. Moreover, our solution proved to be better than Kang J. et al. [13] when we compared the performance of the two approaches. As for future perspectives, we intend to further reduce the tracking ratio by improving the change strategy.

References

1. Kaiwartya O, Abdullah AH, Cao Y, Altameem A, Prasad M, Lin CT, Liu X (2016) Internet of Vehicles: motivation, layered architecture, network model, challenges, and future aspects. IEEE Access 4:5356–5373
2. Yang FC, Wang SG, Li JL et al (2014) An overview of Internet of Vehicles. China Commun 11(10):1–15
3. Mu MP, Khan KUR (2015) Vehicular cloud computing: leading towards tomorrow's Internet of Vehicles. J Wirel Sens Netw 2(1):1–10
4. Lucero S (2016) C-V2X offers a cellular alternative to IEEE 802.11p/DSRC. IHS TECHNOLOGY Internet Everything 3:1–3
5. Hou XS, Li Y, Chen M et al (2016) Vehicular fog computing: a viewpoint of vehicles as the infrastructures. IEEE Trans Veh Technol 65(6):3860–3873
6. Qin B, Wu QH, Ferrer JD et al (2011) Preserving security and privacy in large scale VANETS. In: 13th International conference on information and communications security, Beijing, China
7. Pfleeger CP, Pfleeger SL, Margulies J (2015) Security in computing, 5th edn. Prentice Hall, Upper Saddle River, NJ
8. Benarous L, Kadri B, Bouridane A (2017) A survey on cyber security evolution and threats: biometric authentication solutions. In: Jiang R, Al-maadeed S, Bouridane A, Crookes P, Beghdadi A (eds) Biometric security and privacy. Signal processing for security technologies. Springer, Cham
9. Singh DR, Yadav RS (2018) A state-of-art approach to misbehaviour detection and revocation in VANET: survey. Int J Ad Hoc Ubiquitous Comput 28(2):77–93
10. Khodaei M, Papadimitratos P (2018) Efficient, scalable, and resilient vehicle-centric certificate revocation list distribution in VANETs. In: Proceedings of the 11th ACM conference on security & privacy in wireless and mobile networks
11. Fangchun Y, Shangguang W, Jinglin L, Zhihan L, Qibo S (2014) An overview of Internet of Vehicles. China Commun 11(10):1–15
12. Gerla M, Lee EK, Pau G, Lee U (2014) Internet of Vehicles: from intelligent grid to autonomous cars and vehicular clouds. Internet of Things (WF-IoT), IEEE World Forum
13. Kang J, Yu R, Huang X, Jonsson M, Bogucka H, Gjessing S, Zhang Y (2016) Location privacy attacks and defenses in cloud-enabled internet of Vehicles. IEEE Wirel Commun 23(5):52–59
14. Warren SD, Brandeis LD (1890) The right to privacy. Harvard Law Review, pp 193–220

15. Lukács A (2016) What is privacy? The history and definition of privacy, University of Szeged
16. Boualouache A (2016) Security and privacy in vehicular networks. Dissertation, University of sciences and Technology Houari Boumediene (USTHB)
17. Petit J, Schaub F, Feiri M, Kargl F (2015) Pseudonym schemes in vehicular networks: a survey. IEEE Commun Surv Tutor 17(1):228–255
18. Boualouache A, Senouci SM, Moussaoui S (2017) A survey on pseudonym changing strategies for vehicular ad-hoc networks. IEEE Communications Surveys & Tutorials
19. Committee of Intelligent Transportation Systems (2013) IEEE standard for wireless access in vehicular environments–security services for applications and management messages. IEEE Std 1609:2
20. Sampigethaya K, Li M, Huang L, Poovendran R (2007) AMOEBA: robust location privacy scheme for VANET. IEEE J Sel Areas Commun 25:8
21. Xingjun S, Huibin X (2014) An effective scheme for location privacy in VANETs. J Netw 9(8):2239
22. Freudiger J, Raya M, Félegyházi M, Papadimitratos P, Hubaux JP (2007) Mix-zones for location privacy in vehicular networks. In: ACM workshop on wireless networking for intelligent transportation systems
23. Memon I, Chen L, Arain QA, Memon H, Chen G (2018) Pseudonym changing strategy with multiple mix zones for trajectory privacy protection in road networks. Int J Commun Syst 31:1
24. Arain QA, Memon I, Deng Z, Memon MH, Mangi FA, Zubedi A (2018) Location monitoring approach: multiple mix-zones with location privacy protection based on traffic flow over road networks. Multimed Tools Appl 77(5):5563–5607
25. Guo N, Ma L, Gao T (2018) Independent mix zone for location privacy in vehicular networks. IEEE Access 6:16842–16850
26. Freudiger J, Shokri R, Hubaux JP (2009) On the optimal placement of mix zones. In: International symposium on privacy enhancing technologies symposium. Springer, Berlin, Heidelberg
27. Lu R, Lin X, Luan TH, Liang X, Shen X (2012) Pseudonym changing at social spots: an effective strategy for location privacy in VANETS. IEEE Trans Veh Technol 61:1
28. Network simulator 2. https://www.isi.edu/nsnam/ns/. Accessed 22 Sept 2018
29. Statista (2016) IoT number of connected devices, Statista, November, 2016. https://www.statista.com/statistics/471264/iot-number-of-connected-devices-worldwide/. Accessed 22 Sept 2018
30. Emara K (2016) Safety-aware location privacy in vehicular ad-hoc networks, Dissertation, University of München
31. Liao J, Li J (2009) Effectively changing pseudonyms for privacy protection in VANETS. In: 10th IEEE international symposium on pervasive systems, algorithms, and networks (ISPAN)
32. Boualouache A, Moussaoui S (2017) TAPCS: traffic-aware pseudonym changing strategy for VANETs. Peer-to-Peer Netw Appl 10(4):1008–1020

Chapter 12
Securing Packet Transmission Through Trusted Shortest Network Path Using Fuzzy Forecasting for Mobility of MANET Nodes

Soham Bandyopadhyay and Sunil Karforma

Abstract Mobile Ad hoc Network (MANET) is mostly a decentralized, dynamic configured approach. With the changing of time instances, the topological change in the position of MANET nodes is one of the massive challenges for transmitting data packets. As the MANET nodes move, the distances between these nodes change. Due to changing distances, observation of link failure and new links generation between any two nodes become the biggest challenges for secure transmission of packets through a trusted network path. Many researchers are already working to derive secure trusted network paths for packet flows and to minimize the delay for packet transmission using different decision-oriented statistical measures. Time series forecasting is one of the significant areas for the prediction of mobility of the nodes. With this approach, for the future structure of MANET nodes with the variation of time, forecasting becomes easily possible. In this chapter, we elaborate on the use of least squares time series forecasting, with interval-based fuzzy mathematics on historical dataset, to forecast the future positions of nodes of MANET; and from it, we foretell the link status between two nodes at different time slots in near future. Using these details, we predict the secure shortest paths (using the Dijkstra algorithm) for transmitting packets from one node to another with optimized residual energy utilization for different topological structures for near future for different time slots.

Keywords MANET · Time series · Membership function · Least squares method · T-distribution · Defuzzification · Fuzzy logic · Fuzzy forecasting · Dijkstra · Euclidian distance · Regression

S. Bandyopadhyay (✉)
Dr. B. C. Roy Polytechnic, Durgapur, India
e-mail: sohamban@gmail.com

S. Karforma
The University of Burdwan, Burdwan, India
e-mail: sunilkarforma@yahoo.com

Z. Mahmood (ed.), *Security, Privacy and Trust in the IoT Environment*, https://doi.org/10.1007/978-3-030-18075-1_12

12.1 Introduction

In the area of wireless technology, many researchers are working on several aspects of Mobile Ad hoc Networks (MANET). Analyzing the decentralization and abrupt movement of nodes of MANET, researchers have already worked on different protocols for adapting the dynamic movement of hosts [1]. On the other hand, analysis of several mobility models of MANET offers the researchers several choices to evaluate the performance of MANET using several different parameters [2]. Quality of service improvement through the efficient routing mechanism and minimization of delay [3–6] has also enriched the research in mobile ad hoc technologies and infrastructures. As the topological changes in MANET nodes are highly abrupt in nature, forecasting of the future behavior of nodes becomes significant, especially when taking the preventive measures at earlier stages to resist unwanted packet drop or link breakage problem in near future. By predicting the delay using neural networks, generation of intelligent routing in a wireless network is one of the noteworthy research areas of wireless technology [7]. Embedding time series forecasting for MANET, researchers have come up with remarkable results with respect to performance evaluation of future at earlier stages [8–11], which seems to have resolved the problems like packet drop, delay in transmission, insecure flow controls, etc.

In this chapter, we apply least squares method of time series forecasting with fuzzy statistics [12] to predict the probable links breakages and new links generation at changing topological structures of MANET nodes at different future time slots. Using this prediction, we also generate most trusted and shortest network paths with optimum energy utilizations for transmitting data at different network structures of MANET for those time slots.

In real-life scenarios, estimated results for predicting future are not easily possible, as several environmental and other constraints also affect the results at different observations. Here, we apply the fuzzy time series forecasting method for predicting possible future coordinates of nodes. Using least squares technique and fuzzy regression analysis together, we get the fuzzy forecasted positions of nodes in interval-based form; then applying Euclidean distance on it, we forecast secure shortest transmission path. On the other hand, applying Heinzelman's energy model [13] on shortest path technique, we generate the most optimized energy usage for transmitting packets through shortest network paths from source to destination at different network structures of MANET for different time slots of near future.

We arrange the rest of the chapter as follows: In Sect. 12.2, we describe the general view of packet transmission through MANET with different routing protocols and present challenges for frequent topological changes in their structures with time. In Sect. 12.3, we articulate time series forecasting approach with its promised benefits and applications. In Sect. 12.3.1, we explain the mathematical model of time series forecasting with the least square's method approach. In Sects. 12.3.2 and 12.3.3, t-distribution and Euclidean distance [14, 15] derivations are shown mathematically. Section 12.3.4 is the most important section where fuzzy mathematics is blended with time series forecasting approach using the application of chi-square and t-distribution approach. The next two subsections of Sect. 12.3 explain the Dijkstra shortest path algorithm [16] and show how the algorithm which generates secure shortest path and optimal energy sends data through that path. In Sect. 12.4, we consider a simple MANET with five nodes and for each node, we observe their coordinates for six different time slots using Network Simulator NS-2.35. Using the dataset in Sects. 12.4.1 and 12.4.2, we predict the future mobility of nodes with their changing coordinates and from it, we forecast the probable link breakages and new links generation between two nodes at different time slots. Using Dijkstra algorithm, the forecasted details generate the secure and trusted shortest paths for packet flow at different topological structures for different time slots. In Sect. 12.4.3, we predict residual energies [13] for packet transmission through those secure, shortest linked network paths at different time slots. Finally, in Sect. 12.5, we conclude the chapter with future scope for further improvement of our suggested approach.

12.2 Generic Ideas on MANET Packet Transmission

MANET can be explained as the type of network architecture which is proficient in being shaped anywhere and which is auto-configured without having proper structure—refer to Fig. 12.1. The increasing utilization of laptops and 802.11/Wi-Fi wireless networking has opened a new area of research relevant to MANET, since the 1990s. Many research papers provide suggestions for increasing the efficiency of data transmission through MANET subjects to improve the security, trust, and energy consumption as well as the quality of service of the nodes.

Different protocols can be generated based on a few unavoidable constraints to measure the packet drop rate, average routing load, average end-to-end-delay, and other relevant measures. The elucidations for routing protocols are classified into three categories: proactive, reactive, and hybrid routing protocols. However, reactive protocols have a significant contribution to MANET routing. The three categories are as follows:

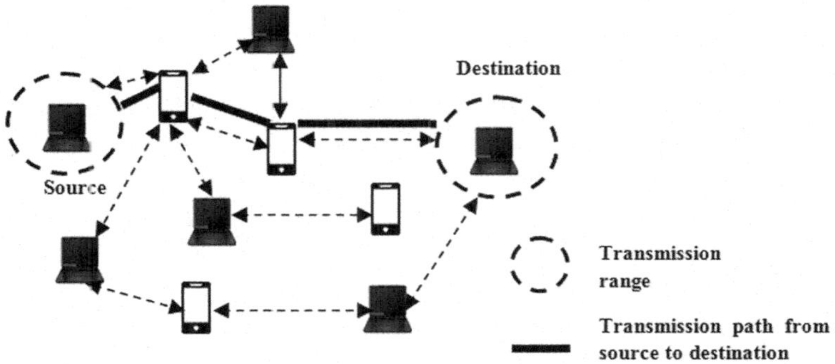

Fig. 12.1 Structure of MANET

- Proactive Protocols—Proactive routing protocols are also named as table-driven routing protocols. In this type of routing, each node maintains routing table for preserving information about the network topology. Every node in the network has one or alternate routes to any possible destination in its routing table at any given time. The routing tables are restructured periodically whenever the network topology is changed. Proactive protocols are inappropriate for bulky networks as they require for sustaining node entries for each and every node in the routing table of every node. Various proactive routing protocols are DSDV, OLSR, WRP, etc.
- Reactive Protocols—Reactive routing protocols are also known as on-demand routing protocol. In these protocols, route is discovered according to its necessity. Reactive protocols do not maintain updated routes to any destination in the network and do not generally exchange any periodic control messages. Searching the route in reactive routing is basically on-demand and establishes the link subject to data transmission between source and destination. Using flooding technique, route request process is stretched over the entire network on the basis of route demand.
- Hybrid routing protocols—These protocols are the combination of the best features of the above two categories. Node within a certain distance from a given node or within a certain geographical area is concern is called routing zone of that given node. For routing within this zone, a table-driven approach is used and beyond this zone, an on-demand approach is used.

All these routing protocols generate and transmit packets on the basis of present demand and the current topological structure. As the packet transmission depends on proper network pathfinding, it is an issue of time consumption. In many cases, frequent changes in topological structures increase the chance of link breakage between two nodes, generate unwanted packet drop and decrease the QOS. The best possible solution for such problems is to predict the future locations of nodes and through which the possible distance between two nodes at different future time slots can be predicted at present time. Here, time series forecasting is the best approach. But as we discuss the future possible results, it is not easily possible to predict the exact location of any node. The location can be predicted within a range of values. Here, we introduce fuzzy time series forecasting to generate the nodes' locations in approximation. In the next part of this chapter, we describe the forecasting method mathematically.

12.3 Mathematical Modeling of Fuzzy Forecasting

To work on fuzzy forecasting method, we construct a MANET structure with m number of nodes using NS-2.35 simulator. For every node, n number of time slots are observed and using NS-2.35 simulation, the coordinates of every node are collected as the reference dataset for predicting future coordinates of every node. In the current study, we apply the fuzzy time series forecasting method on simulated coordinates and predict coordinates of every node for future time slots. Some of the significant processes along with their detail description related to our discussion are as follows.

12.3.1 Time Series Forecasting

Time series is a series of data points which are indexed in the time order. It is basically a discrete sequence of time slots, and by observing the values of those time slots, the future values can be predicted at different future time slots.

Time Series Analysis
Time series forecasting has strong impact on different statistical analyses, as briefly mentioned here.

- Descriptive analysis—It is used to decide the trend or pattern in a time series using graphs or other tools. This helps to identify cyclic patterns, overall trends, turning points, and outliers.
- Spectral analysis—It is used for the analysis of frequency domain; it attempts to separate periodic or cyclical components in a time series.
- Forecasting—It is used extensively in business forecasting, budgeting depending on historical data.
- Explanative analysis—It studies the cross-correlation or relationship between two time series and the dependence of one on the other.

Time series forecasting can be implemented in several ways, e.g., auto moving average method, vector auto-regression, simple exponential smoothing, Holt Winter's exponential smoothing, least squares technique, etc. In this chapter, we choose the least squares method as a forecasting technique. We now explain this method with a mathematical derivation.

Least Squares Method
The least squares method is one of the most significant approaches to generate future values using regression analysis, where the discrete time slot is considered as an independent variable and generated result is used as a dependent variable. Here we show the mathematical model of the least squares' technique.

Suppose, t_i, is a time instance to observe a result φ_i where $i = 1, 2, 3, \ldots\ldots n$

So, total observed results are $\varphi_1, \varphi_2, \ldots\ldots\ldots\ldots\ldots, \varphi_n$

For any particular time instance t_j, if the observed result is φ_j then

$$\varphi_j = \alpha + \beta.\left(t_j - t_k\right) \tag{12.1}$$

where $t_1 \leq t_k \leq t_j$ where t_k is the time slot through which the origin is passed. Here $\alpha\ and\ \beta$ are constant values.

Now, we have

$$\sum_{i=1}^{n} \varphi_i = \alpha.n + \beta.\sum_{i=1}^{n} (t_i - t_k) \tag{12.2}$$

$$\sum_{i=1}^{n} [(t_i - t_k).\varphi_i] = \alpha.\sum_{i=1}^{n} (t_i - t_k) + \beta.\sum_{i=1}^{n} (t_i - t_k)^2 \tag{12.3}$$

From Eqs. (12.1) and (12.2), we find that

$$\beta = \frac{\sum_{i=1}^{n}\left[(t_i - t_k).\varphi_i\right] - \frac{\sum_{i=1}^{n}(t_i - t_k).\sum_{i=1}^{n}\varphi_i}{n}}{\sum_{i=1}^{n}(t_i - t_k)^2 - \frac{\left[\sum_{i=1}^{n}(t_i - t_k)\right]^2}{n}} \tag{12.4}$$

$$\alpha = \frac{\sum_{i=1}^{n}\varphi_i - \beta.\sum_{i=1}^{n}(t_i - t_k)}{n} \tag{12.5}$$

$$\sigma^2 = \frac{1}{n}\sum_{i=1}^{n}\left[\varphi_i - \alpha - \beta.\left(t_i - \bar{t}\right)\right]^2 \tag{12.6}$$

where

$$\bar{t} = \frac{\sum_{i=1}^{n} t_i}{n}$$

Using the constants $\alpha\ and\ \beta$, we can predict values for future time slots. For future time instance t_l where $t_n \leq t_l$ using Eq. (12.1), we get the predicted future result as

$$\varphi_l = \alpha + \beta.(t_l - t_k) \tag{12.7}$$

12.3.2 T-Distribution

A t-distribution is a type of probability distribution that is used for estimating the population parameters for small sample sizes and unknown population variances with specific level of significance for specific degree of freedom.

Suppose, x has a normal distribution with a population mean μ for sample size n; and the sample mean and sample standard deviations are x and s, respectively [16]. Then, we have

$$\mu = \bar{x} \pm t_{n-1,\frac{\alpha}{2}}.\frac{s}{\sqrt{n}} \tag{12.8}$$

The degree of freedom and level of significance with two tail tests are n − 1 and $\alpha/2$, respectively.

Suppose the sample mean of any population is 40.2 with standard deviation 4.35 and sample size of 9, the t-distribution representation for population mean is

$$\mu = \left[\bar{x} - 1.45t_{8,\frac{\alpha}{2}}, \bar{x} + 1.45t_{8,\frac{\alpha}{2}}\right]$$

Here, the population mean is shown in Fig. 12.2.

We use t-distribution technique to represent regression constants in fuzzy interval-based format to predict the mobility of MANET nodes with interval-based coordinates.

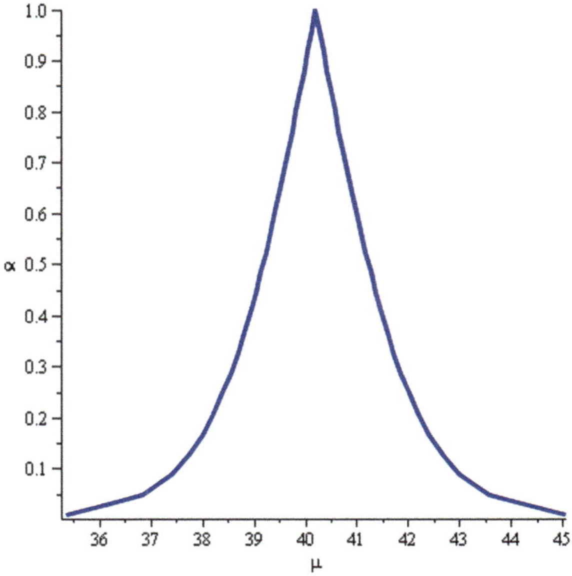

Fig. 12.2 t-distribution for population mean

12.3.3 *Euclidean Distance*

For Cartesian coordinates, if $\delta = (\delta_1, \delta_2, \delta_3 \ldots\ldots \delta_n)$ and $\rho = (\rho_1, \rho_2, \rho_3 \ldots\ldots \rho_n)$ are two points in Euclidean n-space, then the distance $e(\delta, \rho)$ from δ to ρ, or from ρ to δ as suggested in [16] is given by

$$e(\delta, \rho) = \sqrt{(\delta_1 - \rho_1)^2 + (\delta_2 - \rho_2)^2 + (\delta_3 - \rho_3)^2 + \ldots\ldots\ldots + (\delta_n - \rho_n)^2} \quad (12.9)$$

Depending on the dimensions, Euclidian distance is calculated on one-, two-, three-, and multi-dimensional spaces.

One-Dimensional Space

If δ and ρ are two points on a real line, the distance between them is

$$e(\delta, \rho) = \sqrt{(\delta - \rho)^2} = (\delta - \rho)$$

Two-Dimensional Space

If $\delta(\delta_1, \delta_2)$ and $\rho(\rho_1, \rho_2)$ are two points, the distance $e(\delta, \rho)$ between them is

$$e(\delta, \rho) = \sqrt{(\delta_1 - \rho_1)^2 + (\delta_2 - \rho_2)^2}$$

Three-Dimensional Space

If $\delta(\delta_1, \delta_2, \delta_3)$ and $\rho(\rho_1, \rho_2, \rho_3)$ are two points, the distance $e(\delta, \rho)$ between them is

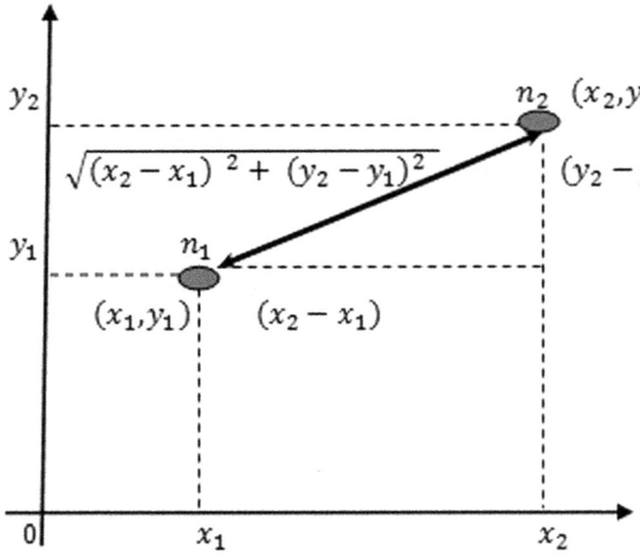

Fig. 12.3 Euclidian distance between two nodes in MANET

$$e(\delta,\rho)=\sqrt{(\delta_1-\rho_1)^2+(\delta_2-\rho_2)^2+(\delta_3-\rho_3)^2}$$

Multi-Dimensional Space

If $\delta(\delta_1,\delta_2,\delta_3\ldots\ldots\delta_n)$ and $\rho(\rho_1,\rho_2,\rho_3\ldots\ldots\rho_n)$ are two points then the distance $e(\delta,\rho)$ from δ to ρ, or from ρ to δ is given by

$$e(\delta,\rho)=\sqrt{(\delta_1-\rho_1)^2+(\delta_2-\rho_2)^2+(\delta_3-\rho_3)^2+\ldots\ldots+(\delta_n-\rho_n)^2}$$

In this chapter, we consider that the nodes of MANET at different topological structures belong to two-dimensional spaces.

According to Fig. 12.3, we find that the Euclidian distance between two nodes $n_1(x_1,y_1)$ and $n_2(x_2,y_2)$ for two-dimensional spaces is

$$\sqrt{(x_1-x_2)^2+(y_1-y_2)^2}$$

or

$$\sqrt{(x_2-x_1)^2+(y_2-y_1)^2}$$

We use this process of distance calculation between two nodes in Sect. 12.4 and generate secure shortest path for data transmission.

12.3.4 Fuzzy Time Series Forecasting

In this section, fuzzy interval-based mathematics on t-distribution technique is incorporated with least square method of time series. According to Eqs. (12.4) and (12.5), we generate the constants α, β for single linear regression equation [12]. Here, we convert these two constants in fuzzy interval format using the following equations:

$$\tilde{\alpha} = \left[\alpha - t_{\gamma/2}\sqrt{\frac{\widetilde{\sigma_L}^2}{(n-2)}}, \alpha + t_{\gamma/2}\sqrt{\frac{\widetilde{\sigma_R}^2}{(n-2)}}\right] \tag{12.10}$$

$$\tilde{\beta} = \left[\beta - t_{\gamma/2}\sqrt{\frac{c_{1L}}{c_{2L}}}, \beta + t_{\gamma/2}\sqrt{\frac{c_{1R}}{c_{2R}}}\right] \tag{12.11}$$

Here, we use t-distribution technique for two tail tests with level of significance $\gamma/2$ for $(n-2)$ degrees of freedom where

$$\tilde{\alpha}_L = \alpha - t_{\gamma/2}\sqrt{\frac{\widetilde{\sigma_L}^2}{(n-2)}}, \tilde{\alpha}_R = \alpha - t_{\gamma/2}\sqrt{\frac{\widetilde{\sigma_R}^2}{(n-2)}}$$

$$\tilde{\beta}_L = \beta - t_{\gamma/2}\sqrt{\frac{c_{1L}}{c_{2L}}}, \quad \tilde{\beta}_R = \beta + t_{\gamma/2}\sqrt{\frac{c_{1R}}{c_{2R}}}$$

$$c_{1L} = n.\widetilde{\sigma_L}^2 \quad , \quad c_{2L} = (n-2)\sum_{i=1}^{n}\left(t_i - \bar{t}\right)^2$$

$$c_{1R} = n.\widetilde{\sigma_R}^2 \quad , \quad c_{2R} = (n-2)\sum_{i=1}^{n}\left(t_i - \bar{t}\right)^2$$

The standard deviation generated from Eq. (12.6) can be represented as fuzzy interval-based format in the following way:

$$\tilde{\sigma} = [\widetilde{\sigma_L}, \widetilde{\sigma_R}]$$

$$\tilde{\sigma}^2 = \left[\frac{n\tilde{\sigma}^2}{\chi 2_{R,\tau/2}}, \frac{n\tilde{\sigma}^2}{\chi 2_{L,\tau/2}}\right] \tag{12.12}$$

where

$\chi 2_{R,\tau/2} = (1-\gamma)\chi 2_{R,0.005} + \gamma(n-q)$
$\chi 2_{L,\tau/2} = (1-\gamma)\chi 2_{L,0.005} + \gamma(n-q)$

$\chi 2_{R,\tau/2}$ and $\chi 2_{L,\tau/2}$ are fuzzy unbiased estimators with chi-square two-tailed test for $\tau/2$ level of significance with n degree of freedom and total number of constants are q. At t_l future time instance, if the predicted future result is φ_l, then

$$\varphi_l = \tilde{\alpha} + \tilde{\beta}.(t_l - t_k) \tag{12.13}$$

Applying fuzzy time series concept, Eq. (12.13) can be represented as

$$\widetilde{\varphi_l} = \left[\tilde{\alpha}_L + \tilde{\beta}_L(t_l - t_k), \tilde{\alpha}_R + \tilde{\beta}_R(t_l - t_k)\right] \tag{12.14}$$

12.3.5 Dijkstra Shortest Path Algorithm

To calculate the shortest and secure paths between source and destination for different time slots/instances, we use Dijkstra shortest path method in Sect. 12.4 and its subsections. The conventional Dijkstra algorithm is used for implanting mathematical results at our simulation part. The main steps of the algorithm are as follows:

1. Create a graph of vertex set Q with n number of vertices.
2. Initialize the distances from source to all other vertices as "INFINITY", where distance from source to source (from n: n distance matrix) is initialized as 0.
3. The distances from source vertex to all other vertices are changeable according to different iterations.
4. Search the vertex u in vertex set Q that has least distance from source vertex which is represented as dist[u].
5. Let length (u, v) represent the weight of the edge, joining two neighbors u and v.
6. Here, as in the following algorithm, variable d is the path length from the root node to the neighbor vertex v, if it passed through u. Distance d is calculated as the summation of dist[u] and length (u,v).
7. Using step 4, calculated current shortest path from source vertex to v is dist[v].
8. Now comparing d and dist[v], if it is found that d is shorter than dist[v], current shortest path is replaced with d and this distance is considered as permanent distance.
9. Repeat steps 4–8 until reset of all unvisited vertices get shortest route (permanent distance) to the source vertex.

Pseudocode for the algorithms is along the following lines:

```
function Dijkstra (Graph, source):
create vertex set Q
for each vertex v in Graph:          // Initialization
     dist[v] ← INFINITY              // Unknown distance from source to vertex v
     prev[v] ← UNDEFINED             // Previous node in optimal path from source
     add v to Q                      // All vertices initially in vertex set Q (unvisited vertices)
     dist[source] ← 0                // Distance from source to source is zero
while Q is not empty:
u ← vertex in Q with min dist[u]     // Vertex with the least distance from source
                                     // will be selected at first
remove u from Q
for each neighbor v of u:            // where vertex v is still in Q (unvisited vertices set)
    d ← dist[u] + length(u, v)
    if d < dist[v]:                  // A shorter path from source to v has been found
    dist[v] ← d
    prev[v] ← u
return dist[], prev[]
```

12.3.6 Transmission Path and Energy Optimization Algorithm

In Sects. 12.3.1–12.3.5, we discussed mechanisms for forecasting link breakage problems of future time slots/instances and resolved them earlier by predicting trusted secure shortest network path and optimized transmission energy utilization. A simulation of the overall algorithm is derived in Sect. 12.4. Here, we present the steps of the algorithm.

1. Get coordinates of all the nodes from NS-2.35 simulator and generate the reference dataset of coordinates for different time slots.
2. Use conventional time series forecasting least square method with reference datasets to generate equations for both x- and y-coordinates.
3. Solving the equations, we generate two constant terms $[\alpha, \beta]$ for both x- and y-coordinates.
4. Using t-distribution technique, we convert α, β in interval-based fuzzy format for both x- and y-coordinates. During conversion technique, we use fuzzy unbiased estimator with chi-square distribution.
5. Use the fuzzy interval-based constants α, β to generate fuzzy regression equations and from these equations generate forecasted coordinates of nodes in interval-based format for different future time slots.
6. From the predicted coordinates, we design the location of the nodes of MANET for different future time slots.

7. Using Euclidian distance method, we generate direct distance between every pair of nodes and prepare the distance dataset for all timeslots.
8. Considering a certain distance as threshold value (as discussed in Sect. 12.4.2), we check whether the intermediate direct node distances for different topological structures are greater than the threshold distance and mark those distances as link breakage distances and predict the probable packet drops at different future time slots due to link breakage.
9. Using Dijkstra shortest path method at reference dataset and predicted coordinates of nodes, we forecast the shortest paths between every pair of nodes in MANET for different topological structures at different time slots.
10. For data transmission, we choose those forecasted shortest paths which are shorter than threshold distance and resolve the probable link breakage problem of future time slots.
11. After predicting secure shortest paths, using Heinzelman's energy model, we also predict most optimized energy utilization to transmit data through those paths at different future time slots for different topological structures.

Using the above algorithm, in the next section, we simulate the overall system mathematically and generate decision-oriented observations.

12.4 Simulation of the Proposed Algorithm

In order to forecast secure shortest network paths and optimized energy utilization to flow data through different topological structures for different future time slots, it is of the utmost importance to predict the node-to-node link breakage and new link generation for those topological structures and future time slots. Here, we generate a dataset of five nodes, where the 2-d coordinates of five nodes are considered at different time slots. Using NS-2.35, the coordinates' details of five nodes are generated.

Table 12.1 shows the dataset of nodes at six time slots. Using this dataset, we formulate the interval-based fuzzy regression equation and try to predict the coordinates of nodes in interval-based format for different future time slots. The C language, NS-2.35, Maple12, and Microsoft Excel 2007 are used as the simulators. The unit of time is considered as second and distance unit as meter.

According to our MANET network structure, total nodes are five. Total number of time slots for observing the locations of MANET nodes is six. So, as we consider the time slots as t_i, where $i = 1, 2, 3, 4, 5, 6$:

$$t_1 = 2.2\,s,\ t_2 = 3.08\,s,\ t_3 = 5.11\,s,\ t_4 = 7.7\,s,\ t_5 = 9.6\,s\ and\ t_6 = 12.07\,s$$

Using the NS-2.35 simulator, we get the coordinates of nodes as shown in Table 12.1 for the six time slots. In the next subsection, we use these coordinates to

Table 12.1 2D coordinates of nodes at six time slots

Time slot (in second)	n_1	n_2	n_3	n_4	n_5
2.2	104.113, 376.867	36.076, 85.9985	327.338, 65.3536	183.836, 365.421	113.751, 254.288
3.08	108.154, 368.944	44.8357, 65.0035	318.483, 65.5402	184.921, 356.77	117.476, 246.35
5.11	107.104, 350.181	63.7116, 79.005	299.458, 67.449	181.408, 337.803	131.101, 232.514
7.7	111.91, 324.77	88.6229, 75.0102	278.223, 81.265	179.996, 341.589	136.793, 210.64
9.6	111.91, 307.127	98.9705, 61.5253	278.388, 88.1853	179.473, 296.128	134.36, 192.353
12.07	112.64, 284.838	92.9574, 69.8774	255.101, 95.0964	178.953, 275.031	136.413, 171.101

predict the coordinates of these nodes at three future time slots of 13.09, 15.03, and 16.8 s using fuzzy time series forecasting.

12.4.1 Future Forecasted Node Position Prediction

We already explained the fuzzy time series forecasting method in Sect. 12.3.4. Here, we use this method on current dataset of coordinates to predict the coordinates of nodes at different future time slots and foretell different topological structures of MANET.

Using NS-2.35 simulated dataset (Table 12.2) and considering time slot 5.11 s to be passed through origin, from Eqs. (12.4) and (12.5), we generate the values of α and β for all five nodes.

Here, we use Eqs. (12.2) and (12.3) such that

$$\sum_{i=1}^{n} \varphi_{ix} = \alpha.n + \beta.\sum_{i=1}^{n} (t_i - t_k)$$

$$\sum_{i=1}^{n} [(t_i - t_k).\varphi_{ix}] = \alpha.\sum_{i=1}^{n} (t_i - t_k) + \beta.\sum_{i=1}^{n} (t_i - t_k)^2$$

where φ_{ix} is the x-coordinate value of any node.

In the same way, for y-coordinates, φ_{iy} signifies the y-coordinate value.

The derived α and β values for five nodes are all point estimated. Using Eqs. (12.8) and (12.9), we convert these to interval estimated fuzzy values. Now, we try to use t-distribution technique with degree of freedom 4 with two-tailed test for 5% level of significance and fuzzy standard deviation.

Table 12.2 NS-2.35 simulation parameter

Simulation parameters	Values
MAC protocol	IEEE802.11
Physical protocol	IEEE802.11b
Number of nodes	5 (can be increased as per the need)
Transmitting frequency of each node	5 Mz
Network protocol	IPv4
Network structure	All the nodes are interconnected
Transport protocol	UDP
Simulation area (square meter)	1000 × 1000
Protocol	AODV
Level of significance	5%
$t_{4,0.025}$ (t-distribution)	2.78

$$\tilde{\alpha}_x = \left[\alpha_x - t_{\gamma/2}\sqrt{\frac{\widetilde{\sigma_{Lx}}^2}{(n-2)}}, \alpha_x + t_{\gamma/2}\sqrt{\frac{\widetilde{\sigma_{Rx}}^2}{(n-2)}}\right]$$
$$\tilde{\beta}_x = \left[\beta_x - t_{\gamma/2}\sqrt{\frac{c_{1L}}{c_{2L}}}, \beta_x + t_{\gamma/2}\sqrt{\frac{c_{1R}}{c_{2R}}}\right]$$
$$\tilde{\alpha}_y = \left[\alpha_y - t_{\gamma/2}\sqrt{\frac{\widetilde{\sigma_{Ly}}^2}{(n-2)}}, \alpha_y + t_{\gamma/2}\sqrt{\frac{\widetilde{\sigma_{Ry}}^2}{(n-2)}}\right]$$
$$\tilde{\beta}_y = \left[\beta_y - t_{\gamma/2}\sqrt{\frac{c_{1L}}{c_{2L}}}, \beta_y + t_{\gamma/2}\sqrt{\frac{c_{1R}}{c_{2R}}}\right] \tag{12.15}$$

To generate fuzzy standard deviations for both x- and y-coordinates of all five nodes, we use Eq. (12.6) as

$$\left.\begin{aligned} \sigma_x^2 &= \frac{1}{n}\sum_{i=1}^{n}\left[\varphi_{ix} - \alpha - \beta.\left(t_i - \bar{t}\right)\right]^2 \\ \sigma_y^2 &= \frac{1}{n}\sum_{i=1}^{n}\left[\varphi_{iy} - \alpha - \beta.\left(t_i - \bar{t}\right)\right]^2 \end{aligned}\right\} \tag{12.16}$$

Using Eqs. (12.15) and (12.12) separately, we generate fuzzy standard deviation for x- and y-coordinates separately. We note that Eq. (12.12) can be represented as

Table 12.3 Interval-based regression constants

Node	φ_x		φ_y	
	α	β	α	β
n1	106.35, 111.11	0.08, 1.51	335.91, 373.54	−15.02, −3.75
n2	48.54, 82.66	1.37, 11.59	74.26, 88.04	−4.20, −0.07
n3	292.30, 322.69	−11.54, −2.44	63.02, 81.47	1.00, 6.52
n4	181.15, 184.37	−1.07, −0.11	325.97, 370.05	−15.39, −2.18
n5	119.32, 134.36	0.04, 4.54	218.13, 251.98	−13.48, −3.34

$$\left.\begin{aligned} \tilde{\sigma}_x &= [\widetilde{\sigma_{Lx}}, \widetilde{\sigma_{Rx}}] \\ \tilde{\sigma}_x^2 &= \left[\frac{n\sigma_x^2}{\chi 2_{R,\tau/2}}, \frac{n\sigma_x^2}{\chi 2_{L,\tau/2}}\right] \\ \tilde{\sigma}_y &= [\tilde{\sigma}_{Ly}, \tilde{\sigma}_{Ry}] \\ \tilde{\sigma}_y^2 &= \left[\frac{n\sigma_y^2}{\chi 2_{R,\tau/2}}, \frac{n\sigma_y^2}{\chi 2_{L,\tau/2}}\right] \end{aligned}\right\} \tag{12.17}$$

Using Eq. (12.17), we generate fuzzy variances of x- and y-coordinates for all nodes in MANET and use them to calculate regression constants at the next portion. Here, we show fuzzy variance of node n_1 for both x- and y-coordinates with Eqs. (12.12) and (12.17) in the following way:

$$\tilde{\sigma}_{xn1}^2 = \left[\frac{19.488}{(1-\gamma)21.955 + 6\gamma}, \frac{19.488}{(1-\gamma)1.344 + 6\gamma}\right]$$
$$\tilde{\sigma}_{yn1}^2 = \left[\frac{1217.56}{(1-\gamma)21.955 + 6\gamma}, \frac{1217.56}{(1-\gamma)1.344 + 6\gamma}\right]$$

where

$\sigma_x^2 = 3.248$
$\sigma_y^2 = 202.927$
$\chi 2_{R,\tau/2} = (1-\gamma)21.955 + 6\gamma$
$\chi 2_{L,\tau/2} = (1-\gamma)1.344 + 6\gamma$

From the above equations, we graphed the fuzzy estimated value of $\tilde{\sigma}_{xn1}^2$ and $\tilde{\sigma}_{yn1}^2$ and these are shown in Figs. 12.4 and 12.5.

Using fuzzy variances in Eqs. (12.15) and (12.17), we find the regression constants in fuzzy format (Table 12.3) for all the nodes in MANET. Here, we show the fuzzy regression constants of node n_1 using fuzzy variances $\tilde{\sigma}_{xn1}^2$ and $\tilde{\sigma}_{yn1}^2$ as

$$\tilde{\alpha}_x = [108.69 - 0.9.t_{\gamma/2}, 108.69 + 0.9.t_{\gamma/2}]$$
$$\tilde{\beta}_x = [0.08 - 0.256.t_{\gamma/2}, 0.08 + 0.256.t_{\gamma/2}]$$

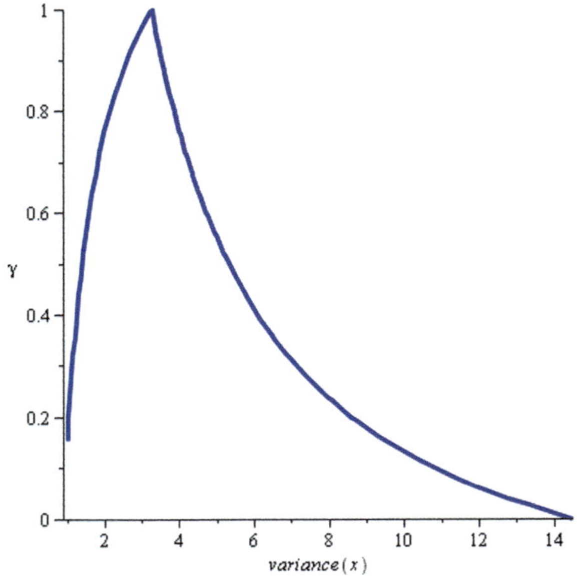

Fig. 12.4 Fuzzy t-distribution graph for $\tilde{\sigma}_{xn1}^2$

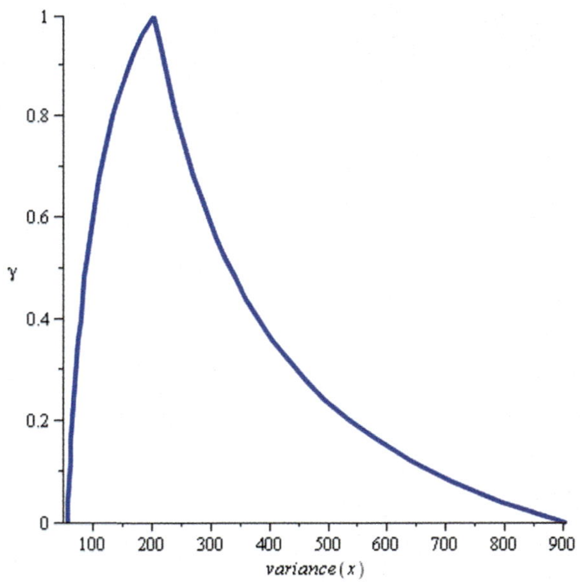

Fig. 12.5 Fuzzy t-distribution graph for $\tilde{\sigma}_{yn1}^2$

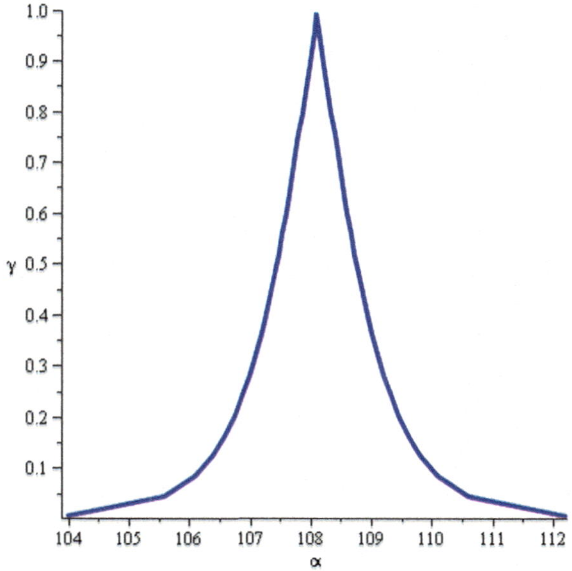

Fig. 12.6 Fuzzy t-distribution graph for $\tilde{\alpha}_x$

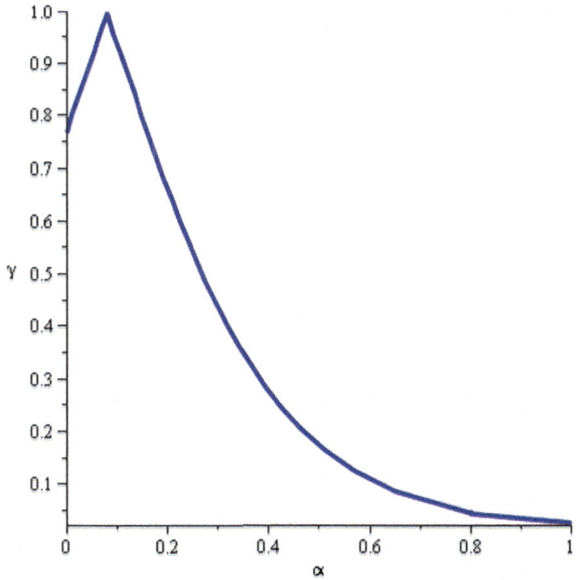

Fig. 12.7 Fuzzy t-distribution graph for $\tilde{\beta}_x$

$$\tilde{\alpha}_y = \left[349.69 - 3.561.t_{\gamma/2}, 349.69 + 3.561.t_{\gamma/2}\right]$$
$$\tilde{\beta}_y = \left[-9.39 - 2.02.t_{\gamma/2}, -9.39 + 2.02.t_{\gamma/2}\right]$$

Using the above equations, the graphs of $\tilde{\alpha}_x$, $\tilde{\beta}_x$, $\tilde{\alpha}_y$, and $\tilde{\beta}_y$ for node n_1 are shown in Figs. 12.6, 12.7, 12.8, and 12.9.

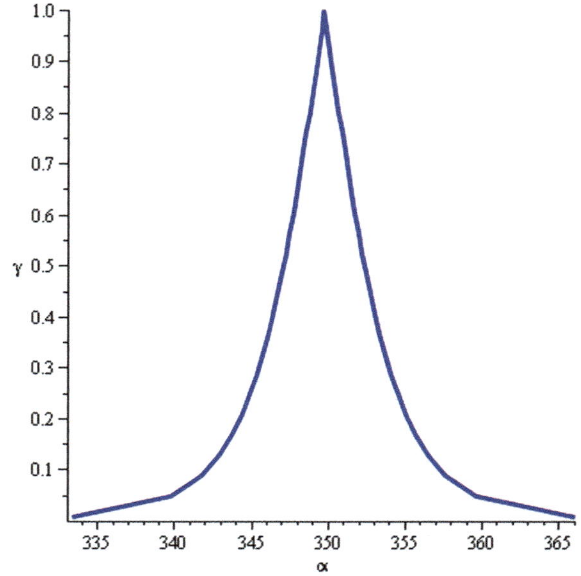

Fig. 12.8 Fuzzy t-distribution graph for $\tilde{\alpha}_y$

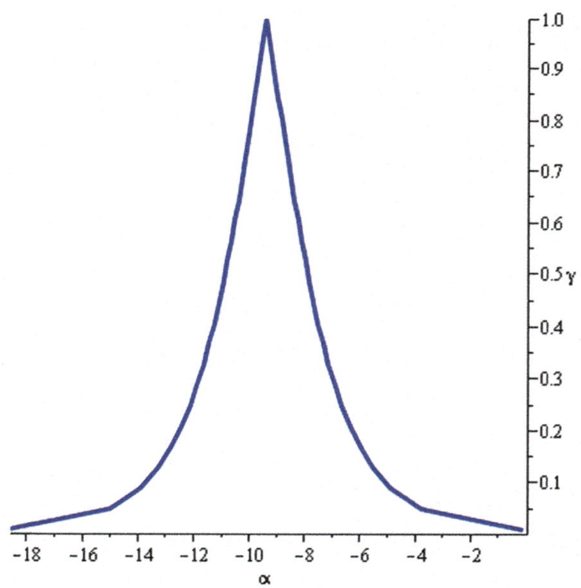

Fig. 12.9 Fuzzy t-distribution graph for $\tilde{\beta}_y$

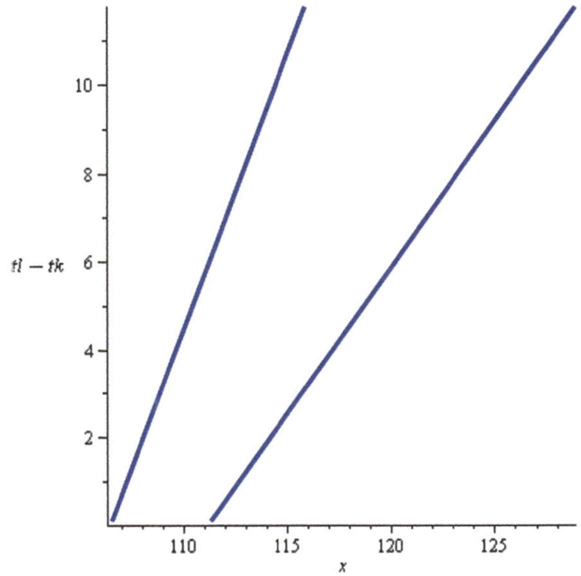

Fig. 12.10 Fuzzy regression graph of x-coordinate for node n_1

Using t-distribution technique for degree of freedom 4 with two-tailed test for 5% level of significance on above equations, we get regression constants for node n_1; using the same procedure, we generate the regression constants for other nodes as given in Table 12.3.

At t_l future time instance, the predicted fuzzy coordinate of any node will be $(\tilde{\varphi}_{lx}, \tilde{\varphi}_{ly})$:

where

$$\left.\begin{aligned}\widetilde{\varphi_{lx}} &= \left[\tilde{\alpha}_{xL} + \tilde{\beta}_{xL}(t_l - t_k), \tilde{\alpha}_{xR} + \tilde{\beta}_{xR}(t_l - t_k)\right] \\ \widetilde{\varphi_{ly}} &= \left[\tilde{\alpha}_{yL} + \tilde{\beta}_{yL}(t_l - t_k), \tilde{\alpha}_{yR} + \tilde{\beta}_{yR}(t_l - t_k)\right]\end{aligned}\right\} \quad (12.18)$$

Here, node n_1 and the regression lines for both x- and y-coordinates from Eq. (12.18) are shown in Figs. 12.10 and 12.11.

Figure 12.10 shows two regression lines, where the points on leftmost line represent the lower limit values of x-coordinates of node n_1 at different time slots. Similarly, all points on the other regression line represent the upper limit values of x-coordinates for node n_1 at different time slots.

Figure 12.11 shows two regression lines and generates the interval-based y-coordinates (upper and lower limit values) for node n_1 at different time slots. Analyzing these regression lines, we predict the coordinates of node n_1 for different future time slots. Analyzing Eq. (12.18), we also predict the coordinates of other nodes of MANET for different topological structures for different future time slots.

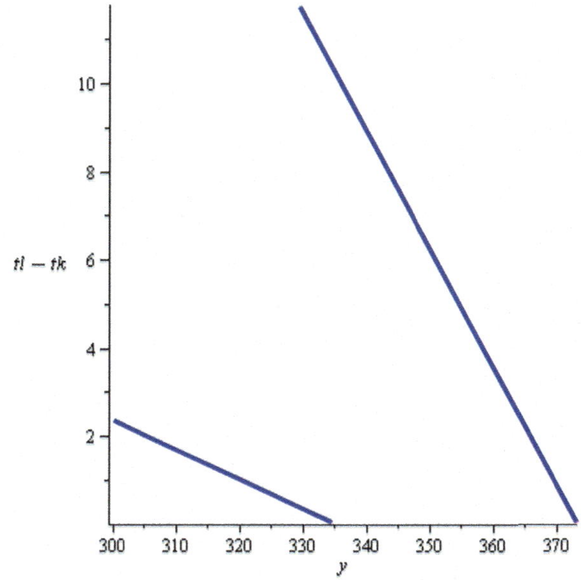

Fig. 12.11 Fuzzy regression graph of y-coordinate for node n_1

Table 12.4 Interval-based predicted coordinates

Time slot	$n_1(\varphi_x, \varphi_y)$	$n_2(\varphi_x, \varphi_y)$	$n_3(\varphi_x, \varphi_y)$	$n_4(\varphi_x, \varphi_y)$	$n_5(\varphi_x, \varphi_y)$
13.09	107.01, 123.15 216.03, 343.58	59.45, 175.14 40.76, 87.47	200.23, 303.23 70.97, 133.50	172.59, 183.49 203.17, 352.62	119.61, 170.59 110.55, 225.29
15.03	107.17, 107.17 186.88, 336.30	62.11, 197.62 32.62, 87.33	177.84, 298.50 72.91, 146.15	170.50, 183.27 173.31, 348.38	119.68, 179.40 84.40, 218.81
16.8	107.32, 128.75 160.29, 329.66	64.53, 218.14 25.19, 87.20	157.42, 294.19 74.67, 157.70	168.61, 183.08 146.08, 344.51	119.74, 187.43 60.54, 212.89

Here, for the three future time slots, we predict the coordinates of the nodes, given at Table 12.4. As we know that the predicted future results are always uncertain, real-life constraints like the physical barrier and probable errors give an approximated result within a range of values in interval-based format. Predicted coordinates of nodes of MANET for future time slots are also represented through approximated range of values in the fuzzy format as shown in Table 12.4.

12.4.2 Future Forecasted Transmission Link and Shortest Path Prediction

For the prediction of shortest and secure network path and optimized energy utilization to flow data through that shortest path, it is required to foretell the possible link breakages and new link generation between two nodes at different topological structures of MANET for different future time slots. So, in the following section, we discuss the link breakage distance, its pictorial representation, and relation with Euclidian distance.

Link Breakage Distance

Using the mean-max technique, we get the defuzzified values of nodes' coordinates.

Assume, at t_i time slot the coordinates of node n_p and n_q are $(\varphi_{xp}, \varphi_{yp})$ *and* $(\varphi_{xq}, \varphi_{yq})$, respectively. Now the Euclidean distance between n_p and n_q according to Eq. (12.9) is

$$d_{pq} = \sqrt{(\varphi_{xp} - \varphi_{xq})^2 + (\varphi_{yp} - \varphi_{yq})^2}$$

If the threshold distance between two nodes for transmitting packets is d_T where $d_T \geq d_{pq}$, then it satisfies the linkage between two nodes for successful packet transmission.

In Fig. 12.12, at t_i time slot, the distance between nodes n_1 and n_2 is d_{pq} and threshold distance is d_T. As at t_i time slot, $d_T \geq d_{pq}$ means the threshold distance is greater or equal to source and destination node distance, the data transmission between n_1 and n_2 will be possible. Here, black straight arrow shows the successful packet transmission. For changing the topological structure at t_j time slot, the distance $d_{pq'}$ crosses the limit d_T, so link breakage occurs which is represented with the dotted line.

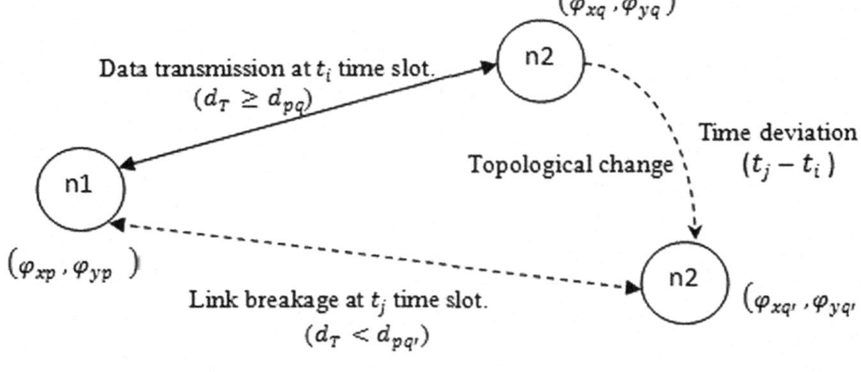

Fig. 12.12 Link breakage with topological change

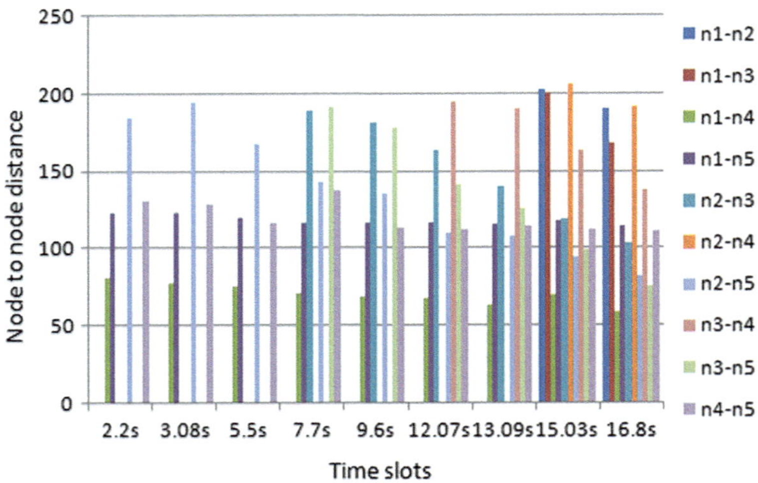

Fig. 12.13 Distance between all pair of nodes

According to Table 12.5, we note that for the historical and future time slots, the direct distance between two nodes is measured using Euclidean distance (Eq. 12.9). Figure 12.13 shows only those pair of nodes to node distances which are shorter than link breakage distance and through this figure, we can easily predict the pattern of all pair of node-to-node distances for different topological structures at different time slots.

In Sect. 12.3.5, we already discussed algorithmic approach of Dijkstra's shortest path method. Here, a mathematical interpretation of the algorithm is given to generate secure shortest path from the dataset provided in Table 12.5.

Mathematical Derivation of Dijkstra Shortest Path Algorithm

Following the approach as presented in [16], consider a topological structure of MANET that is represented by a graph in such a way that

$$G = (V, E, W)$$

where

$V = \{v_1, v_2, v_3 \ldots\ldots\ldots\ldots, v_n\}$
$E = \{e_1, e_2, e_3 \ldots\ldots\ldots\ldots e_k\}$
$W = \{w_1, w_2, w_3 \ldots\ldots\ldots\ldots w_k\}$

Suppose now that Shortest_path (v_i, v_j) is $v_i \rightarrow v_r \rightarrow v_q \ldots .v_s \rightarrow v_j$ where the number of nodes is δ, where Shortest_path (v_i, v_j) signifies the shortest route between two nodes (v_i, v_j) and $\delta \leq n_t$ where n_t = total number of nodes in MANET sub-graph for a particular source and destination.

Then, the total path cost is $\sum_{i=1}^{\delta} w_i$ where for $v_i \rightarrow v_r \rightarrow v_q \ldots .v_s \rightarrow v_j$, and the minimum weights are $\{w_1, w_2, \ldots w_p\}$, respectively.

Table 12.5 Direct route cost between two nodes

	Time slots (in second)								
	2.2 s	3.08 s	5.5 s	7.7 s	9.6 s	12.07 s	13.09 s	15.03 s	16.8 s
n1–n2	298.7198	310.4658	274.6258	250.8431	245.9423	215.8598	215.7014	202.8883	190.2125
n1–n3	383.2362	369.1777	341.9612	294.8808	275.0462	237.2699	224.0632	200.7069	167.9322
n1–n4	80.54047	77.72631	75.32795	70.1326	68.45244	67.03425	62.98896	69.71898	57.81089
n1–n5	122.9573	122.9479	120.089	116.811	116.949	116.1949	115.8424	117.864	113.9475
n2–n3	291.9927	273.6478	236.0295	189.7032	181.3874	164.0931	139.7351	119.1036	103.6049
n2–n4	316.0854	323.6535	284.3041	281.8037	248.0304	222.4483	222.2428	206.2999	192.2232
n2–n5	185.3504	195.354	167.6495	143.9298	135.5297	110.1572	107.4644	93.71853	81.4465
n3–n4	332.6158	320.396	295.0035	278.2393	230.2702	195.3842	190.4906	163.2546	138.4391
n3–n5	285.1589	270.3627	235.7764	191.6777	177.7498	140.9381	125.2377	98.11005	75.08135
n4–n5	131.3866	129.3886	116.6901	137.8918	113.1567	112.2991	114.8022	112.6105	110.8383

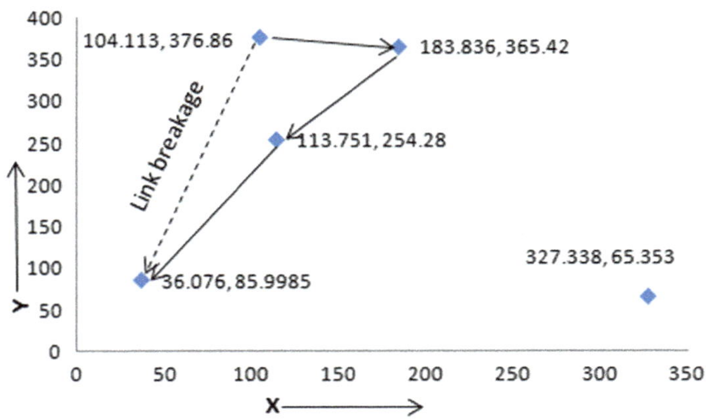

Fig. 12.14 Link status between n_1 and n_2 at 2.2 s time slot

Here, we consider the threshold distance (no intermediate node is considered) between two nodes for packet transmission as 210 m (d_T). According to Table 12.5, direct distance between two nodes larger than 210 m is considered as link breakage distance. For such distances, the intermediate nodes are introduced to break the overall distance into sub distances (less than or equal to 201 m); and different network paths are created for particular source to destination. Using the above Dijkstra's mathematical implication, we choose shortest sub-paths and form overall shortest distance between two particular nodes. As sub-paths are shortest and shorter than 210 m, the link breakage problem can be avoided and data transmission will be more secure. Since Table 12.5 has forecasted distances, using the above technique, we generate Table 12.6 with most secure, trusted, and shortest network paths for different topological structures of MANET at future time slots of 13.09, 15.03, and 16.8 s.

Also, using the NS-2.35 simulation technique, it is found that at 2.2, 3.08, 5.11, 7.7, 9.6, and 12.07 s time slots, n_1 to n_2 direct packet transmissions are not possible for sudden link breakage problem. Using the forecasting technique, we note that at 13.09 s time slots link breakage problem will occur. So, for predicted future time slot at 13.09 s, we can forecast the alternate shortest and trusted route (shorter than link breakage distance) for transmitting packets (using intermediate nodes) from n_1 to n_2 and possibility of packet drop can be reduced. But predicted distance at 15.03 and 16.8 s time slots is shorter than the threshold distance. Thus, it can be concluded that on 15.03 and 16.8 s time slots, the direct link between n_1 to n_2 can be used for data transmission. Figure 12.14 shows the simulated shortest packet flow route for the 2.2 s time period, whereas Figs. 12.15 and 12.16 give the new forecasted shortest and secure route of packet flow from n_1 to n_2 at 15.03 s and 16.8 s time slots, respectively, for three different topological structures of MANET.

From NS-2.35 simulation, for n_2 to n_3 the link breakage is observed for first three time slots 2.2, 3.08, and 5.11 s, where 7.7, 9.6, and 12.07 s allow the packet

Table 12.6 Shortest route cost with direct and indirect paths (time unit in second, distance unit in meter)

	2.2 s	3.08 s	5.11 s	7.7 s	9.6 s	12.07 s	13.09 s	15.03 s	16.8 s
	Shortest path	Shortest path	Shortest path	Shortest path	Shortest path	Shortest path	Shortest path	Shortest path	Shortest path
n1–n2	308.3077	318.3019	287.7385	260.7408	252.4787	226.3521	211.5825	211.5825	190.2125
n1–n3	No transmission	No transmission	No transmission	450.444	433.8661	390.4452	330.6861	330.6861	167.9322
n1–n4	80.54047	77.72631	75.32795	70.1326	68.45244	67.03425	69.71898	69.71898	57.81089
n1–n5	122.9573	122.9479	120.089	116.811	116.949	116.1949	117.864	117.864	113.9475
n2–n3	No transmission	No transmission	No transmission	189.7032	181.3874	164.0931	119.1036	119.1036	103.6049
n2–n4	316.737	324.7426	No transmission	281.8216	248.6864	222.4563	206.329	206.329	192.2232
n2–n5	185.3504	195.354	167.6495	143.9298	135.5297	110.1572	93.71853	93.71853	81.4465
n3–n4	No transmission	No transmission	No transmission	329.5695	430.0738	195.3842	163.2546	163.2546	138.4391
n3–n5	No transmission	No transmission	No transmission	191.6777	177.7498	140.9381	98.11005	98.11005	75.08135
n4–n5	131.3866	129.3886	116.6901	137.8918	113.1567	112.2991	112.6105	112.6105	110.8383

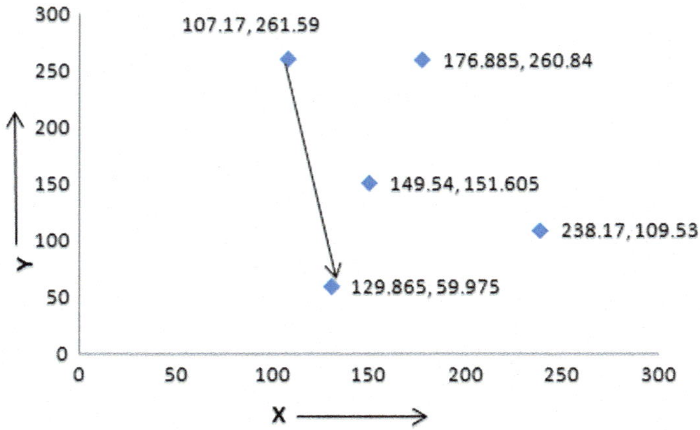

Fig. 12.15 Link status between n_1 and n_2 at 15.03 s time slot

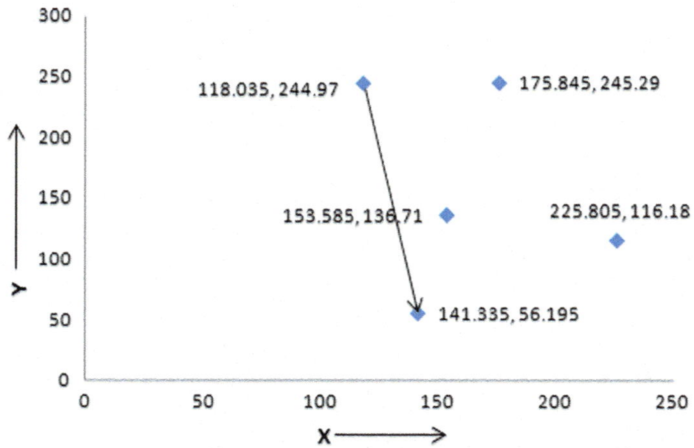

Fig. 12.16 Link status between n_1 and n_2 at 16.8 s time slot

transmission between them without link breakage problem. From predicted future time slots 13.09, 15.03, and 16.8 s, it is forecasted that link breakage problem will not happen. Figures 12.17 and 12.18 show the packet transmission from n_2 to n_3 at two different time slots for two different topological structure of MANET, using shortest path technique.

In Figs. 12.14, 12.15, 12.16, 12.17, 12.18, 12.19, and 12.20, the dotted line represents the link breakage and black arrows show the route for successful packet transmission.

From Fig. 12.19, it is clear that at 7.7 s time slot packets transmission from n_3 to n_4 directly will not possible for link breakage problem which is shown through the dotted line, so intermediate node n_5 is required to flow the packet using shortest

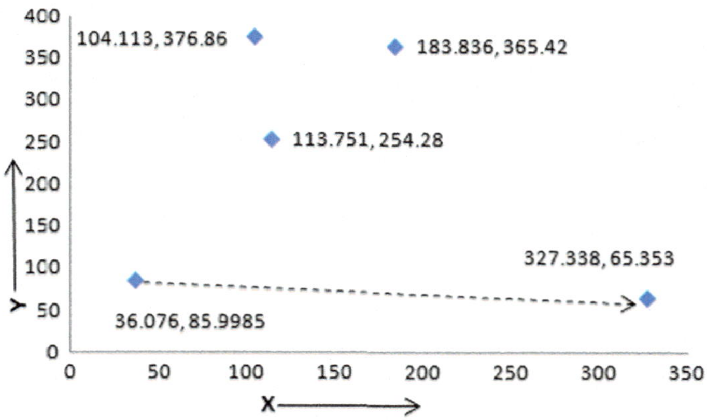

Fig. 12.17 Link status between n_2 and n_3 at 2.2 s time slot

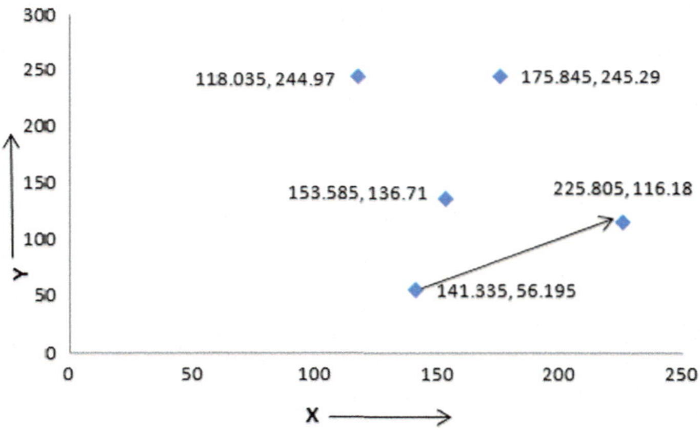

Fig. 12.18 Link status between n_2 and n_3 at 16.8 s time slot

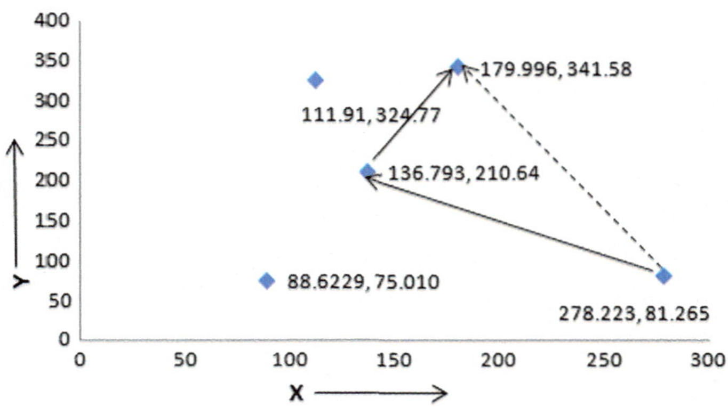

Fig. 12.19 Link status between n_3 and n_4 at 7.7 s time slot

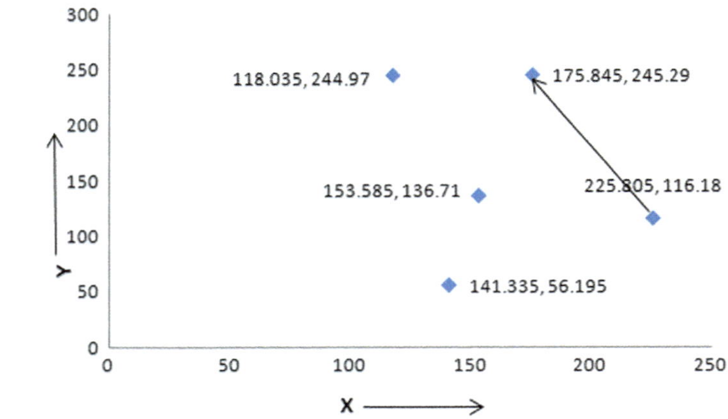

Fig. 12.20 Link status between n_3 and n_4 at 16.8 s time slot

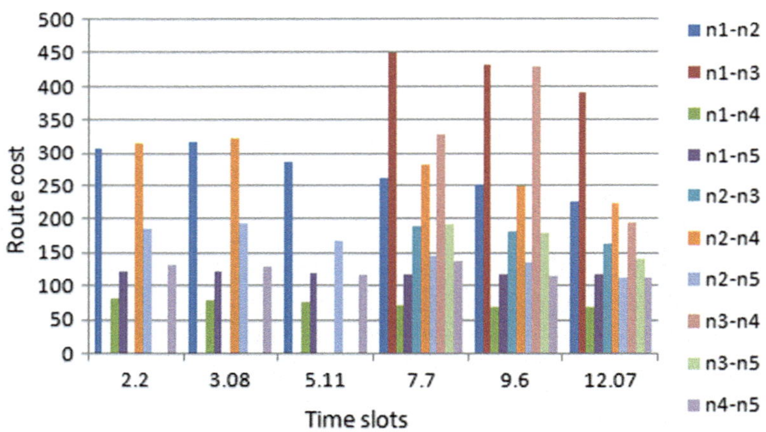

Fig. 12.21 Shortest route cost for optimized packet transmission

path. But through Fig. 12.20, it can be forecasted that at 16.8 s time slot n_3 to n_4 direct data transmission will be possible without link breakage.

Through Table 12.6, the shortest and reliable route (Dijkstra algorithm) between two nodes is shown in such a way that for the direct and intermediate node-based communication, link breakage has no effect for packet transmission. Through Table 12.6, we forecast the most optimized network route for transmitting packets at future time slots. Here, through Figs. 12.21 and 12.22, we show the optimized shortest route cost for historical and future time slots, respectively.

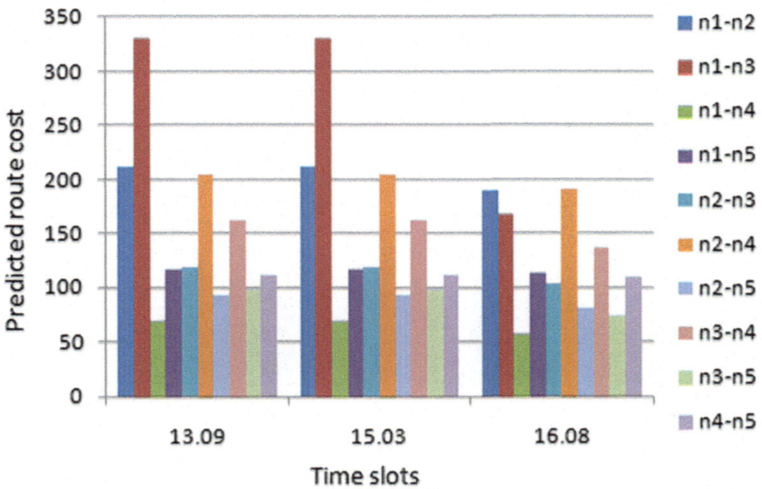

Fig. 12.22 Predicted shortest route cost of future time slot for optimized packet transmission

12.4.3 Future Forecasted Data Transmission Energy Prediction

In an earlier subsection, we already predicted the link breakage, new link generation; and according to that, we generated the shortest and secure routes for different topological structures of MANET at different future time slots without packet drop problem. In this section, we calculate the energy requirement to flow data through those shortest paths for varying MANET structure for different time slots. For less packet drops and improved quality of services, our forecasted energy consumptions will be highly optimized.

Here, we use Heinzelman's energy model [13] to calculate residual energy to transmit packets from one node to another node. While transferring packets in between two nodes, at the sender side, the energy is required to transmit the packet and at the receiver end, energy is required to receive the packet.

Suppose, *k* bit data is transmitted and the distance between two nodes is d (distance unit is considered as meter), then according to Heinzelman's energy model,

energy consumption for transmitting packet is given as

$$E_T(k, d) = E_{elec}.k + E_{amp}.k.d^2 \tag{12.19}$$

and energy consumption for receiving packet is given as

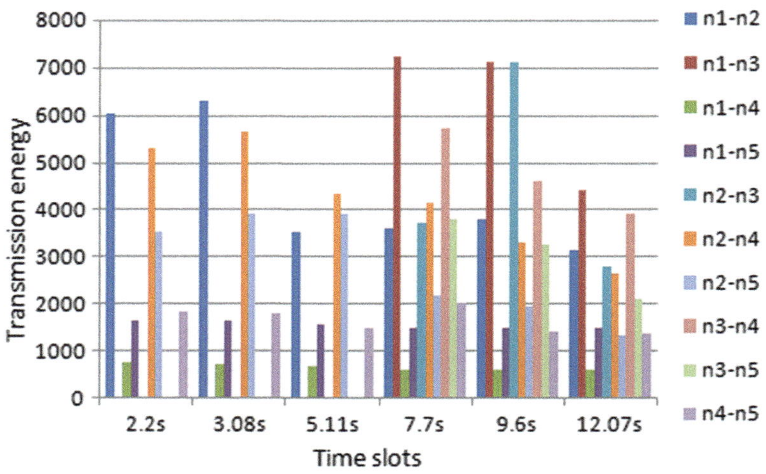

Fig. 12.23 Energy transmission details at historical dataset

$$E_R(k) = E_{elec}.k \tag{12.20}$$

where $E_{elec} = 50\,nJ/bit$ and $E_{amp} = \frac{100\,pJ}{bit}/m^2$

Here, we use 1-bit data to be transmitted from source node to the destination node, so k = 1. Table 12.7 provides the total energy consumption details.

From the forecasted shortest and secure route with the direction of packet flow, we can also predict the residual energy requirement for transmitting packets at future time slots.

As we forecast the secure shortest paths (according to Figs. 12.15 and 12.16) for transmitting packets from n_1 to n_2 at different topological structures of MANET for future time slots 15.03, 16.8 s, we get the required energies for transmitting 1-bit data through those paths from the Eqs. (12.19) and (12.20) as 3223.929 nJ and 3718.08 nJ, respectively.

Similarly, according to Fig. 12.18, required energy for transmitting 1-bit data from n_2 to n_3 at 16.8 s time slot data will be 1173.398 nJ.

The energy required for packet transmission at entire historical and future time slots of Table 12.7 is graphically represented through Figs. 12.23 and 12.24.

Table 12.7 Packet transmission energy through shortest route (time unit in second, energy unit in nano-joule)

	2.2 s	3.08 s	5.11 s	7.7 s	9.6 s	12.07 s	13.09 s	15.03 s	16.8 s
	Transmission energy	Transmission energy	Transmission energy	Transmission energy	Transmission energy	Transmission energy	Transmission energy	Transmission energy	Transmission energy
n1–n2	6010.398	6294.598	3528.065	3586.06	3785.848	3123.929	3173.929	3223.929	3718.08
n1–n3	No transmission	No transmission	No transmission	7234.79	7125.987	4416.858	4466.858	4516.858	2920.122
n1–n4	748.6767	704.1379	667.43	591.8582	568.5737	568.5737	618.5737	668.5737	434.2099
n1–n5	1611.85	1611.619	1542.137	1464.481	1467.707	1450.125	1500.125	1550.125	1398.403
n2–n3	No transmission	No transmission	No transmission	3698.73	7125.987	2792.655	2842.655	2892.655	1173.398
n2–n4	5311.721	5640.46	4322.293	4122.994	3267.274	2624.57	2674.57	2724.57	3794.976
n2–n5	3535.477	3916.319	3916.319	2171.579	1936.83	1313.461	1363.461	1413.461	763.3532
n3–n4	No transmission	No transmission	No transmission	5725.449	4589.943	3917.499	3967.499	4017.499	2016.538
n3–n5	No transmission	No transmission	No transmission	3774.034	3259.499	2086.355	2136.355	2186.355	663.7209
n4–n5	1826.244	1774.141	1461.658	2001.415	1380.444	1361.109	1411.109	1461.109	1328.513

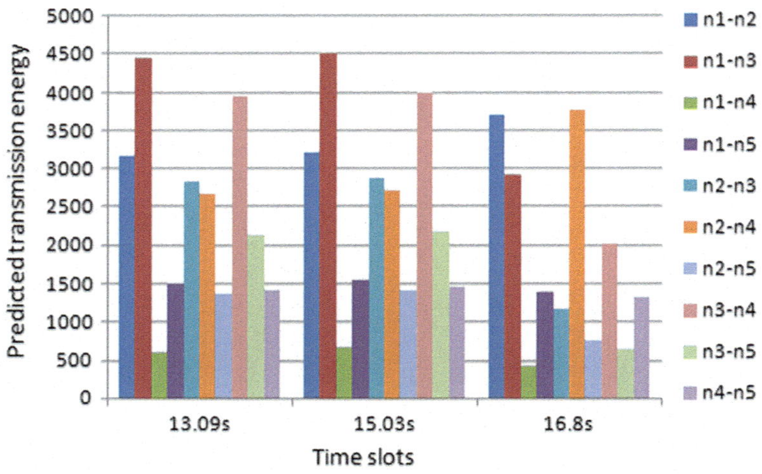

Fig. 12.24 Predicted energy transmission details from future dataset

12.5 Conclusion

Mobile ad hoc networks (MANET) is one of the most promising research areas in the communication systems. Spontaneous movements of nodes like mobile devices, laptops, and other 802.11 wireless-based devices often face the challenges of packet drop, excess energy consumption, and poor quality of services. Searching for the trusted path for optimizing route cost and energy utilization is often not possible for rapid movement of nodes.

In this chapter, we have attempted to propose a method, where the dynamic movement as well as possible link breakage of the nodes can be predicted, so that users get the idea about the transmission path at an earlier stage. We have used, for fuzzy time series forecasting, the least squares method to forecast the mobility of nodes by observing the present and historical dataset of time, node location, and generated most approximated interval-based future coordinates of nodes to locate their position. To predict link breakage in advance, we can generate the optimized network architecture with respect to the shortest path and proper energy consumption. In this chapter, we only predict the link breakage and new links generation to evaluate secure shortest paths at different topological structures of MANET for different future time slots. The node-to-node trust evaluation and trust variation with the changing of time are not considered as predictive parameters in time series forecasting method. If direct, indirect, and communication trust predictions are incorporated with this forecasting approach, the reliability of the prediction will be enhanced. This modified approach can then be implemented by introducing neural fuzzy architecture with time series forecasting technique.

References

1. Johnson DB, Maltz DA (1996) Dynamic source routing in ad hoc wireless networks. Mob Comput 1996:153–181. https://doi.org/10.1007/978-0-585-29603-6_5
2. Camp T, Boleng J, Davies V (2002) A survey of mobility models for ad hoc network research. Wirel Commun Mob Comput (WCMC): Spec Issue Mob Ad Hoc Netw: 483–502. https://doi.org/10.1002/wcm.72
3. Hanzo II L, Tafazolli R (2007) A survey of QoS routing solutions for mobile ad hoc networks. IEEE Commun Surv Tutor: 50–70. https://doi.org/10.1109/comst.2007.382407
4. Sun H, Hughes H (2003) Adaptive QoS routing based on prediction of local performance in ad hoc network. In: IEEE WNCN. IEEE Xplore, New Orleans, LA, USA, 16–20 March 2003, pp 1191–1195
5. Hongyan L, Hong W, Chao G (2006) Internet time-delay prediction based on autoregressive and neural network model. In: International Conference on Communications, Circuits and Systems. IEEE Xplore, Guilin, China, 25–28 June 2006, pp 1758–1761
6. Lee BS, San MN, Lim TM, Yeo CK, Seet BC (2006) Processing delay as a new metric for on-demand mobile ad hoc network routing path selection. In: International Conference on Wireless Communications, Networking and Mobile Computing. IEEE Xplore, Wuhan, China, 22–24 September 2006, pp 1–4
7. Guo Z, Malakooti B (2006) Delay prediction for intelligent routing in wireless networks using neural networks. In: IEEE International Conference on Networking, Sensing and Control (ICNSC '05). IEEE Xplore, Ft. Lauderdale, FL, USA, 23–25 April 2006, pp 625–630
8. Singh J, Dutta P, Chakrabarti A (2014) Weighted delay prediction in mobile ad hoc network using fuzzy time series. Egypt Inform J: 105–114. https://doi.org/10.1016/j.eij.2014.03.001
9. Hwang JR, Chen SM, Lee CH (1998) Handling forecasting problems using fuzzy time series. Fuzzy Sets Syst: 217–228. https://doi.org/10.1016/s0165-0114(97)00121-8
10. Liu H (2007) An improved fuzzy time series forecasting method using trapezoidal fuzzy numbers. Fuzzy Optim Decis Mak: 63–80. https://doi.org/10.1007/s10700-006-0025-9
11. Chen SM (1996) Forecasting enrolments based on fuzzy time series. Fuzzy Sets Syst: 311–319. https://doi.org/10.1016/0165-0114(95)00220-0
12. Buckley JJ (2004) Fuzzy probability and statistics. Warsaw, Poland
13. Haider T, Yusuf M (2009) A fuzzy approach to energy optimized routing for wireless sensor networks. Int Arab J Inf Technol: 179–185
14. Yang Z, Fang KT, Kotz S (2007) On the Student's t-distribution and the t-statistic. J Multivar Anal: 1293–1304. https://doi.org/10.1016/j.jmva.2006.11.003
15. Dokmanic I, Parhizkar R, Ranieri J, Vetterli M (2015) Euclidean distance matrices: essential theory, algorithms, and applications. IEEE Signal Process Mag: 12–30. https://doi.org/10.1109/msp.2015.2398954
16. Bandyopadhyay S, Karforma S (2018) Improving the performance of fuzzy minimum spanning tree based routing process through P-node fuzzy multicasting approach in MANET. Int J Comput Netw Inf Secur: 16–26. https://doi.org/10.5815/ijcnis.2018.06.02

Bibliography

17. Kaaniche H, Kamoun F (2010) Mobility prediction in wireless ad hoc networks using neural networks. J Telecommun: 95–101
18. Ghouti L, Sheltami TR, Alutaibi KS (2013) Mobility prediction in mobile ad hoc networks using extreme learning machines. Procedia Comput Sci: 305–312. https://doi.org/10.1016/j.procs.2013.06.043

19. Su W, Lee SJ, Gerla M (2000) Mobility prediction and routing in Ad Hoc wireless networks. In: Proceedings of IEEE MILCOM. IEEE Xplore, Los Angeles, CA, USA, 22–25 October 2000, pp 491–495
20. Gupta P, Kumar PR (2000) The capacity of wireless networks. IEEE Inf Theory Soc: 388–404. https://doi.org/10.1109/18.825799
21. Desai AM, Jhaveri RH (2018) Secure routing in mobile Ad hoc networks: a predictive approach. Int J Inf Technol. https://doi.org/10.1007/s4187
22. Lee LW, Wang LW, Chen SM (2006) Handling forecasting problems based on two-factors high-order time series. IEEE Trans Fuzzy Syst: 468–477. https://doi.org/10.1109/tfuzz.2006.876367
23. Gamal A, Mammen J, Prabhakar B, Shah D (2004) Throughput-delay trade-off in wireless networks. In: INFOCOM 2004. IEEE Xplore, Hong Kong, China, 7–11 March 2004, pp 464–475
24. Sheu S-T, Chen J (2001) A novel delay-oriented shortest path routing protocol for mobile ad hoc networks. In: IEEE International Conference on Communications (ICC 2001). IEEE Xplore, Helsinki, Finland, Finland, 11–14 June 2001, pp 1930–1934
25. Tabib SS, Jalali AA (2008) Modelling and prediction of internet time delay by feed-forward multilayer perceptron neural network. In: 10th International Conference on computer Modelling and Simulation. IEEE Xplore, Cambridge, UK, 1–3 April 2008, pp 611–616
26. Garg B, Beg MMS, Ansari (2010) A.Q.: inferential historical survey of time series predication using artificial neural network. In: 3rd International Conference on Data Management. Ghaziabad, India, 11–12 March 2010, pp 158–172
27. Thanh MN, Wu Q MJ (2011) Robust student's t-mixture model with spatial constraints and its application in medical image segmentation. IEEE Trans Med Imaging: 103–116. https://doi.org/10.1109/tmi.2011.2165342
28. Tickoo O, Sikdar B, (2008) Modeling queuing and channel access delay in unsaturated random access mac based wireless networks. IEEE/ACM Trans Netw: 878–891. https://doi.org/10.1109/tnet.2007.904010
29. Bisnik N, Abouzeid A (2009) Queuing network models for delay analysis of multihop wireless ad hoc networks. Ad Hoc Netw: 79–97. https://doi.org/10.1016/j.adhoc.2007.12.001
30. Guo Z, Sheikh S, Al-Najjar C, Kim H, Malakooti B (2010) Mobile ad hoc network proactive routing with delay prediction using neural network. Wirel Netw: 1601–1620. https://doi.org/10.1007/s11276-009-0217-7
31. Singh JP, Dutta P, Pal A (2012) Delay prediction in mobile Ad Hoc network using artificial neural network. Procedia Technol: 201–206. https://doi.org/10.1016/j.protcy.2012.05.030

Index

Z. Mahmood (ed.), *Security, Privacy and Trust in the IoT Environment*, https://doi.org/10.1007/978-3-030-18075-1

Printed by Printforce, the Netherlands